Transportation, Energy Use and Environmental Impacts

Transportation, Energy Use and Environmental Impacts

Márcio de Almeida D'Agosto

ELSEVIER

Elsevier
Radarweg 29, PO Box 211, 1000 AE Amsterdam, Netherlands
The Boulevard, Langford Lane, Kidlington, Oxford OX5 1GB, United Kingdom
50 Hampshire Street, 5th Floor, Cambridge, MA 02139, United States

© 2019, Elsevier Editora Ltda. Published by Elsevier Inc. All rights reserved.

This edition of Transporte, Uso de Energia e Impactos Ambientais 1st Edition (9788535228212) by Márcio de Almeida D'Agosto is published by arrangement with Elsevier Editora Ltda.

No part of this publication may be reproduced or transmitted in any form or by any means, electronic or mechanical, including photocopying, recording, or any information storage and retrieval system, without permission in writing from the publisher. Details on how to seek permission, further information about the Publisher's permissions policies and our arrangements with organizations such as the Copyright Clearance Center and the Copyright Licensing Agency, can be found at our website: www.elsevier.com/permissions.

This book and the individual contributions contained in it are protected under copyright by the Publisher (other than as may be noted herein).

Notices
Knowledge and best practice in this field are constantly changing. As new research and experience broaden our understanding, changes in research methods, professional practices, or medical treatment may become necessary.

Practitioners and researchers must always rely on their own experience and knowledge in evaluating and using any information, methods, compounds, or experiments described herein. In using such information or methods they should be mindful of their own safety and the safety of others, including parties for whom they have a professional responsibility.

To the fullest extent of the law, neither the Publisher nor the authors, contributors, or editors, assume any liability for any injury and/or damage to persons or property as a matter of products liability, negligence or otherwise, or from any use or operation of any methods, products, instructions, or ideas contained in the material herein.

Library of Congress Cataloging-in-Publication Data
A catalog record for this book is available from the Library of Congress

British Library Cataloguing-in-Publication Data
A catalogue record for this book is available from the British Library

ISBN: 978-0-12-813454-2

For information on all Elsevier publications
visit our website at https://www.elsevier.com/books-and-journals

Publisher: Joe Hayton
Acquisition Editor: Brian Romer
Editorial Project Manager: Ana Claudia A. Garcia
Production Project Manager: Anitha Sivaraj
Cover Designer: Mark Rogers

Typeset by SPi Global, India

Dedication

I dedicate this book to Emyr D'Agosto, who, long before I recognized and understood the problems addressed here, had already warned me about them.

Contents

About the Author	xi
Preface	xiii
Acknowledgments	xvii

1. Transportation, an introduction

1.1	Introduction	1
1.2	Concepts related to transportation	1
1.3	Transportation modes	4
	1.3.1 Road transportation	5
	1.3.2 Railway transportation	13
	1.3.3 Water transportation	20
	1.3.4 Pipeline transportation	26
	1.3.5 Air transportation	30
1.4	Multimodal transportation	33
	1.4.1 Typical operation plans in multimodal freight transportation	34
	1.4.2 Typical operation plans in multimodal passenger transportation	35
	1.4.3 Conditions for multimodal transportation	38
1.5	Life cycle of a transportation system	39
1.6	An overview of transportation worldwide	40
1.7	Final considerations	44
1.8	Exercises	45
	References	45
	Further reading	46

2. Planning, design, and construction of infrastructure for transportation systems and their environmental impacts

2.1	Introduction	47
2.2	Planning and design of transportation systems	52
2.3	Construction of transportation systems infrastructure	57
	2.3.1 Deforestation of areas and real estate expropriation	60
	2.3.2 Installation, operation, and subsequent deactivation of construction sites	60
	2.3.3 Opening of tracks, accesses, and service paths	61
	2.3.4 Installation and operation of asphalt, concrete, and crushing plants	61

viii Contents

	2.3.5	Opening and recuperation of borrow pits and waste pits	61
	2.3.6	Dredging, rock blasting, and earthworks	62
	2.3.7	Slope stabilization	62
	2.3.8	Drainage works	62
	2.3.9	Paving works	62
	2.3.10	Regular and special civil engineering structures	62
	2.3.11	Operation of machinery and equipment	63
	2.3.12	Works of implementation and installation of guideway accessories	63
	2.3.13	Specific actions and reflexes on the environment	63
	2.3.14	Reflexes on the environment and selected mitigation measures	63
2.4	Demobilization of transportation systems infrastructure		82
2.5	Final considerations		82
2.6	Exercises		83
	Further reading		84

3. Transportation planning and energy use

3.1	Introduction		85
3.2	An overview of energy use in transportation		86
3.3	Transportation planning and energy use		87
	3.3.1	Aspects that impact energy use in transportation	90
	3.3.2	Transportation demand planning and energy use	93
	3.3.3	Transportation management procedures under an energy use perspective	97
3.4	Energy efficiency management in transportation		99
	3.4.1	Energy efficiency and energy consumption in transportation	99
3.5	Tools for energy efficiency management in transportation		106
	3.5.1	Energy efficiency management system in transportation (EEMST)	107
	3.5.2	Life cycle assessment (LCA) applied to transportation	109
3.6	Final considerations		120
3.7	Exercises		120
	References		121
	Further reading		122

4. Propulsion systems and energy use

4.1	Introduction		123
4.2	Movement and propulsion		124
4.3	Road mode		125
	4.3.1	Energy demand in road transportation	125
	4.3.2	Energy supply in road transportation	132
	4.3.3	Conceptual model of a road propulsion system	150
	4.3.4	Conceptual model of final energy use in road transportation	152
4.4	Other modes of transportation		157
	4.4.1	Railway mode	157

Contents **ix**

		4.4.2 Water mode	165
		4.4.3 Pipeline mode	169
		4.4.4 Air mode	171
	4.5	Final considerations	174
	4.6	Exercises	175
		References	176
		Further reading	176

5. Energy sources for transportation

5.1	Introduction		177
5.2	Conventional fuels		185
	5.2.1	Exploration	186
	5.2.2	Production	187
	5.2.3	Transportation and storage	188
	5.2.4	Refining	188
	5.2.5	Distribution	189
	5.2.6	End use	190
5.3	Natural gas		192
	5.3.1	Exploration	194
	5.3.2	Production and processing	195
	5.3.3	Transportation	195
	5.3.4	Distribution	195
	5.3.5	End use	197
5.4	Ethanol		200
	5.4.1	Feedstock production	204
	5.4.2	Ethanol production	205
	5.4.3	Ethanol distribution	207
	5.4.4	Ethanol end use	207
5.5	Biodiesel		208
	5.5.1	Feedstock production—Biomass rich in oils and fats	210
	5.5.2	Feedstock processing	210
	5.5.3	Fuel production—Biodiesel	211
	5.5.4	Distribution	215
	5.5.5	End use	215
5.6	Advanced biofuels		217
	5.6.1	Cellulose ethanol	217
	5.6.2	Sugarcane diesel	218
	5.6.3	Enzymatic biodiesel	219
	5.6.4	Synthetic diesel obtained from biomass	219
	5.6.5	Biokerosene	220
	5.6.6	Bio-oil	220
	5.6.7	Biogas	221
	5.6.8	Dimethyl ether	221
5.7	Advanced energy sources		221
	5.7.1	Hydrogen	222
	5.7.2	Electromobility	222
5.8	Final considerations		223
5.9	Exercises		224

x Contents

	References	224
	Further reading	225

6. Air pollutant and greenhouse gas emissions (GHG)

6.1	Introduction	227
6.2	Air pollution	228
	6.2.1 Negative effects of air pollution on human health, on the existence of living beings, and on material goods	229
	6.2.2 Air pollution caused by the transportation sector	229
6.3	Greenhouse gas (GHG) emissions	234
6.4	Air pollutants and GHG emissions management	239
	6.4.1 Air pollutant emissions inventory	240
	6.4.2 Dispersion and concentration of air pollutants	246
	6.4.3 Measures to control and limit vehicle emissions	248
6.5	Final considerations	254
6.6	Exercises	255
	References	256
	Further reading	257

7. Noise pollution, vibration, visual intrusion, and emission of solid and liquid waste

7.1	Introduction	259
7.2	Noise pollution	260
	7.2.1 Concept of noise pollution	260
	7.2.2 Noise generated by transportation modes	262
	7.2.3 Regulations regarding noise	263
	7.2.4 Management of noises generated by the operation of transportation	264
7.3	Vibration associated with the operation of transportation	271
	7.3.1 Concept of vibration	271
	7.3.2 Effects of vibration on human health	271
	7.3.3 Vibrations caused by transportation	272
7.4	Visual intrusion	274
	7.4.1 Conceptualization of visual intrusion	274
	7.4.2 Visual intrusion caused by transportation	274
	7.4.3 Strategies of land use and occupation integrated to transportation	275
7.5	Generation of solid and liquid waste through the operation of transportation	277
	7.5.1 Conceptualization of solid and liquid waste	277
	7.5.2 Waste generated by the operation of transportation	278
7.6	Final considerations	279
7.7	Exercises	280
	Further reading	280

Index	281

About the Author

Márcio de Almeida D'Agosto is a bachelor in Mechanical and Automotive Engineering and a master in Transportation Engineering at the Military Institute of Engineering (1989 and 1999). He became a doctor in Transportation Engineering at Coppe/UFRJ in 2004. Since he finished his bachelor's degree, in 1989, he accumulated professional experience in the area of freight transportation management in companies such as Companhia Brasileira de Petróleo Ipiranga, SHV/Minasgás S.A. Distribuidora de Gás Combustível and Coca-Cola. In 2005 and 2006, he occupied the position of Transportation Planning Director at the Municipal Superintendence of Urban Transportation (SMTU) of the Municipality of Rio de Janeiro. He was a professor at the Military Institute of Engineering (IME), where he taught the subject of Urban Transportation and at the Brazilian Institute of Capital Market (IBMEC), where he was a professor of Technological Innovation Administration. Since 2006, he is an Associate Professor of the Transportation Engineering Program of Coppe/UFRJ, with experience in the areas of Freight Transportation Planning, Logistics, and Transportation, Energy and the Environment, with emphasis on Transportation Systems Management. For 10 years, he has occupied positions such as director, executive director, and president at the National Association of Research and Education in Transportation (ANPET), and also an acting consultant to the National Council for Scientific and Technological Development (CNPq) of the Ministry for Science and Technology, and evaluator of the Engineering I area (Civil Engineering) at the Coordination for the Improvement of Higher Education Personnel (Capes) of the Ministry of Education and Culture. He was the leading author of Chapter 8 (Transport) of the Assessment Report 5 of the Intergovernmental Panel on Climate Change (IPCC) of the United Nations. He coordinated the Transport Chapter of the Brazilian Panel on Climate Change (PBMC) of the Ministry for the Environment. He is currently the coordinator of the Freight Transport Laboratory (LTC) at Coppe/UFRJ and technical coordinator of the Brazilian Green Logistics Program (PLVB—see www.plvb.org.br) and president of the Brazilian Institute of Sustainable Transportation (IBTS). He has consolidated professional experience in the management of heavy vehicle fleets (trucks and buses) and the management of physical distribution. He currently focuses on the following research lines: sustainability in logistics and prospective future scenarios for energy use in transportation. In the last 10 years, his consolidated experience enabled the publication of 20 scientific

xii   About the Author

articles in top JCR journals such as Transportation Research D, Renewable and Sustainable Energy Reviews, and Journal of Cleaner Production, 84 scientific articles in international and national congresses, 9 book chapters, and 7 books, including the unique Brazilian book in transportation, energy use, and environmental impacts.

Preface

In 1988, when I attended the undergraduate course in Mechanical and Automotive Engineering at the Military Institute of Engineering, studies related to topics associated with engineering and the environment were, to us students, almost a theme of science fiction. I perfectly remember that this subject passed by completely unnoticed in a context in which content addressing machine drawing, thermal engines, transmission systems, and vehicle chassis design was broadly predominant in our daily worries. After all, cars were at the center of our attention and, until the present, they are still fascinating to a large part of the society.

Ten years before, my father, Emyr D'Agosto, already collected newspaper clippings of articles that associated the use of cars to the excessive consumption of fossil fuels, and to the emission of air pollutants and greenhouse gases, although the topic was addressed somewhat differently. "My son, the excessive use of cars is bad for humanity," he once told me. At that time, I was concerned with airplanes and wanted to become an engineer at the Aeronautics Institute of Technology. I did not pay attention to this prediction!

In my first job, at Companhia Brasileira de Petróleo Ipiranga, I had the opportunity of participating in the relevant Brazilian study known as Plangas, which, following the example of countries, such as Italy and Australia, proposed the substitution of diesel oil for natural gas in buses and trucks that operated in urban areas. Our consciousness already began to understand the need for safeguarding energy security and to decrease the intense dependence of road transportation on petroleum-derived diesel oil. Naturally, replacing diesel oil with natural gas in this scenario also brought the environmental benefit of potentializing the reduction of air-pollutant emissions in the cities. This benefit, however, seemed marginal and had to be justified by some sort of financial benefit associated with the lower price of natural gas in terms of energy content.

Approximately 10 years before Plangas, Proálcool had already started introducing a renewable biofuel into the Brazilian transportation energy matrix, also leading to the development of specific vehicular technology. At that time, this action was induced by the need of reducing this dependence on the use of gasoline, in an environment of petroleum crisis. This initiative, taken 50 years ago, reflects the Brazilian position as the largest consumer of biofuels for transportation in the world, with a percentage ranging from 15% to 18% in the national energy matrix, while the world average does not surpass 2%.

xiv Preface

Dealing with large fleets of freight road vehicles in the activity of urban collection and delivery developed at Minasgás S.A. and at Rio de Janeiro Refrescos (a franchise of Coca-Cola in Rio de Janeiro) has enabled me to understand how this activity has the potential of impacting the environment of cities, and allowed the understanding of how the investment in technology to improve the existing equipment, particularly internal combustion engines, helps minimizing these impacts in an environment of regulation and control. However, in this context, the economic development was still the goal to be achieved.

Only in 1997, when I began the master's course in Transportation Engineering, at the Military Institute of Engineering, the environmental focus applied to transportation gained prominence in my activities. The critical analysis of Environmental Impact Reports for transportation enterprises and the financial and environmental assessment of plans for the exploration of roads that would come to suffer the process of concession showed that much still needed to be done in this line of research. This book possibly began to be born at that time.

Also, in the turn of the 21st century, we started to understand that the environmental aspects would begin to have a growing importance in the design, implementation, and operation of transportation activities. In 2000, when I started my doctorate studies at the Transportation Engineering Program of Coppe/UFRJ, under the advisory of Professor Suzana Kahn-Ribeiro, I also began a long period of participation in projects that had the main goal of improving environmental sustainability in transportation. After 19 years, we have the same focus and there is still much work ahead!

From the experience accumulated throughout the years with studies related to transportation and to energy use and its environmental impacts, in 2007, I started to teach the subject of Transportation and the Environment, which was mandatory to students of the Environmental Engineering course of the Federal University of Rio de Janeiro (UFRJ) when I became a professor in 2006. In fact, now I am a professor at the Transportation Engineering Program of the Alberto Luiz Coimbra Institute of Graduate Studies and Research in Engineering (Coppe), with two main research lines: sustainable logistics and future prospective scenarios for transportation and energy use and environmental impacts. Nevertheless, a fortunate combination of knowledge and specific experience in the research line of transportation and the environment has enabled me to establish this cooperation with the Polytechnic School of UFRJ and enjoy the company of excellent students of the Environmental Engineering course. At this moment, it was clear that there was a need for creating and publishing this work as soon as possible. After 7 years, it was possible to publish the Portuguese version of this book and now the opportunity has come to expand its content to the global version in English!

This book has the main purpose of overcoming a gap in the formation of engineers in all specializations that require the understanding of the relationship between the activities of transportation, energy use, and the environmental impacts associated with these activities. The context of its production indicates it as the main reference for disciplines about transportation, energy use, and its environmental impacts in the courses of Environmental Engineering, Civil Engineering with an emphasis on transportation, Production Engineering, Urban Engineering, Mobility Engineering, and Geography. Naturally, it may also be used in courses to form technicians and technologists in the various segments of engineering. My classroom experience allows me to recommend it as a basic reference for the subject of Transportation and the Environment, or any other subject with this kind of focus, for master's and doctorate courses in Transportation Engineering, Production Engineering, Naval Engineering, Mechanical Engineering, Urban Engineering, and Mobility Engineering.

Although I seek to take a broad approach, the book focuses on the operation of transportation since this step is usually associated with the highest level of energy consumption and production of environmental impacts. With that in mind, from this preface on, the book is subdivided into seven chapters.

Chapter 1, presents an introductory view about transportation, a useful subject to the student that did not have any preliminary contact with this activity. Concepts related to the activities of transportation, as well as their elements, systems and subsystems are shown in detail as per the mode of transportation.

The planning, construction, and demobilization of a transportation enterprise along with resulting associated environmental impacts are briefly considered in Chapter 2. I understand that this theme involves enough content to justify a separate publication, specifically focusing on Civil Engineering.

Chapter 3 addresses a procedure for transportation planning under the focus of energy use. Based on fundamental concepts, which relate the activity of transportation and its components to work, under a thermodynamic focus, guidelines are shown that enable the planner to establish how to make transportation more efficient in terms of energy consumption. In this context, the possibility of choosing nonmotorized transportation, individual transportation, and collective transportation directs the energy efficiency of a passenger transportation system. A similar approach is applied to freight transportation.

Chapter 4 presents a specific perspective of propulsion systems and energy use. Greater focus is given to road transportation, due to its importance in the modal split of transportation worldwide. However, applications for the railway, water, pipeline, and air modes are also considered, as well as an overview of future trends on this theme.

The different energy sources for transportation are addressed in Chapter 5, highlighting petroleum derivatives, natural gas, ethanol, and biodiesel, with a description of their productive chains. A brief report of future fuels is also shown.

Chapter 6 addresses the emission of air pollutants and greenhouse gases. Also, the concepts associated with this topic and their specificities are considered. I sought to offer a comprehensive approach, considering all the modes of

xvi Preface

transportation. However, due to its importance, road transportation has special attention.

Finally, Chapter 7 very briefly discusses the environmental impacts associated with sound pollution, vibration, visual intrusion, and waste generation. The approach seeks to present an introductory overview of these topics, keeping in mind that their detailed consideration would justify the development of another book, which may be considered for future editions.

Acknowledgments

I thank all those who contributed somehow to the development of this publication, whose seed was sown more than 20 years ago when I was still a master's student in Transportation Engineering at the Military Institute of Engineering and had the first contact with consistent studies about the environmental impacts of transportation activities.

I especially thank Lísia Carla Lacques, my wife, who supported me along the long journey of knowledge acquisition, which kept me away from her presence very often, culminating in the conclusion of this book. I thank my parents, (in memory) and Nícia Celis Almeida, who created the opportunities for the education and knowledge that enabled me to overcome academic and professional challenges.

Regarding my academic formation, I thank all of the professors of the undergraduate course in Mechanical and Automotive Engineering and of the graduate course in Transportation Engineering at the Military Institute of Engineering for the solid academic formation they have given me, and the professors of the Doctorate in Transportation Engineering, especially professor Suzana Kahn-Ribeiro, who directed my advisory toward deepening the understandings about the environmental impacts related to the activities of transportation.

Regarding the improvement of professional practices, which had strict relationship with topic addressed in this publication, I thank the opportunity of having worked and enjoyed the experience of many colleagues at Companhia Brasileira de Petróleo Ipiranga, of the former Minasgás S.A. Fuel Gas Distributor (currently SHV Energy), of Rio de Janeiro Refrescos (franchise of Coca-Cola in Rio de Janeiro), of CR4 Engenharia e Consultoria Ltda., of the International Virtual Institute of Global Change (IVIG), and of the former Municipal Superintendence of Urban Transportation (SMTU).

I also thank Neide for the support in domestic chores, which relieved me from my housework load and gave me free time to dedicate to this work.

For the financial support throughout my academic life, I thank Alberto Luiz Coimbra Institute of Graduate Studies and Research in Engineering (Coppe) of the Federal University of Rio de Janeiro (UFRJ), the Coordination for the Improvement of Higher Education Personnel (Capes), the National Council for Scientific and Technological Development (CNPq), Carlos Chagas Filho Foundation for the Support of Research in the State of Rio de Janeiro

xviii Acknowledgments

(Faperj), Foundations for Coordination, Research Projects and Technological Studies (Coppetec), and all the institutions that have ever given me support throughout my academic journey.

I thank Pedro Luna, a professional who much dedicated himself to understanding and learning about this topic to translate the full content of this book into the English language.

I finally thank my canine (Layla, Thor, Mel I and Baixus I - in memory - and Luke, Leka, Mel II, Caco, and Baixus II) and feline (Dom Cor Leone) family, who has only given me joy and has helped ease my life of much work.

All have contributed to an environmentally sustainable world!

Chapter 1

Transportation, an introduction

General goal

The general goal of this chapter is to present concepts related to the transportation activity considering its different modes (road, railway, water, pipeline, and air transportation), the structure of each system with its subsystems (way, vehicle, terminal, and control), the steps needed for their implementation (planning, design, construction, operation, and demobilization), and a current overview of the transportation sector around the world.

At the end of this chapter, the reader should be able to understand:

1. The concepts related to the transportation activity, its systems, and subsystems.
2. The different modes of transportation and their subsystems.
3. The different steps needed for the implementation and operation of a transportation system.
4. An overview of transportation around the world.

1.1 Introduction

Transportation is essential to modern life! It supports and enables most social and economic activities. Different modes of transportation are used worldwide to transport people and freight, each mode with specific characteristics of implementation and operation. With that in mind, knowing the subsystems of each mode of transportation is fundamental to understand their functioning and the impacts generated by the different stages of implementation and operation of the transportation systems on the physical, biotic, and anthropic environments, which will be addressed in the following chapters.

To provide a foundation to reader's knowledge about the topic, this chapter presents the concepts related to the area of transportation in Section 1.1. Section 1.2 addresses the transportation system and its elements. Section 1.3 presents the modes of transportation, detailing for each mode its history and subsystems. The phases of the life cycle of a transportation enterprise are presented in Section 1.4. Sections 1.5 and 1.6 give an overview of transportation around the world.

1.2 Concepts related to transportation

Due to its close relationship with the economic and social development of nations, transportation is an indispensable activity in modern society. On the other

Transportation, Energy Use and Environmental Impacts. https://doi.org/10.1016/B978-0-12-813454-2.00001-5
© 2019, Elsevier Editora Ltda. Published by Elsevier Inc. All rights reserved.

2 Transportation, energy use and environmental impacts

hand, transportation has a significant influence on the environment, since it is an activity that depends on the offer of infrastructure, which requires major engineering works for its construction, and whose operation intensively uses energy, which nowadays comes mainly from fossil fuels. But what is transportation and why is it so important?

Transportation is the displacement of mass, either people or freight (goods, assets, residues, etc.), from one point to another. This displacement takes place along a route and consumes a given amount of resources, such as time or an amount of energy, while the latter is responsible for the action of the external force (driving force) that causes the displacement.

Under the economic perspective, transportation, whether of passengers or freight, is a service that not only generates wealth, but also helps to develop the production potential of other activities, adding "time" and "space" value to transported mass. It is through transportation that we can go from one region to another and take products to the places where they are needed. Transportation is part of most human activities in the world and that is why it can be classified as a "fuzzy input."

A transportation system is a set of integrated activities that involve resources (material, human, financial, and intellectual resources) needed for the displacement of people and freight in time along a route.

This system comprises a set of elements that interact with each other aiming to enable the transportation of people and freight. When transportation is service provided by a third party, its elements may be summarized as shown in Fig. 1.1.

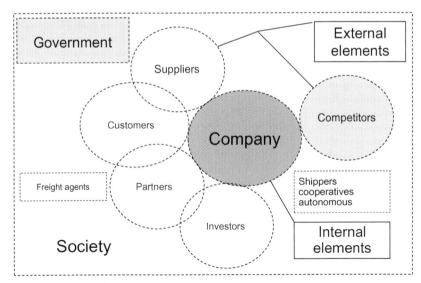

FIG. 1.1 Elements of a transportation system.

In Fig. 1.1, the elements of the transportation system are: customers (e.g., passengers, freight shippers, or service contractors), the company (e.g., passenger transportation operators, freight carriers, cooperatives, or independent carriers), partners (passenger travel agents, freight transportation agents, other carriers, cooperatives, and independent carriers), material or service suppliers (energy, parts, components, and production input suppliers), investors (banks and creditors), competitors (other public transportation operators, other carriers, cooperatives, and independent carriers), society (in different levels of organization and representation), and the government.

The interactions between the elements presented in Fig. 1.1 take place within the social context, where society is the bigger group that includes the other subgroups. The company with its partners, suppliers, and investors seeks to meet the customers' demand so that the latter may act in a way that is favorable to the company's activities. On the other hand, the competitors, as the name suggests, compete within the market.

Each element presented in Fig. 1.1 has its own perspectives and interests regarding the transportation system and it is usually up to the government (public authority) to rule these interests and promote the necessary infrastructure for the good operation of this system, guaranteeing that this be done without compromising the balance of the environment and generating as much social benefit as possible.

The transportation system is usually subdivided into four physical systems: way, vehicle, terminal, and control. These physical subsystems interact with each other to allow the adequate functioning of the transportation system. When analyzing transportation systems, it is important to adopt a systemic view, since a system's optimal level is not always achieved with the sum of the optimal levels of its subsystems.

Way is the space designated for the movement of people and freight. It may be a materialized, well-defined facility of mandatory passage, such as railways, roads, and pipelines, or a simple virtual indicative trajectory calculated for the transportation. In this hypothesis, it is called route and is used for water and air transportation. Even these two modes may have route sections with signaling at terminal access points or at places with potential traffic conflict. In the case of passenger transportation, sidewalks for pedestrian traffic and bicycle paths are also examples of ways.

Vehicle is the equipment that enables the movement of people (driver and passengers) and freight. It is used in the road, railway, water, and air modes, in which the driving force is directly applied to the vehicle to enable the movement of people and freight. In pipeline transportation, however, there is no vehicle in the common sense of the term, and the driving force is applied onto the mass to be transported.

Terminals, stations, and stops are appropriate locations for the exchange of passengers and freight between the transportation system and the environment around it in operations of embarking/disembarking or loading/unloading of

4 Transportation, energy use and environmental impacts

vehicles. They represent points of origin, transfer,[1] transhipment,[2] and/or points of destination for the movement of people or freight.

The stops, in general, are distributed along the way simply for the exchange of passengers or freight. Stations and terminals, on the other hand, may have other functions, such as vehicle maneuvering, replacement, substitution or repair; passenger services; and freight storage.

The adequate and safe working of the transportation system requires a control subsystem. Physically, this subsystem comprises a set of detection, communication, and signaling equipment, which aims to integrate the remaining physical components of the transportation system and regulate its operation with the main purpose of promoting safety, efficiency, and reasonable use. Other aspects also need to be considered within the scope of control, such as all the information technology used in this context, and all the intelligence needed to manage the operation and the business of passenger and freight transportation.

The need for control is related to the spatial freedom of movement within the system. Railways and pipelines, for example, only have one degree of freedom due to the strictness of their guideways, which are necessarily linear.

Roads and waterways have two degrees of freedom, since the movement occurs on a surface, requiring the definition of rules for vehicles to move around to reduce as much as possible the conflicting interferences between them or with the guideway surroundings.

Air transportation has three degrees of freedom, and its vehicles have spatial freedom in three axes, requiring strict universal rules for its operation and an intensive training of the ones responsible for flying the vehicles.

Still concerning control, it is necessary to take into consideration the technical and economic coordination of the modes, so that the elements presented in Fig. 1.1 effectively enjoy the transportation service. For that purpose, the institutional framework is established; it is a set of legal instruments and entities that regulate transportation.

1.3 Transportation modes

The transportation of passengers may be carried out by four[3] modes: road, railway, water, and air. In the case of freight transportation, the pipeline mode may be added. A brief description of a transportation system's subsystems (way, vehicle, terminal, and control) are presented below.

---

1. Transfer: the transfer of passengers between vehicles of the same mode of transportation or of different modes of transportation.

2. Transhipment: the transfer of freight from a segment of a transportation mode to another segment of the same mode or to another transportation mode.

3. Until the date this book was published, the transportation of people through pipelines was not in practice yet. There is an initiative for that called the Hyperloop, which is a system of pipelines meant to transport people and freight.

1.3.1 Road transportation

Roads are the oldest land transportation ways and they appeared as a natural evolution of primitive walking or animal movement tracks. In more developed regions or those with more commercial exchange, roads have gradually received improvements (bricks, stone, wood, oily mixtures) and drainage to provide better traffic conditions during rainy seasons. Thus, in the 18th century BCE it was possible to go from Italy to Denmark by road, and in the 3rd century CE the "Silk Road" was used for land transportation from China to Eastern Europe (Lay, 1992).

The Romans, given their need of keeping roads ready for the passage of military vehicles, at least near Rome, became the best road builders of the Western World in the years before Christ Era. The Appian Way is the best-known example of these constructions, which can still be seen in its preserved sections. Their network of roads extended all throughout Western Europe (Italy, France, Spain, Portugal, Germany, and Netherlands), reaching England, the Middle East, and North Africa, surrounding the Mediterranean Sea. At that moment, there were already concerns with geometric layouts, superficial drainage, special structures (bridges, tunnels, slope containment works, etc.), road bed, and paving (Lay, 1992).

The dominant cultural influence of the northern hemisphere often prevents the noticing of related facts in the South American continent. That is why it is little known that the Incas, with their Royal Road (with 4000 km of length throughout the Andes from the north of Argentina to the west of Venezuela), built a longer and better road in comparison to most roads of ancient western cultures. The Royal Road had heptagonal stone culverts, arc bridges, slope containment works, and pavement that were used until today by motored vehicles (Lay, 1992).

The land roads became the dominant means of transportation where people could walk, ride animals, or use animal traction vehicles until the creation of railways. In Europe and North America, companies dedicated to the regular transportation of freight and passengers were created (Lay, 1992; Heskett, 1998). With the rise of railways and their great capacity to transport both freight and passengers, roads lost their influence, which was only reestablished, in developed countries, with the advent of motored vehicles at the end of the 19th century and beginning of the 20th century (Georgano, 1985). The creation of internal combustion engines with the use of petroleum by-products, that is, gasoline and diesel oil, confirmed this trend (Obert, 1971).

Road transportation became the most usual choice in regions of initial exploration and in countries of a lower degree of development because it is the mode with the lowest investment costs for passenger transport and small and medium freight flows (up to 50 tons per vehicle) in short and medium distances (up to 1000 km) and because it has a fairly simple construction technology.

1.3.1.1 Roads

The way in road transportation is called road or, more popularly, street, avenue, or highway. Its design must meet limitations of vertical alignment (uphill and downhill sections) and horizontal alignment (curves). For that reason, the location where a road will be constructed almost always needs to be submitted to land cuts and fills along the road's layout, consequently leading to earth moving (earthworks). On the other hand, the materials needed for the construction of the road (gravel, sand, crushed stone, clay, etc.) are extracted from places called borrow pits, which must be as close as possible to the construction site.

Road pavement is formed, in its most complete expression, by parts: subgrade, subgrade reinforcement, subbase, base, and surface course; all these together have the technical name of pavement, with thickness usually ranging from 5 to 60 cm, as shown in Fig. 1.2. Usually, the surface course of a road is made with asphalt, which requires the installation of asphalt plants along the region where the road will be constructed. The surface course may also be made of concrete, which renders this pavement layer more resistant to heavier loads, thus suffering less wear and tending to have higher durability.

When the construction site is in an urban area, it is usually necessary to expropriate real estate along the road's layout. In case the construction is out of an urban area, it may be necessary to deforest the perimeter required for the construction of the road.

The projects must also take into considerations regular civil engineering structures (RCES), such as drainage interventions (ditches and culverts), protection (traffic barriers and jersey barriers), landscaping (trees and lawn), signs and markings (signs, surface marks, panels, highway location markers, etc.), and special civil engineering structures (SCES), such as bridges, viaducts, tunnels, and slope containment structures.

1.3.1.2 Road vehicles

Motorized road vehicles are differentiated from each other mainly by their purpose and are categorized as passenger, freight, or mixed vehicles, as illustrated in Table 1.1.

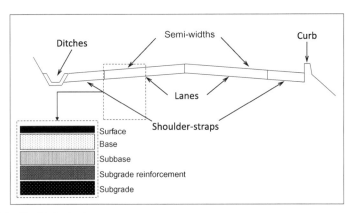

FIG. 1.2 Road infrastructure.

Transportation, an introduction Chapter | 1 7

TABLE 1.1 Characterization of motorized road vehicles

Passenger vehicles	Moped	Two- or three-wheel vehicle with an internal combustion engine with no more than $50\,cm^3$ of engine size and whose maximum speed does not exceed $50\,km/h$.
	Scooter	Two-wheel motorized vehicle operated by a conductor in sitting position.
	Motorcycle[a]	Two-wheel motorized vehicle, with or without a sidecar, operated by a conductor in mounted position.
	Car	Motor vehicle intended for passenger transportation, with capacity of up to eight people, including the conductor.
	Microbus	Collective transportation motorized vehicle with capacity of up to 20 passengers.
	Bus	Collective transportation motorized vehicle with capacity for more than 20 passengers, even if it transports less than that due to adaptations made to increase passenger comfort.
Freight vehicles	Light commercial vehicle	Vehicle used to transport freight with a total gross weight of up to $3500\,kg$.
	Truck	Vehicle used to transport freight with a total gross weight above $3500\,kg$.
	Tractor	Motor vehicle used to pull or drag another vehicle.
	Full trailer	Vehicle designed to be coupled behind a motor vehicle.
	Semitrailer	Vehicle with one or more axles that rests on its tractor unit or is connected to it by an articulation.
Mixed vehicles.	Pickup	Mixed vehicle used to transport passengers and freight in the same compartment.
	Utility van	Mixed vehicle characterized by its versatile use, even off-road.

[a] *This vehicle may be adapted to be used for freight.*
Source: Made by the author based on the Brazilian Federal Law no. 9503, of September 23, 1997.

8 Transportation, energy use and environmental impacts

Thus, motorized road vehicles may be automotive, if they are self-propelled, or towed, if they are not. Currently, the energy used to propel them comes almost exclusively from light petroleum by-products, that is, gasoline and diesel oil, and, to a lesser degree, from other forms such as biofuels (ethanol and biodiesel), natural gas, and electricity. Rolling occurs mostly through the rolling of vehicle wheels with rubber tires over the road's pavement.

In freight transportation, trucks are the most commonly used types of vehicle worldwide. Regarding its construction, this vehicle is made of three main parts: chassis, cabin, and body, as shown in Fig. 1.3.

The chassis is the framework (in the shape of a "ladder," made of longerons and crossmembers) responsible for supporting the weight of the cabin, the body, and the load and, also supporting the remaining components of the vehicle, such as the propulsion, suspension, breaking, and steering systems. An "auxiliary

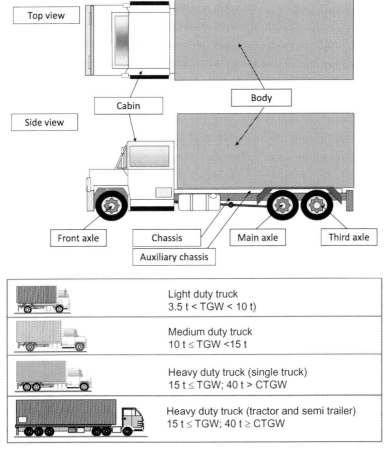

FIG. 1.3 Composition of a truck and truck categories. *TGW*, total gross weight; *CTGW*, combined total gross weight.

chassis" made of wood or steel longerons is usually installed between the chassis and the body to enable the adjustment of the body on the chassis without interferences in other components of the vehicle.

The cabin is the place used by the vehicle driver and the body is the place used to store the freight. It is usually possible to purchase a set including the chassis and cabin from a vehicle manufacturer and the body from a body manufacturer. A set formed by chassis and cabin may receive different bodies such as a box-shaped body, as shown in Fig. 1.3.

For collective passenger transportation, buses (Fig. 1.4A and B) and cars (Fig. 1.5) stand out.

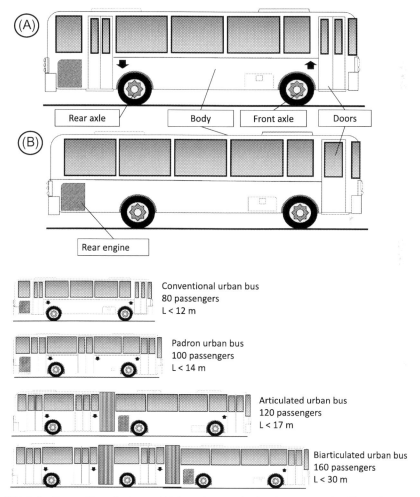

FIG. 1.4 Composition of urban and highway buses and urban buses categories. Figure A represents a conventional urban bus equipped with a two-door body (one for embarking and another for disembarking), and Figure B represents a highway bus, with a front access door body. *L*, length.

10 Transportation, energy use and environmental impacts

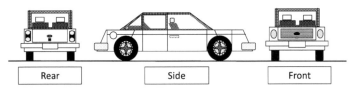

FIG. 1.5 Composition of a car.

Buses may be manufactured from a combination of chassis and body (body-on-frame) or as single block (unibody). In the first composition, the chassis, as in the case of a truck, is a frame (also in the shape of a "ladder" and made of longerons and crossmembers) responsible for supporting the weight of the body and the remaining components of the vehicle, such as the propulsion, suspension, breaking, and steering systems.

The body is the place used by the passengers and the vehicle's driver. It is usually possible to purchase the chassis from a vehicle manufacturer and the body from a body manufacturer.

In the case of buses manufactured as a unibody, a coated structure in the shape of a box or cage supports all the functional components of the vehicle and defines the places designated for the passengers and the driver.

In the case of modern cars, the current standard practice is to build them as a unibody instead of a body-on-frame (Fig. 1.5). In this case, the vehicle is made of one single structure in the shape of a cage that supports all the other components of the vehicle, such as the propulsion, suspension, breaking, and steering systems, and it also protects the driver and passengers.

1.3.1.3 Road terminals

Terminals may be for freight, passengers, or mixed use; they are subdivided into public and private terminals according to their priority and use. In freight transportation, terminals may receive the special designation of warehouses when they are used to store packed and/or bulk freight. Fig. 1.6 shows the morphology of a road terminal used for general unitized freight.

There are terminals for different applications. In the case of freight terminals, they may be used, for example, for bulk, unitized, or containerized freight. These terminals may have specific equipment for vehicle loading and unloading, such as forklifts, pallet trucks, and overhead cranes. In the case of passenger terminals (Fig. 1.7), they may be used for passenger embarking or disembarking, and each may have different morphologies but similar operational procedures.

Still in the case of urban buses, it is common that passengers embark and disembark at specific points throughout the road (bus stops), and in the case of cars, public and private parking lots should be taken into consideration.

Since the road mode enables access throughout the whole road, there may still be what are called "informal terminals," in which access to the system is

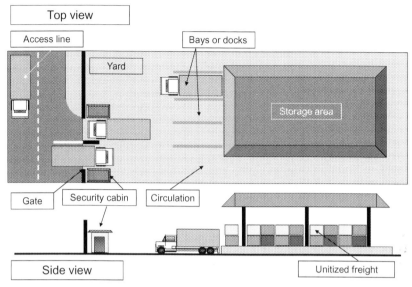

FIG. 1.6 Morphology of a road terminal for general unitized freight.

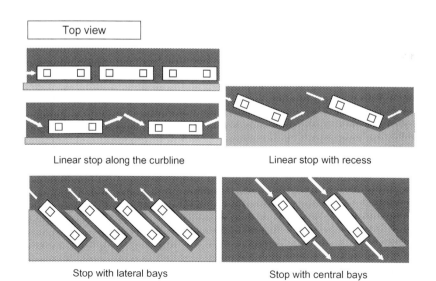

FIG. 1.7 Morphology of passenger road terminals—Top view.

12 Transportation, energy use and environmental impacts

made regardless of specific facilities, such as stops next to sidewalks for cars, buses, or trucks, which makes the mode extremely flexible, especially for small and very disseminated demands.

1.3.1.4 Control

Forms of control, in the current stage of technology application, are mostly external to the vehicles and are usually indicative, in the form of legislation, signs, and police power, which makes education something of vital importance in the conduction of this transportation mode.

It is possible to apply automation in the traffic control of road vehicles, specially using ITS (*intelligent transport system*) solutions. However, although it is available, this technology is still expensive and is more commonly used in developed countries and less applied in developing countries. On the other hand, there is a current belief that this trend will have an accelerated diffusion throughout the following years, including the introduction of autonomous vehicles (without drivers).

It must not be forgotten that traffic control, particularly in the case of automation, heavily depends on information technology, communication systems, and information exchange, and that the availability of this additional infrastructure will have to be made and expanded.

The great expansion of the fleet of private cars, due to their relatively accessible price even in developing countries, the lack of infrastructure, and the slow introduction of effective control mechanisms have originated congestion in cities' urban traffic, which leads to high social and environmental costs. It is possible that the automation of vehicle traffic and a more reasonable use of these resources may lead to ways of minimizing this problem.

Currently, in many cities worldwide, especially in the developing countries, the speed of motorized road vehicles is lower than that of animal traction vehicles in the beginning of the 20th century. In most cases, particularly in central areas, the main component of the problem is the inadequacy of the road network to the type and volume of the current vehicle fleet, and the lack of mass urban public transportation.

Example 1.1   Nonmotorized road transport—Bike sharing systems

As will be presented in Chapter 3, walking and cycling are the two most environmentally friendly ways of transporting people and freight by road as far as travel size, safety, and climatic and geographic conditions allow it. It happens not only because of the limited use of energy but also because of the absence of atmospheric pollutant and greenhouse gas emissions, there is almost no noise and it is beneficial to human health. Compared to walking, cycling allows a faster trip (three times as fast) with less effort (half of it) what makes it the preferred nonmotorized means of transportation for small (5 km) to medium (15 km) trips.

Transportation, an introduction **Chapter | 1**   **13**

Bike sharing systems is one way to improve urban mobility by the use of bikes. In the world, in 2013, it was estimated that there were 52 cities with 635 different bike sharing systems and a fleet of 629,872 bicycles, most of it (70%) in Asia, in particular (20%) in China, where bikes were always used for transportation. Another 20% of the sharing bike's fleet is placed in European countries where people use bikes mostly for transportation needs both for origin to destination trips and to access urban transit modes like buses, LRT, subways, suburban trains, or ferry boats (Midgley, 2013).

1.3.2   Railway transportation

Railways emerged in the mining regions of England, with their *wagonways* that were primitive rough-wood ways over which wagons powered by small animals transported mineral coal and, sometimes, workers. The purpose of these ways was to avoid the formation of wheel channels that would consequently lead to the vehicle getting mired down on rainy days. Installations of this kind spread all through the mining areas of Europe since the 16th century. In the 18th century, the North American mines introduced metal rails and double-flanged wheels to reinforce movement safety. In addition to the constancy of the transportation, considering the meteorological hardships (thus the term permanent way), this mode reduced external friction and, therefore, traction energy consumption, which at that time relied on animal traction (Lay, 1992; Heskett, 1998).

The change from animal traction to an energy-generation mechanism also followed a trajectory of centuries and it was up to James Watt, after 11 years of attempts, to assemble the first effective fixed steam-powered machine in 1775. Murdock, Watt's assistant, built in 1784 a steam locomotive, followed by many other inventors with consecutive improvements such as Blenkisop's rack locomotive in 1811 and Hedley's simple adherence locomotive (Hawkes, 1991; Asimov, 1993; Heskett, 1998).

In 1815, George Stephenson, based on Hedley's experiences, had his first success in the construction of steam locomotives. In 1825, for the railway of 25 km built by Stockton and Darlington, Stephenson won a competition and started the first commercial passenger service (Hawkes, 1991).

Since then, there was continuous progress in the construction of more solid ways and better rolling, as with the locomotives based on other forms of traction such as internal combustion engines running on fuel oil or diesel oil; diesel-electric systems, in which an internal combustion engine running on diesel oil generates electric power for electric traction engines; or electric engines powered by a power distribution network external to the vehicle. The latter was first developed for direct current from 600 to 3000 W and, currently, may use single phase alternating current of up to 25,000 W.

With the growing number of circulating trains, primitive systems of semaphores and telegraphs were created and evolved to the modern automatic systems of total control for trains and their movement in ample territory extensions.

14 Transportation, energy use and environmental impacts

Similarly, the rolling material for traction and transportation was developed per passenger and freight.

Both great stations for passengers and huge automated yards for freight were built as terminals for these compositions. Railways, in developed segments, have an advanced application of computerized automation, with cutting-edge technology such as fiber-optic communication, computer control, and satellite tracking.

1.3.2.1 Permanent way

In railways, the way is called permanent way for the historical reason of having been the only transportation mode to keep land transportation operational during rainy seasons in the 19th century. It is usually subdivided into three parts: infrastructure, superstructure, and complementary works.

Infrastructure essentially comprises earthworks related to the subgrade, at a lower level; the base, which is a superior layer with mechanized treatment to provide more supporting capacity; and the implementation of complementary and special structures (bridges, viaducts, tunnels, containment works, etc.). The superstructure comprises ballast, sleepers, rails, and their fixation, as shown in Fig. 1.8, and it aims to guarantee an easy and safe rolling of the vehicles and allow the distribution of loads over the infrastructure to avoid excessive pressures, besides supporting superficial auxiliary draining.

The ballast, usually made of compressed crushed stone, has a trapezoidal cross section and has three main functions: route layout maintenance, cushioned transmission of train loads (P) to the railway bed, and superficial drainage. Along some sections of high-speed modern railways, the ballast has been replaced by concrete slabs.

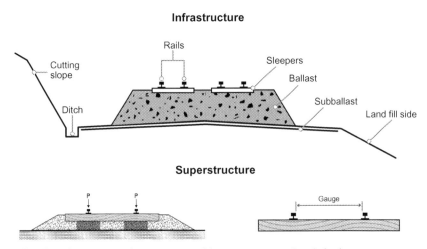

FIG. 1.8 Infrastructure and superstructure of the permanent way. P, train load.

The sleepers have the main purpose of maintaining the gauge.[4] The sleeper also ensures a better distribution of the wheel loads transversally and the good insertion of rail set on the ballast to avoid the displacement of the layout. They may be made of different materials such as wood, concrete, steel, and plastic, although wood is the most common one. The gauge is the main characteristic of a railway's permanent way; the standard gauge is 1.435 m, the broad gauges are 1.567 or 1.600 m, and narrow gauges are smaller than the standard gauge.

The rails, made of carbon steel or special steel alloys, are basically the wheel rolling surfaces, which results in low friction. Their purpose is to fix the railway's layout and to longitudinally distribute the loads. They are longitudinally interconnected by means of fishplates and lately they have been welded in sequence to form a long-welded rail, improving vehicle rolling.

Fastening is the way rails are fixed to sleepers, and it may be rigid or elastic. Rigid fastening seeks to prevent any rail movement in relation to the sleeper and it usually comprises a perforated support plate, where rail spikes or screws are inserted to penetrate the sleepers.

Complementary works include several items concerning the guideway such as fences, slope lawing, placement of way location markers, curve ties, etc.

1.3.2.2 Rolling stock

The vehicles in railways are called rolling stock and are subdivided into powered and unpowered rolling stock (Fig. 1.9). Powered rolling stock includes locomotives, locotractors, and railbuses.

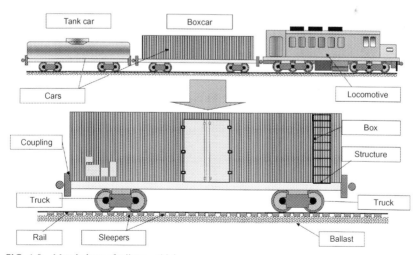

FIG. 1.9 Morphology of railway vehicles.

---

4. Gauge is the distance between the internal faces of rail heads, which are the upper parts of the rails that make direct vertical and horizontal contact with vehicle's wheels.

16 Transportation, energy use and environmental impacts

Type		Purpose
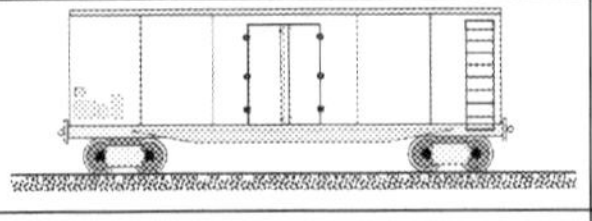	Boxcar	Transportation of solid bulk, bags, boxes, unitized freight and general products that cannot be exposed to the weather.
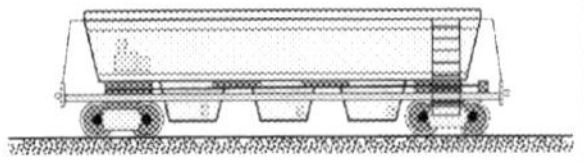	Hopper car	Transportation of corrosive and/or solid bulk (agricultural) that cannot be exposed to the weather when covered or may be an open car for those cargo that can be exposed to the weather.
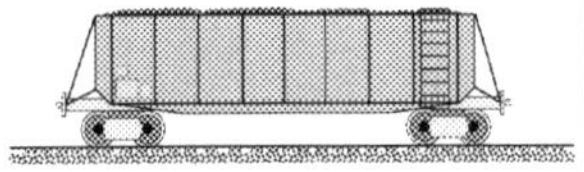	Gondola car	Transportation of solid bulk (ore) and other different kind of products that may be exposed to the weather.
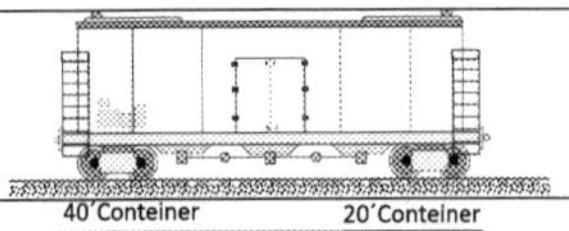	Isothermal car	Transportation of frozen products in general.
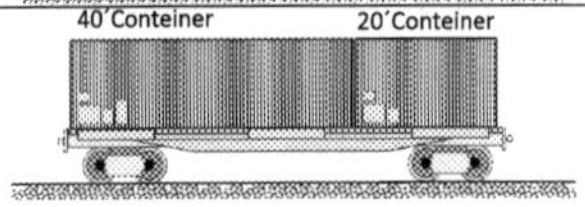	Flat car	Transportation of containers, steel products, big volumes, wood and parts of large dimensions.
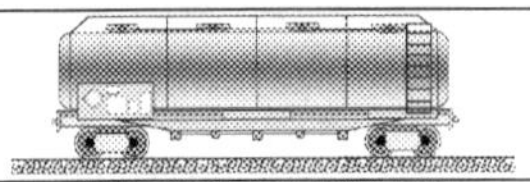	Tank car	Transportation of liquid bulk, like light petroleum products and noncorrosive liquids in general.
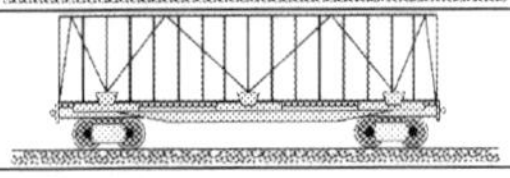	Stock car	Livestock transportation.
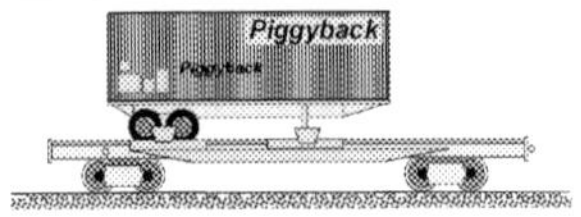	Special cars	Transportation of products with different characteristics than the ones mentioned above, like other vehicles, equipment and special cargo.

FIG. 1.10 Types of freight cars.

The locomotives and locotractors are only used to pull unpowered rolling stock, with various energy sources (firewood and coal to produce steam, diesel oil, and electric power), its power, and purposes (freight, passenger, and mixed transportation).

Railbuses can carry passengers and parcels and are also able to tow light vehicles that have the same purpose. Unpowered rolling stock, however, is subdivided into passenger cars (common, restaurant, sleeping cars, etc.) and freight and maintenance service cars.

In freight transportation, the composition of locomotive and cars is commonly used, as shown in Fig. 1.9. Cars are subdivided into different models, as described in Fig. 1.10.

Railway vehicles move on the rails by means of railroad trucks, which are structural parts containing one to four wheelsets made of one axle with two wheels, usually having a flange on the internal side that keeps the vehicle on rail. The structure of the vehicles usually comprises a box that is placed over a metal framework (underframe) on which the railroad trucks and operational equipment are fixed, such as shock and traction equipment (couplings) and breaking systems (breaks, compressed air or vacuum systems, and safety valves).

Passenger transportation may be made with railbuses, trams, LRT (light rail transit), subway, locomotives, and cars such as urban and regional trains.

Tram and LRT (Fig. 1.11) are urban electric railway systems that have the flexibility of operating with single units or short compositions along guideways that have shared circulation rights, are segregated or exclusive, and may be at-grade, elevated, or underground.

The subway is a metropolitan electric railway transportation system that is implemented in typically urban zones and has an exclusive guideway that is usually underground or elevated, although it may have some at-grade sections. Its most common support and steering are provided through the contact of the steel wheel with the steel rail.

Metropolitan trains may be developed with underground guideways within urban centers and on exclusive guideways in city outskirts and suburbs, however, the most used method is the one installed on exclusive guideways, going from the outskirts to the suburbs.

1.3.2.3 Railway terminals

Terminals are points of access to the railway transportation system, where compositions are formed, loaded and/or unloaded, revised or simply parked for operational reasons, such as crossings between trains going in opposite directions. They may be of passenger, freight, or mixed use, and they may be of public or private access. They may also be extreme or intermediate, according to their situation in

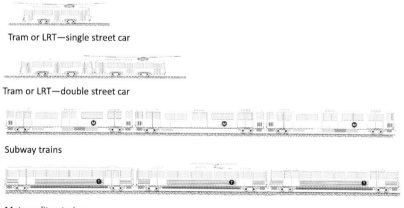

FIG. 1.11 Examples of Passenger transportation rolling stock.

18 Transportation, energy use and environmental impacts

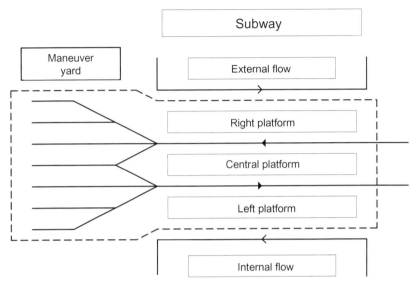

FIG. 1.12 Example of a subway terminal.

relation to sections of the guideway. In the case of freight transportation, it can be of carrier priority, of one or more users, or even of service provider companies.

Fig. 1.12 shows a schematic view of a subway terminal where passenger access (external flow) is made through the sides. In the example presented, the terminal has three embarking and disembarking platforms (right, central, and left). To access the central platform, there must be some sort of connection to the side platforms, which is usually made through elevated walkways. Fig. 1.13 shows an example of a metropolitan train terminal where public access is made through the front, allowing access to all platforms.

There are freight railway terminals with a high degree of specialization that process bulk agricultural products, bulk minerals, bulk liquids (e.g., fuels), and

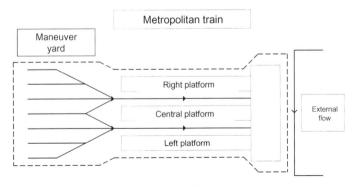

FIG. 1.13 Example of a metropolitan train terminal.

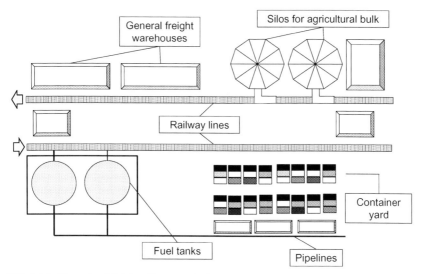

FIG. 1.14 Example of freight railway terminal.

containers. These terminals have specific equipment to process compositions, to quickly load and unload, and to ready the cars (Fig. 1.14).

1.3.2.4 Control

In railway transportation, controls usually comprise signaling, telecommunications, and licensing (permission to move) systems, which become ever more interconnected and coordinated in a computational perspective, being able to reach total train control, even in terms of speed, breaking, and steering. The operation control center (OCC) is the place where trains are controlled, and decisions are made regarding train dispatch and traffic. There are several tools that support traffic controllers, such as dashboards with real-time train tracking, computers, and radios, among others.

An essential factor that must always be considered is that while one train occupies one section of the guideway, no other train should enter this section, which requires the use of operation control systems that may be based on signaling along the sections (European standard called ERTMS[5]) or on the exchange of global positioning system (GPS) data (American standard called PTC[6]).

The section may be subdivided into subsections, called block sections, with limits defined by signals and train detection devices (track circuits). When they are present, they define the rule according to which only one train can occupy the same block section. Their use is controlled by the traffic dispatcher, who is

---

5. ERTMS: European Railway Traffic Management System
6. PTC: Positive train control

20 Transportation, energy use and environmental impacts

the person responsible for the planning, scheduling, and execution of train circulation through the network. This person is the one responsible for all the decisions regarding train crossings. He/she continually monitors their position and transmits instructions resulting from decisions about crossings, routes, stops, etc., with data transmitted by GSM-R[7] (ERTMS) or Radio 256 MHz (currently used) standards.

The integrated operation control systems (signaling, onboard systems, and OCC) based on data networks allow the continuous exchange of information on the position of trains, speed, and licensing characteristics, seeking to guarantee safety and promoting increased transportation capacity.

Example 1.2   The longest and the oldest subway systems in the world (Duddu, 2013)

Seoul subway serving the Seoul Metropolitan Area is the longest subway system in the world with a total route length extended as far as 940 km as of 2013. The first line of the subway was opened in 1974 and the system incorporates 18 lines (excluding the Uijeongbu LRT).

Seoul's subway system is operated by multiple operators including the state-owned Seoul Metro, Seoul Metropolitan Rapid Transit Corporation, Korail, Incheon Transit Corporation, and other private rapid transit operators. The annual ridership of the subway system in 2012 was over 2.5 billion passengers making it the second busiest subway system after Tokyo subway.

The London's subway with 408 km of railways is the oldest electric railway transportation system in the world. Opened in 1863, more than 100 years before the Seoul subway system, the London underground was built as part of a city improvement plan, it was born with only 6 km of rails, but, already in the first year of operation, 9.5 million passengers were transported, averaging 26,000 a day.

1.3.3   Water transportation

Transportation by water has been used by mankind since the most remote past, both in internal bodies of water (rivers and lakes) and in seas all around the world, firstly for the movement of people and for fishing and later for the transportation of commercialized products (Hawkes, 1991; Hoel et al., 2011).

In the beginning, vessels were small and propelled by muscle power or wind power, sometimes taking advantage of natural currents. A great progress was made with the introduction of the steam engine in the beginning of the 19th century, which allowed greater vessel speed and size, besides providing greater safety in face of adverse navigation conditions (Asimov, 1993).

Currently, marine vessels, particularly in maritime transportation, are those of higher unit transportation capacity and the transportation flows in this mode

---

7. GSM-R: Global System for Mobile Communications—Railway

represent more than 90% of international trade, making it an essential part of global economy (ICS, 2018).

Internally, in countries where the river and lake networks are relevant, water transportation usually represents a significant part of the flow of agricultural and mineral bulk products, and liquid fuels. That is the case for the United States, Germany, and France.

For a better approach and presentation of the subsystems, transportation by water may be called waterways transportation when it is carried out through a water guideway, be it in rivers, lakes, or seas, where there is no physical guideway but a calculated route.

Transportation by water is subdivided into: (1) inland navigation and (2) maritime; the latter may be maritime cabotage (coastal navigation) or deep-sea navigation.

Inland navigation is the one carried out along national or international routes through rivers, lakes, canals, lagoons, bays, creeks, coves, and sheltered maritime stretches (inland waterways). Maritime transportation, however, is carried out across oceans and seas.

1.3.3.1 Waterway or navigation routes

Regarding their navigation capabilities, bodies of water (rivers, lakes, and lagoons) may be classified as floatable, rudimentarily navigable, openly navigable, and waterways. Therefore, the author understands that the term waterway (or inland waterway) should be adopted to designate the navigable inland waterways (rivers, lakes, artificial canals, and access channels to ports) that have been prepared, marked, and signaled for a given design vessel,[8] that is, those that offer good safety conditions to vessels, their freight, and passengers or crew, and which have nautical charts.

This group includes the "artificial inland waterways" and the "improved inland waterways" that achieved navigation conditions, or had it improved by means of engineering works (rock blasting, dredging, channeling, installation of ripraps and locks, etc.)

However, considering navigation in a broad sense, the standard practice is to consider a "virtual guideway" based on a calculated line to be followed by the vessel in deep sea, coastal navigation, or in great rivers or lakes. This kind of calculated guideway is called a route.

In early navigation, given the absence of instruments for the calculation of the route, this process was made based on land sight using notable points of reference such as coastal elevations. This process is called coastal navigation and is still used nowadays by small vessels and handcrafted fishing boats. With time, magnetic needles began to be used, they are primitive compasses that pointed to the magnetic north and enabled the estimate of the direction to be followed.

---

8. Design vessel is the name given to the vessel model used in the parameterization of a waterway's design. The design vessel is a design tool and is not a condition to the manufacturing of vessels, at least not in its total features.

22 Transportation, energy use and environmental impacts

Centuries later, celestial navigation began to be used through the calculation of position based on celestial bodies such as the sun and large stars using instruments that evolved from the astrolabe to the sextant and with the help of astronomical tables.

Finally, the electronic navigation era began firstly with the nondirectional beacons and the corresponding direction finders, which were allowed on to find the position of a vessel via triangulation once the locations of two emitting stations were known. Systems with higher precision and rage, such as the *Lorans*, ended this era.

Nowadays, navigation is carried out with precision and ease using specialized geostationary satellites and GPS, which substituted celestial navigation and instantly and automatically provide the precise position of a vessel, regardless of atmospheric conditions.

As a supporting element, when near coastlines, there are nautical charts that can also be digitized and shown on monitors, highlighting geographic features, navigational hazards such as shallow regions and reefs, depth, and aids to navigation such as lighthouses, buoys, and radar reflectors. These are frequently complemented by "guides" with detailed instructions to navigators.

1.3.3.2 Vessels

In water transportation, vehicles receive the general name of vessels. According to their purposes, vessels may be used for passengers, freight, leisure, fishing, services (towing, fire department, rescue, perforation, etc.), and military, such as warships and coast guard vessels. As mentioned before, maritime transportation has a great predominance of freight vessels.

According to the possibility of general or restricted use, they are classified as public or private use and their nationality is attributed considering the port where they were registered, thus carrying a corresponding country flag and belonging to its national territory for civil, tax, and working legislation and for the application of International Law.

In freight waterway transportation, it is common to use convoys of tugs and barges, as shown in Fig. 1.15. In maritime transportation, it is standard practice to use individual ships of larger size (Fig. 1.16) that have been getting even larger throughout the centuries, reaching nowadays capacities above 500,000 tons deadweight (TDW).

Regarding propulsion systems, there was an evolution from nonmotorized systems, which used human power (rowers) and wind power, to those that use steam engines and, more recently, reciprocating internal combustion engines powered by petroleum-derived fuels (fuel oil and diesel oil) and steam turbines, which can use nuclear energy.

The materials used in the construction of the hull and other vessel compartments have also evolved; wood and animal skins were replaced by steel plates, then by lighter metal plates such as aluminum. There were also experiences with cement until recently arriving at plastics and carbon fiber.

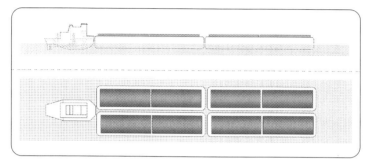

FIG. 1.15 Tug and barges used in waterway freight transportation.

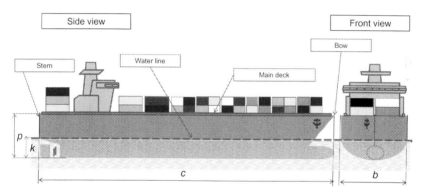

FIG. 1.16 Example of a container ship.

In terms of its dimensions a vessel is characterized by (Fig. 1.16)

- Length (c): the distance from the stern (rear) to the bow (front).
- Beam (b): the greatest distance between the vessel's sides.
- Draft (k): variable height according to the vessel's load and density of water between the waterline and the keel.
- Depth (p): fixed height measured from the keel to the main deck.

The design of a waterway must consider the dimensions (length "c," beam "b," and maximum draft "k_{max}") of the vessels that will operate on it; this is done by specifying a design vessel able to operate on minimal water depth scenario.[9]

1.3.3.3 Terminals

Terminals are the facilities where the transportation by water system may be accessed by other modes of transportation. According to their specifications they may be called ports, terminals, piers, or wharfs. Depending on the body of water in which they are located, they may be maritime, fluvial, or lacustrine.

---

9. Minimal water depth scenario: a situation that considers waterway depth during the dry season.

24 Transportation, energy use and environmental impacts

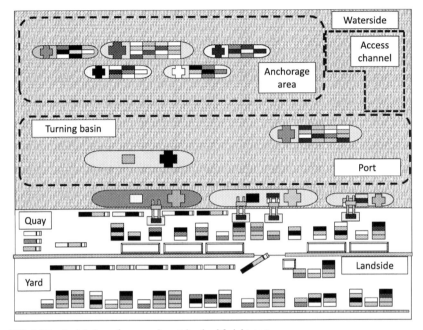

FIG. 1.17 Aerial view of a general containerized freight port.

According to the possibility of general or restricted access, they may be public or private. They may be passenger terminals or freight terminals; if they are used for both passengers and freight, they are called mixed terminals.

Freight ports are subdivided into three consecutive areas: waterside, port, and landside, as shown in Fig. 1.17.

The waterside area is the one adjacent to the terminal, in the body of water, comprising the access channel and anchorage area (the area where vessels wait for permission to access the terminal). The port includes the turning basin, berths, the quay, and the mooring zone, where the equipment used to load and unload the ship are located.

The landside is the land area near the port where there are warehouses; administrative and service buildings; access facilities to land modes, such as railways, roadways, and yards; interfaces with external services, such as the electric power grid and substations; channels and tanks for drinking, industrial, and fire-fighting water; physical telecommunication lines; sewage treatment plant and its drainage to the public grid; physical enclosure; entrance and control gates; and personal and property security cabins.

Hinterland is the name given to the area of direct influence of the water terminal, that is, where it attracts output or export flows from and distributes input or import flows to.

Regarding the products handled in the ports, they may be subdivided into:

- General freight ports, such as boxes, crates, packages, barrels, and isolated objects such as vehicles.
- Liquid and gas bulk terminals, such as those used for crude oil and its derivatives.
- Solid bulk terminals, such as those used for grains and minerals.
- Container terminals for the operation of standardized freight containers.

When compared to freight terminals, passenger port terminals are different essentially at the mooring zone and landside, which, instead of loading and unloading equipment and warehouses, have an infrastructure dedicated to the access embarking and disembarking of passengers.

1.3.3.4 Control

For maritime transportation, control comprises the activities and devices that allow the maintenance of a chosen route. Some of the navigation aid and control tools were described in Section 1.3.3.1, since they help delimiting the route. Considering that there is a certain potential freedom for each vessel to choose its route, in order to avoid collisions and possible shipwrecks, rules for "safety of life at sea" were created centuries ago, including aspects of safety that are intrinsic to the vessels themselves, such as the *Plimsoll Lines*,[10] which mark the maximum loads for each kind of ocean, in each time of the year, and preferences and reciprocal positioning when in interfering routes.

Regarding the aid to navigation equipment, the advances in electronics considerably increased the safety margins of the vessel itself and help meeting the requirements of universal conventions, especially with the radar, which enables the detection of fixed and moving obstacles around the vessel regardless of the available visibility, and the sonar with depth perception. Technological evolution and the use of satellites made it possible to create more precise and detailed nautical charts, while coastal countries intensified the installation of fixed aids, such as lighthouses, buoys, radar reflectors, and service stations.

In waterway navigation, markings, signaling, and nautical charts are instruments of navigational control. Markings on a waterway are understood as the aid to navigation buoys that delimit the navigation channel. Signaling is made with signs placed at the margins of the rivers to guide navigators.

There are waterways of day navigation only and those in which night navigation is allowed depending on the kind of markings and signaling adopted. Since navigation channels cannot be materialized, waterways require nautical charts, which are maps that delimit the navigational routes to provide safety to vessels.

---

10. Standardized marks placed on the hull's side that delimit the position of the waterline according to sea conditions.

26 Transportation, energy use and environmental impacts

Example 1.3   Waterway transportation in China

China has large navigable rivers, especially in Central and Southern China that connect many of its major cities. Moreover, China's geography and the location of its population are exceptionally favorable to inland waterway transportation. All this create the potential for inland waterway transportation to claim a larger share of China's national freight transportation, which today makes up roughly 49.6% of the freight transport in ton-kilometers (see Fig. 1.28).

Many rivers carry large volumes of bulk cargo that are hauled from rural to urban areas for processing. On the rivers' upper sections, limited water depth prevents safe year-round access by vessels with capacity of more than 100t. But for a relatively modest cost, the navigation channels on these rivers could be deepened enough to enable much larger vessels to reach far upstream. An added advantage is that due to the specific conditions in China inland waterway transportation creates less of an impact on the environment than railway or road transportation. Accordingly, to ease the pressure of demand for new roads and improved railways, the government has increased investment in waterways to deepen navigation channels and upgrade navigational aids.

1.3.4   Pipeline transportation

In ancient times, pipelines were used to transport liquid. The Chinese used bamboo to make their pipelines. Egyptians and Aztecs made their pipelines with ceramics and the Greeks made them with lead.

The use of pipelines is also very old in the use of urban equipment, especially in the collection and distribution of water to the population and in the catchment and disposal of residential sewage, functions that characterize this mode as the one with the highest level of use in tonnage and volume, although, regarding its characteristics for this specific purpose, it has not been regarded as pertaining to the transportation sector anymore, but to that of urban sanitation.

Regarded specifically as a transportation mode, pipeline transportation gained importance due to the commercial exploitation of natural gas and petroleum and the distribution of its liquid and gas derivatives, especially in the United States and Russia.

The first oil pipelines were made of cast iron, just as the pipelines used for water transportation. However, this material could not withstand pumping pressures. Positive results were only possible since 1863 with the use of forged iron.

In the beginning, the energy used to transport water in pipelines came from gravity, so that pipelines were only used in lands that favored this mode. With the beginning of the manufacturing of pumps and compressors, more energy was available than that imposed by gravity, thus allowing the transportation through longer pipelines.

More recently, pipeline transportation was reinforced due to its use in the transportation of solid bulk, such as iron ore and mineral coal mixed with water to form a slurry transported through mineral and carbon pipelines.

There is also a network of gas pipelines which is used to distribute manufactured and natural gas and to supply cooking and heating fuel worldwide.

The effective use of pipeline transportation requires continuous operation and, consequently, significant volumes to be transported, which depend on a firm demand for transportation. On the other hand, this mode causes little interference regarding land use and intense security worries with the products due to factors that are external to the system.

1.3.4.1 Pipeline

A pipeline is composed of pipes, usually made of carbon steel, welded or seamless, installed along an outline defined in the design. The sequence of pipes is interrupted at certain points by pumping or compression (in the case of gas products) stations whenever they are needed to maintain the flows, and/or by sets of storage tanks, depending on points of consumption.

The transportation capacity needed is what determines the diameter of the pipes and the power of pumps or compressors (in the case of gas products) to enable design flows with a safety margin.

There is no vehicle in pipeline transportation and driving force is applied to the product being transported. Force is applied, via pumping or compression, to each particle of the freight that, in turn, propels the particle that precedes it, forming a continuous flow directed by the pipes in the pipeline.

Pipelines may be classified according to their construction and the type of products they transport, and they may be (1) subsea or (2) land pipelines. Subsea pipelines are those that are, mostly, submerged at the seabed. Examples of subsea pipelines are the pipelines used to transport oil from offshore platforms to refineries or storage tanks located onshore; and marine outfalls used to discharge wastewater from treated sewage into the sea.

Land pipelines may be underground, on-grade, or suspended. Underground pipelines, as the name implies, are buried at variable depths under the ground. They are usually better protected against the weather, accidents caused by vehicles, and vandalism. On-grade pipelines are those laid visibly on the ground. They are usually built in this way when they are near stations (loading/unloading, pumping, or maintenance stations) or when the land they need to go through is difficult to drill. In this case the pipelines are supported by cradles (small structures made of footing and a concrete block). Suspended pipelines are used in places where there are valleys, water courses, or rough terrain. In this case, towers are built at the ends and at intervals, whenever necessary, to support the pipeline.

According to the type of freight they transport, pipelines may be classified as oil pipelines; mining pipelines; gas pipelines; capsule pipelines; and water pipelines.

Oil pipelines are used to transport fuels, such as petroleum, petroleum derivatives, and ethanol. Mining pipelines are used to transport minerals, cement, and cereals. In this case, it is necessary to use special pumps that are able to propel solid or powder bulk and a carrier fluid that helps in the transportation of the freight along the pipeline. In the case of minerals, water is used; in the case of cement and cereals, air is used.

Gas pipelines are used to transport different kinds of gas, although they are mostly used for natural gas. They are different from oil pipelines essentially due to their propulsion systems. Capsule pipelines[11] may be used to transport mail, coal, or solid waste. In this case, freight is transported in a capsule that is propelled by a carrier fluid (water or air).

Water pipelines are sewage pipes used to transport the water distributed to or produced by households, and water pipes are used to collect water at fountains or sources, transport it to treatment stations, and, later, distribute it to the population.

1.3.4.2 Terminals

Pipeline terminals are facilities used to load, unload, transfer, or store products transported via pipelines. For that reason, they are essentially constructed near pumping or compressing stations and product storage facilities (Fig. 1.18).

Depending on the length of the pipeline, there must be intermediate pumping stations between an origin and a destination, since the increased distance

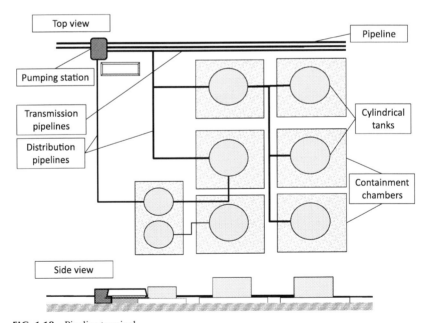

FIG. 1.18 Pipeline terminal.

---

11. The concept of capsule pipelines is the same as that used in the modern proposal of freight and passenger transportation called Hyperloop.

causes pressure drop in the pipe. In the case of gas pipelines, compression stations are used in order to compress the gas and propel it along the pipe. At the destination point, there must be a decompression station, since the gas is commercialized at a lower pressure than the one it transported.

Besides the pumping stations, there are also security and safety stations along the pipeline. These stations have shut-off or block valves, which are used in the case of pressure drop; quick-opening closures, which are used to receive and launch maintenance and monitoring devices from and into the pipes; and pressure-relief stations, which aim to control the pressure inside the pipe to prevent them from bursting.

Pipeline terminals may be connected to waterways, railways, or road terminals where freight is loaded or unloaded, or to locations where freight will be processed, such as water treatment plants or sewage treatment plants, refineries, and minerals or gas processing plants.

1.3.4.3 Controls

Considering that this mode has only one transportation degree of freedom (linear), controls are used to regulate the speed generated by the pumps. These controls aim to avoid both low speeds, which would allow the sedimentation of solid particles inside the pipe, and excessively high speeds which, depending on the type of product, would lead to pipe erosion.

There are also pipeline flow deviation controls to reach storage tank facilities or distribution systems known as maneuver operation controls. Currently, large pipeline networks have OCC that are capable of remotely monitoring in real time all the operations of a pipeline transportation system.

Example 1.4   Pipeline transportation in Russia

The United States lead the list of countries by the total length of pipeline network featuring a network of pipelines with a total length of over 2.2 million km where 10% are devoted to transport petroleum products and 9% to natural gas.

But if the total amount of freight transported by a distance (t.km) is considered (see Fig. 1.28), Russia's pipeline network shares almost half of the total freight transported in the country while in the United States it represents close to 16%. Given the remote location of many Russian's production fields, pipelines have always played a critical role in transporting oil and natural gas. The construction of a vast system of pipelines was often cited as a crowning achievement of the Soviet oil and gas industry. They were designed to move the production first within the Soviet Union and Eastern Europe and second for export to the West.

Because of the vital role of oil and natural gas in the national economy and the need to move those commodities over long distances, pipelines occupy a critical position in the national transportation system. The system includes the Unified Gas System of Russia (UGS), which at 171,400 km, is the world's longest domestic gas trunk transmission system (Newman, 2018).

30 Transportation, energy use and environmental impacts

Natural gas and petroleum pipelines play a crucial role in Russia's economy, both in distributing fuel to domestic industrial consumers and in supporting exports to Europe. Their complex network connects production regions with virtually all of Russia's centers of population and industry. Pipelines are especially important because of the long distances between Siberian oil and gas fields and Russia's European industrial centers as well as countries to the West.

1.3.5 Air transportation

The first airplane was built by Brazilian Alberto Santos-Dumont, who merged the success of Hargraves' gliders with a reciprocating internal combustion engine Antoinette with 50 hp., creating the 14 Bis. The airplane made its first flight in October 1906.

After World War I, aircraft and aerial navigation have undergone considerable technical improvements. After World War II, in the period from 1945 to 1950, there was a great expansion of air transportation due to the surplus military aircrafts. Moreover, the introduction of turbines in the 1950s, which had better energy efficiency than reciprocating internal combustion engines, enabled a significant increase in the autonomy of commercial aircraft, allowing the expansion of airlines and making the air mode the predominant way of transporting passengers in international long-distance trips.

1.3.5.1 Ways

In air transportation, "ways" are calculated routes that were first followed based on visual landmarks, considering the low height of the flights; this was followed by calculations based on astronomical observations using the sextant; the next step was the use of electronic navigation using direction-finders and nondirectional beacons. Nowadays, location is determined using geostationary satellites and GPS.

In all cases, the use of airlines is organized and disciplined by world operation rules discussed and implemented by the International Civil Aviation Organization (ICAO) of the United Nations and complemented by country's internal regulations.

For highly used routes, there are stricter rules of navigation that establish times, flight altitude, and well-established width corridors, forming "airways," with similar procedures of airport approach, forming virtual cylinders to guide the aircraft waiting for permission to land.

1.3.5.2 Vehicles

Vehicles in this mode may be self-propelled, such as airplanes, helicopters, airships, and spaceships, or they may use air currents, especially thermal ones as a propelling system, such as gliders, aerostats, and hang gliders. The self-propelled vehicles use reciprocating internal combustion engines with propellers and powered by aviation gasoline,[12] or jet engines powered by aviation kerosene.

---

12. In Brazil there are small airplanes that use ethanol as fuel.

Regarding their purpose, airplanes may be used for passengers (*full pax*), freight (*all cargo*), mixed use (*combi*), leisure, service, and defense. They may be owned by commercial airline companies, governmental entities, natural persons, and different kinds of legal persons.

Aircraft dimensions are as follows (Fig. 1.19):

- Wingspan (e): distance from the tip of one wing to the tip of the other.
- Length (c): distance from the tip of the nose to the tip of the tail.
- Height (h): distance from the wheel to the upper end of the rudder.
- Track (t): distance between the main wheel axles of the landing gear.
- Wheelbase (b): distance between the nosewheel and the main wheels.

Regarding their nationality, airplanes are considered part of the territory of the country where they were registered. Their passage through and landing on other nations, in the case of commercial aircraft, obey the Chicago Convention and its five freedoms of the air (the first two freedoms regulate the right to innocent overflight and right to technical landing; the three remaining ones regulate the catchment of paying passengers).

1.3.5.3 Terminals

Terminals in the air mode are called airdromes. They may be called civil airdromes when they are used for civilian purposes, and they are subdivided into public and private airdromes.

Organized public civilian airdromes, especially those used for commercial purposes, are called airports. Airports may be classified as freight or passenger

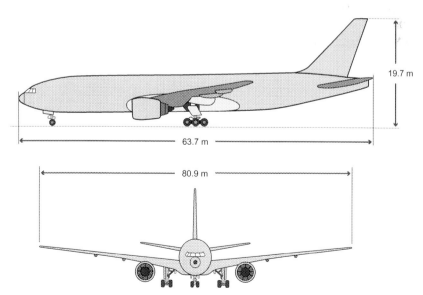

FIG. 1.19 Example of aircraft (airplane). $e = 80.9$ m; $c = 63.7$ m; $h = 19.7$ m.

32 Transportation, energy use and environmental impacts

airports but most of them are of mixed use. The use of their areas and the nature of their equipment will be defined according to their type of use. Public civilian airdromes may also be of restrict use when they have simple facilities. When their purpose is military use, they are commonly called military air bases.

An airport (Fig. 1.20) is characterized according to the technical parameters of its lane(s) and facilities, as follows:

- Number, direction, and height of lanes.
- Length, width, paving, and support capacity of lanes.
- Taxiways and aprons.
- Runway lighting and instrument landing equipment.
- Acquisition and tracking radars, approach radars, and radio communication equipment.
- Management, embarking, disembarking, and storage buildings.
- Customs, sanitation control, and border police services.
- Tanking, fueling, fire-fighting, and personal emergency rescue services.
- Hangars, maintenance, and repair workshops for aircraft, etc.

Other important conditions in airports are their location in relation to urban centers, access to road systems, and predominant weather conditions.

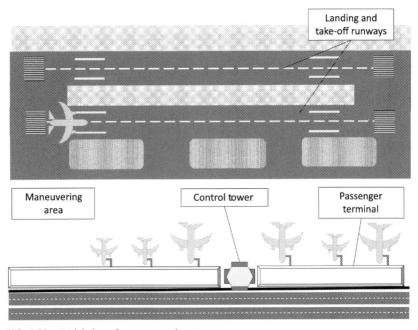

FIG. 1.20 Aerial view of a passenger airport.

1.3.5.4 Control

Since this mode has three dimensions of freedom, the training of pilots and co-pilots is an essential factor, very strictly related to the technical and disciplinary level of air traffic controllers, especially concerning the areas neighboring the airport.

The use of surveillance and high-precision approach radars, and modern ground-to-air telecommunication systems coupled to digital processors has contributed to the efficiency and safety of the essential procedures of landing and takeoff, even under critical weather and visibility conditions and with short operation intervals of even seconds of difference.

Nevertheless, air traffic congestion close to big airports, especially in Western Europe and in the United States, is already close their saturation limit, leading to a search for alternative terminals or the introduction of interval restrictions.

Example 1.5   The largest commercial airplane manufacturers in the world

With thousands of airplanes flying on the runway daily, it is remarkable to note that there are only a few companies manufacturing these aircrafts. The top players in the commercial aircraft industry are Airbus, a European manufacturer and two North American companies, Boeing and McDonnell Douglas.

In addition to the major airplane manufacturers, there are also two smaller players, the Brazilian Embraer and the Canadian Bombardier. Embraer supplies more than 30 airlines with regional service areas. Bombardier provides jet and turboprop aircrafts to American Airlines and other customers.

Airbus and Boeing airplanes are most used for longer distances and these companies build the two biggest airplanes in the world, Airbus A380-800 and Boeing 77-300, both with more than 500 seats. On the other hand, McDonnell Douglas, Embraer, and Bombardier build small- or medium-sized airplanes for medium-range destinations.

1.4 Multimodal transportation

Conceptually, multimodal transportation is that which uses more than one mode of transportation to carry passengers or freight from the origin to the destination.

The practice of multimodal transportation aims to reduce cost if it does not significantly compromise attributes of level of service such as total time or time variation in trips or freight delivery, passenger comfort and safety, rate of failures, safety of freight, and the number of complaints from users of the transportation system.

The use of different modes of transportation is useful when it is possible to combine its advantages, optimizing the operation, reducing trip times, and reducing costs.

If the modes of transportation are available, multimodality may contribute to reduce social costs because it expands accessibility and mobility for people and freight, generating economic, environmental, and social benefits.

34 Transportation, energy use and environmental impacts

TABLE 1.2 Possible combinations between the modes of transportation

Mode	Road	Railway	Air	Water	Pipeline
Road	U	MF-MP	MF-MP	MF-MP	MF
Railway		U	MF-MP	MF-MP	MF
Air			U	MF-MP	MF
Water				U	MF
Pipeline					U

MF, Multimodal Freight; *MP*, Multimodal Passengers; *U*, Unimodal combination.

Theoretically, there are 10 possible combinations of the currently used 5 modes of transportation that enable multimodal freight transportation and 6 combinations for passenger transportation, as presented in Table 1.2.

Only some of the combinations illustrated in Table 1.2 are used in practice and they are common in some cases and specific in others. Usually, the common combinations involve the road mode with railway, air, and water modes. In the case of freight transportation, door-to-door transportation usually cannot be carried out via railway, air, and water modes, thus require complementation via the road mode either in the initial or the final stage of the process.

Furthermore, there can also be a combination of the railway and water modes, including maritime transportation (deep-sea and/or cabotage) and inland waterways. In these cases, there is a trend toward practicing the transportation of specific freight such as solid bulk (e.g., grains, minerals, and coal) and liquid bulk (petroleum, petroleum derivative fuels and biofuels).

In the case of the transportation of petroleum and its derivatives, it is possible to find a combination of water and pipeline modes, mainly when they are being imported or exported. If the pumping of petroleum derivatives is regarded as a transportation segment, there is also the possibility of considering the combination of road and railway modes with the pipeline mode.

In the case of passenger transportation, it is common to use road transportation, either individual or collective to access terminals for urban or interurban trains, subways, airports, and ports. It is also very common to use railway transportation to access airports and ports, in particular by means of urban and interurban trains, subways, trams, and LRT.

1.4.1 Typical operation plans in multimodal freight transportation

For multimodal transportation to achieve its goals, it is desirable that the transportation modes are physically integrated via multimodal terminals that allow

Transportation, an introduction Chapter | 1 **35**

the transfer of freight between the modes in a coordinated, fast, and safe way and at an adequate cost. Ports and airports are typical places where multimodal terminals are located. Ports usually carry out freight transfer between the water mode and the railway, road, and pipeline modes; airports carry out the transfer between the air and road modes.

The easy transfer of freight in multimodal transportation may be carried out using specific equipment dedicated to certain types of freight transported in bulk or using equipment and transportation plans dedicated to the handling of general freight,[13] some of which are: (1) road semitrailer over a railway flat wagon (piggyback); (2) tractor unit with road semitrailer over a flat wagon; (3) road semitrailer that may be coupled to a railway bogie (roadrail); (4) road semitrailer over a barge (fishyback); (5) tractor unit with road semitrailer over a barge; and (6) containers over a flat wagon and/or over a barge.

All the alternatives above seek to keep the transfer of general freight between modes as fast as possible maintaining its integrity. Fig. 1.21 shows the practices of piggyback, roadrail, fishyback, and tractor unit with semitrailer over barge.

Containers stand out as equipment that facilitate multimodal transportation, since they are standardized storage units and there is appropriate equipment to handle and transport them all around the world. Two sizes of containers are widely used: $8' \times 8' \times 20'$ and $8' \times 8' \times 40'$ (width $\times$ height $\times$ length), as shown in Fig. 1.22.

The transportation and stowage of freight in pallets also favors the use of multimodality, since the aggregation of freight allows a quicker loading and unloading. Pallets can also be used in conjunction with containers.

1.4.2 Typical operation plans in multimodal passenger transportation

All over the world, road transportation usually plays an important role in connecting people to long-distance passenger transportation modes like railways, maritime, and air. In this case it is important that terminals are well planned to receive people who come by buses and cars (public, like taxis or private). In this case, well-planned infrastructure considers not only easy access to any kind of transportations modes but also road mass transit terminals and parking stations placed next to rail station, ports, and airports so that the passenger can comfortably walk from one place to another. The same concept can be applied to rail connection to airports and ports.

When talking about urban transit, multimodal passenger transportation plays a major role in improving people mobility. A well-designed transportation network must consider good physical connection within all modes to allow passenger to choose the best way to go from one place to the other. If buses, LRT,

---

13. General freight include the most diverse types of freight, regardless of whether packed in individual volumes or not, shipped in trips of different tonnages of variable unit value. Some examples are: containers, pallets, bags, crates, etc.

Roadrail

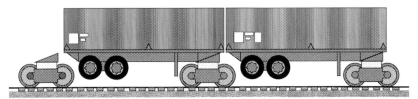

Piggyback

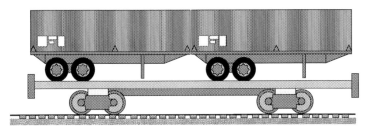

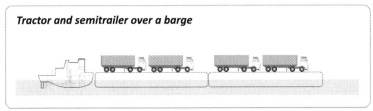

FIG. 1.21 Piggyback, roadrail, fishyback, and tractor unit with semitrailer over barge.

train, and metro station are even spread in the transportation network it will be easy to walk or bike to the nearest place and start the trip in a sustainable way leaving private car at home. Otherwise it will be necessary to drive to the destination, which is not desirable, or to the nearest mass transportation terminal where there will be necessary good access and enough parking stations to leave the car.

For good profit of multimodal passenger transportation in urban areas mass transit vehicles must be designed with good access to passenger, which means large doors for embarking and disembarking with well-signalized access and

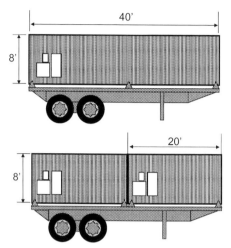

FIG. 1.22 Containers over road semitrailer.

exit flows that should be at same level as that of the stations and terminals platforms. Fare payment should be done before accessing the transportation system. No matter what the situation is, it is important to take for grant the conditions for multimodal transportation as presented in Section 1.4.3.

Example 1.6 Transit integrated network (TIN) que original concept of (Bus rapid transit (BRT) (Cannell, 1995; Curitiba, 2018)

Transit integrated network (TIN) is a bus-based transit system created in the 1970s in Curitiba, the capital of the State of Paraná, Brazil. The TIN was designed as an 80-km network of bus corridors, usually operated by bi-articulated cars that connect the integrated terminals in the various regions of the city and carry almost 2 million passengers daily. Buses have large doors for embarking and disembarking with well-signalized access and exit flows at same level of the stations and terminals platforms. Fare payment is done before accessing the transportation system.

In addition to interconnection by express buses, the terminals are provided with feeder buses, which make up the secondary branch of this system and serve the passengers of the neighborhoods near the terminals. In addition, another category of express buses (light ones) provides fast interchange of passengers between one terminal and another, with different routes and few intermediate stops.

The first TIN line began operating in 1974 and the system was designed not only to transport people but also to drive urban growth. However, the success of the network and population growth have increased demand, which has caused the TIN to begin to show signs of saturation in recent years.

Curitiba's public transportation system has inspired several cities in Brazil and other countries to adopt similar strategies and this kind of transit system concept was widespread as bus rapid transit (BRT). In Brazil, many cities implemented

BRT-like transit systems (e.g., São Paulo, Rio de Janeiro, Belo Horizonte, Brasília). In 1998, Enrique Peñalosa, the then mayor of Bogotá, capital of Colombia, decided to create a BRT system in his city after he visited Curitiba. The well-known TransMilenio, Bogotá's BRT has fast-moving vehicles that run on totally exclusive roads and carries almost 2 million people every day. In addition, Curitiba's TIN also served as inspiration for more than 80 countries around the world.

1.4.3 Conditions for multimodal transportation

One of the most important conditions for the adequate operation of multimodal transportation is the existence of an easy connection between the transportation modes, usually associated with the availability of terminals and the existence of adequate infrastructure for the transfer of passengers and freight between the modes.

Physical integration, expressed by the availability of different modes that have an interconnection between themselves, is necessary but not enough to enable the practice of multimodality. There must also be an operation integration that guarantees the synchronization of the operation of the modes, so that the passengers spend as little time with high regularity as possible in the use of multimodality, and that the practices of receiving, unloading, loading, and clearing vehicles in the different modes are synchronized between themselves. Failures in the operation of one mode or long periods of operational deficiency also compromise the operation of the system, undermining the practice of multimodal transportation.

Besides, in the case of multimodal transportation, there will be passenger transfers or freight transhipment, which represents an additional cost. Fare integration must allow this additional cost not to surpass the benefits achieved with a more cost-efficient use of a mode of transportation.

Considering the above, the conditions for the practice of multimodality may be summarized and represented as shown in Fig. 1.23.

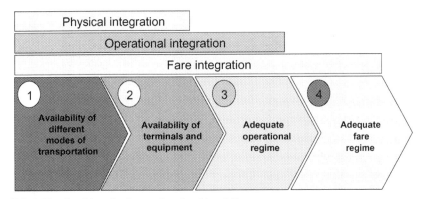

FIG. 1.23 Conditions for the practice of multimodality.

1.5 Life cycle of a transportation system

The life cycle of a transportation system essentially comprises five phases: (1) planning; (2) design; (3) construction; (4) operation; and (5) demobilization, as shown in Fig. 1.24.

The planning phase (1) basically consists in carrying out location and market studies to understand the physical characteristics of the region where the transportation system should be implemented and the demand of that location. This phase also includes technical, economic, political, and social feasibility analyses, and the environmental impact assessment (EIA) with its respective Environmental Impact Report (EIR).

The design phase (2) is the phase that precedes the construction of the infrastructure and comprises the basic design, detailed design, executive design, schedule, and budget of the construction work.

The construction phase (3) comprises the execution of what was planned and designed in the previous phases. The construction phase is when there will be initial interventions in the environment, either related to deforestation and/or expropriation or to the actual execution of works.

When the whole infrastructure of the transportation system is available for use, the operation phase (4) begins; this phase includes the actions resulting from the functioning system, such as the operation of the transportation mode, and the conservation and maintenance of the infrastructure and the transportation system.

In case the transportation system is discontinued, the area occupied by it must be recovered. The demobilization phase (5) seeks to remove the infrastructure

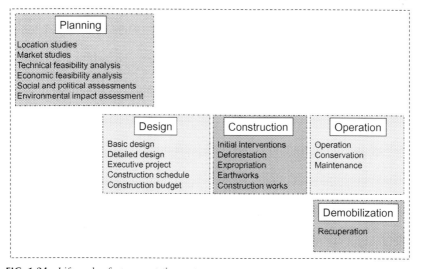

FIG. 1.24 Life cycle of a transportation system.

40 Transportation, energy use and environmental impacts

created for the operation of the transportation system and to restore the original characteristics of the environment where the system was implemented.

1.6 An overview of transportation worldwide

Passenger transportation has the following operational schemes: (1) urban, (2) interurban, (3) interstate, and (4) international. Urban or municipal transportation takes place within a municipality (county), it is usually associated with short and medium distances (less than 100 km), and it is predominantly carried out by road, railway, and water modes. Part of the trips carried out in urban transportation may also occur via nonmotorized ways such as using bicycles or walking. People going from one city to another use interurban transportation (2). This operation, just as with urban transportation, is predominantly carried out via road, railway, and water modes. Interstate and international transportation operations may be carried out via road, railway, water, and air modes. Table 1.3 details the modes of transportation most commonly used in each kind of operational scheme.

To minimize the consumption of natural resources, particularly physical space and energy and, consequently, the generated environmental impact, nonmotorized modes (walking and bicycles) should be privileged for short distances. For distances in which the use of motorized transportation is necessary, the modes with higher capacity and better energy efficiency should be used, for example, high-capacity collective modes such as urban trains, subways and buses. Fig. 1.25 shows the equivalence of capacity.

For the sake of illustration, Fig. 1.26 shows the modal distribution of passenger transportation worldwide, compared to a selection of countries and to the European Union. Worldwide, there is an observable predominance of the road mode (81.9%), followed with a large difference by air transportation (11.4%). In this context, railway transportation has a lower representativeness (6.4%) except for the case of China (31.9%), Russia (28.5%), and India (12.6%). Water transportation of passengers is the least expressive of all cases.

Freight transportation has basically three types of operations: (1) collection, (2) transfer, and (3) distribution. Collection (1) is the activity through which freight is collected at two or more points of origin and transported to a destination place, where it will be sorted, transferred, or distributed. The collection operation usually occurs in urban areas, in short distances (tens of kilometers) using small- or medium-sized vehicles that may have partially used capacity.

Transfer (2) is associated with the transportation of freight from one single point of origin to one single point of destination. The transfer operation usually occurs in long distances (hundreds to thousands of kilometers) and uses modes of higher capacity or road vehicles of larger size that travel fully loaded (in weight or volume).

Distribution is the transportation of freight from one single point of origin to two or more points of destination. As with the collection operation, distribution

TABLE 1.3 Modes usually used for passenger transportation

Mode		Urban (municipal)	Interurban (intermunicipal)	Interstate	International
Road	Walking	x			
	Bicycle	x			
	Motorcycle	x	x		
	Car	x	x	x	x
	Bus	x	x	x	x
Railway	Tram/LRT	x			
	Urban train	x	x		
	Subway	x			
	Regional train		x	x	
	Train			x	x
Waterways	Ferry	x	x		
	Ship			x	x
Air	Airplane			x	x

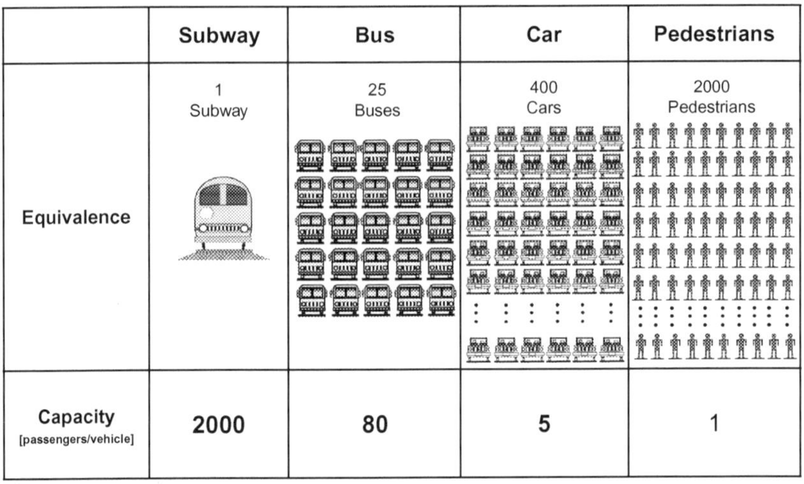

42 Transportation, energy use and environmental impacts

	Subway	Bus	Car	Pedestrians
Equivalence	1 Subway	25 Buses	400 Cars	2000 Pedestrians
Capacity [passengers/vehicle]	2000	80	5	1

FIG. 1.25 Passenger transportation and the use of physical space.

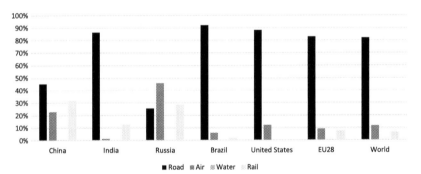

FIG. 1.26 Modal split of passenger transportation worldwide (pass.km). *(Source: IEA and UIC, 2016. Energy Consumption and CO2 Emissions—Focus on Sustainability Targets. International Energy Agency (IEA) and International Union of Railways (UIC), fifth ed. and Gonçalves, D.N.S., D'Agosto, M.de A., 2017. Future Prospective Scenarios for the Use of Energy in Transportation in Brazil and GHG Emissions Business as Usual (BAU) Scenario—2050. Instituto Brasileiro de Transporte Sustentável (IBTS), Rio de Janeiro, RJ.)*

usually occurs in urban areas in short distances and with small and medium vehicles.

Freight transportation may be carried out via the road, railway, water, pipeline, and air modes in an isolated way (unimodal) or through the combination of these modes (multimodal). The road mode, in most cases, is the one capable of carrying out door-to-door transportation, and it is recommended for collection and distribution operations and for transfers, depending on the amount of transported freight and on the distance. The remaining modes are usually adequate for the transfer operation.

Just as in the case of passenger transportation, with freight transportation it is also possible to minimize the consumption of natural resources, especially physical space and energy, and, thus, the generated environmental impact. This is also achieved with the use of modes with higher capacity and better energy performance, such as ships and trains. Fig. 1.27 illustrates this equivalence of capacity for the transportation of agricultural bulk.

Fig. 1.28 shows the modal split of national freight transportation in a selection of countries and in the European Union. If pipeline transportation is not considered, road freight transportation predominates with percentages above 30%, except for Chine, where water transportation predominates (49.60%) and Russia, where railway transportation predominates (86.90%). On the other hand, national freight transportation by air is inexpressive.

If pipeline transportation is considered, the modal split shows changes for Russia and United States, where it represents 48% and 16% of the total t.km transported per year. In Russia railway freight transportation dropped from 86.9% to 45.6% and in the United States both road (56.8%–46.8%) and rail (32.6%–28.7%) transportation loose share to pipeline.

Regarding the modal split of freight transportation worldwide, which includes international transportation, there is a clear predominance of the water mode represented by deep-sea navigation, which contributes with a little over 82% of freight transportation in ton-kilometers, as shown in Fig. 1.29.

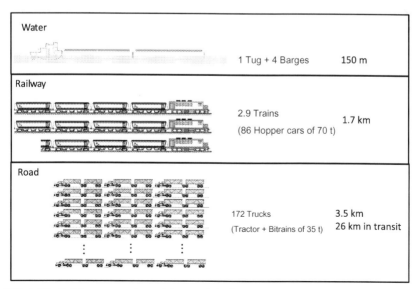

FIG. 1.27 Freight transportation and the use of physical space.

44 Transportation, energy use and environmental impacts

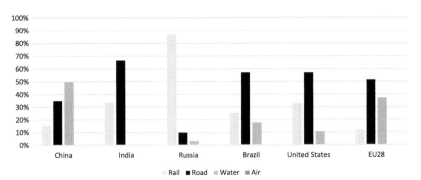

FIG. 1.28 Modal split of national freight transportation (t.km). *(Source: IEA and UIC, 2016. Energy Consumption and CO2 Emissions—Focus on Sustainability Targets. International Energy Agency (IEA) and International Union of Railways (UIC), fifth ed. and Gonçalves, D.N.S., D'Agosto, M.de A., 2017. Future Prospective Scenarios for the Use of Energy in Transportation in Brazil and GHG Emissions Business as Usual (BAU) Scenario—2050. Instituto Brasileiro de Transporte Sustentável (IBTS), Rio de Janeiro, RJ.)*

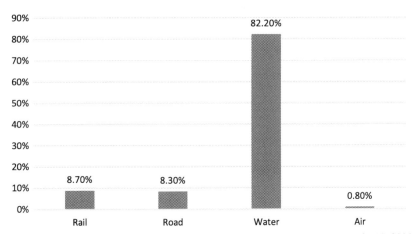

FIG. 1.29 Modal split of freight transportation worldwide (t.km). *(Source: IEA and UIC, 2016. Energy Consumption and CO2 Emissions—Focus on Sustainability Targets. International Energy Agency (IEA) and International Union of Railways (UIC), fifth ed.)*

1.7 Final considerations

This chapter aimed to present: basic concepts regarding transportation systems; an overview of the modes of transportation (road, railway, water, pipeline, and air); the concept, practice and conditions of multimodality; and how transportation systems are structured and correlated. It also described the steps needed for the implementation of a transportation system (planning, design, construction, operation, and demobilization), and provided an overview of freight and passenger transportation worldwide.

Transportation, an introduction Chapter | 1 **45**

These preliminary descriptions will allow the reader to understand how transportation is carried out and to achieve the main goal of this book, which is to associate transportation to energy use and to the impacts on the physical, biotic, and anthropic environments.

1.8 Exercises

1. Define transportation and transportation system, highlighting the difference between these two concepts.
2. List and describe the physical subsystems of a transportation system.
3. List and describe the elements of a transportation system.
4. Which transportation mode is used for the collection and distribution of waste in an urban area? Explain why.
5. Are there any petroleum and its derivatives/by-products (gasoline, diesel oil, and kerosene) that may be transported through pipelines? When is this mode recommended for the transportation of this type of freight?
6. Which transportation mode is most widely used in the world for the importing and exporting of great volumes of freight? Justify your answer.
7. Compare the components of a way for the road and railway modes of transportation, highlighting their similarities and differences.
8. Present the three areas that make up a port terminal and describe their functions.
9. What is the purpose of terminals in a pipeline transportation system?
10. What are the characteristics that determine the use of air freight transportation? Is there any difference when considering passenger transportation?

References

Asimov, I., 1993. Cronologia das ciências e das descobertas, first ed. Civilização Brasileira, Rio de Janeiro.

Cannell, A.E.R., 1995. The Curtitiba Bus ®Evolution. Integrated Transportation System as Mass Transport. In: 4th Thredbo, Transcraft Consultants, Curitiba, Brazil.

Curitiba, 2018. The RIT Today. Curitiba Municipality Website, Curitiba, Brazil. http://www.curitiba.pr.gov.br/siteidioma/progressoonibus.aspx?idiomacultura=2. [(Accessed August 26, 2018)].

Duddu, P., 2013. The World's Longest Metro and Subway Systems. Railway Technology. https://www.railway-technology.com/features/featurethe-worlds-longest-metro-and-subway-systems-4144725/. [(Accessed August 26, 2018)].

Georgano, G.N., 1985. Cars 1886–1930. A. B. Nordbok, Gotemburgo, Suécia.

Hawkes, N., 1991. Vehicles. Marshall Editions Development Ltda, Londres.

Heskett, J., 1998. Desenho Industrial (Industrial Design), second ed. José Olympio Editora, Rio de Janeiro.

Hoel, L.A., Garber, N.J., Sadek, A.W., 2011. Transportation Infrastructure Engineering. A Multimodal Integration. Cengage Learning, Stamford.

ICS, 2018. Shipping Facts, Shipping and World Trade. International Chamber of Shipping, London. http://www.ics-shipping.org/shipping-facts/shipping-and-world-trade. [(Accessed August 28, 2018)].

46 Transportation, energy use and environmental impacts

Lay, M.G., 1992. Ways of the World: A History of the Worlds Roads and the Vehicles That Used Them. Rutgers University Press, Piscataway, NJ.

Midgley, P. (2013). Bike Sharing. Global Consultation for Decision-Makers on Implementing Sustainable Transport. UN-DESA, Sustainable Development Knowledge Platform. (https://sustainabledevelopment.un.org/content/documents/4803Bike%20Sharing%20UN%20DESA.pdf. Accessed 26 August).

Newman, N., 2018. Russia's gas pipeline network revised. Pipeline Gas J. 245 (6).

Further reading

Gonçalves, D.N.S., D'Agosto, M.d.A., 2017. Future Prospective Scenarios for the Use of Energy in Transportation in Brazil and GHG Emissions Business as Usual (BAU) Scenario—2050. Instituto Brasileiro de Transporte Sustentável (IBTS), Rio de Janeiro, RJ.

Hay, W.W., 1961. An Introduction to Transportation Engineering. John Wiley & Sons, Inc., Nova York.

IEA and UIC, 2016. Energy Consumption and CO2 Emissions—Focus on Sustainability Targets, fifth ed. International Energy Agency (IEA) and International Union of Railways (UIC).

Morlok, E.K., 1978. Introduction to Transportation Engineering and Planning. McGraw-Hill, Inc., Nova York.

Obert, E.F., 1971. Internal Combustion Engines (Motores de combustão interna). Globo, Porto Alegre.

Vanek, F.M., Angenent, L.T., Banks, J.H., Daziano, R.A., Turniquist, M.A., 2014. Sustainable Transportation Systems Engineering. McGraw-Hill Education, New York.

Chapter 2

Planning, design, and construction of infrastructure for transportation systems and their environmental impacts

General goal

The general goal of this chapter is to identify the main environmental impacts originated in the phases of planning, design, construction, and demobilization of infrastructure for transportation systems.

At the end of the chapter, the reader should be able to:

1. Identify the activities needed for the planning, design, construction, and demobilization of infrastructure for transportation systems.
2. Know the environmental impacts caused by the construction of infrastructure for transportation systems and associate them with the transportation modes as presented in Chapter 1.
3. Identify, per mode of transportation, measures that mitigate the environmental impacts that occur during the construction of infrastructure for transportation systems.

2.1 Introduction

As with any major construction project, the construction of infrastructure for transportation systems directly interferes with the natural environment, the economy, and the social environment of a region as it takes physical space for the construction of ways, terminals, and control systems.

Usually, the clearing of physical space to build a transportation system leads to the need of carrying out deforestation, underwater blasting, dredging, and owning expropriation, among other kinds of interference that modify the physical, biotic, and anthropic environments of one region.

Interference in the socioeconomic environment may occur given that the built of transportation systems requires a workforce during the construction period, that is, temporary employment, which ends up attracting workers to the region where the intervention is placed, causing migratory movements

---

Transportation, Energy Use and Environmental Impacts. https://doi.org/10.1016/B978-0-12-813454-2.00002-7
© 2019, Elsevier Editora Ltda. Published by Elsevier Inc. All rights reserved.

47

and increasing the chances of cultural conflicts. In addition to the possibility of temporary employment, the implementation of such systems impacts urban mobility and land use, which may increase real estate speculation in the region and cause social segregation.

As shown in Chapter 1, the life cycle of a transportation system (Fig. 1.21) comprises five phases: (1) planning, (2) design, (3) construction, (4) operation, and (5) demobilization. In each of these phases, there are actions that generate positive and/or negative impacts on the environment (anthropic, biotic, and physical) and that must be controlled with mitigation measures aimed at reducing negative impacts. Fig. 2.1 summarizes the relationship between the phases of a transportation system's life cycle and the occurrence of social and environmental impacts.

Table 2.1 illustrates the relationship between the phases of a transportation system's life cycle, a selection of actions for each phase, and their reflexes on the physical, biotic, and anthropic environments. In the planning and design phases the reflexes of the actions affect mainly the anthropic environment, impacting the society through expectations of changes in land use and in speculative population movements. In the other phases, the reflexes are considerably expanded, covering physical, biotic, and anthropic environments.

The social and environmental impacts caused by transportation systems that affect the physical, biotic, and anthropic environments can be classified as positive or negative. The negative impacts are those that are averse to the physical, biotic, and anthropic environments because they cause partial or total destruction of fauna and flora; air, sound, or visual pollution; climate changes; health problems to living beings, specially, to people; and social instability. On the

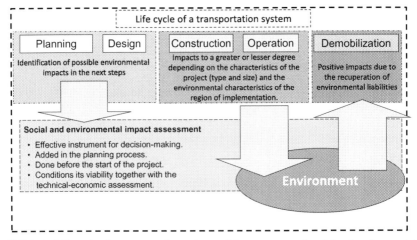

FIG. 2.1 Life cycle of a transportation system and the occurrence of social and environmental impacts. *(Based on Vanek, F.M., Angenent, L.T., Banks, J.H., Daziano, R.A., Turniquist, M.A., 2014. Sustainable Transportation Systems Engineering. McGraw-Hill Education, Boston, MA.)*

TABLE 2.1 Relationship between life cycle of a transportation system, phases, actions, and their reflexes on the physical, biotic, and anthropic environments

Phases	Actions	Reflex on the environment	Environment
Planning	Location study	Changes in land use and occupation	Anthropic
	Market studies	Changes in the real estate market	
	Technical viability analysis	Migratory movements	
	Economic viability analysis	Social reactions	
	Political assessments		
	Social assessments		
	Environmental impact assessment		
	Social impact study		
Design	Basic design	Strengthening of expectations arising from planning actions	Anthropic
	Detailed design		
	Executive project		
	Construction schedule		
	Construction budget		

Continued

TABLE 2.1 Relationship between life cycle of a transportation system, phases, actions, and their reflexes on the physical, biotic, and anthropic environments—cont'd

Phases	Actions	Reflex on the environment	Environment
Construction	Initial interventions (preparation)	Removal of vegetative cover	Anthropic
	Deforestation/expropriation	Property expropriation and demolition	Biotic
		Soil erosion	Physical
	Earthworks • Cut and fill • Waste extraction • Earthworks	Atmospheric pollution Greenhouse gas emissions Water pollution Soil pollution Noise pollution	
	Construction works • Infrastructure • OAC/OAE	Energy waste Social unbalance Salvatage	
	Excavations in borrow pits	Job generation	
	Recuperation of borrow pits	Income distribution	
Operation	Operation	Soil erosion	Anthropic
	Conservation	Atmospheric pollution Greenhouse gas emission	Biotic
	Maintenance	Water pollution Soil pollution Noise pollution Energy waste Social unbalance Animal deaths Increased accessibility Job generation Income distribution	Physical

Demobilization	Initial interventions (preparation)	Restitution of vegetative cover	Anthropic
	Earthworks	Restitution of fauna	Biotic
	• Land recuperation	Atmospheric pollution	Physical
	Reforestation	Greenhouse gas emissions	
	Construction Works	Water pollution	
		Soil pollution	
		Noise pollution	
		Energy waste	
		Job generation	
		Income distribution	

Based on Fogliatti, M.C., Filippo, S., Goudard, B., 2004. Avaliação de Impactos Ambientais. Aplicação aos Sistemas de Transporte (Environmental Impacts Assessment. Transportation Systems Application) Editora Interciência, Rio de Janeiro, RJ and Vanek, F.M., Angenent, L.T., Banks, J.H., Daziano, R.A., Turniquist, M.A. 2014. Sustainable Transportation Systems Engineering. McGraw-Hill Education, Boston, MA. RCES, Regular Civil Engineering Structures (drains, fenders, dams, small bridges, level crossings etc.); ECES, Special Civil Engineering Structures (tunnels, bridges, viaducts etc.).

52 Transportation, energy use and environmental impacts

other hand, the positive impacts are that they have the potential to generate benefits for the region where the intervention will be carried out, such as accessibility, economic growth, job creation, income distribution, and so on.

Mitigation measures are actions that minimize negative impacts and potentiate positive ones, so that the transportation system implementation can guarantee the region's socioeconomic development with environmental responsibility.

This chapter will briefly present the phases of planning, design, construction, and demobilization of infrastructure for transportation systems, comparing the actions needed for the construction of the transportation system, the reflexes of these actions on the environment and the possible mitigation measures. The subsequent chapters will focus on the transportation system's operation phase.

Section 2.2 addresses the phases of planning and design. Section 2.3 deals with the construction and demobilization phases and the final considerations are presented in Section 2.4.

2.2 Planning and design of transportation systems

The planning phase of a transportation system comprises location and market studies; technical and economic viability analyses; political and social assessments; and environmental and social impact assessments.

All these initiatives are carried out to know the physical characteristics (geographic, climatic, and hydrological), social characteristics (land use and occupation by demographic profile), economic characteristics (land use and occupation by the type of economic activity), market characteristics (demand for transportation), the political environment, and the potential impacts on the physical, biotic, and anthropic environments of the region where the transportation system is to be implemented.

Regarding the determination of the potential impacts on the physical, biotic, and anthropic environments, it is worth highlighting the need (in some places, the obligation) to carry out Environmental Impact Assessments (EIA) with the reporting and discussion with the society about the respective Environmental Impact Reports (EIR).

Example 2.1 The process of planning transportation systems

The planning of transportation systems has the objective of adapting the future (short, medium, and long term) transportation needs of an area to its development profile. Two approaches can be found. The first one seeks to establish the means of supplying the demand for transportation generated by a situation of socioeconomic development predicted for the study area. The second one, also known as transport-oriented development (TOD), considers that the supply of transportation induces the socioeconomic development of a region. In both cases, planning is a sequential process that can be divided into steps as shown in Fig. 2.2.

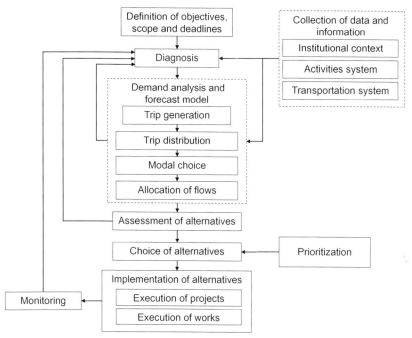

FIG. 2.2 Transportation system's planning process. *(Based on Morlok, E.K., 1978. Introduction to Transportation Engineering and Planning. McGraw-Hill, Inc., New York and Hoel, L.A., Garber, N.J., Sadek, A.W., 2011. Transportation Infrastructure Engineering. A Multimodal Integration. Cengage Learning, Stamford.)*

As shown in Fig. 2.2, the planning of transportation systems may adopt the traditional four-step model (trip generation, trip distribution, modal choice, and allocation of flows in the network), commonly employed in forecasting passenger and freight transportation demand, as described below.

(a) Definition of objectives, scope, and deadlines

The transportation planning process objective is to adapt the service offer to the future transportation demand. Therefore, it is necessary to forecast the amount of the different types of passenger and freight flows that will use a given transportation mode and for which purpose, according to a set of displacement characteristics. This presupposes the knowledge of why this displacement occurs and what factors influence it.

Transportation demand is associated with carrying out activities. Therefore, the analysis of transportation demand cannot be carried out without explicit consideration of the activities system. The activities system consists of people, institutions and activities of many types and quantities, distributed in space, which, when interacting, use the transportation system causing the demand for travels.

Given an activities system, which defines the location of residences, industries, services, businesses, schools, and other activities, the demand for transportation occurs in terms of trips, which are carried out at certain times and between two points of the study area (urban, metropolitan, regional, state, national, or international).

54 Transportation, energy use and environmental impacts

The identification of the study area, its subdivision into traffic zones (TZ) and the identification of the nature of the demand are part of the scope of the application of the transportation planning process.

For the division of the study area into TZs, the following criteria are recommended: (1) compatibility with administrative divisions, especially regarding the census sectors; (2) homogeneity with respect to land use and composition of population and institutions; and (3) compatibility with previously existing zoning, even if done for different purposes.

The configuration of the traffic zones should allow an easy identification of its centroid that are points that represents the origins and destinations of the displacements to and from that traffic zone.

In terms of deadlines, transportation planning may consider short-term (up to 5 years), medium-term (6–15 years), and long-term (16–30 years) deadlines. Most transportation infrastructure projects consider periods between 20 and 25 years.

The final product of the transportation planning process is a set of "expectation lines," which depict the current behavior of transportation system users, as well as the behavior predicted for a predefined time.

(b) Collection of data and information

The collection of data and information involves knowledge about the following aspects: (1) transportation system—characterization of transportation networks in the form of their configuration, supply by mode, and capacity; (2) activities system—characterization of the socioeconomic context of the study area in the form of land use and travel pattern; and (3) institutional context—characterization of political, organizational, and taxation contexts.

As an ideal solution to establish the initial conditions for the transportation planning process, all residents and institutions in the study area should be asked about the characteristics of all trips carried out per year, for example, that used the existing transportation networks, either from the outside to the inside, from the inside to the outside or within the study area.

Unfortunately, the ideal solution is usually impracticable for being expensive and time consuming, thus, a scientific solution is adopted involving the representation of reality through a model that expresses the causal relationship between the activities system and the transportation demand (travel pattern).

It is adopted as a proposition that the travel pattern of a given region is a function of its socioeconomic characteristics. However, as the socioeconomic characteristics vary from region to region, it is necessary to divide the space into zones that have homogeneous characteristics, relevant to the objectives of the study, so that they can be treated individually.

The division of the study area into subareas corresponding to the units of analysis, which form the basis for the characterization of the internal and external displacements of interest for the study, are precisely the TZs.

Regarding the transportation networks that constitute the offer of travel possibilities, it is common to use the resources of Graph Theory, transforming the segments related to any transportation mode into "arcs" and their access points, for transshipment or extremes, into "nodes."

Considering the above, it is possible to represent mathematically the transportation networks within the space corresponding to the study area to enable their treatment using the models of transportation demand.

Usually, the representation of a given TZ in terms of its travel pattern admits an inductive approach and assumes that, based on a sample, it is possible to generalize the behavior of the entire TZ. For that a survey to collect information about the travel behavior of a selected group of households or institutions that generate activities (transportation demand) is carried out through questionnaires applied to the selected group to determine the travel characteristics and build an origin and destination (O/D) matrix.

(c) Diagnosis

The diagnosis seeks to present a description of the current situation that is comprehensive and detailed enough so that the scope of the study may be properly understood. It is much more than the examination of a set of flows in the transportation network and the consequent observations of the lack of capacity in specific segments. Ideally, it should involve the identification of other relevant aspects, as well as the lack of capacity, regarding the impacts of transportation systems on the economic, social, and environmental structure.

(d) Demand analysis and forecasting model use

At the center of the planning process is the use of a demand analysis and forecasting model that has a close relationship with the previously identified actors of the system.

Trip generation has the objective of estimating the production and attraction of trips to each of the traffic zones (TZ) of the study area based on a typical period (day, week, and month) of the future situation. In this case, it is common to use a projection through growth rates or using regression (linear or not), where trip generation is a function of land use (industrial, commercial, and residential) and socioeconomic aspects (jobs, income, number of residences, and number of businesses). The use of this model requires care since studies show that the movement of people and freight can be very much diversified depending on the activity sector and the need of the market where they operate.

Trip distribution has the objective of estimating the number of trips between the TZs by creating an O/D matrix based on the results obtained during the trip generation step. It is common to use the gravitational model or transportation problem.

Modal choice is necessary whenever more than one mode of transportation is available to connect two TZs. In the case of urban transportation, where road transportation prevails, it is possible to infer that different types of vehicles represent different modes. The choice is based on the evaluation of attributes that are specific to each mode, essentially representative of cost, travel time (door to door), and reliability, which are relatively important for the involved actors. These attributes can be considered individually or aggregately in a generalized cost. The models can be deterministic or probabilistic, with the LOGIT model (binomial or multinomial) being often used in the latter case.

The allocation of flows seeks to assess the distribution of trips in the transportation network that already exists or may be created. The choice of routes can be associated with a set of decision factors such as speed, straightness, low congestion, and the shortest route. The use of traffic flow models is typical in the case of an analytical approach otherwise the use of computational simulation is considered.

56 Transportation, energy use and environmental impacts

(e) Assessment of alternatives

Once the traffic expectation lines and the possible alternatives to serve them are identified, it is, then, necessary to apply some method of assessing the alternatives of transportation plans, programs, and projects.

The most used methodology in these cases is the economic assessment of transportation projects that uses the benefit/cost comparison. However, there are other techniques to assess transportation investment alternatives and the most modern ones consider it indispensable that the aspects related to social and environmental impacts be assessed.

(f) Choice of alternatives

The use of any technique for the assessment of the alternatives of transportation plans, programs, and projects produces a rational hierarchy of alternatives as function of increasing socioeconomic benefits. However, decision-making may also depend on the establishment of other priorities which consider aspects of the institutional context and have strong political, legal, and fiscal aspects. More recently, the social and environmental aspects cannot be neglected when choosing alternatives.

(g) Implementation of alternatives

Once the choice for the alternative (or alternatives) has been made, it is followed by the implementation process, with the managing of resources needed for such implementation, which includes the conclusion of all the projects, budgets, and schedules, the construction of the infrastructure and its later operation.

(h) Monitoring and feedback

The efficient and effective performance of freight transportation systems depends on some sort of control tool. This control can be carried out through the monitoring and feedback of the transportation planning process. A useful tool for that is de MRV (monitoring, reporting, and verifying) process.

In addition to the specificities of the role of public authorities in planning transportation systems, there is a growing need to regulate the use of the transportation system to ensure sustainable development.

The design phase is the one that precedes the construction of the infrastructure and, in a brief description, considers the basic, detailed, and executive designs, the schedule, and the budget of the construction. It is worth highlighting the importance of considering these activities in this order, with none of them being suppressed or having their importance minimized, or else there may be a propagation of problems and inaccuracies to the construction phase, with negative impacts on the schedule and budget of the project.

It is also important to consider the need of reassessing the EIA and the respective EIR based on the progress achieved on the knowledge of the problem arising from the implementation of the projects.

The reflexes on the anthropic environment arising from the planning and design phases of transportation systems stem from the expectation created in society about the potential economic, social, and environmental impacts that would be observed if the system were built. These reflexes are related to the potential change in land use and occupation, which can lead, for example, to real estate speculation, migratory movements, and the generation of conflicting social movements.

Infrastructure for transportation systems Chapter | 2 **57**

The planning of a new road system that allows access to an isolated region of a city can cause the expectation of migratory movements to this region, with the consequent potential of real estate speculation by the valuation of real estate located there due to an expectation of easy access.

In the design phase, due to an advance in the detailing of the transportation system's construction, there is a reinforcement of the expectations regarding the potential reflexes of the planning actions.

Example 2.2   The case of bus rapid transit (BRT) Transoeste in the city of Rio de Janeiro, Brazil

Based on the experience of the city of Rio de Janeiro, Brazil, it is possible to exemplify the reflexes on the anthropic environment caused by the planning and design for the construction of a BRT system called Transoeste that is in the west zone of the city, where a rapid population growth was observed in the first decade of the 21st century.

BRTs consist of exclusive bus lanes to which passengers have easy access through special stations where they pay for their tickets in advance and have facilitated boarding access since the station's floor is at the same level as that of the vehicle. The implementation of the BRT systems represented a potential improvement in the collective public transportation system in this region of the city of Rio de Janeiro.

The publicity about the planning and project of the BRT Transcarioca and the potential reduction in travel time between the west zone and the other regions of the city led to an expectation of strong occupation in the neighborhoods of the west zone, followed by a real estate speculation that doubled the price of real estate in the region and by a process of migration to that region.

2.3   Construction of transportation systems infrastructure

In the construction phase, what was planned and designed in previous phases is executed, leading to interventions and modifications in the environment (physical, biotic, and anthropic). It is during the construction phase that the initial interventions in the environment are carried out through the activities of preparation for the physical interventions and the effective execution of civil works associated with the opening of roads, construction of terminals, and implementation of communication and control systems.

To minimize the effects of the construction phase, it is necessary to know the environmental impacts caused by the constructive actions and to indicate mitigation measures for these effects.

Table 2.2 facilitates the understanding and comparison between the actions needed for the construction of the infrastructure by mode of transportation. The "X" indicates the occurrence of the action for the infrastructure construction in a specific mode of transportation.

TABLE 2.2 Actions needed for the transportation system infrastructure construction.

Actions		Transportation modes					
Macro actions	Specific actions	Road	Rail	Pipelines	Maritime[a]	Waterways	Air[a]
Initial interventions	Deforestation of lands[a]	X	X	X	X	X	X
	Expropriation and demolition of real estate	X	X	X	X	X	X
	Installation of construction sites	X	X	X	X	X	X
	Opening of accesses and service paths	X	X	X	X	X	X
	Opening of borrow pits	X	X	X	X	X	X
	Opening of waste pits	X	X	X	X	X	X
	Installation of crushing and concrete plant	X	X	X	X	X	X
	Installation of asphalt plant	X			X	X	X
Earthworks	Dredging works				X	X	
	Rock blasting works	X	X	X	X	X	
	Cut and fill works	X	X	X			X
	Earthworks	X	X	X	X	X	X

Construction works	Operation of construction sites	X	X	X	X	X	X
	Operation of crushing and concrete plant	X	X	X	X	X	X
	Operation of asphalt plant	X			X	X	X
	Slope stabilization	X	X	X		X	
	Drainage works	X	X	X	X		X
	Paving	X			X	X	X
	Construction of regular civil engineering structures	X	X	X	X	X	X
	Construction of special civil engineering structures	X	X			X	
	Operation of machinery and equipment	X	X	X	X	X	X
	Works of implementation and installation of road accessories	X	X	X		X	
Final interventions	Reforestation[a]	X	X	X	X	X	X
	Deactivation of construction sites	X	X	X	X	X	X
	Recuperation of borrow pits	X	X	X	X	X	X
	Recuperation of waste pits	X	X	X	X	X	X
	Recuperation of accesses and service paths	X	X	X	X	X	X

Based on Hay, W.W., 1961. An Introduction to Transportation Engineering. John Wiley & Sons, Inc., New York and Hoel, L. A., Garber, N. J., Sadek, A.W., 2011. Transportation Infrastructure Engineering. A Multimodal Integration. Cengage Learning, Stamford.
[a] There may be works on terminals.

60 Transportation, energy use and environmental impacts

As presented in Table 2.2, it is possible to classify the macro actions according to the cycle of the project as initial interventions, land movement, civil works, and final interventions. The initial interventions consider specific activities that will enable the execution of land movements and civil works. The final interventions seek to restore the original condition of the areas impacted by the works and that are not part of the transportation system after its implementation. Each of the macro actions presents a set of specific actions that will be addressed in the following sections.

2.3.1 Deforestation of areas and real estate expropriation

The construction of roadways, terminals, and control and communication systems for transportation may require large areas of land which should be obtained through deforestation, if the work occurs in an unoccupied area, or through the expropriation of real estate, in the hypothesis of construction in urban areas.

Deforestation involves cutting vegetative cover of a land and clearing it, which, depending on the location, may require mowing, tree felling, and/or stump removal. Mowing is the cutting of shrubs and small plants with the use of a sickle (manual or mechanical). Tree felling, as the name suggests, is the felling of trees located in the construction area and stump removal is the extraction of the stumps of tree trunks that remain on the ground after the felling. Land clearing is the removal of all the material generated in the actions of deforestation or removal of vegetative cover.

Expropriations aim to transfer the ownership of real estate (buildings) and/or areas (land) from individuals or businesses located in the region of interest for the implementation of the transportation system. This may be one of the major costs related to the construction of transportation infrastructure, in the case of construction in a densely occupied area. In addition to the costs of indemnification for the removal of the occupants, it is still necessary to consider the costs with demolition of buildings and removal of debris from the area that will be used for the construction.

Depending on applicable legislation, expropriation can only be carried out with proof that it is a necessary action to carry out a construction that represents an effective contribution to society and is executed by the public administration, being possibly accompanied by an indemnification given to the owner who lost the property.

2.3.2 Installation, operation, and subsequent deactivation of construction sites

Construction sites are temporary facilities that provide logistic support to the infrastructures for the management and execution of the construction works. There are basically four kinds of facilities at a construction site: (1) administrative facilities, (2) community facilities, (3) production facilities, and (4) industrial facilities.

The administrative facilities aim to support administrative work and include offices, workshops, fuel stations, medical facilities, etc. The community facilities are designed to provide site workers with infrastructure such as lodgings, cafeterias, toilets, etc. The production facilities are used to store the equipment that will be used during the construction, also serving as a space for carpentry, metalworking, and molding. The industrial facilities are used to produce all the necessary supplies, parts, and components needed during construction.

2.3.3 Opening of tracks, accesses, and service paths

The trails, accesses, and service paths help and/or allow the flow of labor, raw material, semifinished material, and equipment necessary for the construction of the infrastructure of the transportation system.

Although they are temporary access routes, they must have their layout (horizontal and vertical alignment) safely established with guaranteed traffic condition for different operational situations. This may require the carrying out and maintenance of beaconing, signaling, and drainage works for as long as the construction activities last.

2.3.4 Installation and operation of asphalt, concrete, and crushing plants

These facilities are most commonly used to produce raw material for the construction of roads, railways, and terminals.

Concrete and crushing plants are responsible for producing the raw material (concrete) for activities such as the setting of highways (paved with concrete); duct anchoring; drainage works (gutters, shoulders, curbs, culverts, grates, ditches, and ducts) that are used in all kinds of transportation systems (see Figs. 1.2 and 1.8); special civil engineering works (tunnels, bridges, and viaducts) that apply to road and rail systems; and road or rail terminals, ports, and airports (pavement of access roads and yards, and building structures) (see Figs. 1.6, 1.7, 1.14, 1.17, 1.18, and 1.20).

Gravel can be applied to the permanent way and to the rail (see Fig. 1.8) and port yards. Asphalt plants are facilities that aim to produce all the asphalt mass that will be demanded for the step of asphalt paving of roadways (Figs. 1.2 and 1.6) and road or rail terminals, ports, and airports.

2.3.5 Opening and recuperation of borrow pits and waste pits

Borrow pits are areas used for the acquisition of raw materials such as sand, clay, and gravel for construction. On the other hand, waste pits are areas used to deposit materials that are considered leftover from the construction site and which do not serve as landfills because of their physical characteristics (soil composition) or the excess of foreign material in the landfill, such as construction debris and civil construction parts leftovers.

62 Transportation, energy use and environmental impacts

2.3.6 Dredging, rock blasting, and earthworks

Dredging is a typical work of water environments and aims to remove solid material, sediments, and/or rocks (in which case it is called rock blasting), from the bottom of bodies of water (rivers, seas, and oceans). Usually this action is carried out to open or deepen navigable channels for water modes of transportation.

Rock blasting is the removal of stones or rocks preventing the layout of waterways. It can be carried out with the use of natural or industrial explosives.

Earthworks are services in which earth is moved with purpose of assisting in the preparation of the area for the implementation of the transportation system. The following are among the main interventions associated with earthworks: deforestation or removal of vegetative cover and land clearing; the implementation and exploitation of mineral deposits and borrow pits; cuts and fills; and waste disposal works.

Cuts are operations of excavation and removal of the soil that aim to prepare the area for the installation of the transportation system. Some of the material from the cuts is deposited and compacted in landfills.

2.3.7 Slope stabilization

A slope (see Fig. 1.8) is an inclined plane that limits the terrain. Because it is an inclined plane, it is necessary to carry out stabilization works that aim to avoid or minimize the occurrence of landslides.

2.3.8 Drainage works

Drainage is the action of draining water from the construction site. This drainage may occur with the opening of trenches, ditches, or gutters (see Figs. 1.2 and 1.8) for the flow of excess water or with the use of drainage systems such as geosynthetic tubes.

2.3.9 Paving works

Paving works consist in coating the area that will receive the transportation system (see Fig. 1.2). Paving can be done with crushed stone, cement concrete, or asphalt concrete (see Figs. 1.2, 1.6, 1.7, 1.8, and 1.20).

2.3.10 Regular and special civil engineering structures

Regular civil engineering structures are civil works of lesser complexity and are represented, for example, by drainage works (gutters, shoulders, curbs, culverts, ditches, and ducts) (see Figs. 1.2 and 1.8), installation of pipes, galleries, or small bridges for the transposition of water courses; they are used in all kinds of road and railway systems and terminals like ports and airports.

Special civil engineering structures are works of greater complexity and are represented by the construction of bridges, tunnels, underground passages, which apply to the road and railway systems, aiming to reduce distances and avoid the need for cutting and rock blasting works.

2.3.11 Operation of machinery and equipment

The operation of machinery and equipment is the use of the equipment necessary for the execution of all the works. In addition to the physical installations made up of equipment and machinery of the asphalt, concrete, and crushing plant, other important equipment are the energy-generating groups (usually diesel-electric), pile drivers, compressed air bells, asphalt storage tanks, pipe factory, concrete mixers, road marking machines, hand tools, and conveyors.

Furthermore, there is a set of self-propelled equipment that is required for construction works such as load-haul-dump loaders, excavators, backhoes, graders, rollers, tank trucks, asphalt distributors, concrete mixers, load vehicles, asphalt finishers, and agricultural tractors.

2.3.12 Works of implementation and installation of guideway accessories

The implementation and installation of road and railway accessories are complementary to earthworks.

In the case of the railway mode, which, in addition to the railway area, requires elements that allow the locomotive to circulate, the implementation works represent the placement of ballasts, sleepers, rails, switches, and others.

In the case of water, pipeline, and road modes, these works can be considered as visual works, since they consist, for example, in the installation of accessory elements to the road, such as signs (lane markings, placing of traffic lights, signposts, light poles, tunnel ventilation systems, etc.), in the case of land modes, and the placement of buoys, in the case of water modes.

2.3.13 Specific actions and reflexes on the environment

In the preceding sections, specific actions (sources of impacts) for the implementation of a transportation system were selected. These works are extremely necessary but can generate positive or negative impacts (potential impacts) on the environment.

To identify the impacts that are common among the actions presented in the preceding sections, Table 2.3 was created aiming to relate the specific actions with the expected reflexes on the anthropic, biotic, and physical environments.

2.3.14 Reflexes on the environment and selected mitigation measures

To minimize the potential environmental impacts on the physical, biotic, and anthropic environments resulting from the specific actions carried out during the transportation systems implementation, there is an extensive series of possible mitigation measures. For illustration, Table 2.4 summarizes a selected set of mitigation measures that may be related to the environmental impacts illustrated in Table 2.3. This set does not present an exhaustive list of measures, thus many others could be listed and applied.

64 Transportation, energy use and environmental impacts

TABLE 2.3 Construction of transportation systems—Specific actions and reflexes on the environment

Specific actions	Removal of vegetative cover	Removal of residences	Soil erosion	Atmo- spheric pollution	Green- house gas emissions	Soil pollution	Water pollution
Deforestation of lands	X		X	X	X	X	X
Expropriation and demolition of real estate		X		X	X	X	X
Installation of construction sites			X	X	X	X	X
Opening of accesses and service paths			X	X	X	X	X
Opening of borrow pits			X	X	X	X	X
Opening of waste pits			X	X	X	X	X
Installation of crushing and concrete plant			X	X	X	X	X
Installation of asphalt plant			X	X	X	X	X
Dredging works			X	X	X	X	X
Rock blasting works				X	X	X	X
Earthworks			X	X	X	X	X
Operation of construction sites					X	X	X
Operation of crushing and concrete plant				X	X	X	X
Operation of asphalt plant				X	X	X	X
Slope stabilization				X	X	X	X
Drainage works				X	X	X	X
Paving				X	X	X	X

Infrastructure for transportation systems Chapter | 2 **65**

Noise pollution	Energy waste	Animal deaths	Social imbalance	Sal-vatage	Increased accessibility	Job gener-ation	Income generation and distribution	Flora restoration	Fauna restoration
X	X	X				X	X		
X	X	X	X						
X	X		X			X	X		
X	X	X			X	X	X		
X	X	X				X	X		
X	X	X				X	X		
X	X	X				X	X		
X	X	X				X	X		
X	X	X				X	X		
X	X	X				X	X		
X	X					X	X		
X	X		X			X	X		
X	X		X			X	X		
X	X		X			X	X		
X	X					X	X		
X	X					X	X		
X	X					X	X		

Continued

66 Transportation, energy use and environmental impacts

TABLE 2.3 Construction of transportation systems—Specific actions and reflexes on the environment—Cont'd

Specific actions	Removal of vegetative cover	Removal of residences	Soil erosion	Atmospheric pollution	Greenhouse gas emissions	Soil pollution	Water pollution
Construction of regular civil engineering structures				X	X	X	X
Construction of special civil engineering structures				X	X	X	X
Operation of machinery and equipment				X	X	X	X
Works of implementation and installation of road accessories				X	X	X	X
Reforestation				X	X		
Deactivation of construction sites				X	X	X	X
Recuperation of borrow pits				X	X	X	X
Recuperation of waste pits				X	X	X	X
Recuperation of accesses and service paths				X	X	X	X

Based on Fogliatti, M.C., Filippo, S., Goudard, B., 2004. Avaliação de Impactos Ambientais. Aplicação aos Sistemas de Transporte (Environmental Impacts Assessment. Transportation Systems Application) Editora Interciência, Rio de Janeiro, RJ and Vanek, F.M., Angenent, L.T., Banks, J.H., Daziano, R.A., Turniquist, M.A., 2014. Sustainable Transportation Systems Engineering. McGraw-Hill Education, Boston, MA.

Noise pollution	Energy waste	Animal deaths	Social imbalance	Sal-vatage	Increased accessibility	Job gener-ation	Income generation and distribution	Flora restoration	Fauna restoration
X	X					X	X		
X	X					X	X		
X	X					X	X		
X	X					X	X		
	X					X	X	X	X
X	X					X	X		
X	X					X	X	X	X
X	X					X	X	X	X
X	X					X	X	X	X

68 Transportation, energy use and environmental impacts

TABLE 2.4 Construction of transportation systems—Reflexes on the environment and mitigation measures

Mitigation Measures	Removal of vegetative cover	Removal of residences	Soil erosion	Atmospheric pollution	Greenhouse gas emissions	Soil pollution	Water pollution
Properly calculate the needs of the construction works in order to avoid overpopulation, water and energy shortage, sanitation problems, or food shortage							
Control the emission of liquid effluents and the disposal of solid waste					X	X	X
Adequate treatment of generated solid and liquid effluents					X	X	X
Carry out disease prevention and basic hygiene practices campaigns							
Carry out periodic health inspections							
Periodically check water quality and the level of toxicity in the soil						X	X
Avoid occupying areas near water sources							X

Noise pollution	Energy waste	Animal deaths	Social imbalance	Salvatage	Increased accessibility	Job generation	Income generation and distribution	Flora restoration	Fauna restoration
			X						
						X	X		
X						X	X		
			X			X	X		
			X			X	X		
			X			X	X		
			X						

Continued

70 Transportation, energy use and environmental impacts

TABLE 2.4 Construction of transportation systems—Reflexes on the environment and mitigation measures—cont'd

Mitigation Measures	Removal of vegetative cover	Removal of residences	Soil erosion	Atmospheric pollution	Greenhouse gas emissions	Soil pollution	Water pollution
Carry out environmental education campaigns with workers and suppliers							
Periodically review the operational condition of machinery and equipment				X	X	X	X
Throw water onto the access ways, service paths, and maneuvering yards to settle the dust				X			
Restore the vegetation of the areas deforested to access the construction site or to explore materials	X		X	X	X	X	X
Completely clean the construction site after the works are carried out				X	X	X	X
Control the entry and exit of workers into areas of cut forest	X					X	X
Suppress any kind of aggression to the fauna and flora	X						
Prioritize the hiring of local labor							

Infrastructure for transportation systems Chapter | 2 **71**

Noise pollution	Energy waste	Animal deaths	Social imbalance	Sal-vatage	Increased access-ibility	Job gener-ation	Income generation and distribution	Flora restoration	Fauna restoration
			X			X	X		
X	X								
	X					X	X	X	X
	X		X						
		X		X				X	X
		X				X	X		

Continued

72 Transportation, energy use and environmental impacts

TABLE 2.4 Construction of transportation systems—Reflexes on the environment and mitigation measures—cont'd

Mitigation Measures	Removal of vegetative cover	Removal of residences	Soil erosion	Atmospheric pollution	Greenhouse gas emissions	Soil pollution	Water pollution
Inform workers coming from other locations about the culture and habits of the local community							
Not to install construction sites in urban areas		X					
Install drainage ditches to minimize sediment run-off			X				X
Restoration of natural drainage			X				X
Limit deforestation to the necessary areas	X				X		
Use organic soils to cover the explored areas					X		
Not to burn and/ or expose to the weather the material resulting from deforestation and clearing				X	X	X	X
Carry out controlled removal or incineration of vegetation debris				X	X	X	X
Not to release material resulting from deforestation and clearing in talwegs and water bodies					X	X	X

Infrastructure for transportation systems **Chapter | 2** **73**

Noise pollution	Energy waste	Animal deaths	Social imbalance	Sal-vatage	Increased access-ibility	Job gener-ation	Income generation and distribution	Flora restoration	Fauna restoration
			X			X	X		
			X						
								X	X
								X	X
						X	X		

Continued

74 Transportation, energy use and environmental impacts

TABLE 2.4 Construction of transportation systems—Reflexes on the environment and mitigation measures—cont'd

Mitigation Measures	Removal of vegetative cover	Removal of residences	Soil erosion	Atmospheric pollution	Greenhouse gas emissions	Soil pollution	Water pollution
Store material resulting from deforestation and clearing for further recovery of the explored soil					X	X	X
Control the formation of erosive areas			X			X	X
Adapt the asphalt and concrete plants with grease and oil filters					X	X	X
Protect the material to be transported with tarpaulins or another type of protection that prevents their fall during the journey				X		X	X
Permanently maintain water flow conditions			X			X	X
Install a drainage system			X			X	X
Dispose of waste in compact layers without damaging natural drainage and landscape			X			X	X
Create quarry exploration plans				X	X	X	X
Monitor, control, and adjust quarry exploration plans				X	X	X	X

Infrastructure for transportation systems Chapter | 2 **75**

Noise pollution	Energy waste	Animal deaths	Social imbalance	Sal- vatage	Increased access- ibility	Job gener- ation	Income generation and distribution	Flora restoration	Fauna restoration
								X	
					X	X			
					X	X			
					X	X			
X	X	X		X		X	X	X	
X	X	X		X		X	X	X	

Continued

76 Transportation, energy use and environmental impacts

TABLE 2.4 Construction of transportation systems—Reflexes on the environment and mitigation measures—cont'd

Mitigation Measures	Removal of vegetative cover	Removal of residences	Soil erosion	Atmospheric pollution	Greenhouse gas emissions	Soil pollution	Water pollution
Carry out stabilization works in areas susceptible to landslides			X			X	X
Carry out cuts and fills with slopes compatible with the resistance of materials			X			X	X
Restore the vegetation of the explored area						X	X
Carry out landscaping works trying to maintain the natural species of the region						X	X
Use demolition equipment that has air compressors with noise suppressors							
Establish a waste and vegetation debris collection routine to ensure disposal in appropriate places				X	X	X	X
Use dust filters in crushing facilities and asphalt and concrete plants				X		X	X

Infrastructure for transportation systems Chapter | 2 77

Noise pollution	Energy waste	Animal deaths	Social imbalance	Sal-vatage	Increased access-ibility	Job gener-ation	Income generation and distribution	Flora restoration	Fauna restoration
		X				X	X		
						X	X	X	
						X	X	X	
X									
	X					X	X		

Continued

78 Transportation, energy use and environmental impacts

TABLE 2.4 Construction of transportation systems—Reflexes on the environment and mitigation measures—cont'd

Mitigation Measures	Removal of vegetative cover	Removal of residences	Soil erosion	Atmospheric pollution	Greenhouse gas emissions	Soil pollution	Water pollution
Select the most environmentally appropriate technology for underwater blastings or use less aggressive methods such as removing rocks using hydraulic equipment						X	X
Carry out the detonations close to or shortly after drillings in order to disperse the ichthyofauna							X
Keep machinery and equipment regulated and with noise suppressors				X	X	X	X
Relocate productive activities							
Resettle the population in places that allow working and life conditions that are similar or superior to the areas in which they used to live							
Calculate the appropriate indemnities to be paid in expropriation processes		X					
Treat and give appropriate destination to the solid waste produced during the services				X	X	X	X

Infrastructure for transportation systems Chapter | 2 **79**

Noise pollution	Energy waste	Animal deaths	Social imbalance	Sal-vatage	Increased access-ibility	Job gener-ation	Income generation and distribution	Flora restoration	Fauna restoration
		X							
		X		X					
X	X					X	X		
			X			X	X		
			X						
			X						
						X	X		

Continued

80 Transportation, energy use and environmental impacts

TABLE 2.4 Construction of transportation systems—Reflexes on the environment and mitigation measures—cont'd

Mitigation Measures	Removal of vegetative cover	Removal of residences	Soil erosion	Atmospheric pollution	Greenhouse gas emissions	Soil pollution	Water pollution
Establish and apply procedural rules for the collection, filtration, and recovery of grease, oils, and garbage collection				X	X	X	X
Recycle the related materials or give them appropriate destination				X	X	X	X
Monitor the discharge effluent levels of combustion engines				X	X	X	X
Reforest slopes as a corrective or preventive measure, protecting them from fire				X	X	X	X
Avoid, whenever possible, the felling of arboreal individuals from the riparian forests by performing a simple pruning	X			X	X	X	X
Carry out periodic maintenance of vessels, equipment, and transportation vehicles				X	X	X	X
Not to perform dredging during the period of piracema and larval drift							

Based on Fofliatti et al. (2004) and Vanek, F.M., Angenent, L.T., Banks, J.H., Daziano, R.A., Turniquist, M.A., 2014. Sustainable Transportation Systems Engineering. McGraw-Hill Education, Boston, MA.

Noise pollution	Energy waste	Animal deaths	Social imbalance	Sal-vatage	Increased access-ibility	Job gener-ation	Income generation and distribution	Flora restoration	Fauna restoration
						X	X		
						X	X		
	X					X	X		
	X					X	X	X	
								X	X
X						X	X		
		X							

82 Transportation, energy use and environmental impacts

Example 2.3 Dredging of the Elbe river to deepen the access channel to the port of Hamburg in Germany

Considered as an essential work to facilitate the access of larger freight vessels to the port of Hamburg in Germany, the dredging works of the Elbe River, which includes the correction and deepening of the port access channel bed, with an extension of 130 km and considering the deepening of the river from 12.5 to 14.5 m, have been suspended since 2013 and will only be approved by the German Federal Administrative Court when it is confirmed that the plans for implementing environmental protection measures will be remade.

The dredging of the river has the potential to increase salt content in the water, given the greater possibility of fresh water mixing with salt water of the North Sea during floods, significantly affecting the supply of water for consumption and irrigation in the region.

Example 2.4 Environmental conflict over the high-speed train (HST) connecting the cities of Torino (Italy) and Lyon (France)

The HST connecting the cities of Torino (Italy) and Lyon (France) has become one of the most important generators of environmental conflict in Europe. On the one hand, the project was declared by the European Commission as a priority infrastructure project to connect the west and east of the continent; on the other hand, there has been popular resistance since the 1990s (No-HST Movement) in fear of damages to aquifers and a possible release of asbestos and radioactive materials during the excavation of a tunnel of approximately 57 km that is part of the planned network.

2.4 Demobilization of transportation systems infrastructure

If a transportation system infrastructure reaches the end of its life the demobilization phase begins. In this phase demolition of all the infrastructure is done and the resultant material is processed and recycled. The construction site is restored, and the place is set to its original condition.

In this final phase, almost all specific actions that were addressed in the construction of infrastructure phase are recurrent and the same specific actions and reflexes on the environment and mitigation measures presented in Tables 2.3 and 2.4 should be considered.

2.5 Final considerations

This chapter addressed the identification of the main environmental impacts generated by the planning, design, construction, and demobilization phases of infrastructure for transportation systems (road, railway, pipeline, water, and air).

It was possible to observe that there are specific actions that are common to the planning, design, and construction of infrastructure of all transportation modes; there was also the identification of a selection of reflexes of these actions in the physical, biotic, and anthropic environments; and, finally, the chapter lists a selected set of possible measures to mitigate the effects of these reflexes.

The chapter also presents examples that consider the most commonly used process in transportation systems planning and the potential social and environmental impacts resulting from the planning, design, construction, and demobilization phases.

2.6 Exercises

1. Determine the planning phases of a transportation system by choosing one of the following projects: urban highway, rural highway, interstate railroad for freight transportation, port, or airport.
2. Describe and comment the process of planning transportation systems.
3. Describe and comment the four steps considered in the demand analysis and forecasting model for transportation planning.
4. What reflexes can a project cause, considering the planning phase? Answer based on the choice of one of the following transportation projects: pipelines, inland waterways, metropolitan train, light rail transit, or urban bus network.
5. What reflexes can a project cause, considering the design phases? Answer based on the choice of one of the following transportation projects: pipelines, inland waterways, metropolitan train, light rail transit, or urban bus network.
6. Describe the current situation of a public passenger transportation mode that appears to meet demand in a poor way in your city and explain the reasons why it is so, considering the planning phase of a transportation system.
7. Describe the current situation of a freight transportation mode that appears to meet demand in a poor way in your city and explain the reasons why it is so, considering the planning phase of a transportation system.
8. Imagine you have been hired to carry out a survey of the potential environmental impacts of a BRT in its planning, design, and construction phases. With that in mind, present three examples of actions (sources of impact), identifying the phase in which they occur and what the generated reflex and the impacted environment are.
9. Considering the actions of dredging and rock blasting in ports, identify the main environmental impacts that could have been caused by these actions and the measures that can mitigate them.
10. Present at least three mitigation measures related to the following environmental impacts through the implementation of transportation systems: air pollution, noise pollution, soil pollution, water pollution, energy waste, social unbalance, job generation, and income generation and distribution.

84 Transportation, energy use and environmental impacts

Further reading

Fogliatti, M.C., Filippo, S., Goudard, B., 2004. Avaliação de Impactos Ambientais. Aplicação aos Sistemas de Transporte (Environmental Impacts Assessment. Transportation Systems Application). Editora Interciência, Rio de Janeiro, RJ.

Hay, W.W., 1961. An Introduction to Transportation Engineering. John Wiley & Sons, Inc, New York.

Morlok, E.K., 1978. Introduction to Transportation Engineering and Planning. McGraw-Hill, Inc., New York.

Hoel, L.A., Garber, N.J., Sadek, A.W., 2011. Transportation Infrastructure Engineering. A Multimodal Integration. Cengage Learning, Stamford.

Vanek, F.M., Angenent, L.T., Banks, J.H., Daziano, R.A., Turniquist, M.A., 2014. Sustainable Transportation Systems Engineering. McGraw-Hill Education, Boston, MA.

Chapter 3

Transportation planning and energy use

General goal

The general goal of this chapter is to describe how transportation and energy use are correlated, suggest a way of improving transportation management under a perspective of energy efficiency, and highlight the potential impact it may bring to the environment and to society.

At the end of this chapter, the reader should be able to:

1. Understand and explain the correlation between transportation and energy use.
2. Associate the transportation modes with their respective energy consumption patterns.
3. Compare the energy consumption patterns of different modes of transportation.
4. Analyze the aspects that impact energy use in transportation.
5. Propose a structure of procedures for transportation management under the perspective of energy consumption.
6. Know a set of tools that support the reduction in energy use and environmental impacts of the transportation activity.

3.1 Introduction

A large amount of energy is consumed so that the world can keep moving. However, to ensure the continuity of this movement, three questions must be raised: (1) Why does the world move? (2) How much does the world move? (3) How does the world move? This chapter seeks to address the correlation between transportation and energy use by considering these questions and, while answering them, show how it would be possible to guarantee sustainability in this activity.

After this introduction, the chapter is divided into three sections. Section 3.2 presents an overview of energy use worldwide, highlighting the share used by transportation. A special attention is given to Brazil due to its differential use of biofuels. This overview seeks to highlight not only the amount but also the quality of energy consumed by transportation, aiming to identify the kind of energy most used by transportation under a critical approach.

Then, Section 3.3 presents an approach that seeks to reconcile transportation planning and sustainable energy use. That approach seeks to progressively answer the three questions that precede energy consumption in transportation

Transportation, Energy Use and Environmental Impacts. https://doi.org/10.1016/B978-0-12-813454-2.00003-9
© 2019, Elsevier Editora Ltda. Published by Elsevier Inc. All rights reserved.

86 Transportation, energy use and environmental impacts

leading to a proposed procedure that aims to manage transportation demand under the perspective of energy use and contribute to the use of energy sources (ESs) with higher quality than those currently in use.

Once it is established that transportation is inevitable, Section 3.4 presents the concept of energy efficiency applied to transportation, the measures associated with it, and its forms of management.

Section 3.5 presents two tools used to apply the concepts described in the previous section with the purpose of reducing energy intensity and the environmental impacts caused by transportation systems.

Finally, Section 3.6 presents final considerations regarding the content of this chapter and Section 3.7 provides a set of exercises on this content.

3.2 An overview of energy use in transportation

Petroleum! Transportation worldwide relies on petroleum! According to data from the International Energy Agency (IEA, 2016), in 2015, 64.7% of the petroleum consumed worldwide was used by the transportation sector. This demand has increased by 1.5% per year in the period between 1973 and 2015, when it reached the value of 3.840 million tons of oil equivalent (Mtoe). In 2015, other ESs, such as coal (20.88 Mtoe), natural gas (98.07 Mtoe), electricity (36.48 Mtoe), renewable fuels, and other sources, such as geothermal, solar, electric, thermal, and wind energy, also had their consumption correlated to transportation but in significantly lower proportions than that of petroleum.

The case of Brazil stands out regarding initiatives to revert this scenario considering that, since the beginning of the 19th century, the country started searching for a substitute for petroleum as a source of energy for transportation, which in 2016, according to data from the Energy Research Company (EPE, 2017), answered for 25% of national energy consumption. Despite the great advances in this search and the country's international leadership in the production of biofuels, as shall be addressed in Chapter 6, the Brazilian transportation is still heavily dependent on diesel oil. According to data from the Energy Planning Company (EPE, 2017), in 2015, diesel oil represented 44% of all the energy used by transportation, with a total of 36.2 Mtoe. This value has been constantly growing since the 1970s, when it did not surpass 4.5 Mtoe.

The second most used ES for transportation in Brazil is gasoline, which corresponds to 29% of the total use; in third place comes ethanol, with 17% subdivided into the forms of anhydrous and hydrous ethanol; the former is added to gasoline up to a proportion of 25%.

With the introduction and spreading, in 2003, of *flexible-fuel* vehicles, which can be run on gasoline and/or hydrous ethanol in any proportion, the consumption of the latter tripled from 2003 to 2015. This is a differential of Brazil in relation to other countries in terms of the quality of the energy consumed in road transportation, since ethanol is a biofuel that can be regarded as resulting in zero carbon dioxide emission in its final use, besides being renewable.

Another Brazilian initiative toward the adoption of biofuels as ESs for transportation is the mandatory addition of 10% of biodiesel in volume to diesel oil on a national scale since November 2014. With that, it is estimated that 2.7 Mtoe of biodiesel have been added to diesel oil in 2015.

The Brazilian energy matrix also comprises other ESs such as natural gas (1.9%), used for road transportation; fuel oil (0.6%), for water transportation; aviation gasoline (0.05%) and kerosene (4%), for air transportation; and electricity (0.2%), used in subway and railway transportation.

3.3 Transportation planning and energy use

The beginning of this section calls for a radical statement: "there is no substitute for energy." In the different sectors of socioeconomic activities, an ES may be replaced by another source, but carrying out an activity without the consumption of some form of energy does not seem possible.

The above statement particularly applies to the case of transportation, understood as the displacement of people and/or freight through a route from one place to another in space, during a period, and consuming resources. Among these resources, energy stands out, and in this case, it may be understood in its most elementary form: energy is the capacity to do work, the product of a force by a distance.

More pragmatically, transportation is a necessary resource in the socioeconomic system. Many studies have been trying for a long time to correlate the growth of transportation with economic growth indices, such as a country's gross domestic product (GDP). The work of Schafer and Victor (2000) very clearly presents this result using the per capita income index. The historical series analyzed by the authors suggests that, worldwide, as the per capita income grew, the volume of motorized passenger displacements has also grown. The same can be said about freight transportation in relation to a country's GDP (Gonçalves and de D'Agosto, 2017). In other words, financial gains and mobility, either of freight or passengers, are positively correlated.

In the case of passenger transportation, considering the developed countries, as per capita income grew, the annual per capita traveled distance, expressed by the size of the annual per capita displacement, grew approximately in the same proportion. In this case, motorized displacements (car, bus, train, ship, and airplane) are taken into consideration. For developing countries, this relationship seemed to be less direct. In China, between 1960 and 1990, per capita income tripled, but motorized traffic increased 10 times! This discrepancy reflects the fact that financial gains lead to the replacement of nonmotorized transportation (walking and bicycles) with motorized modes (bus, train, car, ship, and airplane), partly due to the need for a higher number of displacements, with greater length and in a shorter period.

Another aspect of this situation is shown in Fig. 3.1, obtained from a study made by the World *Business Council for Sustainable Development* (CEBDS,

88 Transportation, energy use and environmental impacts

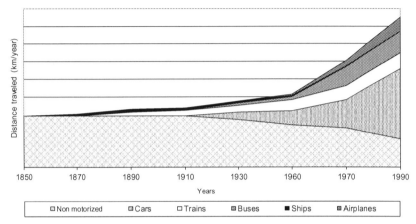

FIG. 3.1 Evolution of the distance traveled per passenger mode of transportation worldwide. Legend: No motorized means walking and cycling. *(Source: CEBDS, 2001. "O transporte do futuro". Desenvolvimento Sustentável, Ano III, n.13, maio-Jun.-Jul. 2001. Conselho Empresarial Brasileiro para o Desenvolvimento Sustentável, p. 4–5.)*

2001). Fig. 3.1 shows the evolution of passenger trips per mode of transportation worldwide between 1850 and 1990. It shows that since the beginning of the 20th century, the number of trips made using motorized transportation has sharply grown, with the use of cars standing out. In the same period, there was a decrease in walking and the use of bicycles.

Considering the above, cars have assumed an important role in the modal split of passenger transportation in the 20th century. According to Schafer and Victor (2000), this dependence would still be maintained worldwide for many years. The percentages presented in Fig. 1.26 (Chapter 1) regarding 2013 leave no doubt about it; one only needs to watch the news in any city in the world today to confirm that prediction.

When predictions for the next 30 years are made, it should be expected that developing countries follow a path of increasing dependence on cars. Considering that their transportation systems are less structured and that investments in other modes of transportation are not always possible, road transportation, and therefore cars, end up assuming the role of satisfying the increasing mobility rates that are typical of developed economies.

Considering freight handling within the national territory of OECD countries, Fig. 3.2 shows that in 40 years, freight handling has tripled, from 4 trillion t.km to 12 trillion t.km, in 2009. In this context, the share of road freight transportation has increased from 19% to 45%, while the share of railway transportation decreased by half (from 60% to 30%). Inland waterways have maintained a small share (between 6% and 8%), and the share of pipeline transportation had a sharp growth from 8% to 21%, a direct reflex of the great dependence of the

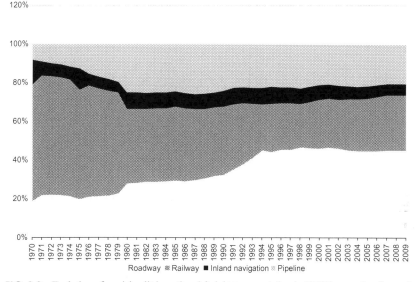

FIG. 3.2 Evolution of modal split in national freight transportation in OECD countries. Legend: percentages calculated over values in t.km. *(Source: ITF (2011). Trends in the Transport Sector, Annual Transport Statistics, International Transport Forum. OECD/ITF, Paris. Disponível em: www.internationaltransportforum.org/statistics/index.html.)*

transportation sector itself on petroleum as an ES. Data from 2013 (Fig. 1.28) confirm this trend.

Fig. 3.2 shows percentages calculated based on t.km data; this can play down the influence of road transportation, which is predominantly used for urban short-distance transportation in OECD (Organization for Economic Cooperation and Development) countries. This calculation basis could emphasize the use of railway transportation, whose vocation directs it to the transportation of large volumes of freight in great distances. However, despite this situation, the share of road transportation is predominant.

Considering that the increase in mobility is a natural trend in a society that evolves economically, and transportation is closely related to energy use, some questions may be raised:

- How is it possible to correlate energy use and measures of transportation demand planning?
- Is the increase in mobility based on the use of cars, or even of motorized road transportation, an option that is coherent with rational energy use?
- How is this applied?

The next subsection attempts to provide the answer to these questions in the form of a methodology that seeks to subsidize transportation planning taking energy use into consideration.

90 Transportation, energy use and environmental impacts

3.3.1 Aspects that impact energy use in transportation

How is it possible to correlate transportation and energy use? Since the transportation activity is directly related to the need for displacement, it is useful to examine in more detail which variables contribute to characterize energy use in the displacement of people and goods. This set of variables may be synthesized into four components:

- the number of trips made;
- the length of trips made;
- the transportation mode used;
- the specific energy use of the transportation mode used.

3.3.1.1 The number and length of trips made

In their study Schafer and Victor (2000) identified that a person spent an average of 1.1 h in daily trips (varying from 1.0 to 1.5 h). The data were updated in 2001 (WBCSD, 2000), and in the last 10 years, this average has increased. It was also possible to identify the length of the trips, which in this case varied from a little more than 5.0 km (in a small village in Tanzania) to a little less than 65.0 km (in the United States). The study did not establish the average number of trips made per day, however, it was based on the fact that home-work trips are predominant at an average speed of 20 km/h. These trips, which are usually two per day (round trip), would have an average length of 22 km.

When considering freight transportation, estimation of the number and extension of trips is a little harder. Nevertheless, the task of minimizing them is a constant activity performed by freight transportation managers as a logistics function, since this effort of reducing the number and length of trips leads to cost reduction.

3.3.1.2 Modes of transportation used and their energy use

Tables 3.1 and 3.2 show the examples of final energy use for the different kinds of passenger and freight transportation vehicles.

In the case of urban passenger transportation, two extremes can be seen. Human-traction bicycle is nonmotorized mode that has the lowest primary energy consumption in kJ/pass.km (kilojoules per passenger times kilometer). On the other hand, the compact car equipped with an internal combustion engine (ICE), regardless of the ES, is the motorized mode of transportation by land that has the highest energy consumption, with values close to the average found for air transportation.

The relative importance of the energy consumption for each mode of transportation should be noted here. When passenger transportation in urban areas is considered, the invention of the bicycle in the 19th century seems to have been the greatest human achievement regarding the rational use of energy for

Transportation planning and energy use Chapter | 3 **91**

TABLE 3.1 Energy use per type of passenger transportation

Type of transportation	Passengers/vehicle	kJ/pass.km
Walking	1	208
Running	1	283
Bicycle—human traction	1	112
Bicycle with gasoline ICE	1	418
Bicycle with EM	1	182
Motorcycle with gasoline ICE	1	1459
Compact car[1] with gasoline ICE	1.3	2766
Compact car[1] with ethanol ICE	1.3	3017
Compact car[1] with CNG ICE	1.3	2785
Medium car[2] with hybrid ICE-EE	1.3	1412
Battery electric vehicle (BEV)	1.3	791
Van[3] with diesel ICE	12	556
Microbus with diesel ICE	20	586
Conventional bus[4] with diesel ICE	60	255
Padron bus[5] with diesel ICE	80	266
Padron bus with hybrid ICE-EE	80	231
Battery electric bus (BEB)	80	100
Subway train[6]	225	183
Metropolitan train[6]	300	196
Long distance train[7]	20	1737
Airplane[8]	96	3138

Legends: ICE—internal combustion engine, EM—electrical motor.
Notes: (1) five places Volkswagen Gol 1.6cc; (2) Toyota Prius; (3) Mercedes Benz Sprinter; (4) conventional urban bus with front engine, 12 m of length and capacity for 80 passengers; (5) padron urban bus with rear engine, 13.2 m of length and capacity of up to 100 passengers; (6) the occupation considers the number of passengers per car; (7) Intercity Amtrak; average value of an interval that may vary from 1500 kJ/pass.km to 4500 kJ/pass.km.
Source: de D'Agosto, M.A., Ribeiro, S.K., 2005. Eco-efficiency management program (EEMP)—a model for road fleet operation. Transp. Res. D 9 (2004) p. 497–511.; D'Agosto, M.A., Ribeiro, S.K., 2009. Assessing total and renewable energy in Brazilian automotive fuels. A life cycle inventory (LCI) approach Renew. Sust. Energ. Rev., 13, 1326–1337.; Davis, Stacy C.; Diegel, Susan W.; Boundy, Robert G., 2009. Transportation Energy Data Book: 28th ed. US Department of Energy. (Edition 28 of ORNL-5198). Disponível em: http://cta.ornl.gov/data/Index.shtml. Acesso em 16 abr. 2010.; Gonçalves, D.N.S., de D'Agosto, M.A., 2017. Future Prospective Scenarios for the Use of Energy in Transportation in Brazil and GHG Emissions Business as Usual(BAU) Scenario—2050. Instituto Brasileiro de Transporte Sustentável (IBTS), Rio de Janeiro, RJ.

92 Transportation, energy use and environmental impacts

TABLE 3.2 Energy use per type of freight transportation

Type of transportation	t/vehicle	kJ/t.km
Van with gasoline ICE	1.5	2712
Light truck with diesel ICE	3.5	1825
Battery electric light truck (BEV)	3.5	510
Medium truck with diesel ICE	7.5	1612
Heavy truck with diesel ICE	12	1277
Tractor and semitrailer with diesel ICE	26	847
Diesel freight train[2]	7500	246
Tug[3] and barges	6600	370
Oil tanker	300,000	66
Freight airplane	20	6900
Pipeline[1]	–	123

Legends: (1) continuous pumping flow; (2) train with two locomotives and 100 cars with 75 t each; (3) one tug equipped with diesel ICE and six barges.
Source: de D'Agosto, M.A., Ribeiro, S.K., 2005. Eco-efficiency management program (EEMP)—a model for road fleet operation. Transp. Res. D 9 (2004) p. 497–511.; D'Agosto, M.A., Ribeiro, S.K., 2009. Assessing total and renewable energy in Brazilian automotive fuels. A life cycle inventory (LCI) approach Renew. Sust. Energ. Rev., 13, 1326–1337.; Davis, Stacy C., Diegel, Susan W., Boundy, Robert G., 2009. Transportation Energy Data Book: 28th ed., US Department of Energy. (Edition 28 of ORNL-5198). Disponível em: http://cta.ornl.gov/data/Index.shtml. Acesso em 16 abr. 2010.; Gonçalves, D.N.S., de D'Agosto, M.A., 2017. Future Prospective Scenarios for the Use of Energy in Transportation in Brazil and GHG Emissions Business as Usual(BAU) Scenario—2050. Instituto Brasileiro de Transporte Sustentável (IBTS), Rio de Janeiro, RJ.

transportation. Compared to the option of walking, the use of the modern bicycle consumes a little more than half the energy at a speed that is three times higher (considering the speeds of 5 km/h for walking and 15 km/h for bicycles).

Although the bicycle enabled a considerable expansion of trip distances, when compared to walking, motorized transportation represented a great differential in terms of mobility because it enabled to travel greater distances in a short time, regardless of the land topography. With that in mind, it is worth highlighting the advantage of collective transportation by land, which uses road or railway technology, over individual transportation (car), because the former reduces by 10 times in average the energy used, when compared with the latter. Furthermore, railway transportation, when electrified, uses a less pollutant ES in its final use.

When freight transportation is considered, energy use decreases as the freight capacity (t/vehicle) increases. Therefore, when it is necessary to choose the road transportation, trucks with higher capacity should be privileged. For the transportation of great masses of freight for long distances, the choice of modes with a higher capacity (railway, water, and pipeline), whenever possible, seems to be the most efficient form in terms of energy.

Nevertheless, the international scenario of energy use in the transportation sector seems not to follow this logic, since the intensive use of road transportation, shown at the beginning of this chapter, leads to a strong dependence on the use of fossil fuels as the ES for the transportation sector, as the technology of car, bus, and truck manufacturing is centered on the use of ICEs to propel vehicles. These engines are usually powered by petroleum-derived fuels and have an energy efficiency varying from 10% to 35% (gasoline: from 10% to 25%; and diesel oil: from 15% to 35%), which partially justifies the high consumption of fossil energy.

Out of the four variables presented at the beginning of this section that are capable of characterizing energy use in the displacement of people and goods, two of them can be determined based on the previous paragraphs: road transportation is the predominant mode, with highlight on the use of cars and trucks; and the energy consumption for this mode is the highest.

3.3.2 Transportation demand planning and energy use

The scenario presented until now seems contradictory if analyzed by point of view of energy use. The displacement needs are met by the mode of transportation that presents the highest energy consumption: the road mode! This fact becomes even more serious if one considers the verified trend of increased use of this mode of transportation (Figs. 3.1 and 3.2).

The historical growth in the use of cars is related to land use patterns. The compact occupation of urban space is being replaced by a decentralized pattern. This is possible due to the availability of cars, which enable the creation of new areas of housing, leisure, and work, which are dispersed and in regions that are far from urban centers. On the other hand, this dispersion would not be possible without the existence of cars, thus leading to a vicious circle of dependence on the use of individual transportation.

Additionally, the dispersion of the activities also leads to the need of freight handling (supply for economic activities and for people's survival) and services. Much of this freight transportation is made in urban areas, where small trucks are the predominant type of transportation due to legal imposition or ease of operation.

Would it be desirable to revert this trend? It is believed so! Measures have been employed in the last decades to either decrease this dependence on individual transportation or reduce the access to trucks in cities. The reasons for that are usually related to traffic problems (traffic jams) or environmental pollution (excessive emissions of atmospheric pollutants, which impact local and regional environment), and are rarely directly connected to the rationalization of energy use.

The need to reduce CO_2 emissions, in the case of fossil fuels, leads to an effort to reduce energy use but, in this case, the focus is environmental and not energetic, and the reduction in energy use is an indirect benefit.

94 Transportation, energy use and environmental impacts

Even so, it is believed that it would be possible to highlight a set of aspects capable of determining a methodology for the planning of transportation demand, with the goal of rationalizing energy use. These aspects are based on the set of variables that contribute to characterize energy use in the displacements of people and freight, as presented above, to create a guide to identify the possible actions that contemplate transportation demand planning and energy use. These aspects are presented below.

3.3.2.1 The need to make trips

This first aspect regards the first of the four variables: the number of trips made. The questions to be addressed are: Is there really the need to make a certain trip? What trips can be avoided? How can the demand for new trips be managed?

From the perspective of energy use, the possibility of "not making trips" or stimulating "no displacement" should be taken into consideration; this would be a situation of null energy use. Considering that, as presented before, there are strong indications that socioeconomic development leads to the need for greater mobility and a higher number of trips, two possibilities of "not making trips" can be imagined: the tribal society and the technological society.

The tribal society is characterized and defended in the book by Illich (1975). It is the society in which trips are unnecessary or highly minimized. If they are necessary, they are made using human muscle energy, with the use of motorized modes of transportation being inadmissible. In this case, the economic and technological developments are placed on the background and social needs are the basic ones, which can be met within walking distance. This situation is like that of indigenous tribes and small extractive, agricultural, or fishing villages, representing a modest and, apparently, utopian reality that seems somewhat unrealistic nowadays.

The other extreme is represented by the technological society. In this case, the need for trips is greatly, if not fully, reduced by the use of telematics (telecommunication + informatics). According to Choo et al. (2004), the idea that telecommunications would be able to reduce the need for trips is as old as the invention of the telephone. However, having worked with this theme for many years, the author of that study showed some skepticism about the power of telematics in suppressing urban trips.

As the main argument, she presented an estimate, based on her research, that at the end of the 20th century, only 16% of the workers, responsible for the highest volume of urban trips, effectively considered telematics to be a work tool. No more than 2% of them actually used this form of suppressing trips, and this percentage represents 0.79% of the total distance traveled by car users (Choo et al., 2004). Twenty years later and with much more resources available for the practice of telematics, the situation seems not to have changed.

It is important to highlight that the use of telematics in the reduction of the number of trips made in a region must be observed with caution. Internet commerce may not generate trips in the acquisition of the product but it ends up generating trips for its delivery, replacing urban passenger trips with freight trips. This phenomenon must be properly understood and controlled.

Encouraging the establishment of a tribal society would be an impractical measure. Seeking ways to stimulate the use of telematics as a way of reducing the number of trips made by people, and the use of energy, may be an applicable measure. However, its efficacy would still be questionable.

3.3.2.2 The length of trips

Once the need for trips and, thus, the number of trips needed have been identified, the next step is to determine the length of these trips. This aspect is related to the second of the four variables presented above and to the criteria of land use planning and management. Initially, two concepts related to this scenario stand out: the compact city and the dispersed city.

Breheny (1995) presents these two concepts and their relationship with energy use for transportation. The author considers a compact city to encompass a variety of urban planning strategies that value the containment of the dispersed growth of cities, in opposition to the strong natural tendency to decentralization, which is a characteristic of the process of a dispersed city. The latter is related to forms of populational and industrial occupation that tend to move away from urban centers.

Although, undoubtedly, the actions involved in the compact city lead to smaller displacements and lead to lower energy use, Breheny questioned the efficiency of this form of planning and argued that the implementation of these actions go in the opposite direction to natural city development trends, which would be of decentralization.

Containing the dispersed city depends on measures that are costly, time consuming, and hardly accepted by the society. In the author's case study, for the metropolitan region of London, the application of urban containment measures would lead to a reduction in energy use ranging from 2.5% (worst scenario) to 30% (best scenario). The author argues that these values could have been equally arrived at with the technological improvement in the modes of transportation being used or by changing the mode of transportation.

For example, Table 3.1 illustrates that a medium hybrid car consumes about 50% less energy than a compact gasoline car, which would represent a reduction in energy consumption 20% higher than the best hypothesis presented by Breheny.

Regarding freight transportation, while the dispersed city would lead to long routes for freight collection and distribution, which, due to a time constraint, is many times a difficult task when trying to take advantage of the freight vehicle's full capacity, the compact city would favor the use of vehicles with higher capacity that would access one point of the city from which the distribution of products and services could be made using nonmotorized modes (human traction carts and bicycles) within short distances.

The work of Banister and Watson (1994) complements the concepts of compact city and dispersed city, characterizing the accessible city. The authors

96 Transportation, energy use and environmental impacts

understand that accessibility should be privileged, seeking the balance between the urban growth containment and dispersion. For that some aspects must be considered when suggesting intervention measures for trip patterns such as a city's housing density, size, and format.

Regardless of compact or dispersed configuration, the reduction in energy use will have better results in areas where it is possible to make a lower number of trips of short length.

3.3.2.3 The choice for the transportation mode with the lowest energy use

Having identified the trip pattern, the transportation mode with the highest energy performance should be searched for. Tables 3.1 and 3.2 enable the identification of modes of transportation that should be privileged. In practice, however, there are other aspects that lead to the choice for a transportation mode and the reality observed is quite different from the recommended scenario under the perspective of energy use, with an observable intensive use of the road mode.

Regarding passenger transportation, a measure that can inhibit the use of cars is the taxation of traditional car fuels (petroleum-derived) and the incentive to the introduction of alternative propulsion systems (PS) or ESs (less pollutant). The international experience indicates that this measure results in a temporary decrease in car use, which is quickly compensated by a gain in technology that ends up boosting the use of cars, resulting in the so-called "rebound effect."

Other possible measures to restrict the use of cars is the creation of urban tolls, the reduction in parking areas, which could stimulate the practice of carpooling or vehicle sharing systems, and the definition of areas of restricted access to cars.

These measures should be supplemented by structural changes in the demand for people displacement. Along these lines, a series of policies that may be employed to influence changes in transportation demand appear, based on regulation, promotion, and investment.

From the perspective of energy consumption, the most immediate measure would be to stimulate walking and the use of bicycles, which are understood as the two modes of transportation with the lowest energy use. This practice applies to a limited range of trip lengths and depends on favorable climate and topography, as well as on the presence of public safety, among other aspects.

Collective transportation, especially railway systems, have the best energy performance results among the motorized modes of passenger transportation. The implementation of collective transportation systems depends on funding availability and is based on the justification of a demand capable of sustaining the operation at some point after its implementation. An adequate planning may indicate the implementation of systems that employ road technology, such as segregated or exclusive lanes for buses, lately called *Bus Rapid System* (BRS) and *Bus Rapid Transit* (BRT). A good planning would indicate that these systems, energetically less efficient than railway systems, should be later replaced by a railway technology of higher capacity and better energy performance, such as light rail transit (LRT), suburban trains, or subways.

The restriction of car use should be accompanied by alternatives for trips, such as incentives to the use of collective transportation. The mere restriction becomes inefficient, since it only affects trips that could already be avoided before and trips that are indispensable, and drivers end up finding ways around the prohibition.

In most cases, these individual policies are more effective if they are jointly and complementarily developed. Measures to restrict the use of fuels and cars must be complemented with measures that privilege walking, cycling, and the use of collective transportation. Options that have lower energy use in transportation must be available in a safe and comfortable way so that they effectively work.

As for freight transportation, the main measures that may be employed regarding rational energy use are associated with adequate modal choice. Therefore, transfers of large volumes of freight over great distances should be made using modes with a lower specific energy consumption, such as railway, water, and pipeline transportation, whenever possible. Nevertheless, this choice requires the availability of transportation infrastructure, which can be inexistent or scarce.

Freight transportation in urban areas is predominantly carried out by road transportation and, thus, a great effort must be made toward taking the most advantage of vehicles' transportation capacity and reducing the number and length of trips. Naturally, all these measures lead to lower cost and energy use, and they are already applied by good managers in freight transportation as a logistics function.

3.3.3 Transportation management procedures under an energy use perspective

Fig. 3.3 shows a flowchart aiming to clarify the procedure to be considered when proposing transportation management planning under an energy use perspective.

For each step of the procedure, there is an associated variable, a possible action, the expected results, and a reference situation. Its application is based on the characterization of a real situation, in which it is sought to apply the planning of the transportation sector considering a rational use of energy. As a first step, the procedure proposes the analysis of the actual need of making trips and the possibility of stimulating "no displacements."

Initially, all the incentives to the absence of displacement are desirable. Trips that cannot be suppressed must, if possible and as part of the second step of the procedure, have its length reduced, following the concept of an accessible city.

As a third step of the methodology, the mode of transportation with the best energy efficiency must be chosen to make necessary trips. In the case of passenger transportation, there is a reference order of privilege for cycling, walking, mass collective transportation (train and subway), and medium capacity collective transportation (bus). Individual transportation (car) should be avoided.

98 Transportation, energy use and environmental impacts

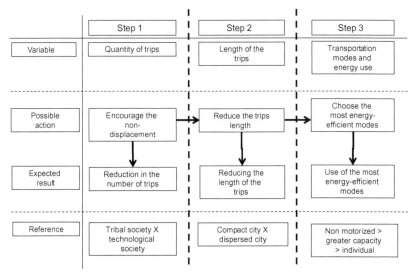

FIG. 3.3 Procedure for transportation demand planning under an energy use perspective.

For the cases in which individual transportation is unavoidable, there is the option of developing technology that is capable of rendering energy consumption in this mode of transportation more efficient, such as hybrid and electric vehicles.

As for freight transportation, the transfers of large masses over great distances should privilege the modes with higher capacity, such as railway, water, and pipeline transportation, when they are available. Urban freight transportation should adopt road freight transportation in a rational way, minimizing the need for trips and their extension and seeking to optimize the use of freight vehicles' capacity. In this context, it would also be possible to develop a technology capable of rendering energy consumption in this mode of transportation more efficient, again with the examples of hybrid and electric vehicles.

As described below, although it is proposed under an energy use perspective, the procedure has a conceptual adherence to other classical approaches adopted to enable the reduction in greenhouse gas (GHG) emissions by transportation, such as the ASI (avoid, shift, improve) and ASIF (activity, structure, intensity, fuel) methodologies.

3.3.3.1 ASI methodology

According to the ASI methodology, established by the German agency GIZ (Deutsche Gesellschaft für Internationale Zusammenarbeit), the energy efficiency of a transportation system may be improved through three strategies (GIZ, 2012): (1) avoid the increase in the transportation activity, reducing demand, that is, the number of trips made by the transportation system as a whole, which is called systemic efficiency; (2) shift the demand to more efficient modes, increasing the energy efficiency of individual trips, which is called trip efficiency; and (3) improve the way making existing trips through the use of vehicles that have better energy efficiency or the use of ESs that emit less GHGs or atmospheric pollutants, which is called vehicle efficiency.

The improvement in the energy efficiency of the transportation systems is achieved through the application of a set of actions that are aligned with the strategies presented before and that act jointly toward reducing energy use in passenger and freight trips. There is a high similarity between the procedure presented in Fig. 3.3 and the ASI methodology.

3.3.3.2 ASIF methodology

The ASIF methodology, introduced by the Intergovernmental Panel on Climate Change (IPCC), considers four strategies focusing on the reduction in GHG emissions resulting from transportation (Oliveira and D'Agosto, 2017): (1) reduction in the activity, which aims to specifically reduce the number of trips or distance traveled in each trip; (2) offer infrastructure, which aims to supply the transportation system with a more complete set of options to transfer trips to modes of transportation with higher energy efficiency; (3) reduction in energy intensity, which aims to stimulate the use of vehicles that have higher energy efficiency; and (4) choice of low-carbon ESs.

The ASIF methodology follows the logic according to which it is possible to increase the energy efficiency of the transportation system as a whole by making the lowest number of trips with the shortest distance possible between the origin and the destination, by using a more efficient mode of transportation in terms of energy use, by reducing vehicles' energy intensity, and by choosing low-carbon ESs.

There is also a high similarity between the procedure presented in Fig. 3.3 and the ASIF methodology, which confirms once again its applicability in transportation demand planning under an energy use perspective.

3.4 Energy efficiency management in transportation

As shown before, the world is strongly dependent on passenger and freight road transportation, and this trend is not expected to change in the following years. Guaranteeing the continuity of this activity requires it to be practiced in an ever more efficient way. For that it is necessary to understand the concept of energy efficiency in transportation and how this efficiency may be improved by means of a management system.

3.4.1 Energy efficiency and energy consumption in transportation

The concept and the basic indicators that correlate energy consumption and transportation usually involve determining the ratio between the quantity of

100 Transportation, energy use and environmental impacts

energy used by the product, the quantity transported, and the distance traveled (Eq. 3.1).

$$C = \frac{E}{Q_t \cdot L} \tag{3.1}$$

where C is the energy consumption; E the total energy consumed; Q_t the transported quantity (passengers or freight); and L the distance traveled.

The interpretation of this relationship indicates the quantity of energy resources needed to produce a given result, represented by the product between the quantity transported and the distance traveled. In this context, energy efficiency may be defined as the opposite of consumption (Eq. 3.2).

$$Ef = \frac{1}{C} \tag{3.2}$$

Therefore, the lower the energy consumption of a given transportation mode, the higher its energy efficiency. Correlating the concepts of consumption and efficiency is necessary because most initiatives toward the improvement in energy efficiency in road vehicles focus on their consumption.

The operation of a given transportation mode requires the consumption of energy directly related to the movement of the vehicles (DIRECT CONSUMPTION) as well as the energy indirectly related to the movement of the vehicles (INDIRECT CONSUMPTION) as shown in Fig. 3.4. The latter involves the energy used in fixed facilities (roadways, railways, waterways, stations, yards, parking lots, garages, signaling, etc.); in recovery, maintenance, and repairs (workshops, shipyards, and hangars; maintenance/repair of fixed facilities; cleaning and inspection of vehicles and fixed facilities; etc.); in vehicles (car, buses, trains, ships, airplanes; etc.), and in management (direct and indirect workforce, and administrative services).

In both cases, the measurement of energy consumed may be done in two ways: GROSS ENERGY and USEFUL ENERGY.[1] The difference between them includes the losses along the energy generation chain and the energy's final distribution and use. In the case of the transportation modes that use petroleum derivatives as fuel, the chain (Fig. 3.4) involves the prospection, extraction, transfer, refining, distribution, storage, supply, and conversion of chemical energy into mechanical energy (final use), as addressed in more details in Chapter 5.

USEFUL ENERGY is equal to GROSS ENERGY minus LOSSES (Fig. 3.4). In practice, the conversion of GROSS ENERGY into USEFUL ENERGY is done by multiplying with efficiency factors.

---

1. Useful energy is understood as the energy available to consumers after the final conversion to their own equipment. It is the energy considered in the final use (the energy supplied to equipment) minus the losses in conversion.

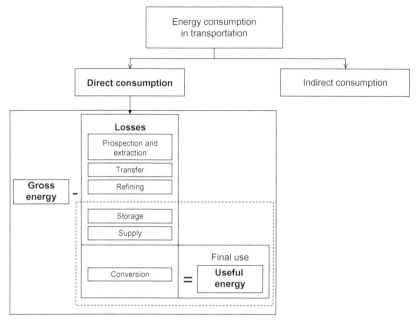

FIG. 3.4 Summary for the measurement of fuel consumption in transportation.

The establishment of this context to determine fuel consumption in transportation helps in the understanding of the scope of energy efficiency programs. As shall be shown, it is common for these programs to act only on the elements outlined by the dashed line in Fig. 3.4, with an emphasis on the final energy use (elements outlined by the thickest line), since these are more easily achieved by the sphere of sectorial influence of each program.

3.4.1.1 Direct consumption of useful energy

Although the losses in storage and supply should not be neglected, which are also considered in more comprehensive energy efficiency programs, a significant part of the initiatives about energy efficiency programs addresses the final energy use. For road transportation, the most used mode worldwide, this share suffers the influence of a set of factors that may be classified into three categories.

(a) Factors related to vehicles.
 * Technology used: type and control of propulsion (cycle of operation of ICE), which can be Otto cycle (alternative four-stroke engine with spark ignition), diesel cycle (alternative engine with compression ignition) or electric motor; type, quality, and specification of the fuel (usually, petroleum-derived gasoline and diesel oil) or battery type; type and control of traction (constitution of the traction system—clutch, gearbox,

102 Transportation, energy use and environmental impacts

drive shaft, half axle of driven wheels and tires); type and control of energy conversion (electronically controlled fuel injection system and ignition with feedback); and the presence of vehicle emission control systems (catalytic converters, λ probe, etc.).
* Design characteristics: weight-power ratio, aerodynamics, number of seats/load capacity, and presence of accessories (power steering, air conditioning, etc.).
* Performance: acceleration rate, deceleration method, and maximum speed.

(b) Factors related to guideway infrastructure.
* Technology used: type of conduction (contact tire/lane—roadway), guideway construction method.
* Design characteristics: guideway configuration, vertical and horizontal alignment, pavement construction characteristics, etc.
* Physical condition: pavement's state of conservation.

(c) Factors related to the operation.
* Traffic regime: maximum circulation speed and its variations, either imposed by traffic volume or by regulation.
* Vehicle drivability: interaction between the vehicle and the driver.
* Relationship between capacity (maximum quantity of passengers or freight that may be transported) and use (quantity of passengers or freight that is effectively being transported) and the determinant of the engine load operations.

Two aspects stand out: (1) the relationship between capacity and use is always undergoing changes and usually has more effect over energy consumed per transported unit than any other isolated factor; (2) considerable reductions both in total energy and in energy consumption per transported unit may be achieved by changing the factors related to the operation. This is the reason why most energy efficiency programs for transportation have focused on these factors.

The energy used to move a vehicle, here considered as final energy use, increases as the load in this vehicle increases, either in passengers or freight being transported. In some cases, this relationship may be linear. The curve of energy consumption per transported unit, as shown in Eq. (3.1), behaves like a hyperbole, having a point of minimum consumption that should be identified and pursued.

3.4.1.2 Efficiency and energy consumption measures

For road transportation, the most usual consumption measure is expressed by the relationship between the distance traveled and the volume of fuel consumed. In the metric system, this relationship is expressed according to Eq. (3.3).

$$C = \frac{L}{V_c} \cdot \left[\text{km} / L \right] \qquad (3.3)$$

where C is the fuel economy (km/L); V_c the volume of fuel (L); L the distance traveled (km).

Although this simple and objective way of representing fuel economy is not dismissed, a way that is quite adequate for the implementation of procedures aimed at measuring fuel consumption in the field, Eq. (3.2) indicates that the efficiency measure, considered to be the opposite of energy consumption, may be expressed in a more complete way based on different factors, but the most common ones are as follows:

- kWh/vehicle.km: it is used for freight and passenger transportation and may be easily measured for each vehicle class, but requires its comparison to other indicators and the creation of vehicles classes with the same physical and operational characteristics;
- kWh/t.km or kWh/passenger.km: it is used for the same purposes as the previous indicator, but it eliminates the inconvenience of the comparison of vehicles with the same physical and operational characteristics;
- kWh/capacity.km (capacity in passengers or tons): it is the basic energy consumption indicator per service offered, but, as the use is not always equal to the capacity, there may be an overestimation of efficiency;
- kWh/use.km (use in passengers or tons of freight): it represents the energy effectively consumed to transport one unit (passenger or freight) per one unit of distance.

The efficiency measures presented seek to correlate energy consumption with the quantity of passengers or transported freight over a distance traveled. These measures are more adequately applied when the vehicle keeps moving most of the time. Otherwise, it would be useful to define an efficiency measure that is correlated with fuel consumption per unit of time. Besides, for certain operations, such as those with stationary engines, a measure that correlates fuel consumption as a function of produced power is also useful. The following are the most usual measures in these cases.

- Fuel consumption per hour of operation [L/h_t]: it only considers the machine's effective hours of production (h_t).
- Fuel consumption per working hour [L/h_f]: considers the whole time in which the machine was working (h_f).
- Fuel consumption per produced power (L/kW.h, g/kW.h): considers fuel consumption in units of volume (L) or mass (g) per unit of produced power.

3.4.1.3 Evolution of the search for energy efficiency in road transportation

Great effort has been put in reducing energy consumption in road transportation, since energy saving consequently leads to cost saving. Nevertheless, some difficulty has been met, mainly when the vehicles are powered by ICEs. This difficulty has grown as higher investments have been made toward energy saving.

104 Transportation, energy use and environmental impacts

Typically, only a small part of the energy stored in the fuel (15%–25%) is effectively used to overcome the vehicle's inertia and rolling and aerodynamics resistances. On average, 30% of the energy is absorbed by the engine's cooling liquid, and 35%, most of it, are eliminated with the exhaust gases. Table 3.3 presents the typical distribution of the energy consumed in a car equipped with ICE.

Although Table 3.3 may serve as a guide to individual actions in the reduction of fuel consumption, a reduction in these losses (e.g., energy lost in exhaust gases) hardly ever reflects directly and in the same proportion on energy consumption. It is important to note that the energy lost in engine cooling (cooling liquid) and in exhaust gases, although it represents most of the losses (65% in average), is extremely hard to be reduced in function of the thermodynamic cycle an ICE is subject to.

Besides the economic gains expected with the reduction of fuel consumption for road transportation, two additional factors should be considered: (1) the local and global atmospheric pollutants emissions; and (2) the correlation of each ES with a nation's political and economic strategies. For a better understanding of these considerations, Example 3.1 provides a summary of the historical evolution of energy use in road transportation in Brazil, a country that has been an example in the use of renewable ESs in transportation.

EXAMPLE 3.1 Summary of the historical evolution of energy use in road transportation—the case of Brazil

- From 1956 to 1971—the car industry consolidated its position in the national market. In this phase, there is little to no worry about the technological sophistication of the products manufactured and sold in the national market. The vehicles' consumer market was quite undemanding and there were, naturally, no worries about energy efficiency. The Brazilian vehicles are usually leftovers of models discontinued in the manufacturers' country of origin.
- From 1972 to 1980—the petroleum crisis of 1973 had a great impact on the car industry and in road transportation, which are strongly dependent on petroleum derivatives. The world effort, led by the United States, toward saving fossil fuels helped in the technological improvement of vehicles' energy efficiency. The consumer market, for reasons that are merely economic, demands vehicles that consume less. In Brazil, for strategic reasons and aiming to further reduce the dependence on road transportation and on the use of gasoline and diesel oil, the National Alcohol Program (Proálcool) was created,[2] period in which a Brazilian technology was developed for a renewable and less pollutant fuel.

---

2 Proálcool was developed aiming to use ethanol, extracted from sugarcane, as an additive to gasoline (anhydrous ethanol) in its first stage started in 1975, and as a fuel (hydrous ethanol) in its second stage started in 1978.

TABLE 3.3 Energy efficiency in a conventional propulsion system

				References			
				1	2	3	4
Components of energy supply							
Energy available in the fuel				100.0%	100.0%	100.0%	100.0%
Components of the propulsion system	ICE	Energy losses	Cooling system	36.0%	30.0%	30.0%	20.0%
			Exhaust gases	38.0%	35.0%	35.0%	35.0%
			Friction of engine components	6.0%	5.0%	5.0%	–
			Engine thermal radiation	–	–	5.0%	20.0%
		ICE efficiency		20.0%	30.0%	25.0%	25.0%
	MTS	Energy losses	Transmission	10.0%	17.0%	40.0%	24.0%
			Tires	15.0%			
		MTS efficiency		77.0%	83.0%	60.0%	76.0%
	Efficiency of the set			15.0%	25.0%	15.0%	19.0%
Final energy offer				15.0%	25.0%	15.0%	19.0%
Components of energy demand (movement resistances)							
Rolling resistance				–	6.0%	–	4.2%
Aerodynamic resistance				8.0%	13.0%	10.0%	10.5%
Energy available to overcome inertia, ramps, and auxiliary equipment				7.0%	6.0%	5.0%	4,3%

Legends: ICE—Internal Combustion Engine; MTS—Mechanical transmission system.
References: (1) typical north-American car operating under common urbano traffic conditions; Ristinen and Kraushaar (1999); (2) European car with oil diesel engine in Euromix cycle; Poulton (1997); (3) typical north-American car, Wiser (2000); (4) typical north-American car, OECD (1997)
Notes: The Euromix cycle considers a route divided into three parts, 1/3 running under urban traffic, 1/3 at a constant speed of 90 km/h and 1/3 at a constant speed of 120 km/h.

106 Transportation, energy use and environmental impacts

- From 1981 to 1989—the problem of world shortage of petroleum derivatives, due to the conflicts in the Middle East, forced the world and national car industries to seek common strategies. A global market was in clear development and the society became aware of its environmental responsibility, leading to a series of measures that improved the performance of traditional engines and the energy performance of vehicles. In 1986, hydrous ethanol was the most used fuel for cars in Brazil. Again, for strategic reasons, in an attempt to reduce the consumption of diesel oil, the National Natural Gas Plan (Plangás) was launched in Brazil aiming to study the viability of the use of natural gas in transit modes and freight road transportation. On the other hand, Conama (National Council for the Environment) published Resolution no 18/1986, which regulates vehicle emissions, by imposing restrictions on the composition of exhaust gases in road vehicles.
- From 1990 to 2003—an irreversible process of technological improvements begun with the import of vehicle to Brazil. The situation of atmospheric pollution in large urban centers became critical and great efforts were made toward reducing the impacts of road transportation on the environment. Although the international petroleum price has stabilized, social awareness about the global environmental problems, such as the climate changes caused by the emission of GHGs, became ever greater. In this scenario, it was worth calling attention to the meeting that brought leaders of more than 150 countries to Rio de Janeiro, Eco-92, aiming to manifest a protocol of intentions that, among other priorities, addressed aspects related to the emission of CO_2, the main GHG, with a decisive impact on vehicle energy efficiency.
- From 2003 to the present days—the world is ever more worried about the consequences of global warming resulting from the burning of fossil fuels. Natural gas is a broadly used fuel in bi-fuel systems (those that use the vehicle's original fuel, which may be gasoline, by adding 25% of bioethanol or bioethanol) in the regions served by pipeline networks. Brazil launched the *flexible-fuel* cars, which may use gasoline and bioethanol in any proportion, and starts to stimulate its commercialization. The Brazilian government launched the National Program for the Production and Use of Biodiesel, according to which *Brazil* had the goal, already achieved, of adding up to 10% of biodiesel to petroleum diesel oil by 2018, then progressively increasing this percentage to 20% in the near future. Brazil became the largest consumer of biofuels for transportation in the world. Hybrid cars, with internal combustion engines and electrical engines, began to be commercialized on a larger scale since 2015. Battery electric vehicles (BEV) already began to be considered and projections for the introduction of this technology indicate it as a trend beginning in 2017.

3.5 Tools for energy efficiency management in transportation

Based on the information shown above, this section seeks to present a selection of tools that enable the improvement in energy efficiency management in transportation.

3.5.1 Energy efficiency management system in transportation (EEMST)

The experience regarding the concepts of energy efficiency presented above indicate that the organization of an energy efficiency program should start with an Energy Management Program (EMP) that aims to determine: (1) how much energy is being used; (2) how this energy is consumed; and (3) where it can be suppressed without losing efficiency in services and fleet operation. Four steps are part of an EMP:

1. Organizing and promoting the program.
2. Conducting an overall audit of the fleet and fuel consumption.
3. Understanding the operation and establishing priorities for energy use.
4. Developing corrective and improvement actions.

The development of an Energy Efficiency Program (EEP) is related to the fourth step, when, having conducted the audit of the fleet and its operation, and having understood and quantified the forms of energy consumption, the focus shifts to starting the development of correction and/or improvement actions in energy use, in search of a more efficient consumption pattern.

The actions toward the improvement of a given result are closely related to the possibility of measuring such results, which implies quantifying this result as precisely as possible. This applies to the development of the EEP, which should include data collection regarding the fleet and its operation. Moreover, it should consider the analysis of energy consumption (fuel), by comparing it with the expected performance pattern, since its goal is to eliminate all the unnecessary energy consumption and achieve maximum productivity with the energy necessary to operate the fleet.

The promotion of the program is of utmost importance, since the lack of interest of those involved may cause the discontinuity of the activities and may reduce the level of trust in actions and information. With that in mind, periodic dissemination of the goals and results achieved may become an incentive to teams so they get involved in the program and guarantee its success. It is worth highlighting the importance of adequately quantifying results, so they are made public in a clear and accurate way.

Initial data gathering should be regarded as the starting point for the development of the EMP and EEP. However, the latter is constantly dependent on the collection of new data, especially due to the need of periodic monitoring of the results. Some of the items that must be analyzed are the ones related to the factors that influenced energy consumption in the operation of road transportation. Furthermore, there is also the need for measuring energy consumption per vehicle type and monitoring of the situation of these vehicles in a program of inspection and mechanical maintenance.

A checklist is quite practical for the periodic monitoring of the fleet's operation. Some items in this list are as follows:

- keeping the vehicles operating within the specified capacity;
- turning vehicles and equipment off whenever they are not being used;

108 Transportation, energy use and environmental impacts

- adapting vehicles to the work being done;
- determining and implementing routes that privilege the reduction in energy consumption—minimizing unnecessary trips;
- keeping data and information on vehicles updated—physical and operational characteristics, maintenance, etc.;
- keeping updated records of fuel consumption;
- keeping updated records of operation and maintenance costs.

Fig. 3.5 summarizes what was addressed in the previous paragraphs.

Splitting the EEMST (Energy Efficiency Management System in Transportation) into an EMP and an EEP is appropriate, since it enables the establishment of responsibilities in the phases of implementation and operation of the EEMST.

The EMP provides the basic information on how much, where, and how energy is spent in the transportation activity. The total energy consumed must be compared to a consumption/efficiency goal or a standard chosen for this value. In case there is the possibility of improvement, the EEP is put in practice; it will indicate where and how this improvement may be implemented. The results will serve as feedback to the system.

The establishment of goals is closely related to the creation of consumption patterns for the vehicles. This pattern may come from a comprehensive regulation, considering the fleet of a region, or it may be sectorial, if it is determined for a given activity sector or for a company individually.

In the implementation phase, all the activities presented in Fig. 3.5 and their participants should be identified and defined by the EEMST manager. This scenario characterizes the influencing action and the aggregated view this participant should have.

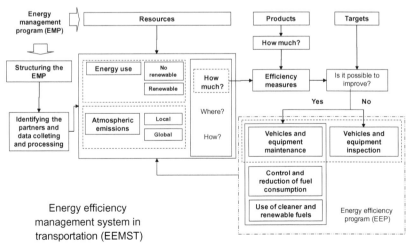

FIG. 3.5 Energy efficiency management system in transportation (EEMST).

Transportation planning and energy use **Chapter | 3 109**

In the operation phase, after the EEMST has been implemented, the manager starts to act only in the activities outlined by the dashed line (Fig. 3.5), which still form the aggregated view, while the remaining participants act on the other activities, still providing support and data needed by the manager.

Table 3.4 presents the scope of the EEMST. Besides the participants, the phases of implementation and the programs, each phase includes what are regarded as the basic responsibilities of each participant.

The manager, being the leader of the process, has the greatest set of responsibilities, which start with the structuring of the EEMST itself and the identification of its participants, even before it is possible to structure the process, define routines, disclose, and implement the EMP and the EEP. Still during the phase of implementation of the EEMST, the efficiency indicators should be defined in function of the relationship between resources employed and products obtained, the measures resulting from these resources and the energy efficiency goals.

In the phase of operation, it is the manager's responsibility to monitor the EMP, collect the data needed to determine indicators, calculate the measures and compare them with the goals to identify the service providers that have nonconformities and realign EEMST results.

On the other hand, it is the participants' responsibility to inform the manager about all the data needed for the implementation and operation of the EMP and the EEP, besides following and improving the EEP defined by the manager.

Regarding the operational data appropriate for the characterization of the service value indicators (Table 3.4) for the manager, they may be obtained by monitoring the data.

All the indicators related to energy consumption may be obtained from the participants, who should monitor the operation of their vehicles and equipment, controlling fueling operations, mileage traveled, hours worked, passengers or freight transported, etc.

Complementing these considerations, it is necessary to detail the process of implementing and operating the EEMST based on the detailing of the EMP and EEP and on the action and control instruments resulting from these programs.

The proposal presented by the EEMST focuses on the final use of energy in transportation. However, it is useful and necessary to also assess the energy needed and the environmental impacts when producing the energy used in transportation, which points to the life cycle assessment (LCA) tool, as discussed in the following section.

3.5.2 Life cycle assessment (LCA) applied to transportation

The life cycle of a product or service is understood as the successive and interconnected stages of a product/service system, since the acquisition of raw materials to the generation of natural resources until the final disposition[3] (ISO, 1998). Fig. 3.6 shows the typical stages of a product's life cycle, also called product system.

---

3. In terms of oil fuels, life cycle assessment is also known as well to wheel (WTW) assessment.

110 Transportation, energy use and environmental impacts

TABLE 3.4 Structure of the EEMST

Participants	Phases	Programs	Responsibilities
Manager	Implementation	EMP and EEP	• Structuring the EEMST • Identifying the participants of the EEMST • Structuring the EMP and EEP • Defining the routine of the EMP and EEP • Promoting the dissemination of the EMP and EEP • Promoting the implementation of the EEP at the service providers • Defining the efficiency indicators and the way of obtaining them • Defining the efficiency measures and the way of obtaining them • Defining the energy efficiency goals, aggregately and per service provider
	Operation	EMP	• Monitoring of the EMP • Collecting data from the service providers • Establishing the efficiency measures • Comparing the efficiency measures with the energy efficiency goals • Identifying the service providers that have nonconformities regarding the energy efficiency goals • Identifying the reasons for the nonconformities regarding the energy efficiency goals and suggesting ways of adjusting them • Reassessing the energy efficiency goals
Participants	Implementation	EEP	• Providing the data requested by the Manager for the implementation of the EMP • Implementing the EEP
	Operation	EEP	• Following and improving the EEP in collaboration with the Manager • Supplying the data requested by the Manager for the monitoring of the EMP

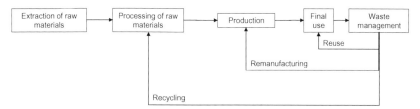

Fig. 3.6 *Life cycle stages. (Source: Rubin, E.S., 2001. Introduction to Engineering and the Environment, first ed., McGraw-Hil Higher Education.)*

The five typical stages of a product's life cycle (extraction of raw materials, processing of raw materials, production, final use, and waste management) are interconnected by flows that indicate the direct sequence of their processing, from the extraction of raw materials to waste management. There is also a separate indication of recycling, remanufacturing, and reuse flows, characterizing a cyclic configuration of part of the resources applied to the product.

The LCA is a tool used to assess the environmental aspects and the potential impacts associated with a product, including steps that start from the extraction of elementary raw materials from nature that enter the product system[4](cradle) to its final disposition (grave). It is possible to interpret the term product in a broad sense of product and/or service that is the result of a desired productive activity (Rubin (2001)).

A great variety of purposes is associated with LCA, among them that stand out are: supporting decision-making, determining environment efficiency indicators that are relevant in the assessment of products, and improving the understanding of the environmental aspects connected to the productive processes in a broad perspective. In this last case, LCA provides subsidies to a change in the traditional philosophy of environmental protection, which considers the mitigation of the environmental impacts after their occurrence instead of its prevention. This fact represents a change in environmental strategy, since it considers the possibility of avoiding environmental impacts before they occur instead of just correcting them.

The phases of LCA, as established by the ISO standard 14.040, are shown in Fig. 3.7, highlighting their relationship and the main aspects considered for each of them.

The goal of the assessment may be to promote some sort of improvement in a product's environmental performance such as improving the eco-efficiency of a conventional (common use) fuel; the need of designing a completely new product, such as an alternative fuel; or simply gathering information about the product to create a database; making a comparison between products or establishing a relationship with the standard.

---

4. The terms product system and productive system do not have the same meaning. The product system includes all the stages of the life cycle, the productive system does not include the stages of final use and waste management. On these terms, product system means the sum of a product's supply chain and final use.

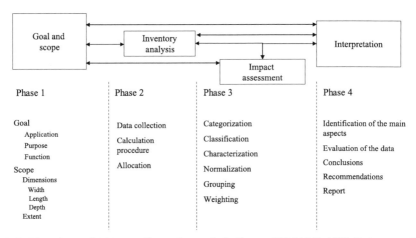

FIG. 3.7 Phases of LCA according to the standard. *(Source: ISO 14.041, 1998. Environmental Management—Life Cycle Assessment—Goal and Scope Definition and Inventory Analysis, International Organization for Standardization.)*

The scope comprises three basic dimensions: length, which indicates where the study should start and end; width, which indicates how many levels of analysis should be included; and depth, which establishes the level of details needed; all are defined to meet what was established in the goals. Determining the scope implies the identification of the boundaries of the product system.

Regarding the function of the system, its functional unit, and performance characteristics, Table 3.5 was adapted to better express the concepts presented. An example in the case of fuels was created according to the goals of this book.

Data quality requirements are understood as data's accuracy, integrity, representativeness, consistency, and reproducibility. The identification of data quality requirements relates to three parameters: temporal, geographic, and technological scopes. Temporal and technological scopes concern data's adequacy to the moment of LCA application, which is representative of their time. The geographic scope creates a relationship of pertinence between the data and its study region.

The inventory analysis is a phase of data collection and processing in which certain criteria must be met in their categorization and inclusion together with the procedures for their collection, validation, aggregation, and allocation. It is clearly the most laborious phase of LCA.

The standard recommends three significant sets to categorize data: (1) inputs—energy, raw materials, auxiliary materials, and other physical inputs; (2) products; and (3) emissions (air, water, land, etc.).

Impact assessment is the third phase of LCA and it seeks to identify, characterize, and assess, quantitatively and qualitatively, potential impacts of the environmental interventions identified in the inventory analysis step, in accordance

Transportation planning and energy use Chapter | 3 **113**

TABLE 3.5 Characterization of function, functional unit, and performance

Attribute description	Attribute characterization	Example—fuels
Function	Possible expected results of a product.	Producing movement, heat, or light.
Chosen function	The function that will be studied according to the goal and scope of the LCA.	Producing movement.
Functional unit	Unit of measurement of the function	Moving 1 passengers over 1 km.
Performance	Relationship between products and inputs.	1 kg/pass.km.
Reference flow	Product volume to be considered as a basis for the study.	1 litter.

with that defined in the study's goal and scope phase. This is done through the structuring, examination, condensation, and simplification of the data to allow their analysis. The standard divides the approach into two parts that involve mandatory and optional elements as presented in Fig. 3.8.

The main recommendation presented regarding the selection of impacts categories, their indicators, and model is that it be done fully based on scientific knowledge. Although the standard is not indicative, it is recommended that the set of categories should include: exhaustion of nonrenewable resources; global warming; reduction in the ozone layer, human toxicity, and ecotoxicity; acidification; photochemical oxidants; and nutrification.

Based on these categories the data obtained in inventory analysis are classified in full, independent, operational, and practical forms. First, the results exclusively related to one impact category should be considered, then those related to more than one impact category, in this case identifying the effects that occur in parallel (one or more impact categories simultaneously) or in sequence (more than one category impact in series).

As each category may comprise one or more data types, after they are classified their contributions are quantified by means of characterization factors. These factors should be strictly backed by scientific knowledge and are used to calculate direct effects. The indirect effects resulting from the modification of the pollutant in the environment are usually not considered.

The result of the characterization is expressed in the form of a set of matrices that express the environmental profile of the studied product system. It is important to highlight that a comparison between the simplicity of the model and the accuracy of results is expected. The results of each matrix may be values

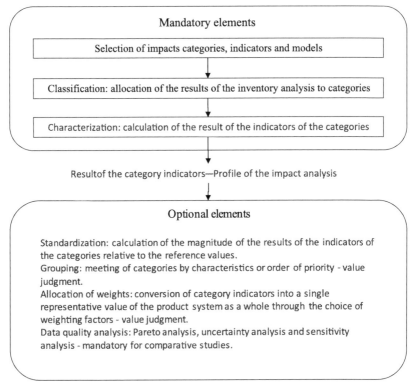

FIG. 3.8 Elements of impacts assessment.

of difficult comparison, requiring their normalization by means of applying a common base, which is already an optional element.

For the optional elements, both the grouping and weighing are made based on value judgment, with the latter being the most controversial, since it is usually developed too subjectively and with little scientific basis. The grouping usually considers a hierarchy, such as high, low, and medium priority.

To better understand the level of significance, the uncertainty, and the sensitivity of the results of the impacts assessment, it is advisable to use techniques that can assess the quality of the data. The standard specifically recommends: Pareto analysis, uncertainty analysis, and sensitivity analysis, but more sophisticated processes such as simulation may also be found.

The last phase of LCA is interpretation. This phase usually progresses in a simultaneous and interactive way in relation to the others, as shown in Fig. 3.9 expanded based on Fig. 3.7. The interpretation of LCA is a systematic technique used to identify, qualify, verify, and assess the results found in the inventory analysis and the impacts assessment, and to present them in a clear and objective way meeting the proposed goals and scope.

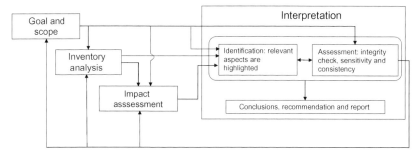

FIG. 3.9 Relationship between the elements of the interpretation phase and the remaining phases of the LCA.

Its objective is to analyze the results, draw conclusions, explain limitations, and provide recommendations for the LCA. Fig. 3.9 shows LCA interpretation and its subdivision into three elements: identification, assessment, and conclusions.

Except for the phase that produces the goals and scope, all the other phases of LCA require the production of a report. In some cases, critical analysis should be used, according to the standard, especially for comparative studies, when this consideration is mandatory.

It is common to apply LCA partially; the phases of goals and scope, inventory analysis, and interpretation comprise the common practice called Life Cycle Inventory (LCI).

EXAMPLE 3.2 Application of the LCI tool to assess energy alternatives for transportation

A first approach to a LCI procedure was drawn up by D'Agosto and Ribeiro (2009) to evaluate total and renewable energy in the life cycle (LC) of Brazilian automotive fuels. The amount of CO_2 emissions from fossil fuel use was also estimated. The procedure is used to compare three fuels—gasoline with 25% ethanol, pure bioethanol, and compressed natural gas—considering their final use in urban passenger car traffic in the municipality of Rio de Janeiro, Brazil. Fig. 3.10 shows the procedure's scheme and serves as a basis for the discussion that follows.

PHASE 1: Goal and scope (STEP 1 and STEP 2)
The goal considers the application of the procedure to transportation fuel alternatives with the purpose to evaluate life cycle total and renewable energy use, and CO_2 emission. The function is to produce movement in urban passenger car traffic.

In STEP 1 of the scope, the consideration of limits to the geographic, temporal, and technological extents restricts and relates the ESs associated with the supply chains, and the PS associated with their final use. Each pair (ES, PS) must be characterized specifically and in as much detail as necessary, considering that a PS

116 Transportation, energy use and environmental impacts

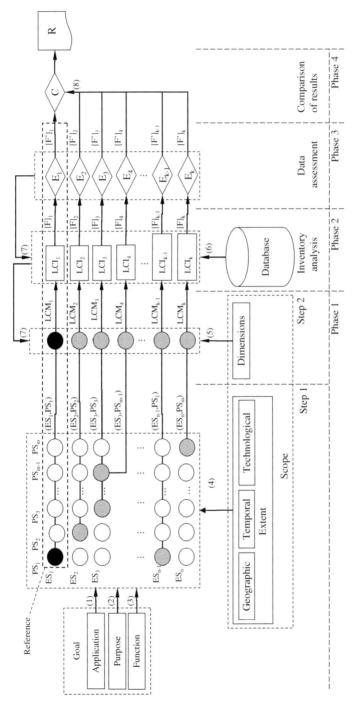

FIG. 3.10 Structure of the procedure. (Legend—(1) Energy sources for transportation; (2) Compare alternatives; (3) Produce movement; (4) Restriction and relationship data; (5) Limits of the product system; (6) Data for the inventory; (7) Data for reassessment; (8) Data for comparison; ES: Energy source; PS: Propulsion system; LCM: Life cycle model; LCI: Life cycle inventory; [F]: Matrix of LCI flows; E: data quality assessment; [F']: Matrix of LCI flows evaluated; C: Comparison of the results; R: Report of the results.) (*Source: D'Agosto, M.A., Ribeiro, S.K., 2009. Assessing total and renewable energy in Brazilian automotive fuels. A life cycle inventory (LCI) approach. Renew. Sust. Energ. Rev. 13, 1326–1337.*)

can use more than one ES; the mixture of two or more ES represents a new supply chain; different production processes lead to different supply chains; and the final use conditions must be specified, because they modify the performance of the PS.

In STEP 2 of the scope, for each (ES, PS) pair, a life cycle model (LCM) is designed that establishes the dimensions of the application and the flows to be considered. A modular structure for designing the LCMs is recommended, as shown in Figs. 3.11 and 3.12, with three depth levels in the form of macro-stages, meso-stages, and micro-stages, allowing successive refinements and guaranteeing the equivalence among the levels. Since the micro-stages are specific for each life cycle, it is recommended that the comparison of alternatives be done at the meso-stage level, where better equality can be achieved.

PHASE 2: Inventory analysis

As a first approach inputs and environmental loads directly associated with the processes should be considered, what is called tier 1 approach. Tier two approach considers inputs and environmental loads necessary to produce tier 1 inputs and tier 3 considers the inputs and environmental loads necessary to produce tier 2 inputs and capital goods.

About inputs and environmental loads, it is common to consider the total energy (TE) renewable energy (RE), and GHGs (mainly CO_2 emissions) from fossil fuels.

For each of the LCMs resulting from PHASE 1 it is necessary to collect data, which is called LCI. For some processes, there will be very reliable data available in the form of historical series, enabling the consolidation of mean values and variation intervals as an expression of their consistency. For data obtained from general use databases, which have less integrity and consistency, the upper limit of available data should be adopted, accompanied by the pertinent justifications and comments. Because of PHASE 2, each LCM is associated with a matrix [F] of flows per process, which will be submitted for data quality evaluation in PHASE 3.

PHASE 3: Data evaluation

The evaluation criteria vary in function of the need of each study. For a preliminary approach, there should be evaluations regarding: (1) the weight the individual inputs and environmental loads of each process have in relation to the respective total flows in the life cycle; (2) the variation interval of the values of each flow; and (3) the origin, which can be specific or general use.

All the flows with weight (W) greater than 10% ($W_{min} = 10\%$) should be assessed regarding the interval of variation and origin. Flows that present $W_{flow} \geq W_{min}$ and interval of variation (T) greater than a maximum (T_{max}) should be evaluated regarding the origin of the data. If these flows have been determined from specific use data, excessive variation can reflect inconsistency. If they have been obtained from general use data, in which case they are called critical flows, it is recommended that their origin be reassessed, and an effort be made to increase their integrity.

It is up to each analyst, according to the limitations of each case, to determine the depth to employ in reassessing the data. Giving priority to reappraising data related to critical flows guides the efforts necessary to improve the LCI and allows the establishment of progressive refinement process, which reduces the time and financial costs of this operation. PHASE 3 produces a matrix of flows [F'] evaluated by meso-stage for each alternative.

118 Transportation, energy use and environmental impacts

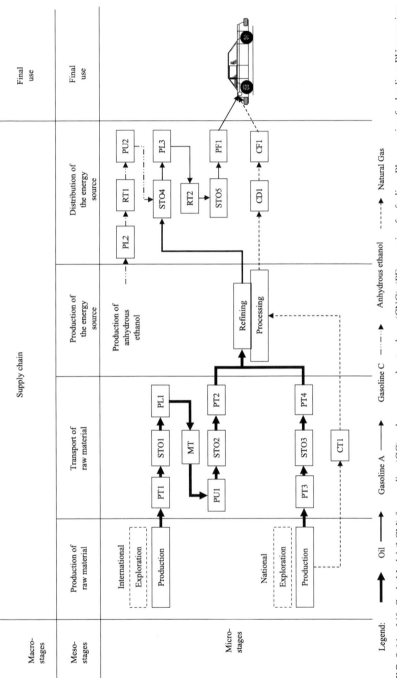

FIG. 3.11 Life Cycle Model (LCM) for gasoline (GC) and compressed natural gas (CNG). (PF: pumping for loading; PU: pumping for unloading; PP: pumping for pipeline transport; STO: storage; MT: maritime transport; RT: road transport; CD: compression for piped distribution; CF: compression for fueling.) (Source: D'Agosto, M.A., Ribeiro, S.K., 2009. Assessing total and renewable energy in Brazilian automotive fuels. A life cycle inventory (LCI) approach. Renew. Sust. Energ. Rev. 13, 1326–1337.)

Transportation planning and energy use **Chapter | 3 119**

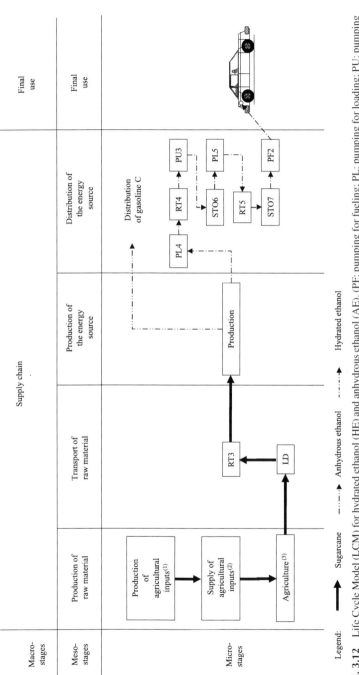

FIG. 3.12 Life Cycle Model (LCM) for hydrated ethanol (HE) and anhydrous ethanol (AE). (PF: pumping for fueling; PL: pumping for unloading; LD: loading; STO: storage; RT: road transport. Notes—(1) Energy embodied in seedlings = 5.87 MJ/tc; fertilizers = 66.49 MJ/tc; lime = 7.14 MJ/tc; herbicides = 11.26 MJ/tc and insecticides = 0.79 MJ/tc (Nogueira, 1987; Centro de Tecnologia da Cana-de-açúcar, 2003); (2) Diesel oil for transporting seedlings, organic and chemical fertilizers equal 8.20.8 MJ/tc (Centro de Tecnologia da Cana-de-açúcar, 2003); (3) Soil preparation, planting and mechanized harvesting.) *(Source: D'Agosto, M.A., Ribeiro, S.K., 2009. Assessing total and renewable energy in Brazilian automotive fuels. A life cycle inventory (LCI) approach. Renew. Sust. Energ. Rev. 13, 1326–1337.)*

120 Transportation, energy use and environmental impacts

PHASE 4: Comparison of the results
The comparison of the results can follow various criteria. For example, the values of [F'] for each alternative can be mutually compared or compared against a benchmark, providing a ranking or parameterization of the alternative outcomes, considering one alternative or the best results of each alternative as a reference. PHASE 4 produces a report [R] to be considered in the LCA impact assessment phase.

3.6 Final considerations

This chapter presented the relationship between transportation and energy use and addressed its potential impact on the environment due to the use of fossil fuels. It showed that there are strategies to reduce energy use in transportation through the adequate planning of this activity. It also made evident that it is possible to achieve energy efficiency gains in road transportation, the most widely used mode of transportation in the world, by means of technological advances or adequate operation management when providing this service.

Worldwide used ASI and ASIF methodologies were considered and aligned with the main concept transportation energy use planning. As tools for energy efficiency management in transportation an entire program was design for road transportation. The concept of LCA was also introduced and an example of how to use it was considered.

3.7 Exercises

1. Which sector is the largest consumer of petroleum and its derivatives in the world? How about in Brazil? Explain it.
2. What is the position of the transportation sector in world regarding final energy consumption? How can this scenario be explained?
3. What fuels are the most used by vehicles of each mode of transportation?
4. What factors influence a transportation user's choice and how he makes trips? Explain it.
5. Regarding passenger road transportation, what makes users prefer to make trips by car?
6. Considering that developed countries provide a good public transportation service to their populations, why do some places that have good public transportation infrastructure still have a higher number of passenger trips made by car?
7. Regarding energy consumption in transportation, what factors should influence the most adequate planning of the transportation sector for a trip? Why?
8. Does the option for the road mode, both for passenger and for freight transportation, represent the best option in terms of the best energy performance? Why is it chosen as the best option?

Transportation planning and energy use **Chapter | 3 121**

9. It is often believed that the improvement in a passenger transportation system should be made through the incorporation of new technologies that guarantee the system's energy efficiency. However, there are other ways of making decisions that can improve the system's efficiency. What are they? Give examples of practical actions that guarantee the system's efficiency.
10. In the case of freight transportation, what aspects could be considered for the planning of a transportation system that promotes energy efficiency? Explain them.

References

Banister, D., Watson, S., 1994. Energy Use in Transport and City Structure. Working Paper 7, Planning and Development Research Centre, Londres. University College.

Breheny, M., 1995. The compact city and transport energy consumption. Trans. Inst. Br. Geogr. 20, 81–101.

CEBDS, 2001. O transporte do futuro. In: Desenvolvimento Sustentável, Ano III, n.13, maio-Jun.-Jul. 2001. Conselho Empresarial Brasileiro para o Desenvolvimento Sustentável. pp. 4–5.

Choo, S., Mokhtarian, P.L., Salomon, I., 2004. Does telecommuting reduce vehicle-miles traveled? Transportation 32 (1), 37–64. 2005. An aggregate time series analysis for the U.S.

CTC, 2003. Use of Energy in the Production of Cane, Sugar and Alcohol and Green House Gas Emissions: Present Situation (2002) and Future Situations (Cogeneration with BIG-GT). Centro de Tecnologia Copersucar, Piracicaba, SP.

D'Agosto, M.A., Ribeiro, S.K., 2009. Assessing total and renewable energy in Brazilian automotive fuels. A life cycle inventory (LCI) approach. Renew. Sust. Energ. Rev. 13, 1326–1337.

EPE, 2017. Balanço Energético Nacional 2016. Empresa de Pesquisa Energética, Rio de Janeiro, RJ, Brasil.

GIZ, 2012. Urban Transport and Energy Efficiency. Sustainable Transport: A Reference Handbook for Policymakers in Developing Cities (Transporte Urbano e Eficiência Energética. Transporte Sustentável: Um Manual de Referência para Elaboradores de Política em Cidades em Desenvolvimento), Módulo 5h. In: GIZ—Deustche Gesellschaft für Internationale Zusammenarbeit. pp. 2012. Brazilia, Brazil.

Gonçalves, D.N.S., de D'Agosto, M.A., 2017. Future Prospective Scenarios for the Use of Energy in Transportation in Brazil and GHG Emissions Business as Usual (BAU) Scenario—2050. Instituto Brasileiro de Transporte Sustentável (IBTS), Rio de Janeiro, RJ.

IEA, 2016. Key World Energy Statistics—2016. International Energy Agency, Paris, France.

Illich, I., 1975. Energia e Equidade, first ed. Livraria Sá da Costa Editora, Lisboa.

Nogueira, L.A.H., 1987. Analysis of the Energy use in the Production of Sugarcane Ethanol (Análise da utilização de energia na produção de álcool de cana de açúcar). Ph.D. Thesis Faculdade de Engenharia de Campinas, Campinas, SP.

OECD, 1997. Eco-efficiency in transport. In: Workshop report and background paper, group on pollution prevention and control, task force on transport. Organisation for Economic Co-operation and Development, Paris, France.

Oliveira, C.M., D'Agosto, M.A., 2017. Guia de referências em sustentabilidade. Boas Práticas para o transporte de carga. In: Programa de Logística Verde Brasil—PLVB. Editora IBTS, first ed.

Poulton, M.L., 1997. Fuel Efficient Car Technology. Computational Mechanics Publications. Ashurst, Southampton, UK.

122 Transportation, energy use and environmental impacts

Ristinen, R.A., Kraushaar, J.J., 1999. Energy and the Environment. John Wiley & Sons, Inc., Hoboken, New Jersey, USA.

Rubin, E.S., 2001. Introduction to Engineering and the Environment, first ed. McGraw-Hil Higher Education.

Schafer, A., Victor, D., 2000. The future mobility of the world population. Transp. Res. A 34, 171–205.

WBCSD, 2000. Measuring Eco-Efficiency. A Guide to Reporting Company Performance. Word Business Council for Sustainable Development, Geneva, Switzerland.

Wiser, W.H., 2000. Energy Resources. Occurrence, Production, Conversion and Use. Springer, New York, USA.

Further reading

Davis, S.C., Diegel, S.W., Boundy, R.G., 2009. Transportation Energy Data Book, 28th ed. US Department of Energy. (Edition 28 of ORNL-5198). Disponível em http://cta.ornl.gov/data/Index.shtml. Acesso em 16 abr. 2010.

de D'Agosto, M.A., Ribeiro, S.K., 2005. Eco-efficiency management program (EEMP)—a model for road fleet operation. Transp. Res. D 9 (2004), 497–511.

ISO 14.041, 1998. Environmental Management—Life Cycle Assessment—Goal and Scope Definition and Inventory Analysis. International Organization for Standardization.

ITF, 2011. Trends in the Transport Sector, Annual Transport Statistics, International Transport Forum. OECD/ITF, Paris. Disponível em www.internationaltransportforum.org/statistics/index.html.

Chapter 4

Propulsion systems and energy use

General goal

The general goal of this chapter is to present an introductory and broad overview of the way different modes of transportation use energy to produce movement and how this may impact the environment.

At the end of this chapter, the reader should be able to:

1. Understand how the modes of transportation use energy to produce movement.
2. Compare how energy is used by the different modes of transportation to produce movement.
3. Associate the modes of transportation, particularly the road mode, which is the most used mode worldwide, to their conventional and alternative propulsions systems.
4. Analyze the aspects associated with the transformation of energy into movement for the different modes of transportation.
5. Present, in summary, the current trends in propulsion systems for transportation.

4.1 Introduction

This chapter seeks to describe how energy is transformed to produce movement in transportation systems. Special attention is given to road transportation, since it is the most used mode worldwide, both for freight and passenger transportation.

Initially, Section 4.2 presents, based on elementary physics, the concepts of propulsive force (PF), forces of resistance to motion (FRM), work, energy, and power. These concepts are a general basis for the understanding of the following sections, which seek to consider the specific characteristics of each mode of transportation.

Due to the quantitative characteristic of the theme addressed in this chapter, application examples are given as the concepts and their applications are presented.

Section 4.3 discusses the application of the concepts presented in Section 4.2 to road transportation, while the other modes of transportation are briefly discussed in Section 4.4. Attempting to establish future trends, Section 4.5 presents a select set of advanced propulsion systems and the final considerations of this chapter are presented in Section 4.6.

Transportation, Energy Use and Environmental Impacts. https://doi.org/10.1016/B978-0-12-813454-2.00004-0
© 2019, Elsevier Editora Ltda. Published by Elsevier Inc. All rights reserved.

124 Transportation, energy use and environmental impacts

4.2 Movement and propulsion

Transportation, understood as the movement of a mass (m) along a certain distance (s) over time (t), depends on the availability of a PF for it to occur. This PF is needed to overcome the FRM and produce changes in speed. In general, and for didactic purposes, different FRMs may be classified as follows.

1. Natural forces of resistance to motion (NFRM): may vary for each mode of transportation, but are usually the aerodynamic, rolling, and friction resistances.
2. Forces needed to change speed (FNCS): the forces needed to change the speed of vehicles in direction and sense. For a vehicle to accelerate in the direction of the motion (changing of sense) or for a vehicle to change direction, changing its position in the horizontal or vertical direction, these forces must be in operation. Examples of that are the force of inertia, the centrifugal force, and weight.

The generation of PF involves the transformation of energy (E) into work (W), understood as the operation of a force along the movement of mass. The rate at which this occurs over time (t) is called power (Pow) and characterizes the way the FRM are overcome by the PF (Eq. 4.1).

$$Pow(t) = \frac{W(t)}{dt} = PF(t).\frac{ds}{dt} = PF(t).v(t) \tag{4.1}$$

where $v(t)$ is the speed of movement.

The total work is done over a period $\Delta t = t_1 - t_0$ during which the power $Pow(t)$ is given by Eq. (4.2).

$$W = \int_{t_0}^{t_1} Pow(t).dt = \int_{t_0}^{t_1} PF(t).v(t).dt \tag{4.2}$$

Assuming, for didactic simplification, a very particular situation in which there is movement in a permanent condition, and the PF remains constant and equal to the FRM in a way that maintains the speed (v) of the mass constant, Eq. (4.2) may be rewritten as follows (Eq. 4.3).

$$W = PF.v.\int_{t_0}^{t_1} dt = PF.v.\Delta t = PF.s = FRM.s \tag{4.3}$$

where $s(t)$ is the distance of movement.

If the energy needed to move the mass is proportional to the work, Eq. (4.3) leads to the usefulness of knowing the FRM for the different modes of transportation, which will enable an estimate of the PF and the minimum power to be applied by the propulsion system to maintain the movement of this mass. This minimum power should be added to the one needed to generate eventual changes in speed.

This will be initially done for the road mode, the most used one worldwide for the transportation of passengers and freight. Then, the remaining modes will be addressed.

4.3 Road mode

Based on basic concepts of physics and chemistry, it is possible to establish the main directives that regulate energy consumption by a road vehicle. The approach chosen is traditional and was born with the development of the car industry in the 1950s.

Its choice allows one to present, via inductive reasoning, a comprehensive and strong way of understanding regarding the definition of the final energy use in road transportation, considering aspects related to the energy source being used, the construction of vehicles, and their operational characteristics.

This way of understanding the problem considers two components: (1) the demand for energy in road transportation, in function of what is required from the vehicle that moves carrying a given load; and (2) the energy supply that the vehicle's propulsion system may offer. The balance between these two components, given a condition of operation, establishes the consumption of energy that the vehicle will present along a route.

4.3.1 Energy demand in road transportation

Consider a vehicle that moves with constant speed along a plane, as shown in Fig. 4.1. In this simplified case, the only forces that resist motion are the NFRM, here considered to be the aerodynamic resistance force (ARF), and the rolling resistance forces (RRF=RRF$_f$+RRFr). The vehicle's weight is P, m is the vehicle's mass, g is the acceleration of gravity, FR$_f$ and FR$_r$ are the forces of reaction to the weight on the front and rear axles, PF$_f$ and PF$_r$ are the PFs on the front and rear axles and ⊗ is its center of mass.

One of the ways of expressing RRF, it being proportional to the weight and speed of the vehicle, is shown in Eq. (4.4).

$$RRF = CR_s.P + CR_v.v^2.P \qquad (4.4)$$

where CR_s is the constant of rolling resistance depending on the position; and CR_v is the constant of rolling resistance depending on speed.

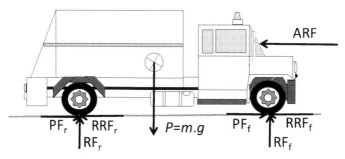

FIG. 4.1 Schematic representation of forces acting on a vehicle that moves with constant speed along the plane.

126 Transportation, energy use and environmental impacts

It is common for the CR terms to be tabulated in function of pavement conditions and speed. Besides, these coefficients increase as a direct function of the deformation of the tire-road pair and as an inverse function of the radius of the set wheel-tire. Thus, it increases as P increases and as tire pressure decreases.

Another way, a little more simplified, of expressing RRF is given by Eq. (4.5), which considers it independent of speed. Because they are an empirical formulation, the CR_s coefficients may be determined to establish approximate results. Table 4.1 presents a set of coefficients that are modified in accordance with the following equation.

$$RRF = CR_s.P \qquad (4.5)$$

Naturally, the distribution of RRF per axle will be proportional to the distribution of weight per axle.

In the case of ARF, this force is proportional to the area of the vehicle's cross section, to air density, and to the vehicle's squared relative speed, as shown in Eq. (4.6).

$$ARF = \frac{1}{2}C_a \cdot A \cdot \rho \cdot (v + v_o)^2 \qquad (4.6)$$

where C_a is the coefficient of aerodynamic resistance; A is the vehicle's frontal area, perpendicular to the direction of movement; ρ is the specific mass of the

TABLE 4.1 Rolling resistance coefficients

Wheel-tire × road relationship	CRs
Car tires over	
Asphalt or concrete pavement way	0.013
Smooth pavement way	0.015
Coarse pavement way	0.02
Rough pavement way	0.025
Non-paved way	0.05
Irregular way	0.1–0.35
Simple truck or bus tires over	
Asphalt or concrete pavement way	0.006–0.01
Irregular way	0.14–0.24
Tractor tires over	
Irregular way	0.07–0.12

Propulsion systems and energy use Chapter | 4 **127**

air; v_o is the component of wind speed perpendicular to A; and v is the component of the vehicle's speed perpendicular to A.

Air density varies very little, in function of the altitude, and is in the range of 1.200–$1.250 \, kg/m^3$. However, C_a depends on the design of the vehicle's body and may assume the values presented in Table 4.2.

In function of the formulated hypotheses, considering that the vehicle in Fig. 4.1 travels at a constant speed (v), it is possible to apply Newton's Second Law, resulting in Eq. (4.7)

$$PF_t + PF_r = PF = RRF_t + RRF_r + ARF = NFRM \tag{4.7}$$

The work $[W]$ and energy $[E]$ related to the PF may be expressed as force times movement (Eq. 4.3). Considering that power $[Pow]$ may be expressed as the ratio of the energy consumed over time, Eq. (4.8) may be obtained.

$$E_{plane} = \left(RRF_t + RRF_r + ARF\right) \cdot s = NFRM \cdot s \tag{4.8}$$

$$Pow_{plane} = \left(RRF_t + RRF_t r + ARF\right) \cdot v = NFRM \cdot v \tag{4.9}$$

where s is the observed movement; and v is the vehicle's speed.

To overcome a slope, additional work must be done against the vehicle's weight. The component to be overcome of the FNCS is the force of resistance to inclination (FRI), given by Eq. (4.10), with the component of the vehicle's

TABLE 4.2 Typical aerodynamic resistance coefficients

Vehicle type		
Cars		C_a
	Open convertible	0.5–0.7
	Van	0.5–0.6
	Sedan	0.5–0.55
	Hatchback	0.3–0.4
	Faired fusiform	0.2–0.25
	Drop-shaped	0.12–0.20
Simple and combined trucks		0.8–1.5
Bus		
	Conventional	0.6–0.7
	Aerodynamic	0.3–0.4
Motorcycles		0.6–0.7

128 Transportation, energy use and environmental impacts

weight (P) being decomposed in function of the slope's angle of inclination (α). For slopes with up to 5% of elevation, it is possible to directly multiply P with the inclination gradient in decimal value (grad).

$$\text{FRI} = P \cdot \text{sen}(\alpha) \text{ or } \text{FRI} = P \cdot \text{grad}(\%) \text{ if grad} < 0.05 \tag{4.10}$$

With this new consideration, Eqs. (4.8) and (4.9) become:

$$E_{\text{slope}} = \left(\text{NFRM} + P \cdot \text{sen}(\alpha)\right) \cdot s \tag{4.11}$$

$$Pow_{\text{slope}} = \left(\text{NFRM} + P \cdot \text{sen}(\alpha)\right) \cdot v \tag{4.12}$$

Additionally, when a vehicle travels along a curve, external forces operate to resist the transversal speed change in the form of forces of resistance to curve (FRC). This force is proportional to the vehicle's weight and speed, and inversely proportional to the radius of curvature (r), according to Eq. (4.13).

$$\text{FRC} = \frac{1}{2} \cdot \frac{v^2 \cdot P}{r} \tag{4.13}$$

Therefore, another FNCS may be added to Eqs. (4.11) and (4.12).

$$E_{\text{slope+curve}} = \left(\text{NFRM} + P \cdot \text{sen}(\alpha) + \text{FRC}\right) \cdot s \tag{4.14}$$

$$Pow_{\text{slope+curve}} = \left(\text{NFRM} + P \cdot \text{sen}(\alpha) + \text{FRC}\right) \cdot v. \tag{4.15}$$

A vehicle rarely travels at a constant speed. So the model must include the energy needed to accelerate the vehicle. In this case, it is useful to use the concept of kinetic energy and its variation, considering that the vehicle reached v_f (final speed) starting at a v_i (initial speed). Therefore, the acceleration energy [E_a] will be the variation in kinetic energy [Ek_f–Ek_i]. It is possible to express kinetic energy in function of a vehicle's mass and its speed, thus:

$$E_{\text{aceleration}} = Ek_f - Ek_i = \frac{1}{2} . m . v_f^2 - \frac{1}{2} m . v_i^2 = \frac{P}{2g}\left(v_f^2 - v_i^2\right) \tag{4.16}$$

Eq. (4.16) only refers to the energy needed for the vehicle to overcome inertia. When considering the energy needed to overcome the remaining NFRMs, the total value is different from the one calculated by using Eqs. (4.14) and (4.15). However, if there is a variation in speed, the component that changes is ARF, since speed is not constant throughout the whole period of acceleration, and ARF increases as speed increases. In the case of a vehicle that has constant acceleration from rest, ARF is given by Eq. (4.17), which leads to Eq. (4.18) for the calculation of the energy required during constant acceleration. For the sake of simplicity, in this hypothesis, it is considered that $v_f^2 = 2.a.d.$, that is, v_i and v_o are equal to 0 and the vehicle moves in a straight line.

Propulsion systems and energy use **Chapter | 4 129**

$$ARF_{aceleration} = \frac{1}{4}.Ca.A.\rho.v_f^{2} \qquad (4.17)$$

$$E_{slope+aceleration} = \left(CR_s.P.\cos(\alpha) + \frac{1}{4}.Ca.A.\rho.v_f^{2} + P.sen(\alpha) + \frac{a}{g}.P \right).d \qquad (4.18)$$

The total energy (E_{total}) consumed by a traveling vehicle may be obtained by adding the contributions of each segment of traffic traveled under certain conditions. For example, Eq. (4.19) presents the total energy of a vehicle that travels along the plane, in a straight line, at constant speed (v_f) over m segments, and with constant acceleration (a) over n segments.

$$E_{total} = \sum_{i=1}^{n} \left(CR_s \cdot P + \frac{1}{4} \cdot C_a \cdot A \cdot \rho \cdot vf_i^{2} + \frac{a}{g} P \right) \cdot d_i + \\ \sum_{j=1}^{m} \left(CR_s \cdot P + \frac{1}{2} C_a \cdot A \cdot \rho \cdot vf_j^{2} \right) \cdot d_j \qquad (4.19)$$

Based on Eq. (4.19) it can be seen that the demand for energy (E_{total}) is the product of the sum of the forces of restriction to motion and the distance (d) to be traveled by the vehicle at each segment, which characterizes a measure of work. It can also be seen that E_{total} is directly proportional to the distance traveled.

Still based on Eq. (4.19), E_{total} is directly proportional to the vehicle's design features, such as its weight (empty weight plus load capacity), size (frontal area), shape (aerodynamic resistance coefficient), and type of contact between tire and pavement (rolling resistance coefficient). In this case, E_{total} is also influenced by the road's construction features (roughness, elasticity, maintenance conditions, etc.).

Considering that force P represents the vehicle's total weight, taken as the sum of its empty weight (tare weight) and transported load (capacity), E_{total} is directly proportional to the vehicle's use in terms of the amount of cargo or transported passengers. Indirectly, the variation in the total weight causes a variation in tire deformation (CR_s) and in the behavior of the RRF.

The greater the final speed, the higher the demand for energy, considering the increase in ARF with squared v_f. However, there is virtually no change in the demand for energy in function of air density, which has a limited range of variation under normal operational conditions.

An expansion of this model's limits of application shows that the demand for energy increases based on the need for overcoming slopes, since a component of resistance to the additional motion, created by the decomposition of the vehicle's weight, will have to be included in Eq. (4.19).

If the vehicle travels at a constant speed, then the term $a \cdot P/g$ no longer exists and the ARF has double importance, since factor ¼ assumes the value of ½, which implies the recommendation of a speed limit when one intends to save energy. The suppression of the term $a \cdot P/g$, when the vehicle is traveling at constant speed, also indicates that speed variations with successive segments of acceleration should be avoided.

130 Transportation, energy use and environmental impacts

Under real operational conditions, external conditions, such as traffic and the driver's style, cause variations in the values of acceleration and final speed in the form of a traffic cycle.

In summary, the demand for energy for road transportation is a function of the vehicle's speed variations, regulated by parameters associated with the vehicle's and the way's physical characteristics, and conditioned to the traffic cycle.

Table 4.3 provides a summary of the equations used to determine the NFRM presented in this section, with the respective measures for their determination.

TABLE 4.3 NFRM for road transportation

NFRM (Natural forces of resistance to motion)	Equation	Terms
ARF (Aerodynamic Resistance Force)		
Uniform motion	$\frac{1}{2}0.0772 \cdot C_a \cdot A \cdot \rho \cdot (v + v_o)^2$	ARF [N] Ca [nondimensional] A [m^2]
Uniformly varied motion	$\frac{1}{4}0.0772 \cdot Ca \cdot A \cdot \rho \cdot (v_f + v_o)^2$	ρ [m^3] v [km/h] v_f [km/h] v_o [km/h]
RRF (Rolling Resistance Force)		
Independent from speed	$CR_s \cdot P$	RRF [N] CRs [non-dimensional] P [N]
Dependent on speed for cars	$CR_s \cdot P + 0.0772 \cdot CR_v \cdot v^2 \cdot P$	RRF [N] CR_s [nondimensional] P [N] $CR_v = 6.99 \times 10^{-6}$ s^2/m^2 v [km/h]
Dependent on speed for trucks	$CR_s \cdot P + 1,47 \cdot CR_v \cdot v^2 \cdot P$	RRF [lbf] CRs = 0.2445 [non-dimensional] P [lbf] $CR_v = 0.00044$ s^2/ft^2 v [mph]
FNCS (Forces Needed to Change Speed)	Equation	Terms
FRI (Force of Resistance to Inclination)	$P \cdot sen(\alpha)$	P [N] α [rad]
FRC (Force of Resistance to Curve)	$\frac{1}{2} \dfrac{0.0772 \cdot v^2 P}{g \cdot r}$	FRC [N] v [km/h] P [N] r [m] g [m/s^2]

Propulsion systems and energy use **Chapter | 4** **131**

Some examples are described below to consolidate the concepts presented so far.

Example 4.1

A simple truck of 20 t of TGW (total gross weight) and a front area of 10 m² travels at a constant speed of 60 km/h going up a ramp of 3% over a very well-maintained asphalt pavement. Calculate the FRM, in Newtons. Assume there is no wind and adopt $C_a = 1.0$, $CR_s = 0.01$, and $\rho = 1.2$. Remember that 1 N = 9.81·1 kgf.

Under the conditions of the exercise, FRM = NFRM + FRI = ARF + RRF + FRI.

Calculation of the ARF.

ARF = 0.5·0.0772·1·10·1.2·60² = 1667.52 N.

Calculation of RRF.

RRF = 0.01·20,000·9.81 = 1962.00 N.

Calculation of FRI:

FRI = 0.03·20,000·9.81 = 5886.00 N.

FRM = 1667.52 + 1962.00 + 5886.00 = 9515.52 N.

Example 4.2

After finishing the drive and stopping, the truck from Example 4.1 had to accelerate along an at-grade segment with constant acceleration of 1.5 m/s² until reaching 80 km/h. What is the total energy consumed in this segment? Assume the same movement conditions as before.

The total energy may be calculated using Eq. (4.18), with due adjustments, since the vehicle is traveling along a plane.

$$E_{total} = \left(CR_s \cdot P + \frac{1}{4} \cdot 0.0772 \cdot C_a \cdot A \cdot \rho \cdot v_f^2 + \frac{a}{g} \cdot P \right) \cdot d$$

$E_{total} = (0.01·20,000·9.81 + 0.25·0.0772·1.0·10·1.2·80² + 1.5/9.81·20,000·9.81)$ $·d = (1962 + 1482.24 + 30,000)·d = 33,444.24·d$.

Distance d must be determined, since a and v_f are known. In this case, application of uniformly varied motion equations results in:

$v_0 = s_0 = 0$.

$t = v_f/a = (80·1000/3600)/1.5 = 14.82$ s.

$s = \frac{1}{2}·a·t^2 = \frac{1}{2}·1.5·(14.82)^2 = 164.72$ m.

$E_{total} = 33,444.24·164.72 = 5,508,935.21$ Nm = 5.51×10⁶ J = 5.51 MJ.

Example 4.3

If, in Example 4.1, the ramp is 500 m long, what is the total energy required?

In this case, one needs only to apply: $E_{total} = FRM·d$.

$E_{total} = 9515.52·500 = 4,757,760$ Nm = 4.76 MJ.

132 Transportation, energy use and environmental impacts

Example 4.4

Assume that the truck in Example 4.3 travels along a plane, with all other conditions remaining the same. What is the total energy demanded in a segment of 500 m?

In this case, the portion of FRI is suppressed.

FRM = 1667.52 + 1962.00 = 3629.52 N.

E_{total} = 3629.52·500 = 1,814,760 N m = 1.81 MJ.

Note that, moving along a plane, the energy demand is reduced by 62%.

4.3.2 Energy supply in road transportation

The energy calculated using Eq. (4.19) is the one needed for the wheels to propel the vehicle. However, the transformation of energy stored in the vehicle into work is directly related to the propulsion system.

The propulsion systems used in road vehicles may be classified into two broad groups: conventional systems and nonconventional systems. Conventional systems were predominant in the market, up to this book's publishing date, and comprise a reciprocating internal combustion engine[1] (ICE) and a mechanical transmission system (MTS). Nonconventional propulsion systems may be of three basic configurations: combustion engines and MTSs; electric engines and MTS, also referred to as electric propulsion system; and hybrid propulsion systems (HPS).

In the first configuration, it is possible to find external combustion engines (ECE, e.g., *Rankine* or *Stirling* cycle), or rotary internal combustion engines (RCE, e.g., *Wankel* engine or gas turbines), in conjunction with an MTS like the one used by conventional propulsion systems. Almost all their uses are in experimental or limited commercialization vehicles.

The electric propulsion system uses electric motors (EM), in which electric power comes from an external source or from inside the vehicle (onboard). In the first case, energy comes from a power network, as with trolleybuses.[2] In the second case, electric power is supplied by batteries (BAT) or fuels, such as fuel cells (FC).

The HPS may be of very different forms but are more frequently a conjugation of components of conventional and electric propulsion systems, arranged in series, when both work simultaneously in a regime of optimized operation, or in parallel, when work alternately, with the control of best performance for each of them.

---

1. The term reciprocating internal combustion engine is used to identify the type of internal combustion engine that is most widely used in the modern automotive industry. Its use is needed to differentiate this kind of internal combustion engine from rotary internal combustion engines, which have virtually no commercial application in the automotive industry. In this study, the acronym ICE (internal combustion engine) will be used to refer to reciprocating internal combustion engines.

2. Trolleybuses are buses with propulsion systems powered by electric motors that use electric power supplied by an air network.

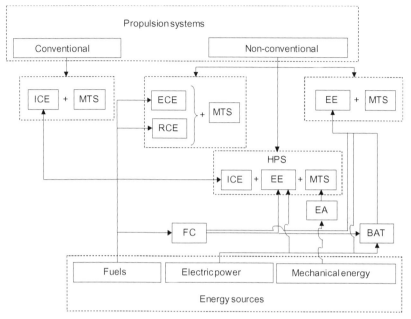

FIG. 4.2 Propulsion systems for road vehicles. (Subtitles: ICE—reciprocating internal combustion engine; MTS—mechanical transmission system; ECE—external combustion engine; RCE—rotary combustion engine; EM—electric motors; HPS—hybrid propulsion system; EA—energy accumulator; BAT—battery; FC—fuel cell).

Fig. 4.2 attempts to summarize these concepts and highlight the energy source used in each propulsion system. In the case of the HPS, the figure also presents the possibility of using mechanical energy stored in an energy accumulator (EA) and delivered straight to the MTS.

4.3.2.1 Conventional propulsion system

Fig. 4.3 shows the propulsion system for road vehicles that is most widely used worldwide nowadays.

Reciprocating ICE

The fuel stored in the fuel tank is mixed with air and burned within the cylinders of a reciprocating ICE, whose main components are represented in Fig. 4.4. The ignition of the air-fuel mixture (A/F mixture) may be produced via spark ignition engine (SIE), when the conventional energy source is gasoline, or via compression ignition engine (CIE), when the conventional energy source is diesel oil. The ignition of the A/F mixture increases the pressure within the cylinder and causes the piston to move downward, producing rotation at the crankshaft; this is called an engine cycle. Therefore, the ICE converts chemical energy from the fuel into torque and power to be used as work and cause the vehicle to move.

134 Transportation, energy use and environmental impacts

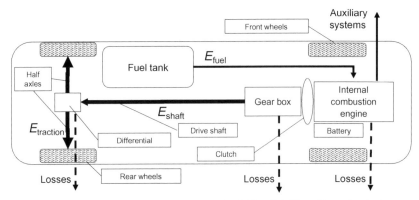

FIG. 4.3 Conventional propulsion system—road vehicle. (Subtitles: E_{fuel}—chemical energy stored in the fuel; E_{shaft}—mechanical energy available at the drive shaft; $E_{traction}$—mechanical energy available at the traction bar (half axles).)

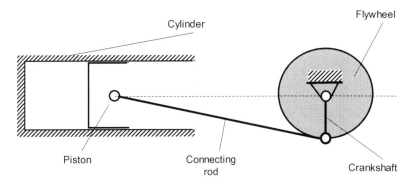

FIG. 4.4 Main components of the ICE.

The engine cycle may be represented by pressure vs volume diagrams ($p \times V$), pressure vs time or crank angle ($p \times t, p \times \alpha$), as shown in Fig. 4.5, which facilitates the understanding of its workings and enables the definition of some relevant variables to determine the efficiency of this thermal machine.

The position of the piston within the cylinder varies from bottom dead center (BDC) to top dead center (TDC), when the A/F mixture is compressed at maximum level, with the same volume as the combustion chamber (V_c). For the best performance when burning the A/F mixture, it is common for the ignition to occur slightly before TDC, a point that is indicated as PI in Fig. 4.5.

When the piston is at BDC, the total volume of the cylinder is the sum of V_c and V_d, the latter is called displacement volume or cylinder capacity. Compression ratio (cr) is the relationship presented in Eq. (4.20).

$$t_c = \frac{V_c + V_d}{V_c} \quad (4.20)$$

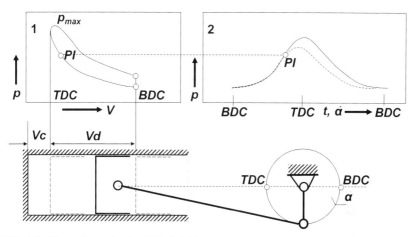

FIG. 4.5 The engine cycle of an ICE. (Subtitles: p—pressure; V—volume, p_{max}—maximum pressure; BDC—bottom dead center; TDC—top dead center; Vc—combustion chamber volume; Vd—displacement volume; PI—point of ignition; t—time; α—crack angle.)

Total displacement (TD) is the product presented in Eq. (4.21), where n_c is the number of cylinders of the ICE.

$$TD = Vd \cdot n_c \quad (4.21)$$

Both SIE and CIE engines may operate with two strokes or four strokes (2S or 4S). This classification regards the cycle of transformation of the chemical energy contained in the fuel into mechanical energy via the rotation of a crankshaft. In 2S engines, each complete revolution of the crankshaft represents one engine cycle. In 2S engines, the engine cycles take place at every two complete revolutions of the crankshaft.

2S engines are cheaper, lighter, and can turn more energy into work per unit of time when compared to 4S engines of the same proportion. That is why they have always been used in motorcycles, tricycles, outboard engines, and small equipment. However, their mechanical configuration and operational features make it difficult to control the burning process, leading them to emit between 20% and 50% of unburned fuel through the exhaust, resulting in undesirable atmospheric pollutant emissions and high fuel consumption, which is the reason for their gradual disuse.

Almost all road vehicles manufactured worldwide use 4S ICEs, which may be SIEs (ICE-SIE-4S), known as Otto cycle engines or CIEs (ICE-CIE-4S). Fig. 4.6A and B synthetically illustrate the four strokes of operation in these engines.

Each stroke has a specific name. For both types of engines, these strokes are called intake, compression, power, and exhaust.

In the case of the ICE-SIE-4S, the intake stroke occurs when the A/F mixture enters the cylinder; with the downward movement of the piston toward BDC, the internal pressure of the cylinder decreases, forcing the intake of the mixture through the intake valve that needs to be open. In the case of ICE-CIE-4S, there is only air intake.

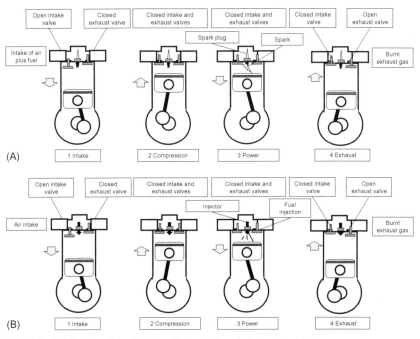

FIG. 4.6 (A) Strokes of the ICE-SIE-4S, (B) strokes of the ICE-CIE-4S.

When going up, the piston compresses the gas mixture, increasing its temperature and pressure. At the PI, slightly before TDC, a spark is produced or, in the case of direct injection (DI) ICE-CIE-4S, fuel is injected.

During the power stroke, the A/F mixture is burned, and the gases expand exerting pressure over the cylinder walls, among which is the upper part of the piston, causing its displacement until BDC and the revolution of the crankshaft.

Once the piston reaches BDC, the fourth stroke, exhaust, begins; during this stroke the burnt gases are expelled from the cylinder as the piston moves toward TDC. From then on, a new operational cycle begins.

Chapter 3 addressed the efficiency of final energy use (Table 4.3) but it is worth mentioning that around 60%–80% of the energy stored in the fuel is lost when the fuel is burned. Moreover, auxiliary systems, such as air-conditioning and hydraulic steering also consume part of the energy available in the fuel. It is estimated that the engine's slow running (with the vehicle stopping) is responsible for consuming around 15% of the energy available in the fuel.

Mechanical transmission system

In the conventional propulsion system, all the ICE operates at a rotation range delimited by two extremes: slow running rotation and maximum rotation. That way, the torque and power generated in the ICE are not uniform throughout the

Propulsion systems and energy use Chapter | 4 **137**

vehicle's operation. Thus, a MTS must be added to transform torque and power supplied by the ICE into power momentarily demanded to move the vehicle.

As shown in Fig. 4.3, the MTS is made of a clutch (elastic mechanical coupling), a gearbox (angular velocity variator), a drive shaft, a differential, and half axles of wheels. This configuration assumes a scenario in which the ICE is located at the front part of the vehicle and traction transmitted by the wheels in the rear axle, which is very common in commercial passenger and freight vehicles. Table 4.4 presents other possible configurations.

The MTS must meet the requirements associated with the operation of road vehicles, including: (1) promoting the transition between a stationary (stopped) and moving vehicle; (2) converting the engine's torque and rotation to meet the vehicle's traffic needs; (3) promoting motion ahead (forward) and backwards (reverse); (4) compensating for the variations in the wheel rotation in curves; and (5) guaranteeing that the ICE keeps working within a rotation range that allows the limiting of fuel consumption and atmospheric pollutant emissions.

The clutch is responsible for interrupting or promoting the connection between the engine and the other components of the transmission. It is necessary when the vehicle is stopped but the engine is still working, when the vehicle needs to start moving, or at the moment of changing gears.

The gearbox changes the engine's torque and rotation to adapt them to the vehicle's momentary traction needs, keeping the power generated by the engine at a relatively constant level. In a car, in its most usual configuration, the gearbox has five ratios; the first three reduce the engine's nominal rotation and the last two either maintain or slightly increase this rotation. In a truck or a bus, the number of gears can get to more than a dozen. Gear switching may be manual or automatic.

The differential allows the set of half axles (see Fig. 4.3) and wheels located at opposite sides to spin at different angular velocities along the curves, guaranteeing a uniform distribution of traction forces.

It is estimated that the energy lost in this set to overcome internal friction is approximately 5% of the energy originally contained in the fuel.

TABLE 4.4 Configurations of the MTS

Configuration	Position of the ICE	Traction axle
Reference	Front and longitudinal	Rear
Front traction	Front, longitudinal, or transversal	Front
Traction on all axes	Front, with the possible occurrence of rear or central position less frequently.	Front and rear permanently or selectively coupled.
Rear traction	Rear, longitudinal, or transversal	Rear

138 Transportation, energy use and environmental impacts

4.3.2.2 Nonconventional propulsion systems

Although they still represent a small share of the propulsion systems used in road vehicles nowadays, we chose to synthetically present nonconventional propulsion systems as alternatives that may be adopted with greater emphasis in the future. This seems to be particularly applicable to the case of electric and hybrid propulsion systems.

Use of nonconventional combustion engines

In addition to reciprocating ICEs, there are other thermal machines capable of converting the fuel's chemical energy into torque and power is made available to power road vehicles. In this case, the MTS either remains unchanged or suffers small adjustments to enable the use of these machines. What follows is a brief description of their operation as well as the advantages and disadvantages of their use.

Wankel engine: it is a spark-ignition rotary ICE that uses a triangular rotor of convex sides and an elliptical combustion chamber. The eccentric movement of the rotor within the combustion chamber causes the volume between rotor's and the chamber's walls to vary, generating the functions of compression and expansion in a way similar to the piston's action in the ICE. To provide a given power, the Wankel engines are smaller, lighter, and produce less vibration and noise than the ICE. Moreover, they have a less complex configuration, which leads to lower maintenance frequency. Its limitations of use are related to a higher consumption of fuel and lubricating oil, and higher emissions of unburned hydrocarbons due to the difficulty in optimizing the shape of the combustion chamber. Wankel engines have high manufacturing costs and cannot be adapted to the use of diesel oil, since their configuration and operation limit the compression rates.

Rankine cycle engines: they are external and continuous combustion engines capable of consuming a variety of fuels and use the heat resulting from the burning of fuel to generate steam. The steam may be used to move a piston within a cylinder (reciprocating motion) or to spin the rotor of a turbine (rotary motion). Due to its mechanical conception, they are large, heavy, and expensive engines. Their great advantage lies in the low-atmospheric pollutant emissions when compared to the ICEs without emission control systems. No information was found reporting that the technology to produce these engines has significantly evolved since the 1970s. At that time, it was possible to produce engines that used the *Rankine* cycle with fuel consumption similar to that of gasoline ICEs. Its application for road transportation seems to be limited to energy cogeneration in heavy vehicles, where it is possible to take advantage of the heat wasted by the exhaust gases of the ICEs.

Stirling engines: they are external and continuous combustion engines capable of consuming a variety of fuels to produce heat and to heat a working fluid that expands within the cylinders, producing reciprocating motion. Due to their high working pressures, they are large, heavy, and expensive engines, capable of generating moderate power, considering their size and weight. Their main advantage lies in the fact they produce significantly lower unburned hydrocarbon emissions, carbon monoxide (CO), and nitrogen oxides (NO_x) than modern ICEs that already have emission control. Furthermore, they are quiet engines and may consume less fuel than the ICE to generate the same power due to its better thermal efficiency. This advantage may be compromised due to need for long heating periods. Their use as the only energy conversion unit (ECU) in road cars does not seem viable in the medium term but hybrid systems with small Stirling engines associated with electric engines are a possible option.

Gas turbines: they are rotary internal and continuous combustion engines that may burn a great variety of fuels. In turbines, the A/F mixture is burned within a combustion chamber and the exhaust gases expand and go through a rotor, causing an axle to spin. The burning of fuel within the combustion chamber uses a poor mixture,[3] producing low levels of atmospheric pollutants, even with virtually no control device. Moreover, they have a smooth operation, with low levels of vibration and noise. Their mechanical design allows long intervals between maintenance routines. Their disadvantages are high manufacturing costs, unsatisfactory response in transient regimes, high fuel consumption, especially with low loads, and little application to low powers.

Table 4.5 presents a summary of the characteristics of nonconventional engines, their main advantages and disadvantages.

Electric propulsion system (electric vehicles)

Vehicles with an electric propulsion system, also known as electric vehicles, are those that are not equipped with reciprocating ICEs as part of the ECU and whose main components of the power unit are electric engines. Fig. 4.7 illustrates the typical configuration of a battery electric propulsion system, a vehicle equipped with a plug-in electric vehicle or battery-electric vehicle (BEV).

There are three ways of providing electric power to the engine throughout a vehicle's operation. In the first way, electric power is supplied by an air network and is not stored or generated in significant amounts in accumulators within the vehicle. Currently, the use of these vehicles is limited to urban collective passenger transportation and they receive the general name of trolleybuses. Transportation by trolleybuses does not properly characterize the use of an electric road vehicle due to the freedom of movement being restricted to the electrified way. In the second way, vehicles have accumulators, represented in Fig. 4.7 by a battery pack that stores electrical energy onboard, making them independent of the existence of an electric power network and, therefore, more versatile. The third way uses a FC, which shall be shown later. The electric propulsion system, equipped with onboard electric power storage, either with a

---

3. A poor mixture is an air-fuel mixture in which the proportion, in moles, of air is higher than the one chemically needed to oxidize 1 mol of fuel. The A/F mixture within the chemically needed proportion is called a stoichiometric mixture.

TABLE 4.5 Nonconventional combustion engines

	Wankel Engine	Stirling *Engine*	*Rankine* cycle engine	Gas turbines
Process type	Internal combustion	External combustion	External combustion	Internal combustion
Fuel	Suitable fuels for the ICE-SIE	Without limitation	Without limitation	Without limitation
Ignition	Depends on external device—spark plug.	Depends on external device—spark plug or torch	Depends on external device—spark plug or torch	Depends on external device—spark plug or torch
A/F Ratio	Stoichiometric or poor	Poor	Poor	Poor
Fluid that produces work	Combustion gases	Hydrogen or Helium	Steam	Combustion gases
Combustion type	Cyclic	Continuous	Continuous	Continuous
Configuration	Rotary	Reciprocating	Reciprocating or rotary	Rotary
Advantages (1)	Smaller size, weight and mechanical complexity. Smoother operation with less noise and vibration. Lower frequency of maintenance.	Lower atmospheric pollutant emissions, quieter. Higher thermodynamic efficiency on permanent operation.	Lower atmospheric pollutant emissions if compared to ICEs of the same generation—reference: 1970s.	Lower atmospheric pollutant emissions, operation with low vibration and noise. Lower frequency of maintenance.
Disadvantages (1)	Higher fuel consumption and price. Higher emissions of unburned hydrocarbons.	Large, heavy, and expensive. Have a high weight-to-power ratio.	Large, heavy, and expensive. Outdated technology.	High manufacturing costs, inadequate response in transient operation regimes and with low loads.

Note: (1) If compared to an ICE used for a similar purpose.

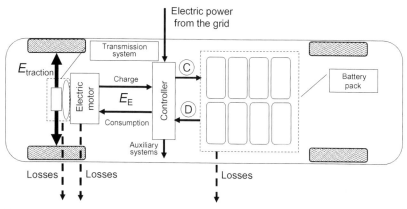

FIG. 4.7 Typical configuration of an electric propulsion system. (Subtitles: C—charge; D—discharge; E_E—electricity; $E_{traction}$—mechanical energy available at the traction bar (half axle).)

battery pack or any other configuration, represents an alternative of great potential to conventional propulsion systems in cars.

In a classification regarding the type of service, these vehicles may be divided into two sets: (1) general-use road vehicles and (2) industrial use vehicles. The first ones may be used as substitutes for road vehicles with conventional propulsion systems; the second ones have a limited use restricted to industrial yards, distribution centers, stations and terminals, transporting passengers, and freight along short distances with a limited speed of 50 km/h.

Regarding general-use road vehicles, in the beginning of the 20th century, around 38% of the North American fleet of road vehicles were electric vehicles (Wright, 1990). On the other hand, in the beginning of the 1990s, the percentage of electric vehicles in the North American fleet was below 0.002% (Ristinen and Kraushaar, 1999). Due to current worries about global environmental impacts, the issues of energy security, mainly those related to the growing dependence on petroleum-derived fuels for transportation, and atmospheric pollution in the cities, the share of electric vehicles in world fleet is expressively changing. Considering that the electric propulsion system represents a promising alternative what is required is highly energy efficient and silent operation that is free of local atmospheric emissions and respects the limits of the autonomy the technology offers, according to the International Energy Agency, in 2015 the world fleet of electric vehicles[4] reached 1 250,000 vehicles, representing 0.1% of total number of light vehicles in the world; an increase of 50 times in 25 years, and in the period between 2015 and 2017 this fleet more than doubled, reaching 3,100,000 in 2017. Most of this fleet (40%), and of the recharging infrastructure (41%), was in China.

---

4. Here we take into consideration battery-electric vehicles (BEV), also called plug-in electric vehicles, and plug-in hybrid vehicles, which shall be defined later in this book.

142 Transportation, energy use and environmental impacts

The main advantages of the electric propulsion system, when compared to the conventional propulsion system, are as follows:

(1) It does not generate local atmospheric pollutant emissions. This characteristic is particularly interesting in the case of vehicles that operate in urban areas. However, attention must be paid to the way electric power is produced, which may involve the emission of atmospheric pollutants outside urban areas.

(2) It has a higher efficiency in overall energy use. Even considering that electric power comes from a thermal source (thermoelectric), in which the efficiency varies between 20% and 35% (Wiser, 2000), since the efficiency of the electric propulsion system is approximately 85% (Riley, 1994), the overall energy use efficiency is between 17% and 30% (Riley, 1994; Wiser, 2000), better than the range of 10%–30% usually found in conventional propulsion systems.

(3) Lower maintenance costs for the MTS. The maintenance of the electric engine is cheaper due to the possibility of coupling the electric engine straight to the axle of the wheel and due to the sheer simplicity of the electric engine's operation, with less mobile pieces than the ICE, much less heat generation, and less items that require lubrication.

The challenges that need to be overcome for a greater diffusion of the electric propulsion system, when compared to the conventional propulsion system, are as follows:

(1) Limited autonomy: while a vehicle that uses fuel has an autonomy between 500 and 600 km (with a tank of 50 L and running 10 km/L), the values for electric vehicles are estimated to range between 200 and 300 km. Nevertheless, this limitation seems to have quickly decreased in the last years and may reach a range of 500–700 km until 2025.

(2) Cruise speed limitation: to guarantee operation with maximum energy efficiency and better autonomy, it is advisable that the electric vehicle should not exceed certain speed limits. As the cruise speed increases, autonomy tends to decrease, causing the need to increase the battery pack and the vehicle's weight. This reality tends to discourage the adoption of general use electric vehicles. However, just as with the autonomy limitation, cruise speed limitation has been quickly overcome in the last decade.

(3) Long recharge time. While a vehicle powered by gasoline or diesel oil may be refueled in 5–10 min, the most common form of recharge for electric vehicles may take from 4 to 8 h. There are fast charge devices that allow this kind of operation to be done in minutes (40–60 min) but never as fast as refueling operations.

(4) Use of space and weight for EAs: even the most modern batteries require a significant amount of space and weight in the vehicles, as can be estimated based on Table 4.6.

Propulsion systems and energy use **Chapter | 4** **143**

(5) Battery replacement costs: with the currently available technology, it is estimated that the lifespan of a battery pack is 1000–3500 recharge cycles. Considering a scenario that demands daily recharges, the lifespan of the battery pack would be 4–12 years, with a replacement cost of around 150–360 US$/kWh for battery packs ranging from 20 to 100 kWh, which can still be deemed a high cost, when compared to the maintenance costs of a fuel-powered car. Furthermore, the final disposition of batteries, after their use, may also become an environmental problem.

Example 4.5 The recent evolution of batteries

In the beginning of the 1990s, several manufacturers in Europe and in the United States determined that the performance profile of electric vehicles required an autonomy of 120–50 miles (192–80 km), cruise speed of 80 km/h, and a battery recharge time of 12–6 h for tensions between 110 and 220V. The battery pack would be made of lead-acid batteries, weighing about 500 kg, and its cost would be around US$ 1500.00, with a maximum lifespan of 20,000 miles (32,000 km). This profile included mainly the operation of small- and medium-sized cars, performing home-to-work round trips in urban centers.

A great evolution has already been achieved in this scenario and the limitations imposed to electromobility are being overcome mainly via the development of lighter and cheaper batteries that are able to store more energy per unit of mass. For example, Table 4.6 illustrates that lithium-ion batteries have a lifespan up to seven times higher than that of lead-acid batteries, with an energy density up to four times higher and a proportional increase in costs. There is high indication that recent technological developments will allow the remaining challenges regarding the spread of electric vehicles to be overcome.

As a reference, one should consider the values of energy density and specific energy for gasoline, which range from 9000 to 12,000 Wh/L and from 9500 to 13,000 Wh/kg, considering the tank's weight (Ristinen and Kraushaar, 1999).

Considering that the main limitation to the use of electric vehicles concerns the storage of energy in batteries, FCs are an alternative that is being developed. FCs are devices that convert the chemical energy of a substance, almost always hydrogen, straight into electric energy by means of a reaction with an oxidizer, usually oxygen.

Fig. 4.8 illustrates the typical configuration of an electric vehicle powered by FC. We chose to represent on the same platform two different ways of feeding the FC with hydrogen, although this does not happen in practice. In the first way, hydrogen is stored in tanks, usually at low temperatures. In the second way, a substance of easier storage (fuel) is used, which can then be converted to hydrogen to be used in the FC.

The fuel is an intermediate vector of hydrogen, a substance that has a high amount of hydrogen in its composition and that works as carrier, releasing

TABLE 4.6 Types of batteries for electric vehicles

Type of material in the battery	Specific power [W/kg]	Specific energy [Wh/kg]	Estimated cost [US$/kWh]	Cycles
Lead-acid VRLA	250	35–45	160–210	400–500
NiMH	350	70	780–930	1350–1550
NiNaCl$_2$	150–200	90–125	300–700	1000–3000
Lithium ion	400	150–200	900–1200	1000–3500
Lithium polymer	300	150	–	–
Nano-lithium-titanate	1250	80–100	2000	25,000
Lithium-sulfur	–	500	–	–
Lithium-air	–	5000	–	–

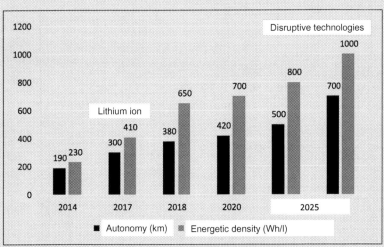

Legend: VRLA—valve regulated lead-acid, NiMH—nickel, magnesium, and hydrogen, NiNaCl$_2$—nickel, sodium and chlorine.

Source: IEA (2018). Global EV Outlook 2018. Towards cross-modal electrification. International Energy Agency, Paris, France.

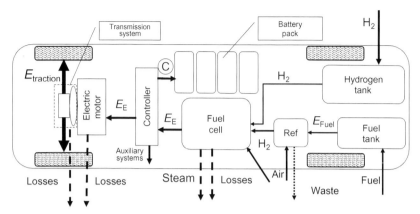

FIG. 4.8 Electric propulsion system with fuel cell. (Subtitles: E_E—electricity; REF—reformer; E_{fuel}—chemical energy stored in the fuel; $E_{traction}$—mechanical energy available at the traction axle.)

hydrogen on demand for the vehicle's operation through a specific process. The intermediate vectors may be some kinds of alcohol (methane and ethanol), hydrocarbons (gasoline, natural gas), metals, and hydrides. In the case of alcohols and hydrocarbons, the process usually adopted to release hydrogen is steam reforming and partial oxidation, which are done using a reformer (REF). For metals and hydrides, reactions with water, acids, and bases are used.

Physically, a FC consists of two electrodes: the anode, which is the electrode at which oxidation occurs, and the cathode, where reduction occurs. They are immersed in an electrolyte that facilitates the movement of ions. The feeding of electrodes with reactants results in a potential difference that produces electric current. In this aspect, the difference between an FC and a conventional battery is the fact that in FCs the reactants are fed continually and externally, while in batteries the reactants are stored.

FCs are differentiated according to the kind of electrolyte used but among all the kinds of FCs, the PEMFC—*polymer electrolyte membrane fuel cell*—is the predominant one in automotive vehicle prototypes.

The energy conversion presented in Fig. 4.8 is more efficient than the one found for ICEs, whose efficiency varies from 10% to 25% depending on the engine cycle and the operational conditions. A system that uses a FC may operate with an efficiency of 48%, in the case of direct use of hydrogen, and 37%, in the case of methanol use. The FC, by itself, has an efficiency of around 60%.

Although hydrogen is the main substance to be studied for use in FCs, there is also the possibility of directly using other substances, without the need for the previous acquisition of hydrogen. The most advanced studies are particularly contemplating the alcohols (methanol and ethanol) but the performance achieved so far has still proven inferior to that of using hydrogen.

146 Transportation, energy use and environmental impacts

Regarding the environmental issue, the use of FCs has some particularities that deserve to be mentioned. The first one is the fact that FCs, along with EMs, are very quiet and have very low levels of atmospheric pollutant emissions. The second one is the fact that FCs use materials that are far less aggressive to the environment, such as graphite and aluminum, unlike the heavy metals used in the most common batteries. A serious environmental problem in traditional batteries is their difficult final disposition after wear. Since their chemical components have high toxicity and cause cumulative effects in living organisms, the direct final disposition at sanitary landfills is extremely dangerous.

The main disadvantage of FCs is the issue of hydrogen storage. Hydrogen storage systems take more space and are heavier than the equivalent ones for traditional liquid fuels because the physical dimension of hydrogen is the lowest among all chemical elements. This ends up facilitating its permeability through the molecular structure of the most diverse kinds of materials, including steel, causing micro fissures and weakening. Another disadvantage of its use is the need for keeping the liquid hydrogen at low temperatures, which includes constant energy consumption expenses or the use of pressure relief valves with continuous hydrogen losses to the environment.

Example 4.6   A bit of history about fuel cell vehicles

The first steps toward the development of vehicles powered by fuel cells were taken in 1966, when the first electric vehicle in the United States powered by a pack of fuel cells (alkaline) fed by hydrogen was constructed. In 1982, tests with an electric bus began at the Georgetown University (USA). The vehicle was powered by fuel cells with hydrogen obtained from methanol. In 1993, the Canadian company Ballard Power Systems began testing an electric bus with 20 seats, equipped with proton-exchange membrane fuel cells (PEMFC), fed by hydrogen stored in cylinders within the vehicle. Since then, the development of these vehicles has not stopped. Almost all car manufacturers in the world and some research institutions already have prototypes of this kind of vehicle, which may be seen in the examples presented in Table 4.7.

Hybrid propulsion systems

In a broad sense, the term hybrid propulsion applies to vehicles that use more than one propulsion system to move. The HPS may incorporate different devices to store energy, with their respective converters. Originally, HPS were associated with electric vehicles that had a complementary propulsion system that increased their autonomy.

The purpose of the development of HPS was to combine components of different propulsion systems so that the advantages of their use, under different operational conditions, surpass the additional costs of their configuration. Table 4.8 presents an illustrative selection of combinations of propulsion system components that characterize HPS found in German buses and trucks.

TABLE 4.7 Examples of electric vehicles powered by fuel cells.

Institution/Manufacturer	Prototype
Georgetown University	*Bus (methanol fuel cell)*
ZEVCO	Taxis in London (Hydrogen AFC) Light truck in Westminster (Hydrogen AFC)
Ballard Power Systems	Three municipal buses in Vancouver and three buses in Chicago (hydrogen fuel cell)
Ford	Vehicle P2000 SUV (methanol fuel cell)
Daimler Chrysler	Vehicle Necar 1 (hydrogen PEMFC) Vehicle Necar 2 (stored hydrogen PEMFC); Vehicle Necar 3 (reformed methanol PEMFC); Vehicle Necar 4 (stored liquid hydrogen PEMFC); Vehicle Necar 5 (reformed methanol PEMFC);
Nissan	Fuel cell vehicle
Toyota	Vehicle RAV4
Volkswagen	Vehicle Golf (methanol fuel cell)
General Motors/Opel	Vehicle Zafira (methanol fuel cell)

PEMFC—Polymer Electrolyte Membrane Fuel Cell; AFC—Hydrogen Alkaline Fuel Cell.

The HPS that combine reciprocating ICEs with electric propulsion systems were the most developed ones worldwide. In terms of performance and autonomy, the use of ICE in propulsion systems has so far proven to be difficult to overcome. Nevertheless, the ICEs have low efficiency, especially when operating with partial loads, besides emitting atmospheric pollutants resulting from the burning of fuels. When dimensioning a conventional propulsion system, it is necessary to provide the vehicles with ICEs that meet different conditions of torque and power. When the vehicle is intensely accelerated, the engine's power is used to the maximum. Thus, the higher an engine's volumetric capacity, the higher its operating rotation and the higher its available power. In most situations, this maximum power is not needed, which leads to the dimensioning of an ICE of greater size and power than needed for most of the vehicle's time of operation.

The HPS that combine an ICE and an electric propulsion system allow smaller ICEs that operate at rotations that are close to maximum energy efficiency and are capable of meeting average power demands for vehicle operation. When additional power is needed, as in the case of intense acceleration, this power is provided by the electric power storage units.

The components of this system may have two basic setups: serial and parallel. In the serial setup, the vehicle's traction is provided by one single component

TABLE 4.8 Examples of different compositions of hybrid propulsion systems

Energy conversion unit	Reciprocating internal combustion engine (ICE)								
	PT	**PT**					**FT**	**FT**	**FT**
	Electric engine			**PT**	**FT**	**RS**	**RS**	**FT**	**FT**	**FT**
Mechanical energy storage	Flywheel (mechanical energy accumulator)	PT			FT	RS				FT
	Pressure accumulator		PT							
Storage/Electric energy generation	Battery			PT	FT	RS	RS	FT		
	Fuel cell						RS			
	External supply (network)			PT	FT				FT	
Vehicle example		1	2	3	4			5	6	7

Subtitles: PT—vehicle prototype; RS—vehicle in research; FT—vehicle in field tests. (1) Daimler Bens/MAN Gyrobus; (2) MAN Hydrobus; (3) DUO bus Esslingen; (4) Neoplan trolleybus, Basel; (5) Daimler Bens hybrid electric bus and MAN distributor truck; (6) DUO bus Essen; (7) Solenoid motor bus Munich.
Source: SAE, 1996. Automotive Handbook, fifth ed. Society of Automotive Engineering (SAE), Warrendale, USA.

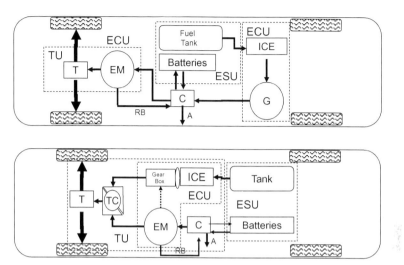

FIG. 4.9 Hybrid propulsion system setups. (Subtitles: T—transmission; TC—torque coupling; EM—electric motor; C—controller; ICE-internal combustion engine; G—generator; TU—traction unit; ESU—energy storage unit; ECU—energy conversion unit; RB—regenerative braking; A—load of accessories.)

of the propulsion system, usually an EM. In the parallel setup, traction is alternately provided by two components of the propulsion system, usually an EM and an ICE. Fig. 4.9 briefly illustrates the most common form of these setups. In both cases, the system comprises an ECU, energy storage units (ESU), and traction units (TU). A brief discussion of this technology is presented below.

The ECU is responsible for transforming chemical energy, stored in the form of fuel or in the batteries, into mechanical energy needed to power the vehicle.

As shown in Fig. 4.9, in the case of a serial setup, one part of the ECU is part of the TU, generating electric power by means of an engine-generator set made of a reciprocating ICE coupled to an electric generator (G). This set feeds the EM, which may depend on a MTS to supply traction to the wheels, as shown in Fig. 4.9, or may be directly connected to them.

In the case of a parallel setup, the ECU is within the TU. In this case, the vehicle is equipped with a conventional propulsion system and an electric propulsion system, which operate alternately and, together, form the HPS. For operations in which greater autonomy and higher speed are needed, the conventional propulsion system is used. That occurs in trips from the periphery of a city to the urban center. Once the urban center is reached, where moderate speed and shorter trips are needed, the electric propulsion system is used.

The connection of the conventional or electric propulsion system to the traction bar may be done via a torque coupling (TC) or by connecting the EM straight to the gearbox, as represented by the dashed line in Fig. 4.9. In the first case, it is not possible to take advantage of the reduction and multiplication capability of the gearbox, leading to the need of dimensioning an electric engine

150 Transportation, energy use and environmental impacts

that is capable of providing all the torque and power ranges needed for the vehicle's operation, which invariably increases its size and weight. On the other hand, efficiency in transmission is higher. In the second case, the electric engine is dimensioned to provide similar torque and power ranges as those of the ICE.

The ESU are of two types: fuel storage for the ECU and energy storage to be directly used by the TU. The first type consists of a fuel tank and the second one may consist of batteries and/or ultracapacitors to store electric power, or flywheels to store mechanical energy. In the serial setup, the ESU for direct use supply during peak energy demand, allowing the ICE to operate at a constant rate, thus rationalizing its dimensioning. For both configurations, it is possible to take advantage of part of the energy generated during the vehicle's deceleration by means of a system called regenerative braking (RB), achieving greater energy efficiency in the conversion of energy to traction. For that, the EM must be reversible and act as a generator at the moment of deceleration.

In both setups, the batteries may be recharged by the ICE when the vehicle does not need all the power that is being generated by this component. Again in both cases, it is also possible to feed the propulsion system through an air network, as seen in the operation of trolleybuses, or to charge the batteries via a charger connected to the power grid. In the last case, the vehicle is called a plug-in hybrid vehicle.

Both setups require the use of a controller (C). In serial setups, the controller is an electronic component with the main purpose of: managing the power demand of the EM; controlling the share provided by the engine-generator set and, in peak demands, by the batteries; maintaining their charging; allowing the engine-generator set to work constantly; and managing the operation of RB. For parallel setups, the controller manages the demand of the EM and other vehicle components. The parallel setup is predominant in light vehicles, such as passenger cars; in the case of buses, the serial setup is more common.

It is worth noting that the hybrid propulsion technology represents an intermediate stage in the development of more modern technological alternatives, both in terms of energy efficiency and in terms of atmospheric pollutant emissions, as is the case of vehicles with exclusively electric propulsion or those that use FCs using hydrogen as an energy vector.

4.3.3 Conceptual model of a road propulsion system

Regardless of the propulsion system being used, it is possible to use a model to determine the energy that is available to move the vehicle. No matter what kind of energy is stored in the vehicle, it must be converted into mechanical energy and transmitted to the wheels, which assumes the existence of energy conversion and transmission systems. Fig. 4.10 illustrates this model.

The energy conversion system is responsible for converting any kind of energy into mechanical energy. In the conventional propulsion system, this is done by the ICE. The energy transmission system is responsible for transmitting

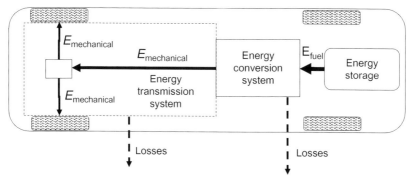

FIG. 4.10 Energy conversion and transmission systems in road vehicles.

mechanical energy to the wheels through a mechanical coupling (clutch, gears, axles, fittings, etc.) and it is called the MTS.

Based on this model, it is possible to calculate the energy offered to the wheels to produce the desired movement (E_{of}) using Eq. (4.22).

$$E_{of} = E - \Sigma Losses \qquad (4.22)$$

where E is stored energy and Σ Losses is the sum of the losses in the energy conversion and transmission systems.

There are two key.

The lower the losses, the lower will be the difference between the stored energy (E) and the offered energy (E_{of}). Losses are closely related to the energy source being used (fuel, electric power, and mechanical energy) and to the configuration of the propulsion system, thus, the definition of its value is only possible after determining this pair. In practice, the operational conditions also influence the losses, with lower values in a regime of permanent operation and small variations in speed.

The concept of efficiency was more widely addressed in Chapter 3 but it is worth presenting the definition of efficiency in a vehicle's propulsion system (η), as shown in Eq. (4.23).

$$\eta = \frac{E_{of}}{E} \qquad (4.23)$$

Just as efficiency was defined for the whole propulsion system, it is possible to define an expression for the efficiency of each of the main components of this system. In the case of the conventional propulsion system, it is enough to consider only the two main components: (1) the ICE, including the auxiliary systems; and (2) the MTS. Therefore, two new efficiency expressions are presented:

$$\eta_{ICE} = \frac{E_{axle}}{E} \qquad (4.24)$$

152 Transportation, energy use and environmental impacts

$$\eta_{MTS} = \frac{E_{of}}{E_{axle}} \tag{4.25}$$

The term E_{axle} represents the mechanical energy delivered to the MTS at the engine's output. Based on Eqs. (4.23)–(4.25), Eq. (4.26) may be defined.

$$\eta = \eta_{ICE}.x\eta_{MTS} \tag{4.26}$$

It is possible to generalize this expression for other propulsion systems, considering that this system may be divided into two parts: (1) an ECU, which can convert any form of energy into mechanical energy for vehicle traction; and (2) an MTS, which receives mechanical energy from the ECU and makes it available at the wheels. Thus, Eq. (4.27) assumes the following form:

$$\eta = \eta_{ECU} \times \eta_{MTS} \tag{4.27}$$

Usually, the term η_{ECU} is calculated considering the individual efficiencies of each ECU component.

In practice, the efficiency of the propulsion system varies according to operational conditions, having higher efficiency in a regime of permanent operation and small variations in speed.

4.3.4 Conceptual model of final energy use in road transportation

Considering all that was already discussed so far, it is possible to present a conceptual model to determine final energy use in road transportation. Fig. 4.11 illustrates this model and shows that the improvement in final energy use aiming at lower energy consumption is associated with two actions: (1) reduction in demand—loads imposed on vehicles; and (2) increase in the energy efficiency of the propulsion system.

If E_d is the energy demand at the wheels, for the vehicle to perform displacement d, with the same assumption as E_{total} [Eq. (4.19)], and E_{of} [Eq. (4.22)] is the energy supplied to the wheels to generate the desired movement, it is possible to equate them, leading to Eq. (4.28). The mathematical model shows how the stored energy (E) transforms into demanded energy (E_d). As the equation indicates, this transformation is subject to the operation conditions.

$$
\begin{aligned}
E_{operational\ condition} = {}& = \sum_{i=1}^{n} \left(CR_s.P + \frac{1}{4}.Ca.A.\rho.v.f_i^2 + \frac{a}{g}.P \right).d_i \\
& + \sum_{j=1}^{m} \left(CR_s.P + \frac{1}{2}.Ca.A.\rho.v.f_j^2 \right).d_j + \sum losses
\end{aligned} \tag{4.28}
$$

The main parameters and variables presented in this model are conditioned by factors related to the vehicles' design characteristics (vehicle and propulsion

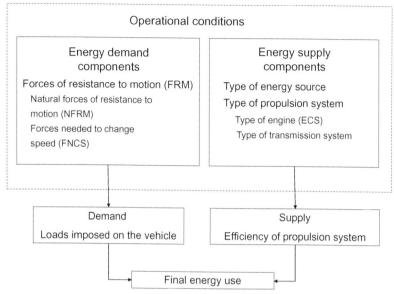

FIG. 4.11 Final energy use in road transportation.

system design), energy conversion method (propulsion system design), and kind of energy source used (propulsion system design and technology available).

The distance to be traveled (*d*) is a determining variable for final energy use and is related to transportation planning, as already discussed in Chapter 3. Moreover, the result of the model's application depends on conditions connected to the operation of the vehicle that directly or indirectly influence energy demand and losses. Table 4.9 attempts to summarize these considerations.

The flowchart shown in Fig. 4.12 makes it easier to understand how it is possible to reduce final energy use in transportation influencing energy supply and demand. Its original conception was developed for light duty vehicles (vans and pickup trucks) with conventional propulsion systems (ICE + MTS). However, except for the actions described within the dashed rectangle, the other actions may be generally applied.

The vehicle's weight (*P*) is a critical parameter for energy saving and is directly influenced by the vehicle's design and the technology available. Regarding the design, the reduction in vehicle dimensions, making them more compact, is an effective way of reducing empty weight, as long as safety standards are maintained. Furthermore, value engineering studies vehicle parts and components to reduce their quantity. With available technology to process materials, it is possible to replace steel, raw material that is traditionally used in the manufacturing of vehicle components, with aluminum, lighter plastic components, and even carbon fiber.

TABLE 4.9 Summary of factors that influence final energy use in road transportation

Component	Parameter	Variables	Description	Conditions
Energy demand E_d	P		Total Gross Weight (TGW) = empty weight + load capacity	Vehicle design and its use
	A		Vehicle's cross-sectional area	Vehicle design
	C_a		Vehicle's aerodynamic resistance coefficient	Vehicle design
	CR_s and CR_v		Rolling resistance coefficient (tire × pavement)	Vehicle and tire design, and road design and physical conditions
	α		Road or ramp inclination	Road design
	ρ		Air density	Climate conditions
	g		Acceleration of gravity	Geographical position
		v_f	Speed at the end of acceleration or speed chosen for traffic	Vehicle and propulsion system design, road design and conditions, traffic regime, driving style
		a	Acceleration	Vehicle and propulsion system design, road design and conditions, traffic regime, driving style
		d	Distance traveled	Transportation planning
Energy supply E_{of}		E	Energy that is stored or supplied to the propulsion system	Vehicle and propulsion system design in function of available technology
		ΣLosses	Sum of losses in the energy conversion and transmission system	Vehicle and propulsion system design in function of available technology

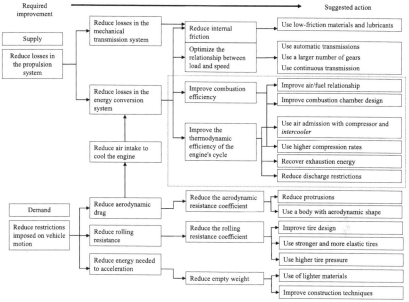

FIG. 4.12 Actions to reduce energy consumption in road transportation.

A vehicle's design determines its capacity through the number of passengers or the amount of load the vehicle can transport. A vehicle's use, that is, the relationship between its capacity and what is effectively transported, is what determines the weight of the vehicle in operation. An increase in the load results in an approximately linear increase in energy consumption.

A reduction in the vehicle's cross section and shape may decrease ARF. The cross-sectional size is closely related to the vehicle's size, and its shape determines the aerodynamic resistance coefficient (C_a). In both cases, the predominant influencing factor is vehicle design. Since the ARF varies with speed, the operational condition also influences in this case. In urban traffic, however, in which final speeds are mostly low, this component has little influence.

Rolling resistance may be decreased through the improvement in tire-pavement contact conditions. In this case, the use of low rolling resistance tires is a possible measure to be adopted. Nevertheless, the kind of pavement and its maintenance condition may decisively influence this item.

The road's vertical alignment, which will determine its inclination, is essentially related to road design. Horizontal alignment may also be a source of variation in energy consumption due to the need for reduced traffic speed and increased traveled distance.

Regarding supply, the main parameter that influences final energy use is the amount of loss in the energy conversion system, which is associated with

156 Transportation, energy use and environmental impacts

its efficiency. This parameter depends on vehicle design, more specifically on propulsion system design, on the technology available to manufacture the engine, and on the energy to be used. There is a limited possibility of improving ICEs, considering the natural thermodynamic limitations of combustion engines. A significant progress may be achieved using EMs, which is estimated to happen soon.

The dynamic operation conditions, due to variable speed and acceleration, closely interact with the other components to characterize final energy use. The design of the vehicle and the propulsion system will determine the engine's power (rate of conversion of stored energy into mechanical energy over time) and its load capacity; the maximum rate of acceleration; and the maximum speed the vehicle may reach.

On the other hand, the driving style, imposed by the traffic conditions and depending on the driver's behavior, determines how energy will be transformed into work as the vehicle travels (traffic cycle).

The proposed model considers that the final energy use is adequately characterized by the balance between the energy supply and demand components, given a certain operational condition. Some more examples of application of the concepts presented in this chapter are presented below to help you stabilize this knowledge.

Example 4.7

A simple truck equipped with a conventional propulsion system of 20 t TGW and frontal area of 10 m^2 travels at a constant speed of 60 km/h up a 3% ramp over very well-maintained asphalt. Calculate the power needed for the displacement, the power to be supplied by the engine, and the diesel oil consumption. Assume there is no wind and adopt $C_a = 1.0$, $CRs = 0.01$ and $\rho = 1.200$. Remember that 1 N = 9.81 kgf.

As already shown in Example 4.1, FRM = NFRM + FRI = ARF + RRF + FRI and, in this case, FRM = 9515.52 N.

Assuming that PF = FRM, we find that Pow_E = FRM. v is the power needed at the drive shaft.

$Pow_E = 9515.52 \cdot 1000/3600 \cdot 60 = 158,592$ N m/s = 158,592 J/s.

$Pow_{E(hp)} = 158,592 \cdot 1.341 \times 10^{-3} = 212.67$ hp.

Assuming that $\eta_{STM} = 0.90$.

$Pow_{UCE(hp)} = 158,592/0.90 = 176,213.33$ J/s = 236.3 hp.

Assuming that $\eta_{UCE} = 0.25$, energy consumption will be.

$C_{energy} = 176,213.33/0.25 = 704,853.32$ J/s = 0.7 MJ/s.

Assuming that 1 L of diesel oil has 38.31 MJ, we find that.

$C_{energy} = 0.7/38.31 = 0.018$ L/s = 64.80 L/h.

Considering the speed of 60 km/h, it is possible to estimate an energy performance of.

$R_{energy} = 60/64.8 = 0.92$ km/L.

Propulsion systems and energy use **Chapter | 4** **157**

Example 4.8

Find out the energy consumption and the performance of the vehicle described in the previous exercise if it were traveling along a plane.

In this case, FRM = 3629.52 N.

$Pow_E = 3629.52 \cdot 1000/3600 \cdot 60 = 60,492$ N m/s = 60,492 J/s.

$Pow_{E(hp)} = 60,492 \cdot 1.341 \times 10^{-3} = 81.12$ hp.

Assuming that $\eta_{STM} = 0.90$.

$Pow_{UCE(hp)} = 60,492/0.90 = 67,213.33$ J/s = 90.13 hp.

Assuming that $\eta_{UCE} = 0.25$, energy consumption will be.

$C_{energy} = 67,213.33/0.25 = 268,853.32$ J/s = 0.27 MJ/s.

Assuming that 1 L of diesel oil has 38.31 MJ, we find that.

$C_{energy} = 0.27/38.31 = 0.007$ L/s = 25.37 L/h.

Considering the speed of 60 km/h, it is possible to estimate an energy performance of.

$R_{energy} = 60/25.37 = 2.36$ km/L.

4.4 Other modes of transportation

Based on the concepts established for road transportation, it is possible to present an approach to address energy use in the remaining modes, as shown below. Most cases are of empirical formulation developed in countries that adopt the English system, so whenever necessary the conversion to the international system will be presented.

4.4.1 Railway mode

Based on the concepts established in Chapter 2, it is known that a train is a set formed by locomotives or railbuses and freight or passenger cars, respectively. As with road transportation, it can be assumed that train displacement depends on energy supply and demand, as presented below.

4.4.1.1 Energy supply in railway transportation

Consider a train that travels along a plane at constant speed with no wind. In this case, the American Railway Engineering and Maintenance-of-Way Association suggests that the NFRM (Natural Forces of Resistance to Motion) can be summarized according to Eq. (4.29).

$$NFRM_{train} = B_1 \cdot P + B_2 \cdot n + B_3 \cdot P \cdot v + C_a \cdot A \cdot v^2 \tag{4.29}$$

where B_1, B_2, and B_3 are constant;

P is the total weight of the locomotive, railbus, freight car, or passenger car;

n is the number of axles of the locomotive, railbus, freight car, or passenger car;

v is the speed;

158 Transportation, energy use and environmental impacts

C_a is the aerodynamic resistance coefficient;
A is the vehicle's cross-sectional area.

Eq. (4.29) is known as Davis formula and its empirical modeling was developed in 1926, remaining the same until today.

Eq. (4.29) considers: (1) rolling resistance forces (RRF) related to the friction between the wheel and the rail, between the axle and the wheel bearings and losses that vary with speed, particularly friction at the wheel flange and looseness, slips and bumps resulting from oval or rough wheels; (2) ARF, last term in Eq. (4.29), which is directly proportional to the vehicle's cross-sectional area, its shape, and the squared speed.

To overcome a slope, in the case of trains, it is also possible to consider a component of the FNCS (forces needed to change speed) with Eq. (4.10). However, due to constructive restrictions, railway ramps are very smooth, usually lower than 5%, assuming $FRI = P \cdot grad$.

Still regarding the FNCS, it is possible to determine the FRC in the case of trains. Opposite to the case of road vehicles, though, this force depends on the friction between the wheel flange and the rail, on wheel rolling, and on the radius of curvature. Based on tests performed by the American Railway Engineering Association on trans that currently operate in the United States, it is possible to adopt the rate of $4\,\text{N/t}.^{\text{o of curvature}}$ (Newton per ton × degree of curvature). This rate is applicable to vehicles equipped with three-axle bogies and standard gauge. It is also possible to estimate the FRC using Eq. (4.30), recommended by the Canadian National Railways.

$$T_{RC} = 0.279 \cdot RG \qquad (4.30)$$

where T_{RC} is the rate of resistance to curvature in $\text{N/t}.^{\text{o of curvature}}$; and RG is the rail gauge [m].

It is worth highlighting that the FRC observed when initiating the displacement in a train is around two times the value found with the train in motion.

When considering uniform movement in the direction of the displacement, Eqs. (4.14) and (4.15) may be used to determine the energy and the power needed to keep the train moving, using the same appropriate forms of determining the NFRM and FNCS. In the case of uniformly varied rectilinear motion, Eq. (4.16) may be employed to estimate the kinetic energy required to change speed.

Table 4.10 illustrates the usual ways of determining the NFRM for railway transportation.

4.4.1.2 Energy supply in railway transportation

As shown before, it is possible to correlate the power [*Pow*] needed to move a vehicle with the propulsive force [PF], at a speed [*v*], according to Eq. (4.1). Assuming that one wishes PF=FRM, it is possible to determine what energy supply is needed to meet the displacement need of a train.

TABLE 4.10 Usual ways of determining the NFRM—railway mode

Equations for the English metric system

Vehicle type	Equation	Terms
Locomotives	$NFRM = 1.3 \cdot P + 29 \cdot n + 0.030 \cdot P \cdot v + C_a \cdot A \cdot v^2$	NFRM [lbf] P [ton] n: number of axles v [mph] C_a: 0.0017–0.0024 A: 105–120 [ft^2]
Conventional freight car	$NFRM = 1.5 \cdot P + 18.5 \cdot n + B_3 \cdot P \cdot v + B_4 \cdot v^2$	$n = 4$ B_3: 0.015–0.045 B_4: 0.043–0.055
Passenger car	$NFRM = 1.3 \cdot P + 29 \cdot n + 0.030 \cdot P \cdot v + C_a \cdot A \cdot v^2$	$C_a = 0.00034$ A: 110–120 [ft^2] 70–110 [ft^2]
Road semitrailer over railway platform (piggy back)	$NFRM = 0.6 \cdot P + 20 \cdot n + 0.010 \cdot P \cdot v + 0.20 \cdot v^2$	

Equations for the international system

Vehicle type	Equation	Terms
Conventional freight car	$NFRM = 2.943 \cdot P + 88.977 \cdot n + 0.030 \cdot P \cdot v + g \cdot 0.0123 \cdot v^2$	NFRM [N] P [t] n: number of axles v [km/h] $g = 9.81$
Road semitrailer over railway platform (Piggy back)	$NFRM = 2.943 \cdot P + 88.977 \cdot n + 0.030 \cdot P \cdot v + g \cdot 0.028 \cdot v^2$	
Container car	$NFRM = 2.943 \cdot P + 88.977 \cdot n + 0.030 \cdot P \cdot v + g \cdot 0.0164 \cdot v^2$	
Conversion factors	1 ton = 0.907 t 1 lbf = 4.448 N 1 mph = 1.610 km/h ft. = 0.305 m	

Urban trains and subways for urban passenger transportation predominantly use the electric propulsion system, where coupling of the electric engines straight to the bogies of the railbuses or motor cars causes the composition to move. The same happens in the case of long-distance passenger trains, which have electric locomotives.

In the electric propulsion system, electric power is supplied directly to the vehicles via air networks (pantographs connected to the grid) or a third rail (electric power supply through mobile contact between the vehicle and a device

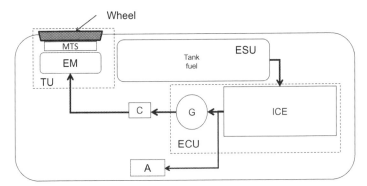

FIG. 4.13 Diesel-electric railway propulsion system. (Legend: EM—electric engine; C—controller; G—generator; ICE—internal combustion engine; TU—traction unit; ESU—energy storage unit; ECU—energy conversion unit; MTS—mechanical transmission system; A—load supplied to auxiliary organs.)

fixed between the rails of the permanent way). In these cases, the power available to meet the energy demand for the displacement is made available by the EM, subtracted from the losses associated with the MTS, usually a set of gears that couple the electric engine directly to the wheels.

Freight trains, in turn, predominantly use the diesel-electric propulsion system, as shown in Fig. 4.13.

The diesel-electric railway propulsion system is very similar to the series-HPS presented for the road mode. In this propulsion system, an ICE, usually of diesel cycle (ICE-CIE-4S), activates an electric generator (G) making up an ECU that generates electric power to activate the TU, which comprises an EM directly coupled to the traction bar or to the wheel.

The power available for railway displaced may, thus, have the following classification, according to the position it is measured.

1. Indicated power (Pow_I): the power at the locomotive's primary engine. In an electric locomotive or railbus, it is the power at the electric engines. In an ICE locomotive, it is the power supplied by the ICE. In the case of the diesel-electric locomotives, it is called gross power (Pow_B).
2. Effective power (Pot_E): it is the power at the wheels of the locomotive; it equals the Pow_I multiplied by the efficiency of the transmission system from the engine to the wheels. In the case of the diesel-electric locomotives, it will be the power delivered to the generator (Pow_G), considering the power supplied to the auxiliary organs (auxiliary generator, air compressor, brakes, blowers, fans, etc.) multiplied by the efficiency of the TU.
3. Useful power (Pow_U): it equals the Pow_E subtracted from the power needed to traction the locomotive itself, and it equals the net power needed to traction the cars.

Considering that in the diesel-electric propulsion system the ICE operates in a regime of best performance, efficiency is assumed to be around 28%–30%

Propulsion systems and energy use **Chapter | 4 161**

$(0.28 \leq \eta_{ICE} \leq 0.3)$. A small share of Pot_I (Pot_B), around 8%, is consumed in auxiliary organs at the electric generator ($\eta_{A/G} = 0.92$). The TU, in turn, has an efficiency of 85% ($\eta_{TU} = 0.85$). Assuming that Pot_E is the power needed at the wheels of the locomotive, railbus, or motor car to overcome the FRM, it is possible to determine Eq. (4.31).

$$Pow_I = Pow_B = \frac{FRM.v}{\eta_{TU}.\eta_{A/G}} \tag{4.31}$$

Energy consumption will be calculated using Eq. (4.32).

$$C_E = \frac{FRM.v}{\eta_{TU}.\eta_{A/G}.\eta_{ICE}} \tag{4.32}$$

Some more examples of application of the concepts presented in this chapter are presented below to help you stabilize this knowledge.

Example 4.9

Consider a train made of:

4 Diesel-electric locomotives, each weighing 136t, with 4 axles and cross-sectional area of 120 ft^2;

20 Empty freight cars, each weighing 30t and with 4 axles;

20 Loaded freight cars, with a payload of 40t and with 4 axles;

10 *Piggy-back* platform cars, each with 4 axles, carrying 2 empty road semitrailers, the full set weighing 47 t;

10 *Piggy-back* platform cars, each with 4 axles, carrying 2 full road semitrailers, the full set weighing 70t;

1 Passenger car at the end of the composition to accommodate the crew, with 4 axles and weighing 30t.

At a speed of 50 mph, traveling on a plane, what is the total resistance to motion of this train?

Using the equations in Table 4.10, for the English metric system, it is possible to calculate the NFRM for each component of the train. The sum of the resistances of each component will be the total resistance to motion.

For one locomotive:

$NFRM_{Loco} = 1.3 \cdot 136 + 29 \cdot 4 + 0.03 \cdot 136 \cdot 50 + 0.0024 \cdot 120 \cdot (50)^2 = 1216.8$ lb.

For four locomotives:

$NFRM_{4Loco} = 4 \cdot 1216.8 = 4867.2$ lb.

For one empty freight car:

$NFRM_{Empty\ car} = 1.5 \cdot 30 + 18.5 \cdot 4 + 0.015 \cdot 30 \cdot 50 + 0.055 \cdot (50)^2 = 279$ lb.

For 20 empty freight cars:

$NFRM_{20\ empty\ cars} = 20 \cdot 279 = 5580$ lb.

For one full freight car:

$NFRM_{full\ car} = 1.5 \cdot 70 + 18.5 \cdot 4 + 0.015 \cdot 70 \cdot 50 + 0.055 \cdot (50)^2 = 369$ lb.

For 20 full freight cars:

$NFRM_{20\ full\ cars} = 20 \cdot 369 = 7380$ lb.

For one empty *piggy-back*:
NFRM$_{empty\ piggy-back}$ = 0.6·47 + 20·4 + 0.010·47·50 + 0.20·(50)^2 = 631.7 lb.
For 10 empty *piggy-backs*:
NFRM$_{10\ empty\ piggy-backs}$ = 10·631.7 = 6317 lb.
For one full *piggy-back* car:
NFRM$_{full\ piggy-back}$ = 0.6·77 + 20·4 + 0.010·77·50 + 0.20·(50)^2 = 664.7 lb.
For 10 full *piggy-back* cars:
NFRM$_{10\ full\ piggy-backs}$ = 10·664.7 = 6647 lb.
For one passenger car:
NFRM$_{Passenger\ car}$ = 1.5·30 + 29·4 + 0.030·30 50 + 0.055·(50)^2 = 343.5 lb.
NFRM$_{Train}$ = 4867.2 + 5580 + 7380 + 6317 + 6647 + 343.5 = 31,134.7 lb.

Example 4.10

Calculate Pow_I and C_E for the same railway composition described in Example 4.9.

In this case, Pow_E, power at the wheels of the locomotive to overcome the NFRM, should be: Pow_E = 31,074.5·50/375 = 4143.27 hp.

Assuming η_{TU} = 0.85 e $\eta_{A/G}$ = 0.92, we find that.

Pot$_i$ = 4143.27/(0.85·0.92) = 5298.29 hp.

In this case, each of the four locomotives should have 5298.29/4 = 1324.57 hp. Since the power range of Brazilian locomotives is from 1500 to 3000 hp., this value does not seem to be exaggerated.

Energy consumption may be found assuming that η_{MCI} = 0.3.

C_E = 5298.29/0.3 = 17,660.96 hp.

C_E = 0.746·17,660.96 = 13,175.07 kW.

Thus, total energy consumption will be 13,169.81 kWh in 1 h of operation. Assuming that 1 kWh = 3.6 MJ and that 1 L of diesel oil has 38.31 MJ, it is possible to determine the consumption of diesel oil in 1 h of operation.

$C_{E(hour)}$ = 13,175.07·3.6/38.31 = 1230.06 L/h.

In this case, each of the four locomotives has a consumption of 309.51 L/h.

4.4.1.3 Railway nonconventional propulsion system

Traditionally, the railway propulsion system depends on wheel-rail contact to enable the vehicle's displacement. An alternative way of producing vehicle displacement that is being currently tested for passenger transportation is the magnetic levitation system or *Maglev*.

Magnetic levitation consists in forming a ferromagnetic surface under the edges and on the sides of T beam, usually made of reinforced concrete. Supports on the vehicle in the shape of arms, which have electromagnets, are attracted to the ferromagnetic surface with an approach controlled by optical sensors that place the train at about 10 mm of vertical and horizontal distance (Fig. 4.14). This configuration energizes the electromagnets and gives support to the composition. Since the support surrounds the T beam, and the train is wide enough, the configuration provides better stability than wheel-rail contact in the conventional system, which usually makes it harder for a *Maglev* train to derail.

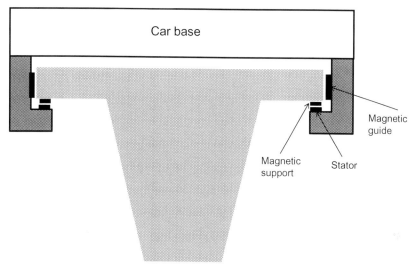

FIG. 4.14 Example of a *Maglev* propulsion system.

The operation of a *Maglev* train has many environmental advantages because it does not produce rolling resistance; it gets electric power via electromagnetic induction rather than by physical contact with an air network through a pantograph; it is powered by a linear motor without friction, which is capable of overcoming any ramp and is being supported on elevated ways. *Transrapid*, a system of trains with *Maglev* propulsion implemented in China in 2002, consumes 34 Wh/pass.km at 300 km/h. When compared to the consumption of German *Inter City Express* systems, with 51 kW/pass.km, the Chinese system results in an economy of 30%, even considering 1.7 kW consumed to levitate and guide each ton of the train. The main disadvantage of this technology is its implementation cost and the limitation regarding the weight that can be supported by the magnetic levitation system, when compared to conventional railway propulsion systems.

One can still consider that *Maglev* technology is evolving and undergoing improvements, such as electrodynamic levitation and superconductor levitation, the last one under development in Brazil at the Federal University of Rio de Janeiro. These technologies may even further improve the magnetic levitation propulsion system.

4.4.1.4 Improving energy use in railway transportation

Either due to the growing increase in energy cost or to further improve the environmental performance of the railway mode in relation to the road mode, we believe there will be incentives to increased energy efficiency of locomotives in the future. There are two key aspects regarding this topic: reducing the ARF in long compositions, making them able to travel at speeds of around 100 km/h, and reducing the mass of the railway composition (locomotives and cars) without losing load capacity and traffic safety.

164 Transportation, energy use and environmental impacts

The ARF may be reduced by adjusting locomotive and car designs, adopting a body that has no sharp tips and edges and reducing protrusions. This practice, however, also has improvement opportunities that do not require the replacement of the rolling stock. It is possible to, for example, minimize the distance between the cars, install a cover on open cars, in the case of bulk products transportation (minerals and cereals), or optimize the loading of cars, reducing the space between the containers in the case of intermodal freight transportation.

In the case of mass reduction, the replacement of steel, usually used in the manufacturing of locomotives and cars, with other materials such as aluminum and composite materials allow the reduction of the composition's mass, reducing energy consumption and increasing transported payload, which leads to an improvement in energy efficiency in the set. However, there are two main challenges to mass reduction measures: safety and the current costs of alternative materials to steel. Despite the expected increase in transported payload, the use of alternative materials may impact the cars' capacity of withstanding elevated loads and, eventually, reduce safety in transportation.

In addition to train manufacturing issues, the replacement of mechanical control equipment in the rolling stock with electronic ones may also help further reduce weight.

Although they operate in different regimes, the research being conducted to improve energy performance in diesel oil engines that power road vehicles may be adapted to engines used in railway transportation, reaching efficiency improvements of up to 10% (McKinnon et al., 2010).

Locomotives that have diesel-electric propulsion systems may be equipped with a battery pack and operate in a way similar to that of a road vehicle equipped with a serial hybrid-electric propulsion system. This configuration may recover part of the kinetic energy wasted during the braking process, accumulating it in the battery pack. Moreover, locomotives equipped with hybrid-electric propulsion systems may operate the generator group at an optimal rotation, maximizing efficiency in electric power generation and, thus, reducing fuel consumption.

Besides the possibility presented by hybrid-electric propulsion systems for locomotives, the incorporation of other systems that allow the recovery of kinetic energy for later use is also seen in electric trains. Currently, there are solutions already available that are based on energy storage via mechanical EAs, such as flywheels, the supercapacitors for fast recovery, and discharge of electric power (McKinnon et al., 2010). Besides, the development of new engine control technology based on power electronics has generated additional improvement opportunities.

Where railway systems powered by diesel-electric locomotives predominate for freight transportation, there is a possibility of making investments in its electrification. The electrification of railways represents a unique opportunity of evolving from segmented (disconnected) supply chain configurations and the use of fossil fuels in ICEs with low energy efficiency (from 25% to

Propulsion systems and energy use **Chapter | 4** **165**

40%) to integrated systems of decentralized generation, transfer, distribution, and use of electric energy supplying electric engines of high efficiency (80%). The efficiency values adopted in this case are maximum efficiency in energy generation and minimum loss possible in final use. The main limitation for the electrification of railway networks is the availability of resources for the initial investments, which may be costly.

On the other hand, when electrification is not viable, there should be continued investments in improving engines that use fuels that cause less atmospheric pollutant emissions, such as diesel oil with low levels of sulfur and biofuels, such as biodiesel, which will be presented in Chapter 5.

4.4.2 Water mode

The study of the forces involved in the movement of vessels is beyond the scope of this book, however, an introduction about the NFRM and the determination of the PF in the case of vessels may be presented just as was done for land transportation modes.

4.4.2.1 Energy demand in water transportation

The most important NFRM that have to be overcome by vessels are: (1) surface friction force (SFF), which is the friction caused by calm water on the hull's wet surface in the form of laminar flow; (2) hydrodynamic drag (force of resistance to motion created from the contact of water with the vessel's hull); (3) resistance to turbulent flow; and (4) wave resistance. Usually, these resistances are measured with calm waters, constant speed, and no wind. Additionally, it is also necessary to take into consideration aerodynamic resistance—found using $ARF = C_a \cdot A \cdot v^2$—caused by the portion of the vessel that remains above the water. Despite that, the low speed and the aerodynamic shape of the vessels keep the ARF from being excessive, with the SFF being responsible for 50%–85% of the FRM. The SFF may be estimated using Eq. (4.33).

$$SFF = f.15,6\sqrt{D.L.v^{1.83}} \qquad (4.33)$$

where SFF [lbf], f=0.01 – hulls of 20 ft., 0.0085 – hulls of 600 ft., D is the displacement [ton], L is the length [ft], and v is the speed [knot = 6080 ft./h].

Except for the ARF, the remaining NFRM, referred to as forces of residual resistance (FRR), may be estimated using Taylor's formula, Eq. (4.34).

$$FRR = 12.5.\beta.D.\left(\frac{v}{\sqrt{L}}\right)^4 \qquad (4.34)$$

where FRR [lbf], $\beta = V/L \cdot B \cdot t$ [block coefficient], V= volume of displaced water; L=length; B=mouth; t=draught, D: displacement [ton], and v: speed [knot = 6080 ft./h].

166 Transportation, energy use and environmental impacts

The total of the NFRM will be given by the sum: FNRM = SFF + FRR + ARF. Summing these forces and dividing them by the displacement, it is possible to find Eq. (4.35), which estimates the NFRM in function of the vessel's displacement.

$$\text{NFRM}(D) = \frac{f.15.6.\sqrt{D.L}.v^{1.83} + C_a.A.v^2}{D} + 12.5.\beta.\frac{v^4}{L^2} \tag{4.35}$$

where A [ft^2], and $C_a = 0.002$.

4.4.2.2 Energy supply for water mode

The PF that powers the vessels is given by the thrust (E) generated by the propeller and the power that must be supplied by the propeller to overcome the FRM, it is also called effective power (Pow_E).

The capacity of generating thrust by means of a propeller depends on a series of complex factors that involve, for example, the configuration, position, and flow of the fluid surrounding the blades of the propeller and the formation of air pockets between the blades and the fluid, which is called cavitation. The study of this system is far beyond the scope of this book, so a reasonable estimate considers that an efficiency of 50% is acceptable ($\eta_P = 0.50$).

Additionally, the coupling of the ECU (engine) to the propeller is, usually, made through an MTS (axle), whose efficiency is within the range of 92%–95% ($0.92 \leq \eta_{MTS} \leq 0.95$). Therefore, the power to be supplied by the ECU may be estimated using Eq. (4.36) and energy consumption using Eq. (4.37).

$$Pow_{ECU} = \frac{E.v}{\eta_P.\eta_{MTS}} \tag{4.36}$$

$$C_E = \frac{E.v}{\eta_P.\eta_{MTS}.\eta_{ECU}} \tag{4.37}$$

Once again, examples of application of the concepts presented in this section are presented below.

Example 4.11

A general freight ship has displacement of 50,000 t, length of 600 ft., front area of 1000 ft^2, block coefficient of 0.7, and travels at 12 knots. Calculate the NFRM considering the displacement.

In this case, the following applies:

$$\text{NFRM}(D) = \frac{f.15.6\sqrt{D.L}.v^{1.83} + C_a.A.v^2}{D} + 12.5\beta.\frac{v^4}{L^2}$$

NFRM(D) = $(0.0085 \cdot 15.6 \ (50{,}000 \cdot 600)^{1/2} \cdot 12^{1.83} + 0.002 \cdot 1000 \cdot 12^2)/50{,}000 + 12.5 \cdot 0.7 \cdot (12^4/600^2) = (68{,}549.73 + 288)/50{,}000 + 0.504 = 1.38 + 0.504 = 1.88$ lbf/ton.

Propulsion systems and energy use Chapter | 4 **167**

Example 4.12

What is the power required to move the vessel described in the previous exercise?
$Pow_{ECU} = E \cdot v / \eta_P \cdot \eta_{MTS}$.
Assuming that thrust (E) should equal the NFRM, we find that.
$Pow_{ECU} = (1.88 \cdot 50,000 \cdot 12 \cdot 6080/3600)/(0.95 \cdot 0.5) = 4,010,667$ lbf ft./s.
$Pow_{ECU} = 4,010,667 \cdot 0.0018 = 721,920$ hp.

4.4.2.3 Improving energy use in water transportation

In general, vessels have very efficient architecture and propulsion systems in terms of energy use when compared to road transportation and even railway transportation. Even so, its performance may be improved by means of interventions regarding the improvement in vessel design focusing on energy efficiency, the development of alternative technologies for the main propulsion system or for the auxiliary energy generation systems, and the replacement of fossil fuels with other energy sources.

Vessel design improvements that lead to the improvement in their architecture to reduce hydrodynamic and ARFs acting on the vessels may reduce up to 25% energy consumption in deep-sea and cabotage maritime transportation (McKinnon et al., 2010).

The improvement in vessel architecture must be considered during the design process, since it involves basic assumptions such as speed, form of displacement, and hull design. For that, it is possible to: taper and elongate the bow and install a lateral appendix; install a stern flap (a relatively small plate that extends the rear part of a ship); use a flap rudder or a stern flat; reduce the roughness of the ship's hull (through constant cleaning to remove fouling); and installing antifouling films.

Currently, vessels are mostly propelled by compression ignition engines. Improving the thermal efficiency of these engines, the coupling systems, and propeller design may increase the energy efficiency of vessels from 2% to 15% (McKinnon et al., 2010; Singh and Pedersen, 2016).

Regarding the state of the propellers, their surface condition influences energy consumption, leading to the need of reducing fouling and roughness (through the constant polishing of the blades), using contra-rotating propellers and propellers combined with a rudder, performing advanced selection of propellers, and using a nozzle with hydrodynamic profile surrounding the propeller.

The use of POD propulsion (Azipod) has been increasingly adopted when allowed by the vessel's type of operation. Its main advantages are the expansion of useful space in the hull due to the absence of conventional propellers and its coupling system, improved maneuverability capacity, better reversion capacity during navigation, better response in case of deceleration, and low levels of noise and vibration.

One growing way of improving energy efficiency in propulsion systems is the use of the hybrid-electric system, in which a compression ignition

168 Transportation, energy use and environmental impacts

engine powers a generator that, in turn, powers electric engines that move the propellers. Besides allowing the ICE to operate at its point of best energy efficiency, the advantages of this system are its capacity to respond to sudden changes, the possibility of speed control, and the low levels of noise and vibration.

The adoption of the hybrid-electric propulsion system results in an improvement of 14% in energy efficiency and a proportional reduction in the emission of CO_2 and other atmospheric pollutants such as NO_x and SO_x in bulk carrier ships, which corresponds to 1.8% of the world fleet's emissions (Dedes et al., 2012).

The use and progressive improvement in energy recovery systems, which involve the better efficiency of turbo compressors, the use of power turbines, steam turbines and combined turbines (steam and gas), and the development of engine exhaust heat recovery systems, before they are released into the atmosphere, may increase the energy efficiency of vessels from 5% to 10% (Attah and Bucknall, 2015).

Replacing compression ignition engines with turbines, which can use fuels other than diesel oil (such as natural gas), allows the achievement of high power in relation to its weight and volume, low levels of noise and vibration, low emissions of NO_x and SO_x (compared to compression ignition engines), easy installation automation, and fast start and deceleration.

Auxiliary systems may take advantage of the wind to generate a supplementary PF or to feed auxiliary power generation systems. In this case, it is possible to use rigid sails, airfoils, *flettner* rotors, wind turbines, and kite sails. Therefore, it can be said that the installation of four *flettner* rotors (height of 27 m and diameter of 4 m) on a freight ship for maritime transportation, traveling at an average speed of 16 knots, may reduce fuel consumption by 30% and 40%. The installation of kite sails between 100 and 200 m high and the installation of airfoils may reduce fuel consumption up to 30% and 15%, respectively (Leloup et al., 2016).

Another possibility is to explore sunlight through photovoltaic cells. The installation of solar panels on top of a freight ship, depending on the area available, may reduce up to 20% fuel consumption for auxiliary equipment in the vessel (McKinnon et al., 2010).

Besides using wind and sunlight, which may be converted into electric power, alternative energy sources other than fossil fuels may be used in ships aiming to minimize the emission of CO_2 and atmospheric pollutants. In this context, natural gas stands out, either in dedicated engines or in a dual-fuel system (diesel-gas); biofuels, such as ethanol, biodiesel, and bio-oil; and nuclear energy. Some of these solutions are presented in Chapter 5.

Improving the energy efficiency of vessel propulsion systems, reducing the consumption of fossil fuels using electric power generated by the wind or by sunlight, or replacing fuel oil and/or diesel oil with other energy sources collaborate to minimize the emission of greenhouse gases and atmospheric pollutants,

Propulsion systems and energy use **Chapter | 4 169**

especially sulfur oxides (SO_x) and nitrogen oxides (NO_x), the main atmospheric pollutants associated with water transportation.

Because it uses fossil fuels of a lower quality (with a higher level of impurities, especially sulfur) than the ones used in road and railway transportation, water transportation is one of the contributors to the emission of sulfur oxides (SO_x). For that reason, the International Maritime Organization (IMO) has currently limited the mass percentage of sulfur in fuel oil to 4.5%, a value that must drop to 1.5% by 2020.

Reducing the level of sulfur in the fuel oil will also support the progressive reduction in nitrogen oxides (NO_x) emissions, since it enables the installation of SCR catalytic converters on engine exhaust systems.

Another action that may be taken to reduce atmospheric pollutant emissions by vessels when they are operating at ports is supplying them with electric power. This is being done at Long Beach port, California, with a reduction in the concentration of SO_x, NO_x, and PM.

4.4.3 Pipeline mode

As presented in Chapter 1, in conventional pipeline transportation, the PF is applied directly to the material being transported so that it may overcome the FRM, as discussed below.

4.4.3.1 Energy demand in pipeline transportation

Pumping pressures and resistance to flow in pipelines may be treated in the same way as FRM. Resistance to flow mainly consists of: (1) resistance due to friction between the liquid and pipe walls, which depends on roughness and diameter, and on the number and type of gaskets and connections; (2) resistance of the fluid itself, which is related to its viscosity and temperature; and (3) type of fluid flow within the pipe, which may be laminar or turbulent.

A practical and commonly used way of determining pressure drop in pipe through which passes laminar flow is described in Eq. (4.38).

$$P = \frac{962,000.Q.\mu}{d^4} \tag{4.38}$$

where P is the pressure drop [lbf/ft^2]; Q is the flow [ft^3/s]; μ is the absolute viscosity [ft.lb.s]; and d is the pipe diameter [pol].

In the case of turbulent flow, Eq. (4.39) is used.

$$P = \frac{229,610.f.Q.\rho}{d^5} \tag{4.39}$$

where P is the pressure drop per mile [lbf/ft^2];
f is the friction coefficient—tabulated;
Q is the flow [ft^3/s]; and ρ is the density [lb/ft^3].

170 Transportation, energy use and environmental impacts

4.4.3.2 Energy supply in pipeline transportation

The power required (Pow_E) to move the fluid and overcome pressure drop will be given by Eq. (4.40).

$$Pow_E = P.Q \tag{4.40}$$

Usually, centrifugal pumps are used to pump liquid; these pumps are powered by EMs. Thus, the power demanded from the EMs will be given by Eq. (4.41) and energy use by Eq. (4.42).

$$Pow_{EM} = \frac{P.Q}{\eta_{PUMP}} \tag{4.41}$$

$$C_E = \frac{P.Q}{\eta_{PUMP}.\eta_{EM}} \tag{4.42}$$

The following example will help the reader stabilize the knowledge presented in this section.

Example 4.13

What is the power needed to pump $5000\,ft^3/h$ of petroleum with absolute viscosity of 0.876 through a pipe of 10 pol over a distance of 30 miles? Assume laminar flow.

The application of $P = \dfrac{962,000.Q.\mu}{d^4}$ results in.

$P = (962,000 \cdot 5000/3600 \cdot 0.876)/(10)^4 = 1,170,433.33/10,000,000 = 117.04$ lbf/pol² mile.

$P_{30\,miles} = 117.04\ 0.30 = 3511.3$ lbf/pol².

$Pow_E = (P_{30\,miles} \cdot Q)/\eta_{PUMP} = (3511.3 \cdot 144 \cdot 5000/3600)/0.9 = 702,260/0.9 = 780,288.89$ lbf.ft./s.

$Pot_E = 780,288.89 \cdot 0.0018 = 1418.87$ hp.

4.4.3.3 Nonconventional pipeline transportation methods

The transportation proposal called Hyperloop considers the use of capsules traveling within tubes and being able to reach a speed of up to 1200 km/h. The transportation of capsules within tubes is not a new idea when considering small-scale networks restricted to industrial facilities. However, a proposal for long-distance pipeline transportation was launched in 2013 aiming to shorten trip times and reduce the environmental impacts of people and freight transportation.

This system consists of pipes supported by pillars above the ground. Aerodynamic capsules are inserted into the pipes; these capsules are made of light and resistant materials, and are used to carry passengers, freight, or both. The air inside the pipes is partially evacuated, allowing the capsules to move

Propulsion systems and energy use **Chapter | 4 171**

under the influence of low ARF. This enables the capsules to reach high speeds without consuming much energy, so that the magnetic induction propulsion system that would power the Hyperloop could be powered by solar panels.

This proposal is still in the phase of implementing a prototype that will be evaluated regarding its functionality, operability, and safety. There is still no definition of implementation and operation costs or load capacity.

4.4.4 Air mode

As with the water mode, the study of the forces involved in the displacement of aircraft is far beyond the scope of this book. Thus, a greatly simplified approach will be presented.

4.4.4.1 Energy demand in air transportation

The FRM involved in the displacement of aircraft are usually known as drag. During a flight, there are no RRF due to the contact with the ground or bearings. In this book, our approach will only be to consider the case of aircraft that are heavier than the air, have fixed wings (airplane), and flying at cruise speed, which is the flight speed established as the one that considers the highest operational efficiency.

From fluid mechanics, Eq. (4.43) describes the resistance of a fluid to the passage of a body.

$$\text{FR} = C_A \cdot \left(\frac{\rho}{2} \right) . S . v^2 \tag{4.43}$$

where FR is the force of resistance; C_A is the drag coefficient, which depends on the shape of a body and incorporates resistance in function of either laminar or turbulent flow; ρ is the air density, which depends on the altitude; S is the surface of the wings; and v is the speed of the body.

This equation is similar to the one used to determine lift force (LF), except for the C_A coefficient. Both equations, for FR and LF, are components of the decomposition, in sine and cosine, respectively, of the total force acting upon a wing or airfoil of an aircraft.

Drag comprises two elements: (1) parasitic drag, caused by frontal air pressure and its friction with the parts of an aircraft; and (2) induced drag, which is inherent to the production of an aircraft's lift and due, mainly, to the turbulence caused at the trailing edges of wings. Therefore, it is possible to decompose C_A into C_{Ap} and C_{Ai}, which are, respectively, the coefficients of parasitic and induced drag, respectively. The values of these coefficients vary according to the shape of the airfoil (shape of the wing) and are determined in a wind tunnel.

The C_{Ap} coefficient is determined by the configuration of the aircraft, and depends on the cross section of the wings, fuselage, tail, and engine compartments.

172 Transportation, energy use and environmental impacts

The C_{Ai} coefficient depends only on the aircraft's wingspan; an increase in the wingspan decreases induced drag.

As could be seen in Eq. (4.43), FR increases with squared speed, but decreases with altitude, once air density decreases. A reduction in the wingspan reduces parasitic drag but, on the other hand, reduces lift. Therefore, an aircraft designer must determine whether the most desirable feature is high speed or load capacity at moderate speeds, for a given thrust and power.

In summary, the gross load capacity of an aircraft in level flight, without wind, at constant speed and at an altitude depends on: (1) speed; (2) air density, which is factor of altitude; (3) drag, which depends on wingspan and wing's angle of attack; and (4) engine capacity. Drag divided by the gross load capacity determines the aircraft's unit resistance.

4.4.4.2 Energy supply in air transportation

The power needed (Pow_E) to move an aircraft may be given by Eq. (4.44).

$$Pow_E = E.v \qquad (4.44)$$

where E is the thrust; and v is the speed.

Replacing thrust with drag enables the definition of the power needed to win the FRM. At level flight, drag and thrust must be at least the same, to maintain a constant speed. Naturally, the engine's power must be determined based on Pow_E and the efficiency of this device, and it varies depending on whether the aircraft is powered by propellers or turbo reactors.

The example below helps stabilize the knowledge presented in this section.

Example 4.14

A plane flies at a constant speed v at an altitude of 1000 and 6000 m. Knowing that air density decreases by around 50% for this height difference, estimate the power that must be considered to maintain the same speed.

The following is applied: $Pow_E = FR.v = C_A \cdot (\rho/2) \cdot S \cdot v^2 \cdot v = C_A \cdot (\rho/2) \cdot S \cdot v^3$.

$Pow_{E1000} = C_A \cdot (\rho_{1000}/2) \cdot S \cdot v^3$ – at 1000 m.

$Pow_{E6000} = C_A \cdot (\rho_{6000}/2) \cdot S \cdot v^3$ – at 6000 m.

But it is known that $\rho_{6000} = \frac{1}{2} \rho_{1000}$ – replacing in Pow_{E6000}.

$Pow_{E6000} = C_A \cdot (\rho_{1000}/4) \cdot S \cdot v^3 = \frac{1}{2} C_A \cdot (\rho_{1000}/2) \cdot S \cdot v^3 = \frac{1}{2} Pot_{E1000}$.

At 1000 m, half the power needed to keep the aircraft at constant speed at 6000 m would be enough.

4.4.4.3 Improving energy use in air transportation

As previously mentioned, the air mode is the highest consumer of energy among the modes of passenger or freight transportation. Nevertheless, the current configuration of aircraft considers a series of aspects aiming at the improvement in their environmental performance considering that, in 40 years, the energy efficiency of commercial aircraft improved by 70% and, in 20 years, noise emissions decreased by around 75% (ICAO, 2007).

Even so, there is still potential to further improve aircraft environmental performance in the next 40 years. However, due to the characteristics of the aeronautical industry, the cycle of development, implementation, and diffusion of new technologies with this purpose may take >50 years (Airbus, 2008).

Some ways of improving environmental performance in aircraft, especially regarding energy use, are the improvement in aircraft design and their propulsion systems, the optimization of the air traffic management system, the increase in their load capacity, and the use of alternative energy sources.

According to studies by the Committee on Climate Change (2008), improving the design of commercial aircraft could lead to an increase in their energy efficiency between 20% and 30% from 2006 to 2025. This would happen through the following measures: use of a growing percentage of composite materials lighter than duralumin in the aircraft's structure; improvement in the aerodynamic profile of the fuselage, which may reduce fuel consumption by up to 20%; substitution of hydraulic flight control systems for lighter electronic systems (fly-by-wire); and the installation of winglets at the tips of the wings, with the potential of improving aircraft energy efficiency by 4%–6%.

Regarding the improvement in the propulsion system, an improvement of 15%–25% in engine efficiency may be achieved from 2006 to 2025 (Committee on Climate Change, 2008).

The optimization of air traffic management involves both in-flight aircraft route control and its operation on the ground. It is estimated that savings of 10%–15% in energy consumption may be achieved by: (1) reducing the operation time of aircraft on the ground and in the air, (2) through the optimization of landing and takeoff procedures, and (3) the optimization of air routes and flight profiles (ACARE, 2008).

Regarding the increase in freight capacity, efforts are being made to increase up to 50% the capacity of freight compartments in passenger aircraft, and up to 20% the capacity of freight airplanes until 2026 (Hanson and Guiliano, 2004; Airbus, 2008).

Although it is likely that aviation kerosene will be the predominant fuel for air transportation in the next decades, as a way of reducing CO_2 emissions in its final use, there already are initiatives aiming to use biokerosene in turbines and ethanol in reciprocating ICEs. This will be covered in Chapter 5.

The efforts toward reducing fuel consumption in air transportation are directly related to the reduction in GHG emissions in final use. Two other environmental impacts related to this mode of transportation are the emission of nitrogen oxide (NO_x) and aircraft noise. Thanks to the application of technological improvements in engines and to air transportation operation management, in 15 years the emissions of NO_x were reduced by 50% and the exposure of the population to aircraft noise decreased by 35%.

174 Transportation, energy use and environmental impacts

Example 4.15

The new paradigm shift in air transportation—electric airplanes, unmanned aerial vehicles (UAVs), and airships.

The path to arrive at the first totally electric airplanes started in the 1950s and continued until today resulting in few small and light aircraft models with potential for serial production. These vehicles use electric power that may be supplied by the sun (photovoltaic), FCs, or batteries. Even with limitations regarding energy storage due to the weight of the batteries, totally electric aviation seems to be a technically viable alternative in the future when ultralight and highly resistant materials, such as composite materials, may enable the design of lighter aircraft that will demand lower energy intensity to be propelled. It is estimated that when batteries can produce 400Wh/kg, with a power-to-weight ratio between 0.7 and 0.8, transcontinental electric airplanes will be economically viable.

The use of electric power in air transportation seems to be a closer reality in the case of UAVs. Small autonomous aircraft with 4, 6, or 8 rotors distributed in quadrangular, hexagonal, or octagonal shape and powered by EMs have been developed to deliver small packages in rural areas and to provide services such as surveillance and monitoring of operations. There are innovative projects that propose the use of UAV for urban delivery individually or complementing the operation of other modes of transportation. It is also possible to transport passengers, in projects of air taxis, which may be manned or not.

The use of aircraft that are lighter than air, such as airships, is also an alternative for air transportation. This kind of equipment is particularly useful in remote areas of difficult access, such as the region of the Amazon Rainforest. These aircraft are capable of carrying up to 100t of freight and flying at over 100km/h with higher energy efficiency than commercial planes, since their lift does not depend on speed; they may perform freight transportation from a point of origin to a point of destination without the need for big areas to take off and land.

4.5 Final considerations

This chapter addressed, in summary, how it is possible to determine the FRM for the different modes of transportation. It was shown that the FRM may be divided into NFRM and FNCS.

For the land, road, and railway modes, the NFRM are subdivided into RRF and ARFs. The former depends on the vehicle's total weight and its type of support (tire-road or wheel-rail). The latter are determined in a similar way and depend on the vehicle's configuration, air density, and the speed of movement.

For the water mode, the main NFRM is the SFF between the fluid (water) and the vessel's hull.

In the case of pipeline transportation, restrictions to the pumping of a fluid result from physical characteristics of pipes, such as their diameter and roughness, and from characteristics of the fluid, such as viscosity.

For air transportaion, considering the scope limitations of this book, it was shown that drag is responsible for resistance to motion in aircraft.

Propulsion systems and energy use **Chapter | 4 175**

Regardless of the mode of transportation, the power needed to overcome the FRM is the one that produces a PF that at least cancels the FRM. However, for such a power to be generated at the place of action of the FRM, the efficiency of the components that make up a propulsion system must be considered.

The chapter also presented nonconventional propulsion systems for the road and railway modes, especially for the former, and described the electric propulsion system, whose use has sharply increased in the last years, and the hybrid system. For the air mode, in addition to the ways of improving energy use and potential impacts of atmospheric pollutant emissions, the chapter presented a nonconventional energy source, electric power, that may equip small passenger or service aircraft and UAVs, which, along with airships, are nonconventional methods of air transportation. A nonconventional method of transportation was also shown for pipeline transportation: the Hyperloop.

4.6 Exercises

1. Which forces act on a moving vehicle? Explain it.
2. What is a propulsion system? Explain its function and indicate its basic components.
3. For the conversion and transmission of energy in a vehicle, the energy stored is not fully supplied to the vehicle due to losses in the system. What actions should we take to reduce losses in energy supply?
4. Regarding energy demand, what actions should we take to reduce losses?
5. Make a diagram of a conventional propulsion system, indicating its main components.
6. What are the types of reciprocating internal combustion engine (ICE)? What is the difference between them?
7. Make a diagram of an electric propulsion system, indicating its main components.
8. What are the advantages of a fuel cell propulsion system and what makes it different from the electric propulsion system?
9. What are the possible fuels that may be used in a fuel cell electric propulsion system? What are its advantages and disadvantages?
10. Define the main elements of a hybrid-electric propulsion system and differentiate the series hybrid from the parallel hybrid by making a diagram.
11. Determine the difference in ARF between a passenger car and a simple truck traveling, both, at 100 km/h. Assume that the cross section of the passenger car is 3 m^2 and that of the simple truck is 10 m^2. Choose C_a and ρ at your convenience.
12. Determine the rolling resistance of a passenger car that weighs 1 t and is traveling along a plane, on excellent quality asphalt pavement, at 100 km/h.
13. Determine the RRF of a train made of conventional freight cars traveling at 30 km/h on a plain and straight segment of the way, considering that the load per axle is 18 t and the train has 16 cars of 4 axles each.

176 Transportation, energy use and environmental impacts

14. A simple truck with three axles is traveling along an interstate highway at 80 km/h and is approaching a horizontal curve with a radius of 280 m. Determine the FRC that acts on the truck while it makes the curve. The weight at each axle is 2300 t.

15. Calculate the power needed to operate a train of 16 cars that makes a curve of 2° at 50 km/h on a plain segment of the way. The load per axle is 20 t and the train has 64 axles, including the electric locomotive.

16. A passenger car of 1300 kg is traveling at 90 km/h at a plain segment of the way when it makes a horizontal curve with a radius of 300 m. If the vehicle's cross section is 3 m^2 and it receives frontal wind at the opposite direction at a speed of 30 km/h, determine the power needed to overcome the NFRM.

References

Airbus, 2008. Flying by Nature: Global Market Forecast 2007–2026. Airbus, Paris.

Attah, E.E., Bucknall, R., 2015. An analysis of the energy efficiency of LNG ships powering options using the EEDI. Ocean Eng. 110, 62–74.

Committee on Climate Change, 2008. Building a Low Carbon Economy Part III. Committee on Climate Change, London.

Dedes, E.K., Hudson, D.A., Turnock, S.R., 2012. Assessing the potential of hybrid energy technology to reduce exhaust emissions from global shipping. Energy Policy 40, 204–218.

Hanson, S., Guiliano, G., 2004. The Geography of Urban Transport, third ed. Guilford Press, London.

ICAO, 2007. ICAO Environmental Report 2007. ICAO. Mont.

Leloup, R., Roncin, M., Bles, G., Leroux, J.B., Jochum, C., Parlier, Y., 2016. A continuous and analytical modeling for kites as auxiliary propulsion devoted to merchant ships, including fuel saving estimation. Renew. Energy 86, 483–496.

McKinnon, A., Cullinane, S., Browne, M., Whiteing, A., 2010. Green Logistics—Improving the Environmental Sustainability of Logistics. Editado por Kolgan Page. Reino Unido.

Riley, R.Q., 1994. Alternative Cars in the 21st Century. A new Personal Transportation Paradigm. Warrendale, Society of Automotive Engineers, Inc.

Ristinen, R.A., Kraushaar, J.J., 1999. Energy and the Environment. John Willey & Sons, Inc.

Singh, D.V., Pedersen, E., 2016. A review of waste heat recovery technologies for maritime applications. Energy Convers. Manag. 111, 315–328.

Wiser, W.H., 2000. Energy Resources. Occurrence, Production, Conversion and Use. Springer, Nova York.

Wright, K., 1990. The shape of things to go. Automakers turn to high technology in the search for car that is clean, safe and fun. Sci. Am. 262 (5), 58–67.

Further reading

IEA, 2018. Global EV Outlook. International Energy Agency, Paris, France, p. 2018. Towards cross-modal electrification.

Chapter 5

Energy sources for transportation

General goal

The general goal of this chapter is to present energy sources for transportation, identifying both those considered to be, up to the present date, conventional energy sources and those considered alternative sources.

The chapter also presents a summary of the reasons that led both to the adoption of petroleum derivatives as conventional energy sources for transportation and to the spread of internal combustion engines (ICEs) as the main element of propulsion systems in vehicles. The arguments reinforce the interrelationship between the energy source and propulsion systems.

The concepts of conventional energy sources and alternative energy sources for transportation are presented before detailing the options, to highlight their meaning and clarify their dependence on the application reality in different places of the world.

At the end of this chapter, the reader should be able to:

1. Know the conventional and alternative energy sources used in transportation.
2. Know the production chains of a selection of energy sources used in transportation worldwide.
3. Analyze the aspects associated with the use of alternative energy sources in transportation and the mitigation of environmental impacts.
4. Know a set of alternative energy sources that are under development and have potential application for transportation in the future.

5.1 Introduction

In the 17th century, the Industrial Revolution brought great progress in the control of energy from the burning of fuels, mainly coal, in steam-powered machines. These machines, initially, were only used industrially and, in the case of transportation, for railway and vessel traction, mainly due to their high weight-to-power ratio and because they required the storage of a great volume of fuel.

Only after the emergence of the ICE in the mid-1860s, created by French inventor Jean-Joseph-Étienne Lenoir, it was proven that it was possible to create a machine capable of using an easy-storage fuel with great energy potential, when compared to the sources available at the time. This engine was initially powered by lighting gas and, later, adapted to the use of crude oil, but with a

Transportation, Energy Use and Environmental Impacts. https://doi.org/10.1016/B978-0-12-813454-2.00005-2
© 2019, Elsevier Editora Ltda. Published by Elsevier Inc. All rights reserved.

177

limited power of 3 hp. (horsepower). Another French inventor, Beau de Rochas, was responsible for improving Lenoir's engine and creating the four-stroke (4S) ICE, similar to the modern engine. However, the application of this invention was spread by a German inventor named Nikolaus August Otto, who patented what was called the spark-ignition (SI) 4S reciprocating ICE in 1876, which became known as Otto cycle engine.

The development of the ICE was followed by the use of gasoline as fuel, with continual improvements being added to its operation with time. These improvements only reinforced the fundamental quality of this invention to produce, with little machine and fuel weight, much more useful power than what was produced by a steam engine of similar dimensions. By winning the great Paris-Bordeaux-Paris race, in 1895, the car created by *Panhard & Levassor* showed this property, enabling the birth and progress of road transportation.

Parallel to these events, another German inventor, Rudolphe C.K. Diesel, developed and patented, in 1895, the engine that would be universally used in heavy road vehicles, locomotives, and vessels. It was the compression-ignition reciprocating ICE, which came to be used predominantly as a fuel a petroleum derivative named after the creator of the engine: diesel oil.

Despite these inventions, at the turn of the 19th century, the United States, which became the birthplace of the world car industry, had only 22% of its car fleet running on gasoline. The remainder of the fleet was split between steam-powered vehicles (40%) and electricity-powered vehicles (38%) (Wright, 1990). The high percentage of vehicles running on electric power is surprising; this source was almost entirely replaced by petroleum in the following years and now is being reconsidered due to issues of energy security and environmental impacts.

In 1901, the discovery of a vast petroleum reserve in Beaumont, Texas, placed gasoline-powered cars and the United States at a leading position in the world car industry. The great availability of gasoline, a subproduct of the refinement of petroleum, whose main derivative at the time was lighting kerosene, at a low price was surely one of the main factors that promoted the subsequent success of ICEs for road vehicles.

Both steam vehicles and electric vehicles had characteristics that pleased users at the time, such as little noise and good handling. However, besides the low price of gasoline, some limitations, such as delayed start, operational complexity (steam propulsion), and low autonomy (electric propulsion) also collaborated to the spread of ICEs). With the creation of the electric start engine, ICEs reached a combination of economy, autonomy, and ease of operation that the remaining alternatives could not reach at the time, thus ICEs dominated the market. The subsequent technological development resulted in durable and reliable equipment.

In parallel, due to its characteristics of compactness, robustness, and its ability to generate high starting torque and high power at low rotations, the compression-ignition ICEs, which used heavier petroleum derivatives than

Energy sources for transportation **Chapter | 5** **179**

gasoline as their main energy sources, such as diesel oil and fuel oil, started to progressively substitute steam engines in power generation for heavy road vehicles (trucks and tractors), locomotives, and small vessels. This substitution became more intense after World War II and, currently, the diesel-cycle engine is the predominant choice when powering buses, trucks, locomotives, and vessels of different sizes. There are exceptions such as metropolitan railway transportation systems (urban trains and subways) and high-speed trains (interurban long-distance trains), which widely use electric power, and the use of different types of turbines to power large vessels (ships).

The characteristics of compactness with the possibility of producing high power at high rotations caused the ICE of large volumetric capacity and SI, such as Otto-cycle engines, to become the only choice when equipping aircraft since their invention, in the first decade of the 20th century, until the mid-1950s, when commercial turbines and reactors started to be used. The latter, due to their characteristics of relative operational simplicity and energy performance that was superior to that of the ICE, started to dominate this segment of application, using as an exclusive energy source petroleum-derived kerosene.

The dependence on petroleum derivatives as the conventional energy source for transportation is related to the historical context briefly described before, and everything indicates that the engines powered by petroleum-derived fuels will still dominate the market for the next few years.

This situation has two inconveniences. The first one is of strategic nature and results from the dependence on a finite resource whose reserves are heterogeneously distributed around the world; most proven and probable[1] petroleum reserves are located in the Middle East (Bentley, 2002). The second one is environmental nature and results from the emission of air pollutants of local, regional, and global action due to the burning of petroleum-derived fuels.

To minimize these inconveniences, efforts must be made to: (1) better use conventional energy resources, improving their supply chain and end use without compromising the service provided—people and freight transportation; (2) find alternative energy sources that allow results at least like those obtained with conventional resources associated to a rational supply and end use.

Alternative energy source for transportation is defined here as one that is different from the one conventionally chosen for end use in each study region and that has proven technical viability. This conception is sufficiently broad to allow a regional approach and the inclusion of energy sources that are still in early stage of proving their economic viability.

---

1. Proven reserves represent the energy volume of known reserve that, according to the analysis of the geology and engineering data, may be estimated with reasonable certainty of being commercially recoverable under regular economic conditions and using the recovery methods in practice at the time of the assessment. Probable reserves represent the unproven energy volume about which geology and engineering data suggest there is a greater recovery risk in comparison to the proven reserve.

180 Transportation, energy use and environmental impacts

The Brazilian example shows that regional characteristics that are appropriate to the culture of sugarcane, in addition to political and economic circumstances, favored the use of ethanol (sugarcane alcohol) as the fuel for transportation on scale not found anywhere else in the world, thus resulting in an alternative energy source to the use of gasoline in passenger cars.

The North American experience, with the introduction and use of alternative fuels and propulsion systems for transportation, shows that even if a given technology for road transportation does not have broadly proven economic viability, its use may be economically viable in a specific market niche. This is also applicable to other countries, such as the European and South American ones, where the use of compressed natural gas (CNG) is technically viable as a substitute for gasoline and diesel oil in certain specific transportation sectors, as in the case of urban buses or taxi fleets.

Conventional energy sources are those used in most of the vehicle fleet in a region. For road transportation, conventional energy sources are petroleum-derived gasoline and diesel oil all around the world. In the case of railway transportation, diesel oil and electric power are considered to be conventional energy sources. For water transportation they are diesel oil and fuel oil and for air transportation, aviation kerosene and aviation gasoline, with the latter being used for small aircraft. For pipeline transportation, pumping and compression are carried out by electric equipment that may obtain their energy from different sources, such as petroleum derivatives and natural gas (NG). Table 5.1 summarizes the energy sources currently available for transportation.

Besides classifying energy sources as conventional or alternative, the ones considered renewable were specified. This concept is associated with the time needed to transform energy emitted by the sun into some form of energy applicable to transportation. In the case of nonrenewable energy sources, such fossil fuels (petroleum, natural gas, coal, etc.), this time passes in geological scale, since petroleum originates from the decomposition of organic matter accumulated at the geologic strata over thousands of years, a process that has started many years before the appearance of humans on Earth. For renewable energy sources, such as biomass fuels (biofuels), this time passes on a scale that can be reproduced by humans, since it is possible to plant vegetable crops from which biofuels are produced.

Due to the geographic and climate conditions in certain countries, there is good agricultural productivity, which enables the privileging of biomass renewable sources (biofuels), responsible for generating rural jobs, in some cases intensively, with positive economic and social consequences.

Moreover, biofuels apply both to conventional propulsion systems, which allows their implementation with little effort, and to nonconventional and advanced technology propulsion systems, such as their use to power fuel cells, favoring the development of cutting-edge technology.

Because they are widely used alternatives, petroleum-derived gasoline, diesel oil, kerosene, and fuel oil are resources available all around the world and

TABLE 5.1 Energy sources for transportation

Classification	Energy source	Usual production processes	Resource type	Mode of transportation	Ways of final energy use
Conventional	Gasoline	Petroleum refining	Nonrenewable	Road and air	Spark-ignition (SI) ICE fuel in conventional or hybrid propulsion system. Use of fuel cell for electric power.[6]
	Diesel oil			Road, rail, and water	Compression-ignition (CI) ICE fuel in conventional or hybrid propulsion system.
	Fuel oil			Water	Compression-ignition (CI) ICE fuel in vessels.
	Kerosene			Air	Turbine fuel (jet fuel)
	Electricity	Hydroelectric power generation	Renewable	Road, rail, and pipeline	Energy source for electric road and railway systems and pipeline transportation.
		Thermoelectric generation	Nonrenewable		

Continued

TABLE 5.1 Energy sources for transportation–cont'd

Classification	Energy source	Usual production processes	Resource type	Mode of transportation	Ways of final energy use
Alternatives[8]	Gasoline[1]	Petrochemical process or synthesis from natural gas and mineral coal[3]	Nonrenewable	Idem conventional gasoline.	
		Synthesis from biomass	Renewable		
	Diesel oil[2]	Petrochemical process or synthesis from natural gas or mineral coal[3]	Nonrenewable	Idem conventional diesel oil.	
		Synthesis from biomass	Renewable		
	Liquefied petroleum gas (LPG)	Petroleum refining, petrochemical process, separation, and/or synthesis from natural gas	Nonrenewable	Road	Spark-ignition (SI) ICE fuel in conventional or hybrid propulsion system. Usually used in bi-fuel form with gasoline.
	Natural gas (NG)	Purification, dehumidification and compression (compressed natural gas—CNG) or cooling (liquefied natural gas—LNG)	Nonrenewable	Road, rail, and water	Spark-ignition (SI) ICE fuel in conventional or hybrid propulsion system. May also be used in compression-ignition (CI) ICE. May be used in bi-fuel form ICE-SI with other liquid fuels or in dual-fuel form in ICE-CI. Use in fuel cell for electric power.[6]
	Biogas	Biomass bio-digestion	Renewable	Road, rail, and water	Idem natural gas

Methanol	Chemical synthesis from coal or natural gas	Nonrenewable	Road	Spark-ignition (SI) ICE fuel in conventional or hybrid propulsion system. May be used as a mixture with gasoline or ethanol.[4] Use in fuel cell for electric power.[6]
	Fractioning and distillation of biomass (wood), chemical synthesis from biogas	Renewable		
Ethanol	Chemical synthesis from natural gas or petroleum	Nonrenewable	Road and air[10]	Spark-ignition (SIE) or compression-ignition (CIE) ICE in conventional or hybrid propulsion system. May be used in a mixture with gasoline[4] or diesel oil.[5] Use in fuel cell for electric power.[6]
	Processing and distillation of biomass (sugarcane, cassava, corn, etc.)	Renewable		
Hydrogenated vegetable oils	Oil extraction from oilseed biomass	Renewable	Road	Compression-ignition[7] (CI) ICE fuel in conventional or hybrid propulsion system. May be used in a mixture with diesel oil.
Biodiesel	Conversion of oil obtained from oilseed biomass	Renewable	Road, rail, and water	Compression-ignition (CI) ICE fuel in conventional or hybrid propulsion system. May be used in a mixture with diesel oil.
Biokerosene			Air	Turbine fuel (jet fuel). May be used in a mixture with kerosene.
Bio-oil			Water	Compression-ignition (CI) ICE fuel in conventional or hybrid propulsion system. May be used in a mixture with fuel oil.

Continued

TABLE 5.1 Energy sources for transportation–cont'd

Classification	Energy source	Usual production processes	Resource type	Mode of transportation	Ways of final energy use
	Hydrogen	Steam reformation from coal, petroleum, or NG.	Nonrenewable	Road	Spark-ignition (SI) ICE fuel in a conventional propulsion system. Ideal to be used with fuel cell for electric power.
		Electrolysis of water or reforming of renewable fuel	Renewable[9]		
	Electricity	Hydroelectric, wind or photovoltaic power generation	Renewable	Road, air, and water	Use of exclusively electric propulsion system (battery electric vehicles—BEV— or overhead power line supply, in the case of road transportation).
		Biomass thermoelectric generation			

Notes: (1) Includes reformulated gasolines with a reduction of aromatics and addition of petroleum-derived oxygenated compounds; (2) includes diesel oil with low sulfur content; (3) may be obtained from biogas, when it will be considered renewable; (4) may have an ICE dedicated to the mixture or *flexible-fuel* technology, (5) by means of an emulsifier additive (a technology that is in test and development phase); (6) use of embedded reformer; (7) adapted CI engine or Erbest engine; (8) due to the low incidence in the consulted references, the use of DME (dimethyl ether) was not considered; (9) considering hydroelectric generation; (10) used in Brazil in small aircraft.

Energy sources for transportation Chapter | 5 **185**

are usually adopted as reference for comparison, requiring a more detailed explanation of their supply chain and end use (Section 5.2). Besides them, other options that have become attractive all around the world in the last decades will be detailed in the following sections, especially NG (Section 5.3), sugarcane ethanol (Section 5.4), and biodiesel (Section 5.5). Furthermore, Section 5.6 presents some examples of biofuels considered advanced and Section 5.7 describes examples of other advanced alternatives for transportation. The final considerations of this chapter are presented in Section 5.8.

5.2 Conventional fuels

Petroleum-derived conventional fuels are: gasoline, kerosene, diesel oil, and fuel oil. They are mixtures of substances whose molecules are made of carbon (C) and hydrogen (H) that are called hydrocarbons.

Crude oil is a mixture of a great variety of hydrocarbons, including light gases, of simple chemical structure, such as NG, and heavy liquids, of complex chemical structure, such as asphalts, tar, and residues, as presented in Table 5.2.

The values presented in Table 5.2 vary and the composition of the gasoline may include substances of 4–12 carbon atoms, considered liquid light petroleum fractions. For diesel oil, there is an even higher tolerance; hydrocarbon mixtures with chains from 6 to 30 carbon atoms may be considered, making it slightly denser than kerosene and distilled within the range of 250–400°C (CONCAWE, 2014).

TABLE 5.2 Classification of petroleum fractions in function of the amount of carbon

Number of carbon atoms in the molecules	Distillation range (°C)	Typical fractions[1]
1–4	Until 40	Gases
5–10	40–175	Gasoline
11–12	175–235	Kerosene
13–17	235–305	Light fuel oil
18–25	305–400	Heavy fuel oil
26–38	400–510	Lubricants
>38	>510	Asphalt and residues

Note: (1) Diesel oil has a distillation range between 250°C and 400°C.
Source: Made by the author based on CONCAWE, 2014. Petroleum Substances. Workshop on Substance Identification and Sameness, Helsinki.

186 Transportation, energy use and environmental impacts

Gasoline, kerosene, diesel oil, and fuel oil are in liquid state at normal temperature and pressure conditions and their physicochemical properties make them quite significant to be used as energy source for transportation in almost all use conditions all around the world. The basic composition of these fuels remains virtually unchanged since the emergence of ICEs.

There are usually regulatory agencies that establish the specifications of conventional fuels to help the final consumer in search of improving burning and energy performance in engines. With that in mind, it is important to pay attention to the sulfur content limit in fuels used in urban centers and due to the technological demands in modern exhaust gas posttreatment systems, which forced extremely low levels of this contaminant, in the order of 50–10 ppm (ppm).

Regarding their conversion into mechanical energy by means of propulsion systems, the main physicochemical characteristics of petroleum-derived conventional energy sources are highlighted in Table 5.3.

Gasoline, kerosene, diesel oil, and fuel oil are fuels that are usually obtained from petroleum refining. In this case, the supply chain of these fuels is, in part, analogous to the petroleum exploration chain, which is usually subdivided into six phases: exploration, production, transportation, storage, refining, and distribution.

5.2.1 Exploration

The first step of the exploration stage is prospection, which aims to detect the existence of petroleum in the deposits located within the Earth's crust, either *onshore* or *offshore*. It is a process of elimination that reduces the areas with petroleum production potential; it is difficult, time consuming, uncertain, and expansive. The failure index in pioneering perforations ranges from 80% to 90%.

TABLE 5.3 Relevant physicochemical characteristics of petroleum-derived conventional energy sources

Energy source	Lower calorific value[1] [kcal/kg]	Density [kg/L]
Gasoline[2]	10,550	0.742
Aviation gasoline	10,600	0.726
Maritime fuel oil (MFO)	9700	1.013
Diesel oil	10,350	0.852
Aviation kerosene (jet fuel)	10,350	0.799

Notes: (1) lower calorific value is used because it considers the liquid energy available to be converted into work by the thermal machine, (2) used in road transportation.
Source: Made by the author based on CONCAWE, 2014. Petroleum Substances. Workshop on Substance Identification and Sameness, Helsinki.

Scientific prospection follows three types of techniques: geological, geophysical, and geochemical. The geological techniques are based on the knowledge of processes of formation and evolution of different rocks, including deformations (fractures, folds, displacements, etc.); it is possible to assess the potential occurrence of petroleum in part of the underground rock structure based on its topography, rock outcrops, and other geological factors.

Some of the geophysical techniques that stand out are: gravimetry (registration and analysis of surface variations in the force of gravity caused by more or less dense rock layers); magnetometry (registration and analysis of the surface of magnetic variations also caused by underground rock layers); and seismology (registration and analysis of reflections and refractions of shock waves produced on the surface by underground rock layers). Seismology is the most used geophysical technique.

The geochemical techniques include analyses that detect the presence of gas hydrocarbons in soil, water, or air in a region, which suggests migration to the surface from underground reservoirs.

The interpretation of data obtained via prospection methods allows the exclusion of regions where the possibilities of finding petroleum are remote. In other regions, drilling surveys must be carried out to confirm the presence of petroleum. Drilling rigs are equipped with drills powered by engines and have towers capable of maintaining its alignment and allowing the inclusion and removal of the pipes that are used as guides. Through the drill pipe, a fluid made of water, clay, and chemical products is pumped to cool the drill, to remove fragments of the drilled rock, and to prevent the uncontrolled leakage of gas or petroleum. Current drilling equipment are capable of drilling through any rock type and are adaptable to vessels and platforms, allowing them to be used in deep sea. Drilling may reach up to 9 km of depth and may be vertical, directional, and horizontal, allowing branching within the petroleum reservoir to facilitate its flow.

5.2.2 Production

Once the exploration phase is finished, and after it is confirmed that the surveyed region has potential, the production phase begins. Petroleum is impregnated in porous rocks called reservoirs that have layers of NG, petroleum, and water that are submitted to high pressures. The drilling of well creates a path so that the pressure naturally boosts these constituents to the surface. In low-pressure reservoirs, or when the initial pressure drops after the initial extraction period, it may be necessary to use some method to assist in the extraction of petroleum. The conventionally used methods are: pumping, using reciprocating suction pumps, and the injection of gas or water, which is called secondary recovery. This method aims to increase the pressure within the reservoir. It is also possible to use nonconventional methods, such as steam injections, in situ combustion and chemical substance injection, aiming to facilitate petroleum flow by heating it, increasing its pressure, or reducing its viscosity.

188 Transportation, energy use and environmental impacts

Once it is produced, petroleum is transported to a separator to be separated from gas and water. This equipment is usually located next to the extraction location and is the first stage of petroleum processing. At this stage, NG and light petroleum fractions are separated. This is done by passing the humid gas mixture through an absorption tower, in which a low-volatility oil absorbs liquid droplets. Dry NG leaves the absorption tower and the liquid phase is extracted from the oil through heating, producing a virtually ready-to-use derivative called natural gasoline (C_5^+).

5.2.3 Transportation and storage

Once produced, petroleum is transported to storage centers, and loading and unloading terminals, initiating the transportation phase. Usually, transportation between the point of production and storage centers is done by pumping petroleum through oil pipelines. For long distances, as in the case of petroleum import or offshore production, transportation is carried out by ships, and it is convenient to use large vessels dedicated to petroleum transportation called oil tankers. In the case of onshore production, it is possible to use trucks, trains, or barges or even waterways transportation.

Storage centers must be in convenient places for the whole supply chain. In the case of offshore petroleum extraction, as is the predominant case in Brazil, the storage centers are located on the coast, along with loading and unloading terminals; this is an ideal location to receive imported petroleum and to export surplus. From the storage centers, petroleum is pumped through oil pipelines to storage tanks at refineries, where the refining phase takes place.

5.2.4 Refining

The refining phase consists in a set of physical and chemical processes that aim to transform the petroleum originating in production areas, also known as crude oil, into its commercially used derivatives, such as gasoline and diesel oil. The main processes to which petroleum is submitted at a refinery may be classified into two subgroups:

- Refining processes: it is also known as separation processes. They are always of physical nature and aim to split crude oil into its more basic fractions or process a fraction that has been previously generated to obtain, from it, a given product through temperature or pressure change, or using solvents that carry out the desired separation. The main refining process is distillation, atmospheric or vacuum; the former is the most basic process applied to crude oil at a refinery.
- Conversion processes: those that are of chemical nature and use reactions of molecular cracking, unification, and rearrangement to transform petroleum fraction into products of greater economic interest. These processes change the structure of hydrocarbon molecules to obtain smaller, larger, or better-quality

Energy sources for transportation **Chapter | 5** **189**

molecules. Its use is very common when trying to produce high-octane fuels, such as gasoline. These processes are quite varied, but the following stand out: coking, cracking (thermal and catalytic), and chemical treatments.

Due to the diversity and complexity of the processes carried out at a refinery, we chose to present a basic refining scheme, capable of considering the essential elementary processes at a modern refinery.

Crude oil, coming from the refinery's storage tanks, is heated and is submitted to a process to remove corrosive salts, metals, and suspended solids (desalting). Later on, it is preheated in tubular furnaces and introduced into an atmospheric distillation tower that has many separation stages (trays), one for each desired fraction. The products of this process are, mainly, refinery gas (methane and ethane), liquefied petroleum gas (LPG), naphtha, gasoline, kerosene, fuel oils (such as diesel oil), and atmospheric residue (reduced crude oil or asphalt). These fractions, extracted throughout the column in its several stages of separation, should be treated to be transformed into final products or be sent as feedstock to other refining processes.

Atmospheric residue, which is the heaviest fraction found at the bottom of the distillation tower after a new heating, is submitted to a second fractioning, now in vacuum (vacuum distillation), generating types of fuel oil (light and heavy) and vacuum residue, made of hydrocarbons of high molecular weight and impurity, which, according to specifications, may be commercialized as fuel oil or asphalt.

The fractions generated at the vacuum distillation tower are used in the conversion processes that aim to create products with lower molecular weight and higher added value; among these processes, the following stand out: fluidized bed catalytic cracking, whose main products are LPG and gasoline; and vacuum residue coking, which generates LPG, naphtha, diesel oil, and petroleum coke, a mixture of solid carbon, hydrocarbons, and impurities. The products obtained in these conversion processes are submitted to treatment processes and transformed into finished products.

Fig. 5.1 summarizes the production scheme described above, which can be considered a basic refining scheme, considering the flexibility and productivity usually obtained with this set of processes. In this case, the average coking fractions are submitted to hydrotreating, enabling the increased offer of good-quality diesel oil. With this configuration, it is possible to find greater balance in the supply of gasoline and diesel oil at the refinery.

Once produced, the derivatives are pumped by pipelines into storage tanks at the refinery. Then they are delivered straight to fuel distributors, who have their own storage tanks at their distribution bases. The transportation between the refinery and bases is usually carried out by pipelines, trains, or ships.

5.2.5 Distribution

The last stage of the supply chain of conventional fuels is distributions, carried out by companies called distributors. The fuel is received from the refinery

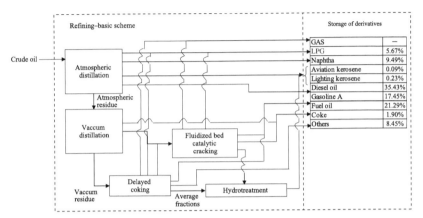

FIG. 5.1 Basic scheme of petroleum refining. *(Source: Made by the author based on CONCAWE, 2014. Petroleum Substances. Workshop on Substance Identification and Sameness, Helsinki.)*

terminals, stored in tanks, and distributed to the network of resale stations spread throughout the influence area of the distribution base. The transportation between the distribution base and resale stations is mostly carried out by the road mode using tank trucks. The loading of tank trucks is done by pumping, and the unloading, at the service station tanks, by the force of gravity. Vehicle fueling is also done by pumping.

Kerosene and aviation gasoline are supplied to airports, and diesel oil and fuel oil to ports, to fuel aircraft and vessels. This transportation is usually made by the road mode, but in case of proximity and in function of large demands, there may be connections of bases with ports and airports via pipelines, trains, or vessels.

5.2.6 End use

The conventional propulsion system, made of reciprocating ICE and mechanical transmission system (MTS), is the most used technology in the end use of conventional fuels, which are also considered as energy sources for most nonconventional propulsion systems because their supply chain is already consolidated.

Although the basic configuration of the ICE and MTS set has remained the same for almost one century, its main improvements are related to vehicle performance (rates of acceleration, speed recovery, and top speed), energy efficiency, and environmental impacts.

Nowadays, in almost the whole world, vehicles that use gasoline as fuel are equipped with a reciprocating ICE of Otto cycle, that is, with SI and 4S cycle. The engine feeding system consists of the air intake and fuel indirect injection devices (IID); air flow and fuel injection rates are electronically controlled. Furthermore, to comply with air pollutant emission legislation, it is common

Energy sources for transportation Chapter | 5 **191**

for these engines to have exhaust gases control and conversion devices called posttreatment devices.

Vehicles that use diesel oil as fuel are equipped with reciprocating ICEs of diesel cycle, that is, with compression ignition (CI) and 4S cycle. In this case, the engine feeding system also consists of air intake and injection devices; the latter may be of two types: (1) direct injection (DI) devices and (2) IID.

In the case of the ICE-CI-4S-IID, diesel oil is injected in a combustion pre-chamber, in which the ignition of the mixture begins; then, the fuel propagates to the combustion chamber, continuing the burning process. This technology is mostly employed in engines with low volumetric capacity in high-rotation regimes, as with passenger cars, and it is found in Europe, in the United States, and in part of Asia.

In ICE-CI-4S-DI, fuel is injected directly inside the combustion chamber, in which it is mixed with air at high temperature and pressure, then it burns. When compared to indirect injection engines, it has higher power, better fuel economy, and noisier operation. Its use is broadly adopted in light commercial vehicles (pickup trucks and vans), medium, heavy, and ultraheavy trucks, all kinds of buses, locomotives, and vessels.

Diesel cycle engines are usually more robust and tolerant to variations in the characteristics of the fuel. Even so, the characteristics that have the greatest impact on energy efficiency and air pollutant emissions are: the cetane number, which measures a fuel's resistance at the beginning of the burn, and the fuel's chemical composition, specifically regarding aromatic hydrocarbons and sulfur contents.

The cetane number is a characteristic that determines the mixture's capacity of autoignition. Thus, variations in this characteristic of diesel oil may lead to incomplete combustion and efficiency loss in the ICE-CI-4S-DI. The cetane number is indirectly related to the aromatic hydrocarbon content in the chemical composition of diesel oil, creating a relationship between these two characteristics.

For gasoline, the measure of resistance to autoignition is the number of octanes, which determines the Anti-Knock Index (AKI). The higher the AKI, the higher the gasoline's resistance to spontaneous combustion when submitted to pressures and temperatures in the combustion chamber. Therefore, gasolines with a high AKI withstand higher compression rates and may operate in engines with better thermodynamic efficiency.

Gasoline, diesel oil, and fuel oil in vehicles are stored in tanks that have shapes and dimensions adjusted to the vehicle's operational needs and design. Depending on the tank size, which is a function of the vehicle's desired autonomy, it may be made of plastic, aluminum, or galvanized steel.

In addition to the low efficiency in energy conversion, another inconvenience of using ICEs is the generation of air pollutants, especially carbon monoxide (CO), hydrocarbons (HC), nitrogen oxides (NOx), and particulate matter (PM). Emission rates vary in function of the specification of the fuel and the type of technology being used.

192 Transportation, energy use and environmental impacts

Keeping the same operational conditions, the reduction in air pollutant emissions by ICEs is associated with the modification of the type of fuel or the engine's design and its components. These actions may influence fuel consumption, which is one of the aspects addressed in Chapter 4.

Kerosene is the fuel used in aircraft turbines. The specification of the kerosene used in aviation must follow an international regulation, being compatible with the North American system *Aviation Fuel Quality Requirements for Jointly Operated Systems (AFQRJOS) for JET A-1*. It is required that it remains liquid and homogeneous until the combustion area in the aircraft; has the highest calorific value possible; has chemical and physical resistance to temperature and pressure variations; and has good lubricant characteristics.

5.3 Natural gas

NG is a general designation of a mixture of hydrocarbons in gaseous form. Its formation results from the accumulation of decomposed organic matter buried at great depths due to the process of accommodation of the Earth's crust. It occurs in nature by accumulating in porous rocks underground frequently accompanied by petroleum, constituting a reservoir or a deposit. The way NG occurs is therefore subdivided as associated or nonassociated petroleum gas. In the form of associated gas, it is dissolved in petroleum or it forms a gas cap. In this case, gas production is basically determined by petroleum production. Nonassociated gas is the one which is free or has very small amounts of petroleum.

The composition of NG varies depending on its original reservoir, on the fact of being or not associated with petroleum, and also on having or not been processed at industrial units; it is formed by a mixture of hydrocarbons, mostly methane (CH_4)—80%–90%—and ethane (C_2H_6), which, at room temperature of 25°C and pressure of 1 atm, remains in gaseous state. The heaviest hydrocarbons such as propylene, butane, and pentane are associated with these two gases at lower and more varied proportions. Depending on the deposit, other elements such as water, carbon dioxide, and hydrogen sulfide (H_2S) may be found.

Table 5.4 presents the typical composition in volume % of NG in its associated or nonassociated form. The last column shows the composition of NG after its processing at natural gas processing unit (NGPU). Processing eliminates heavy components from the gas (i-butane, n-butane, i-pentane, n-pentane, hexane, and superior heptanes) and increases methane content, in this example, by 8% for associated gas and 3% for nonassociated gas.

Just as was done for conventional fuels, Table 5.5 presents the relevant physicochemical characteristics of NG.

The use of gas fuels is as old as the internal combustion system itself but the extensive use of NG as fuel in cars began in Italy, in the last century, around 1930. After World War II, with the economic restrictions and the abundance of petroleum-derived products, this fuel discretely remained in the Italian market, although it was restricted to some regions. In 1970s, during petroleum crises

TABLE 5.4 Typical composition of natural gas in volume (%)

Component	Typical analysis (vol%)	Range (vol%)
Methane	94.9	87.0–96.0
Ethane	2.5	1.8–5.1
Propane	0.2	0.1–1.5
Isobutane	0.03	0.01–0.3
n-Butane	0.03	0.01–0.3
Isopentane	0.01	Trace to 0.14
n-Pentane	0.01	Trace to 0.14
Hexane	0.01	Trace to 0.06
Nitrogen	1.6	1.3–5.6
Carbon dioxide	0.7	0.1–1.0
Oxygen	0.02	0.01–0.1
Hydrogen	Trace	Trace to 0.02

Source: Demirbas, A., 2010. Methane gas hydrate, Chapter 2, Natural Gas, Springer. http://www.springer.com/978-1-84882-871-1. Access 31 July 2018.

TABLE 5.5 Relevant physicochemical characteristics of natural gas

Energy source	Lower calorific value (kcal/kg)	Density (kg/L)
Wet natural gas	9.408	0.000856
Dry natural gas	10.295	0.000745

Source: Demirbas, A., 2010. Methane gas hydrate, Chapter 2, Natural Gas, Springer. http://www.springer.com/978-1-84882-871-1. Access 31 July 2018.

and in face of the need of energy diversification, NG proved to be a viable alternative as automotive fuel.

Besides the strategic aspect, the growing awareness about the environmental impacts caused by transportation has strengthened the use of NG as a cleaner fuel alternative, considering that its use leads to a reduction in the emissions of carbon monoxide (CO) and non-methane hydrocarbons (NMHC).

Keeping NG under pressures that vary between 200 and 230 atm (3000–3600 psi or 20–23 MPa) is the most widely used method of storing this fuel in vehicles. This method of using NG in vehicles is called CNG. Another way of storing NG is through its liquefaction at a temperature of approximately −162°C,

194 Transportation, energy use and environmental impacts

which is then called liquefied natural gas (LNG). The world experience with the use of LNG is lower than that with CNG, although the former allows fuel storage systems with approximately half the weight and volume of those used for CNG.

Table 5.6 presents the 10 largest road fleets powered by NG, according to the statistics of the *International Association for Natural Gas Vehicles* (IANGV, 2018). In 2017, the world fleet of vehicles powered by NG was estimated to be around 26.2 million. In the beginning of the 1990s, this number was around 700 thousand.

The NG supply chain may be divided into the following stages: exploration, production, processing, transportation, and distribution.

5.3.1 Exploration

As with petroleum, exploration is the initial step of the supply chain of NG and consists of two phases: (1) prospection, which is the reconnaissance and study of the geological structures that favor the accumulation of petroleum and/ or NG; and (2) drilling the well to confirm the existence of these products in a commercial level.

The details of NG production are very similar to that was already described in the case of petroleum, so there is no need to repeat them. Thus, the onus of exploration is usually attributed to petroleum instead of NG.

TABLE 5.6 Estimation of the fleet of vehicles converted to NG

Country	NGV population	% All NGVs in world
China	6,080,000	23.2
Iran	4,502,000	17.2
India	3,090,139	11.8
Pakistan	3,000,000	11.5
Argentina	2,185,000	8.4
Brazil	1,859,300	7.1
Italy	1,004,982	3.8
Uzbekistan	815.000	3.1
Colombia	571.668	2.2
Thailand	474.486	1.8

Source: IANGV, 2018. Natural Gas Vehicle Fleet—2017. International Association on Natural Gas Vehicles. http://www.iangv.org/current-ngv-stats/. (Access 31 July 2018).

5.3.2 Production and processing

When being produced, the gas initially needs to go through separator vessels, which are a kind of equipment designed to remove water, liquid hydrocarbons, and solid particles (dust, impurities, products of corrosion, etc.). If the gas is contaminated with sulfur compounds, it is sent to desulfurization units, where these contaminants are removed. After this step, in the case of associated gas, part of the gas is used in the production system itself in processes known as re-injection and gas lift aiming to increase petroleum recovery from the reservoir.

The remainder is sent to the NGPU, where it will be fractioned to have methane and ethane removed, forming processed or residual gas, propane and butane, which is a component of LPG and a product called C_5^+ or natural gasoline.

The production of NG may occur in regions that are far from consumption centers and are often difficult to access. For this reason, both production and transportation are usually critical activities in the system. In maritime platforms, for example, the gas must be dehydrated before being sent to land so as to avoid the formation of hydrates, which are solid compounds that may block the pipelines. Another situation that may occur is the reinjection of gas into the reservoir if it is not consumed.

5.3.3 Transportation

In its gaseous state, NG may be transported through gas pipelines or, in very specific cases, in high-pressure cylinders in the form of CNG. In its liquid state, as LNG, it may be transported via ships, trains, barges, or trucks equipped with cryogenic tanks. In this case, the gas is stored at $-162°C$ and its volume is reduced by around 600 times, facilitating its storage. LNG must be revaporized to be used.

5.3.4 Distribution

Distribution is the system's final step, when the gas reaches the final consumer, which may be energetic, residential, commercial/public, industrial, and for transportation; the last one is exclusively for use in cars. In this stage, the gas must meet the standards established for consumption.

To be used in the form of CNG, the gas must be distributed quite comprehensively within the urban network and throughout the roadways, serving the liquid fuel service stations. The pipeline network used to feed the stations must withstand service pressures of 8–10 atm and flow rates of 600–1000 m^3/h.

There are two basic methods of refueling vehicles with CNG: fast fueling and slow fueling. In the first case, vehicle fueling times are similar to those observed in the case of conventional fuels. Fast fueling is the most common method and its peculiarities may be seen in the schematic diagram presented in Fig. 5.2, which represents only the equipment directly related to the fueling of natural gas. In the case of service stations dedicated to fueling this product, these will be the only

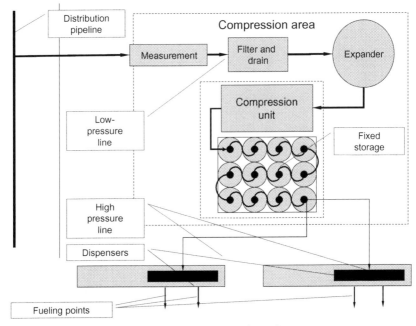

FIG. 5.2 Basic scheme of a compressed natural gas service station.

facilities available. However, if liquid fuel (conventional fuels) service is already provided, these facilities will be added to the existing ones.

NG is provided by the local distribution company that serves the region where the service station is located. The product is supplied via a gas pipeline, as indicated in Fig. 5.2. The gas distribution line is a low-pressure line (5–10 atm). The gas supplied is measured at the metering station and goes through a filtering system and a pressure vessel (expander) before feeding the compressors. At the compressors, the gas reaches pressures of around 250 atm and is ready to be made available at the fueling stations or sent to fixed storage, commonly known as "lung," which is made of a set of cylinders, like the ones used when adapting vehicles; they are interconnected through pipes and designed to withstand high gas pressures.

Each fueling point, also known as *dispenser*, works as a fuel pump, similar to a gasoline, diesel oil, or hydrous ethanol pump. The fueling point is equipped with devices capable of supplying the product to a storage system that is compatible with the vehicle's fueling valve, and capable of summing up the volume of NG supplied.

An average fueling station, with a flow rate of approximately 1000 m^3/h, is capable of fueling 100 cars or 10 buses in a period of 12 h.

5.3.5 End use

NG is a gas fuel whose chemical properties are well adaptable to the substitution of conventional fuels for reciprocating ICEs that use SI, and are 4S (Otto cycle) or two-stroke engines. When designing these engines, it is common to use gasoline as the fuel. The characteristics that facilitate the use of NG are as follows:

- Methane (CH_4), which is the main component of NG, is the hydrocarbon with the lowest carbon content and, therefore, the highest hydrogen/carbon ratio (4:1). This allows the combustion of this product to have emission indicators lower than those of conventional fuels used in engines.
- Because it is a gas fuel, its mixture with air, required so that it can burn in the engine, is much more homogeneous and uniform, which optimizes carburetion and distribution within the cylinders. This brings benefits to the engine's performance both regarding cold start and the stability of its operation.
- Its combustion is more efficient than that of other fuels, that is, the formation of unwanted products is minimized so that less deposits are formed and, consequently, the lifespan of the lubrication system components increases (oil, filters) and the wear of engine components also decreases.
- Its autoignition temperature is very high and it also has excellent resistance to knocking, which are important properties in SI ICEs.

Vehicles may have engines designed to use only NG or those that operate with two fuels (bifuel), NG and one of the conventional fuels, according to the engine's cycle of operation. Fig. 5.3 shows several options of NG use as a fuel in vehicles equipped with ICEs.

In the case of using NG in its compressed form (CNG), whatever the option presented in Fig. 5.3, the basic equipment that comprises the conversion device is shown in Fig. 5.4. This equipment allows the converted vehicle to use NG as a fuel along with the original fuel, in the case of a bifuel application for SI reciprocating ICEs, or the complete substitution of the original fuel, in the case of diesel engines. In this case, there still must be some sort of adaptation in the engine.

NG is able to maintain regular engine performance both at slow running (slow rotations and no load) and in scenarios of high power demand (high rotation and load) or high torque demand (slow rotations and heavy load), and it is also able, if well regulated, to effectively inhibit the knocking problem, without requiring the addition of polluting substances to the fuel, considering its high octane rating, when compared to conventional fuels.

The vehicles whose engines were designed to use exclusively CNG as a fuel use the Otto cycle engine, since this cycle allows the optimization of the competitive advantages of gas in relation to conventional fuels. An engine specially designed for NG use usually operates at high compression rates (from 14/1 to 16/1), allowed due to the high anti-knocking power (high octane rating) inherent to gas, and thus has a superior[2] thermal efficiency when compared to gasoline or hydrous ethanol engines.

---

2. This concept is better detailed in Chapter 4.

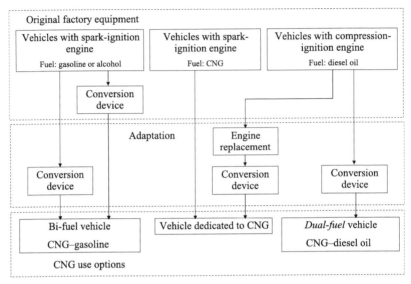

FIG. 5.3 Options for using CNG as automotive fuel.

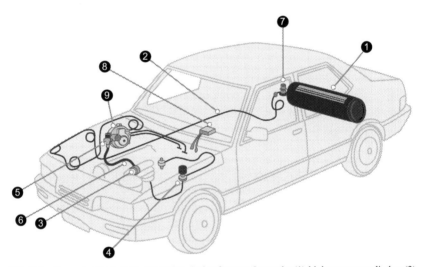

FIG. 5.4 Example of a typical conversion device for cars. Legends: (1) high-pressure cylinder; (2) high-pressure pipeline; (3) CNG-air mixer; (4) fuel selection electro valve; (5) CNG fueling valve; (6) low-pressure pipeline—feeding; (7) cylinder head valve; (8) CNG gauge; (9) pressure regulator valve.

The first engines that used NG in an Otto cycle engine were much simpler than the equivalent ones running on gasoline but resulted in a power loss of about 10%. To optimize the performance of these engines with NG, in each generation of engines, the manufacturers have been continually incorporating changes so as to maximize its power. Currently, the technological advancements

Energy sources for transportation **Chapter | 5 199**

incorporated to the feeding and combustion systems in engines of this type have already enabled a significant reduction in the above-mentioned difference.

In the case of heavy vehicles, especially applicable to urban buses, there are many engine manufacturers, among which the following stand out: Culmmins, Scania, Volvo, Daimler-Chrysler, and MAN. One of the disadvantages of the vehicles that use this type of engine is the total dependence on NG to fuel the vehicle, which limits its autonomy to regions that have adequate fueling facilities.

In the case of using NG in engines designed to use gasoline or hydrous ethanol, it is common to operate in bifuel form, preferably using gas but with the possibility of using the original fuel when needed. Vehicles that have this type of adaptation may be manufactured in this way, coming from factory with the possibility of choosing the fuel to be used, or may be adapted at accredited workshops where they undergo the conversion process with the installation of a device briefly made of the elements presented in Fig. 5.4.

Due to the need of reconciling the operation in bifuel form, the converted vehicles must maintain the original compression rates of their gasoline engines (9/1) or hydrous ethanol (12/1). This situation affects power, since in a SI reciprocating ICE power depends on the ratio $PCI/(1 + V_a)$ and on the thermal performance η_t,[3] where PCI is the lower calorific value of the fuel being used and V_a is the amount of air needed to burn one volume unit of gas. The thermal performance depends on r, on the compression rate, and on factor $k = C_p/C_v$ (C_p: specific heat at a constant pressure and C_v: specific heat at a constant volume). In theory, considering that the ratio $PCI/(1 + V_a)$ for gasoline is 960 and for methane it is 836, the use of NG (mostly methane) would be responsible for a 14% drop in power.

Conversion devices have continually evolved to follow the technological development incorporated by the car industry in fuel dosing and injection systems in vehicle engines; the evolution is shown by the fact that most recent devices include elements to make the operation with conventional fuels compatible in vehicles equipped with single-point or multipoint electronic injection systems.[4]

One of the great advantages of this type of vehicle for its owner is trip autonomy, since, in the absence of CNG fueling stations, the vehicle may be fueled with its original fuel.

In any vehicle running on gasoline or any other fuel adequate to Otto cycle engines, it is possible to install a conversion device to use NG, if there is room for the installation of the gas cylinder. There are many manufacturers of conversion devices that may be installed by any of the accredited workshops.

However, it is worth pointing out that, as already mentioned before, it is necessary to assess whether the technologies of the conversion device and the vehicle are compatible to maximize vehicle performance with any of the fuels.

---

3. Where: $h_t = 1 - (1/(r.(k-1)))$.

4. In single-point electronic fuel injection, fuel is injected through one point at the intake manifold. In multi-point electronic fuel injection, fuel is injected at one point for each cylinder.

200 Transportation, energy use and environmental impacts

Dual-fuel vehicles were developed so that CNG could replace diesel oil in compression ignition engines. However, as described before, in engines that operate on diesel cycle, combustion begins with the fuel's autoignition. As the ignition temperature of NG is very high, this reaction does not occur as required. To work around this problem *dual-fuel* systems use "pilot injection" of diesel oil in the cylinders in a quantity that is just enough to begin the burning of the air + gas mixture so that the vehicle operates in a mixed cycle, since it has characteristics of diesel cycle, until the pilot-injection, and others of Otto cycle after that. Therefore, unlike bifuel engines, *dual-fuel* engines do not allow the vehicle to operate at times with the alternative fuel (CNG) and at others with the conventional fuel (diesel oil).

Although the development phase of NG use in vehicles has already been surpassed, the manufacturers have invested very little in this type of engine, comparing to investments carried out in the development of new technologies applicable to conventional fuels. Therefore, significant improvements in this technology are still expected.

Some chemical characteristics of NG, such as the fact it is almost fully made of methane (CH_4), has no carbon–carbon bonds, and has low contaminant content, especially regarding sulfur, are its greatest strengths in comparison to conventional fuels, since the combustion process tends to be simpler and there is a lower probability of an incomplete combustion of long-chain hydrocarbons. As the NG engine does not require the mixture enrichment device for cold start, the emissions in this condition tend to be lower than that in the case of liquid fuels. Finally, if the gas storage facilities are sealed, evaporative emissions should be irrelevant.

Considering what was already described in the previous section regarding design improvements and the introduction of new technologies in light vehicles, the environmental advantages of a conversion to CNG depend on several factors, among which is the compatibility between vehicle technologies and conversion devices.

5.4 Ethanol

Ethanol[5] or ethyl alcohol, a chemical substance of formula C_2H_5OH, is the most widely used renewable alternative fuel in the world and its highest consumption for transportation is in Brazil. The product is known as an automotive fuel for more than one century and when Henry Ford designed its Model T he thought the car could run on ethanol produced from corn.

Ethanol's physicochemical characteristics are compatible with its use in SI reciprocating ICEs, among which the most used ones are Otto cycle engines. It is a simple substance, an oxygenated compound, that, at normal temperature and pressure, is found in liquid form; its specific weight is higher than that of gasoline and lower than that of diesel oil.

---

5. Some authors also refer to ethanol as bioethanol when it is originated from biomass.

Energy sources for transportation Chapter | 5 **201**

TABLE 5.7 Relevant physicochemical characteristics of ethanol

Energy source	Lower calorific value (kcal/kg)	Density (kg/L)
AEAF	6.735	0.791
HEAF	6.317	0.809

Source: Mateus Henrique Rochan, Rafael Silva Capaz, Electo Eduardo Silva Lora, Luiz Augusto Horta Nogueira, Marcio Montagnana Vicente Leme, Maria Luiza Grillo Renó, Oscar Almazándel Olmo (2014). Life cycle assessment (LCA) for biofuels in Brazilian conditions: a meta-analysis. Renew. Sust. Energ. Rev. 37, 435–459.

In Brazil, used as automotive fuel in ICEs either dedicated to ethanol combustion or designed to equip flexible-fuel vehicles, ethanol is commercialized with up to 7.4% of water and is called hydrous ethyl alcohol fuel (HEAF). To be used as oxygenating additive in gasoline, at the average proportion of 25% in volume, ethanol may only have a maximum of 0.7% of water and it will be called anhydrous ethyl alcohol fuel (AEAF). Table 5.7 illustrates the relevant physicochemical characteristics of ethanol.

In both cases, the Brazilian National Petroleum Agency (ANP), via the Technical Regulation, establishes the specifications for the commercialization of these fuels throughout the national territory.

EXAMPLE 5.1   A brief history of the use of ethanol as automotive fuel in Brazil

In Brazil, ethanol could be classified as a conventional fuel because since the 1980s ethanol is used in the road fleet. Its large-scale use began with a Federal Government program called Proálcool (National Alcohol Program), which was considered strategic to reduce the dependence on imported petroleum. Through the formation of partnerships with the private sector, the program was initially developed and then became a social, environmental, and technological success. However, a series of political and economic factors have made it difficult to consolidate the participation of ethanol in the national market of car fuels.

In 1973, year of the first petroleum crisis, the price of a petroleum barrel went up from US$ 2.70 to US$ 11.20. This increase caused a great impact on the Brazilian trade balance, since approximately 80% of the petroleum consumed in Brazil was imported. In face of that, the Brazilian government started to invest in research to find alternative energy sources to diesel oil, fuel oil, and gasoline. Proálcool, established in 1975, sought to facilitate the substitution of gasoline for ethyl alcohol produced from sugarcane. The incentives were directed to: the production of hydrous and anhydrous ethyl alcohol (ethanol) at the independent sugar units and distilleries; the development of production infrastructure; the financing of

202 Transportation, energy use and environmental impacts

the development of engines by the car industry; and the formation of an extensive fuel distribution network.

Hydrous alcohol (second phase of Proálcool) was intended to fully replace gasoline in cars equipped with ICEs dedicated to this fuel in the beginning of the 1980s. Anhydrous ethanol (first phase of Proálcool), however, was introduced in the market as an additive to gasoline, to increase its octane rating and substitute tetraethyl lead, which is an additive usually used in gasoline to improve its properties of resistance to pre-knocking[6] in engines. The initial proposal was that the fuel blend should only have 10% of anhydrous ethanol but, since 1980, a percentage of 22% was adopted in all over the country.

In 1979, with the second petroleum crisis, when its price reached US$ 34.00 per barrel, the Brazilian government accelerated Proálcool. Many investments were made in the sector, with the concession of loans and government subsidies to farmers and to the production plants, guaranteeing financial return to investors.

In 1986, the reduction in petroleum consumption by importer countries led OPEC,[7] aiming to guarantee its market, to reduce the price of petroleum barrel to US$ 10.00. Under these conditions, alternative solutions became no longer that advantageous. Brazil could not abandon Proálcool but it started to cut funding, subsidies, and discounts offered to alcohol producers and vehicle manufacturers.

Nevertheless, ethanol kept being used and, thus, Brazil reached a production of 26 billion liters of ethanol in 2009, equivalent to approximately 100 million petroleum barrels, 58% of this volume was produced in the state of São Paulo. Besides, anhydrous ethanol is used, at a proportion of 25%, as an additive to gasoline, which represented, in 2016, a consumption of 11.6 million cubic meters.

In the period between 2001 and 2003, the policy of cutting subsidies led to a certain disorganization of the market, requiring a search for a new balance between the many actors in the national energy scenario. Aiming to accelerate the return to an intensive use of ethanol in Brazil, vehicles capable of running on both gasoline and ethanol at the same time and at any proportion (*flexible-fuel* vehicles) started to be commercialized, considering that the main issue reported by users of this alternative fuel was the risk of fuel shortage, which was critical in the case of dedicated fuel vehicles but not in the case of *flexible-fuel* vehicles.

The first manufacturer to launch a *flexible-fuel* vehicle in Brazil was Volkswagen, which launched in March 2003, Gol 1.6 Total Flex, with a market price that was only 3% higher than gasoline-exclusive Gol Power 1.6. This initiative was followed by the remaining manufacturers, which started to offer *flexible-fuel* vehicles in their product lines.

A vehicle with factory *flexible-fuel* and bifuel compatibility was also launched; it could use ethanol and gasoline or CNG. Adaptations are possible and throughout Brazil there are already *flexible-fuel* vehicles adapted to run on CNG.

Until the present time, ethanol in Brazil is produced from sugarcane, which guarantees a higher yield than that of corn processing (widely practiced in North

---

6 Pre-knocking is the phenomenon in which the mixture burns in the engine before the piston achieves top dead center (see Chapter IV). This problem is popularly known as "pinging."

7 OPEC—Organization of the Petroleum Exporting Countries. Its members are Saudi Arabia, Iran, Iraq, Kuwait, Venezuela, Qatar, Indonesia, Libya, Abu Dhabi, Bahrain, Algeria, Nigeria, Ecuador, and Gabon.

America) and beet (European practice) and will either be added to petroleum-derived gasoline in a proportion of up to 25% or used in pure form, once most Brazilian vehicles have already been produced with *flexible-fuel* capability.

Ethanol may be produced using NG or petroleum as feedstock. In this case, it will be a nonrenewable fossil fuel obtained through the catalytic hydration of ethylene (C_2H_4), produced from methane or petroleum derivatives. This way of obtaining ethanol is not an alternative to the use of exhaustible energy sources.

As a renewable energy source, the most commonly used inputs are sugarcane, beet, grape, corn, cassava, and several vegetables that enable the production of starch or sugar. When the inputs used are rich in saccharides ($C_{11}H_{22}O_{11}$), as is the case of sugarcane, beet, and grape, ethanol will be obtained simply by fermentation and distillation. In the hypothesis of using inputs that are rich in starch ($C_6H_{10}O_5$), as is the case of corn and cassava, a step prior to fermentation is required to break starch into sugar.

Although studies are being carried out with several inputs, the international experience indicates that the United States chose to produce ethanol from corn, while in France the best option is the combination of beet and wheat. In the French case, decision makers intended to add 7% of ethanol to gasoline, producing the additive from the cultivation of $5100\,km^2$ (150,000 ha of beet and 350,000 ha of wheat to generate 1.5 million liters).

Germany, the United Kingdom, and Switzerland proposed similar projects, the last two considering the surplus in the production of wheat and barley. However, the large-scale adoption of the North American option seems to be facing some sort of opposition due to the adverse effects of dedicating large farming areas to produce fuel instead of food. Moreover, with current technology, the energy required to produce ethanol from corn is usually higher than the energy contained in the fuel.

It is also possible to produce ethanol through the process of hydrolysis of any type of plant that contains cellulose, which is the most abundant substance in the woody parts of a plant and constitutes one-third of all plant matter. In this case, the component being considered is a carbohydrate, it is the most abundant natural compound, and it has no feeding function for humans. Therefore, the inputs to produce ethanol would be leftover wood, paper, pruning twigs, forest waste, roots, cereal chaff, bagasse, grass, organic waste, etc. The cellulose molecules are more complex than those of starch, but it is possible to break them into saccharides by means of enzymatic or acid hydrolysis. Once broken, the process will follow the logic of fermentation and distillation.

Following the Brazilian experience, it seems promising to produce ethanol in large scale from sugarcane. The supply chain of sugarcane ethanol may be subdivided into the following steps: feedstock production (agricultural input), ethanol production, distribution, and end use, as shown next.

204 Transportation, energy use and environmental impacts

5.4.1 Feedstock production

Sugarcane is a kind of grass plant that has high energy potential; each ton is equivalent to 1.2 barrel of petroleum. This plant develops by forming clumps with aerial sections (culms and leaves) and underground sections (rhizomes and roots). The varieties are chosen for their productivity, resistance to diseases and pests, saccharide content, ease of sprouting, soil demands, and useful industrialization time.

To provide feedstock to the distillery throughout the whole season, which lasts around 6 months, the sugarcane crop must have early, medium, and late varieties, that is, varieties in which sugarcane matures at the beginning, middle, and end of the season.

Sugarcane better develops in deep, clay soil with good fertility and high water-retention capability but not subject to waterlogging. The desirable acidity index (pH) will be between 6.0 and 6.5. Usually, when preparing the soil for planting, there is a need of mixing lime with the soil so that the pH reaches these levels. Moreover, there is a common need of fertilizing the soil with nitrogen (N), phosphorus (P), and potassium (K), based on the analysis of the soil and the nutritional needs of the crop.

After the soil is plowed and harrowed, the soil is simultaneously furrowed and fertilized with a spacing of 1.00–1.35 m between the furrow lines. At the bottom of the furrows, the culms[8] are deposited and covered with earth. The plant buds,[9] which are located at the "nodes" of the culms, will give rise to a new plant.

Sugarcane, once planted, would keep producing for 4–5 years consecutively, then productivity greatly decreases, and the sugarcane crop is reformed. The first cut of sugarcane is called "cana planta" (plant cane); the second cut is called "cana soca" (1st ratoon); and from third cut onwards it is called "ressoca" (second ratoon, third ratoon, and so on). Planting from February to May will produce the sugarcane known as "ano e meio" (year-and-a-half), and planting from October to December will produce the "cana de ano" (year cane).

Mechanized harvesting is already widespread. After being cut and having its tips removed, sugarcane is piled in heaps in seven rows. These heaps will be placed in trucks and/or sets of trucks and trailers using a loader, and then transported to the power plant.

Taking the Brazilian experience as a reference, it is possible to estimate that 1 ha of land supplies between 40 and 100 t of sugarcane, depending on the cultivation, fertilization, and irrigation methods and on choice for the varieties that are most adequate to a given region.

---

8. Segment of the stem in grass plants located between the root and the shank.
9. Part of the plant susceptible to its reproduction.

5.4.2 Ethanol production

Arriving at the sugarcane production plant, the sugarcane must be milled within 72 h after the cut, otherwise there is a possibility of infestation by fungi and bacteria that hamper the juice fermentation process and loss of part of the sucrose through culm respiration. The first step in the process is weighing, followed by unloading using cranes; part of the sugarcane is stored to be milled at night, when there is no transportation. The other part is immediately forwarded to the feeder table, where it is washed to be industrialized. Washing aims to remove impurities, such as earth and sand, that would be prejudicial to the good performance of the manufacturing process.

On a conveyor belt, sugarcane is transported to the shredder, where it is cut into pieces that are forwarded to the fiberize, which aims to open the cane cells to facilitate the next step, which is the extraction of the juice made with the mills. Sugarcane passes through a total of four sets of three-roll mills. To maximize juice extraction, the bagasse is soaked in diluted juice after passing through the first and second sets and in water after passing through the third set.

This milling process produces sugarcane juice and bagasse. The juice represents 26%–30% of sugarcane's weight. The energy content of the bagasse is very high, around 2257 kcal/kg with a water content of 50%. Even so, it is common practice to burn part of it in boilers to produce steam that will provide all the power used in the industrial complex. Another part of the bagasse may be used as animal feed.

An alternative destination to the surplus bagasse generated at the production plant is the production of alcohol through hydrolysis, as mentioned above. Still based on the Brazilian experience, it is estimated that 1 t of bagasse may produce around 180 L of alcohol. This process is recommended, considering that bagasse is already at the plant, which minimizes transportation costs.

After its extraction, sugarcane juice is sieved to separate the small fragments of bagasse resulting from the milling process. Almost all the sugar present in sugarcane will be in this juice, which is called mixed juice. The mixed juice is pumped to the heaters, where it is heated to temperatures between 90°C and 105°C. Then, the mixed juice is moved to the decanter, where its impurities are decated. The result of this step is called clarified juice; after this a mass called mud is left at the bottom of the decanter. The mud is sent to rotary vacuum filters that aim to maximize juice retrieval resulting in clean juice and filter cake. This cake is used as crop fertilizer, since it is rich in mineral salts.

The clarified juice is pumped to a tank and then passes through a heat exchanger to be cooled down and to follow to the fermentation process. Fermentation is the process that transforms sugars into alcohol by the action of the yeast added to the juice. This mixture will react in the reactors from 6 to 8 h. The fermented juice produces the wine, which is centrifuged to be separated into two parts. The first part produces the yeast milk, which was responsible for the fermentation and will be used in new fermentations after it undergoes

206 Transportation, energy use and environmental impacts

adequate chemical treatment. Some percentage of the yeast milk is dehydrated and used as animal feed. The second part is yeast wine, which contains 7%–8% of alcohol.

Considering that alcohol has a boiling temperature of 78.5°C, lower than water, it is possible to separate both through a process of distillation. In practice, the industrial distillation of alcohol is done using what are called distillation towers, similar to those found at petroleum refineries. The columns are heated at the bottom and cooled at the top part, so that yeast wine, which feeds the base of the tower, evaporates. Due to the different boiling temperatures of alcohol and water, as it goes up, steam is enriched with alcohol; this mixture is condensed and collected on trays throughout the tower. On the trays that are closer to the top of the column, the percentage of alcohol in the condensed mixture is higher.

In principle, it is possible to design trays with a given height and number of trays so that the last tray has the highest possible alcohol content, which, in this process, would be 96%. However, for technical reasons, the industry commonly uses three towers to reach this concentration.

The industrial waste of the distillery is called vinasse, which is the aqueous part of yeast wine and is a high-importance by-product to farming because it is rich in mineral salts (N, P, K, Ca, Mg) but it is also an environmental polluting agent. If it is not treated and used rationally, it can pollute rivers, threatening animal life and human populations that use this water. The production of 1 L alcohol leads to the production of 6–13 L of vinasse, which, after being deposited in natural tanks, is sent to crops through channels, being pumped and distributed to be used as fertilizer.

Another use for vinasse is the production of biogas through its anaerobic decomposition, that is, through the action of microorganisms without the presence of air. This use reduces the amount waste, produces fertilizer, and increases the amount of total energy produced by the plant.

In Brazil, it is possible to produce around 85 L of ethanol per ton of sugarcane; the most commonly reported variation interval is between 70 and 80 L per ton. This way, a reasonable yield average may consider to be 5000 L of alcohol per planted hectare. It must also be highlighted that this yield almost doubled from 1979 to the mid-1990s.

Brazil has also developed industrial technology to produce alcohol from vegetables containing starch, as is the case of cassava. In this case, the starch is decomposed with appropriate enzymes, turning into sugars that are fermented and distilled, in a way similar to that is done with sugarcane. A ton of cassava can produce 180 L of alcohol. The studies on the improvement in this production process indicated the possibility of reaching a productivity level of 25–30 t of cassava per hectare, which would lead to a proportion of 4500–5400 L of alcohol per hectare, again similar that is produced with sugarcane.

Two aspects confirm the continuity of research regarding the use of cassava as input for ethanol production: (1) this plant does not require fertile earth to develop; (2) the production of such a strategic fuel for the country's interests

Energy sources for transportation **Chapter | 5** **207**

would not be restricted to only one raw material, sugarcane. Thus, the offer of ethanol would be less dependent on international variations of the price of sugar, which would bring more stability to Proálcool.

5.4.3 Ethanol distribution

Once produced, ethanol is stored in distilleries and transported via road or pipeline modes to the distribution centers, the same used for the distribution of conventional fuels. If not already in operation, it is necessary to build storage tanks, pumping systems, and pipelines to store and distribute the product. These components must be resistant to the chemical characteristics of ethanol and, mainly, must prevent the absorption of water, considering the high affinity between water and alcohol. When using ethanol as an additive, one must be even more careful, since small amounts of water may lead to the separation of the phases and lead to corrosion of the facilities and the engines in end use.

Due to its lower energy density, a higher volume of ethanol storage will be needed to meet the needs that were previously met by gasoline use. The ratio between the volume of ethanol and gasoline is 1.4–1.5. In Brazil, this whole structure is already present and available both at fuel distribution centers and at fuel stations. Even with the reduction in the consumption of HEAF, the existing infrastructure was maintained, and the product may be distributed all over the country.

5.4.4 Ethanol end use

The use of ethanol as fuel in vehicles assumes the design of an ICE with an operation that is conceptually identical to that of a gasoline engine but with components that are adequate to the physical and chemical characteristics of this fuel. Thus, designers must plan for the substitution of engine components made of metal alloys and plastic polymers that are susceptible to chemical attack by alcohol.

Among the engine components that must be planned for, the following stand out: injectors, galleries, filters and fuel pumps, fuel tank and its accessories, and spark plugs. The main problems resulting from the use of inadequate materials in engines that use ethanol are increased fuel consumption, torque and power loss, acceleration failures, damage to the catalytic converters, and increased emissions.

The higher octane rating of ethanol may also be used by increasing the compression rate of the engines dedicated to this fuel, thereby increasing its thermal efficiency. On the other hand, to maintain the same autonomy, the vehicle will need a bigger fuel tank due to the lower energy density of alcohol when compared to gasoline.

Due to its low cetane number, the use of ethanol replacing diesel oil in compression-ignition engines depends on modification or adaptation that may be made through one of the following methods:

208 Transportation, energy use and environmental impacts

- Modification of the original engine to a *dual-fuel* system, similar to the one described for CNG use, in which ethanol becomes the main fuel and diesel oil is used as pilot spark to begin the burning of an air-fuel mixture.
- Adaptation of dual-feed system in which ethanol is mixed with air and partially compensates for the volume of diesel oil required.
- Modification of the original engine so that it starts to operate as a SI engine in a way that diesel oil may be fully replaced by ethanol.
- In a compression-ignition engine especially developed to use ethanol with the addition of a knocking additive allows the fuel to burn as it is injected into the combustion chamber.
- Promoting the mixture of diesel oil with ethanol through the use of emulsifier substances so that part of the diesel oil consumed by the vehicle starts being replaced by ethanol. The emulsifier is usually an ester with properties similar to those of biodiesel.

Flexible-fuel technology exists in the United States since the beginning of the 1990s; they were introduced in Brazil in 2003 and rapidly gained acceptance due to the high availability of ethanol as a fuel in the market.

In case ethanol is produced from sugarcane, it is possible to consider that 100% of carbon emissions, in the form of CO_2, are absorbed by the plant during its growth, thus compensating the amount liberated when burning the fuel. Besides, its use reduces local air pollutant emissions such as sulfur oxides (SO_x) and toxic organic compounds such as benzene and 1,3-butadiene.

Its main disadvantage is the emission of acetaldehyde, which is a toxic compound. Besides, ethanol vapors react in the atmosphere, generating more acetaldehyde, forming peroxyacyl nitrate, which is one of the precursors of tropospheric ozone, also toxic. The emission of formaldehydes from the burning of ethanol is similar to what is expected in gasoline vehicles.

5.5 Biodiesel

The use of vegetable oils to replace diesel oil has been addressed in national and international studies for many years. Because they have high cetane number and high calorific value, their use *in natura* enables its burning in diesel cycle engines, as the inventor of this engine already assumed in 1900 by presenting a model capable of burning peanut oil.

As the molecules of vegetable oils have glycerin, if they are used without any adaption in engines designed to burn diesel oil, they may lead to carbonization problems, deposits on injectors and valve seats, and premature wear of pistons, piston rings, and cylinders. Other problems are related to: dilution of lubricating oil, difficulty in cold starting, irregular burning, reduced thermal efficiency, unpleasant odor of exhaust gases, and emission of toxic substances (Parente, 2003). As a result, *in natura* vegetable oils are not used as large-scale substitutes for diesel oil.

To minimize or work around these problems, there are a few options: (1) use of vegetable oil and diesel oil blends in proportions of up to 30%; (2) use of fatty acid esters obtained through the chemical transformation of vegetable oil; and (3) use of cracked vegetable oils.

A common alternative worldwide is the use of fatty acid esters, which are commonly referred to as biodiesel. The most common way of producing this fuel is the reaction of vegetable oils with methanol or ethanol in the presence of a catalyst in a chemical process known as transesterification, whose products are the mixture of fatty acid ethyl or methyl esters, which are the components of biodiesel itself, and glycerin, whose main constituent is glycerol.

Although there are several kinds of feedstock capable of producing biodiesel, including both vegetable oils (such as palm, peanut, soy, cotton, avocado, and castor bean) and animal fats and fatty residues, the international experience in industrial production has focused on the use of rapeseed oil, which is an edible species (*Brassica oleracea*) whose seed produces oil (great predominance), soy oil, and sunflower oil (in lower quantity). In all cases, the properties of biodiesel must follow the specification of the regulatory agencies of the countries where they are produced.

The use of biodiesel on a larger scale was seen in the European Community (EC), which studies, since the 1970s, the applications of this fuel in agricultural equipment and for road transportation. The EU production of biodiesel in 2016 was 11.6 million tons, while the North American production, the second largest, was 5.1 million tons (EBB, 2018).

In Europe, biodiesel is predominantly produced from rapeseed. In lower quantity, this fuel may also be produced from sunflower oil. Historically, the first experiences began in Austria (in the 1970s), but the three largest European producers and consumers of biodiesel currently are Germany, France, and the Netherlands (EBB, 2018).

Germany, nowadays, is the largest consumer of biodiesel, and it even has crops dedicated to energy production. In the period from 2006 to 2009 its consumption more than doubled due to the expansion of offer in the distribution network. France and the Netherlands also stand out regarding the growth of biodiesel use.

The following may be listed as the main arguments for the production of biodiesel: the use of lands not dedicated to the cultivation of food, the heating of the agricultural market, the strategic substitution of petroleum derivatives, and the fact that it is a way of reducing liquid greenhouse gas emissions, mainly CO_2.

The biodiesel supply process is partially associated with the origin of inputs that may be used in the production of this fuel. They may be classified as follows:

- Residual inputs: include used frying oil, fatty acids, animal fat, and sanitary sewage. As these inputs are considered pollutants, the production of fuel from them is deemed an activity that uses materials with no market value, which contributes to the reduction of production costs and is characterized as sanitary treatment. The feedstock in the process has immediate availability in urban centers, however, in small quantity when compared to the energy demand.

- Extractive inputs: these are the resources originating from plant extractivism, such as babassu, buriti, and Brazil nut. This feedstock also has immediate availability, but it is found far from urban centers. It is found in a larger quantity than residual inputs.
- Cultivated inputs: include, for example, soy, castor bean, oil palm, sunflower, peanut, rapeseed, and coconut; these are inputs that do not have immediate availability because they already have a consolidated market and their price may suffer variation due to market fluctuations.

The origin of inputs has greater impact on the method of obtaining feedstock than on fuel production. Once feedstock is available, fatty acid esters may be produced through the transesterification of triglycerides within the feedstock or through the process of hydrolysis of triglycerides in fatty acids and later the esterification of fatty acids. The option will depend on the composition of the feedstock, which may be rich in triglycerides or fatty acids, but both cases rely on chemical processes to be carried out at an industrial plant.

5.5.1 Feedstock production—Biomass rich in oils and fats

An attractive alternative to produce fuel for urban road transportation would be the combination of residual inputs, already available at urban centers, and cultivated inputs. In this case, it is possible to explore the use of frying oil residues as a complement in the production of biodiesel from soy or palm oil, which are predominant options in the United State, Brazil, and Asia.

Therefore, there are two possibilities to combine the production of biodiesel from frying oil residues, available at urban centers, with the use of surplus soy oil: (1) the consumption of biodiesel being prioritized at the urban centers of the regions where there is the largest production of soy and oil; (2) the production of biodiesel in the regions where there are the largest productions of soy and oil.

In the case of residual frying oil, the main aspect to be assessed in the process that precedes the production of biodiesel regards the logistics of feedstock collection, since it is scattered across many points within the urban network.

The production of biodiesel from virgin soy oil depends on the steps of agriculture and oil production. Based on the Brazilian experience, it is possible to produce an average of 2.3 t of soy per cultivated hectare. The process of planting and harvesting is fully mechanized, and the seeds are transported to oil extraction centers (crushing) by means of road or rail transportation.

5.5.2 Feedstock processing

The processing of feedstock for its conversion into biodiesel aims to create better conditions to carry out the chemical reaction, achieving the maximum conversion rate. In the case of biomass rich in vegetable oil, the first step is to obtain oil,

Energy sources for transportation Chapter | 5 **211**

TABLE 5.8 Oil extraction method and recommended situation

Oil extraction method	Recommended situation	Oil content	Typical feedstock
Mechanical	Small and medium capacities, usually below 200t of grain per day.	High (>35% in weight)	Castor bean, peanut, babassu
Solvent	High capacities, usually above 300t of grain per day.	Low (<25% in weight)	Soy
Mixed	Medium and high capacities, usually above 200t of grain per day.	Medium (between 25% and 35% in weight)	Castor bean, peanut, babassu, sunflower, cotton

Source: Made by the author based on Ejaz M. Shahid and Younis Jamal (2011). Production of biodiesel: a technical review. Renew. Sust. Energ. Rev., 15, 9, 4732–4745.

which may be done through mechanical extraction (crushing), solvent extraction, and/or mixed extraction.

At first, the selection of the oil extraction method depends on two factors: productive capacity and oil content found in the biomass. Table 5.8 illustrates the extraction method, the most adequate situation for its use, and the type of feedstock that may be used.

Regarding residual inputs, it may be necessary to extract oil, as with animal oil and fats, which is done using water and steam. The processing of sewage fatty materials is still in phase of research and development, but it also requires a process of fat extraction, which can be done with a solvent.

In the specific case of soy, before being crushed, the seeds are washed and dried. After extracted, the oil is degreased to remove carbonates and free fatty acids. This is done through washing with hot water. A ton of processed soy produces around 190 kg (19%) of degreased oil and 780 kg (78%) of bran. The soy bran is chiefly used as high-protein animal feed.

5.5.3 Fuel production—Biodiesel

It is possible to create a flowchart of the biodiesel production process from oils and fats rich in triglycerides, the main feedstock in obtaining this fuel, as shown in Fig. 5.5.

Before beginning the chemical reaction, it is necessary to prepare the feedstock so that it has minimum acidity and water content, which is possible by submitting it to a neutralization process through washing with alkaline solution of potassium or sodium hydroxide, followed by an operation of drying and dehumidification.

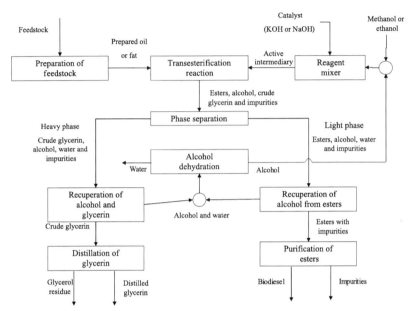

FIG. 5.5 Biodiesel production process. *(Source: Made by the author based on Ejaz M. Shahid and Younis Jamal (2011). Production of biodiesel: a technical review, Renew. Sust. Energ. Rev., 15, 9, 4732–4745.)*

The chemical reaction, usually called transesterification, is the step of conversion of the oil or fat into fatty acid methyl or ethyl esters that make up biodiesel. Eqs. (5.1) and (5.2) show these reactions:

$$\text{Oil or fat} + CH_3OH \Rightarrow \text{Fatty acid methyl ester} + \text{glycerol} \quad (5.1)$$

$$\text{Oil or fat} + C_2H_5OH \Rightarrow \text{Fatty acid ethyl ester} + \text{glycerol} \quad (5.2)$$

From an objective point of view, both reactions are equivalent, since both methyl and ethyl esters are considered biodiesel and are capable of replacing diesel oil. Both reactions happen in the presence of a catalyst, which may be sodium hydroxide (NaOH) or potassium hydroxide (KOH). It is very difficult to generically decide which of the two catalysts should be used, leaving the decision to be made for each case. Table 5.9 briefly summarizes the characteristics of the production.

All around the world, biodiesel has been produced from methanol but where ethanol is available, like in Brazil and in the United States, the advantages of using the ethyl process are related to the availability of the product, and the supply chain and infrastructure. From an environmental perspective, ethanol also has advantages over methanol, since the latter is produced from petroleum derivatives or NG and is a toxic substance. This environmental advantage may not exist if methanol is produced from biomass.

TABLE 5.9 Biodiesel production characteristics in function of the chosen route

Production characteristics	Process type	
	Methyl	Ethyl
Amount of alcohol consumed per 1000 L of biodiesel	90 kg	130 kg
Average alcohol price	US$ 190/kg	US$ 360/kg
Recommended alcohol surplus recoverable through distillation after the reaction	100%	650%
Recommended reaction temperature	60°C	85°C
Reaction time	45 min	90 min

Source: Made by the author based on Ejaz M. Shahid and Younis Jamal (2011). Production of biodiesel: a technical review, Renew. Sust. Energ. Rev., 15, 9, 4732–4745.

On the other hand, considering that in Brazil ethanol has already been widely used as automotive fuel and additive in gasoline, producing biodiesel from methanol obtained from NG may be a way of better using the national resources of this fossil energy source and diversifying the Brazilian energy matrix, taking less dependence and shortage risks. The same reason may be used to choose the biodiesel route for any country that has the same diversity of fuel options as Brazil.

The product of the transesterification reaction may be subdivided into two phases: the heavy phase, made of a mixture of glycerin, alcohol, water, and impurities; and the light phase, made of ester (methyl or ethyl), alcohol, water, and impurities. It is possible to find traces of glycerin in the light phase and of ester in the heavy phase.

The heavy phase is submitted to the alcohol recovery process, which is made through evaporation. The alcohol and water mixture that vaporizes this process is sent to the alcohol dehydration process through distillation. Raw glycerin is submitted to the process of glycerin distillation.

Evaporation is also used to eliminate the alcohol and water mixture from the ester, which is then submitted to the purification process. The alcohol and water mixture are submitted to dehydration.

The dehydration process is much easier with the methanol and water mixture than with the ethanol and water mixture because the volatility difference between methanol and water is very high and there is no azeotropism[10] to make the separation difficult, which is not the case with ethanol.

---

10. Azeotropism: phenomenon presented by the solutions of two or more substances that, under constant pressure, have a perfectly determined isothermal vaporization temperature. The water and ethanol mixture form a homogeneous azeotrope, since the mixture has only one phase in which the constant pressure boils at constant temperature.

Once it has undergone the process of alcohol recovery, the ester must be submitted to a purification process in which it is washed through centrifugation and dehumidified so that its characteristics perfectly match the desired specifications. This is a very critical phase and must be thoroughly controlled so that all the impurities are eliminated, especially glycerin residues.

Raw glycerin is a commercial product, but a higher market value is attributed to purified glycerin, which is produced through vacuum distillation, resulting in a clean and transparent product commercially called distilled glycerin, which has applications in the chemical and pharmaceutical industries. Studies are still being carried out regarding the applications of the residue of this process, containing 10%–15% of glycerin.

The description of the production process presented before has a general application in the production of biodiesel from oils and fats rich in triglycerides. Considering the potential of soy as feedstock to produce biodiesel, we decided to highlight the particularities of this process, which will be presented next.

Soy oil is made of triglycerides (97.7% in weight), carbonates (0.02% in weight), nonsaponifiable material (1.5% in weight), and free fatty acids (0.719% in weight). Once extracted and transported to the biodiesel production plant, this oil must undergo a neutralization process to remove free fatty acids (acidity removal), which generates soap as a residue.

To remove soap, refined oil is washed with hot water and, later, undergoes a drying process before following to the transesterification process, in which it reacts with a product considered an active intermediary, originating from the reaction between alcohols and a base, thus producing fatty acid ester and glycerin.

The active intermediary is a result of the reaction between the alcohol, usually methane, with a base, usually sodium (NaOH) or potassium (KOH) hydroxide, which works as a catalyst. Anhydrous ethanol might also be used, with a maximum tolerable percentage of 2% of water, since water acts as an inhibitor of the reaction. This reaction occurs preferably with alcohols of low molecular weight such as methanol, which has been preferred due to its high reactivity and attractive price in the world market, causing the fatty acid methyl ester to be the biodiesel produced all around the world.

The productive process occurs in two steps. Initially, methanol is mixed with the catalyst to produce the active intermediary. The latter is then pumped to a reactor, in which it will come in contact with soy oil to result in the transesterification. After the reaction glycerin is separated in decantation tanks or through centrifugation and methyl ester is removed and distilled.

On average, the reaction of degreased soy oil with 11% in methanol weight results in 88% of biodiesel and 9.2% of glycerin (Ferrés, 2001). The difference is in the form of soap. In the case of ethanol, it is necessary to use 13%–15% in alcohol weight, obtaining 85% of biodiesel and 8.8% of glycerin.

Energy sources for transportation Chapter | 5 **215**

5.5.4 Distribution

The biodiesel distribution stage is very similar to that of diesel oil. If it is used as an additive to be mixed with diesel oil, biodiesel must be made available at the distributors, who will be responsible for mixing it at the specified proportion, as is done with anhydrous alcohol. If it is used in pure form, meeting specific market niches, there should be tanks to store it at the distributors and at the service stations. In this case, special care must be taken regarding water contamination, which may accelerate product degradation.

5.5.5 End use

One of the great advantage of biodiesel is its adequacy to diesel cycle engine, since, the application of other fuels that are cleaner than the conventional ones (such as CNG) requires the adaptation and/or replacement of engines, the combustion of biodiesel does not require great changes, becoming a renewable fuel alternative that is capable of powering the whole existing diesel oil fleet.

Based on the European experience, problems may happen due to the inadequate use of fatty acid methyl esters. These problems may occur due to the existence of contaminants resulting from the production process, due to the properties of the fuel itself or due to its degradation.

Current knowledge indicates that there should be a standardization of the properties of fatty acid esters and its quality control, which, if taken into consideration, guarantee the use of biodiesel in engines originally designed to use diesel oil without the need of adaptations, thus minimizing the probability of failures.

Regarding the North American experience about the results of 20 studies that tested (with permanent or transient dynamometer tests) biodiesel or its blends (B10 to B100) with diesel oil in engines (several models and manufacturing years), the authors concluded that it is not possible to identify any power loss or consumption increase with the use of biodiesel or any of its blends at the significance level of 90%.

The possible explanation for the results is that biodiesel's higher calorific value, which is inferior to that of diesel oil (around 9.6% lower than diesel oil), is virtually compensated by its higher density (around 3.5% higher than diesel oil) and higher cetane number (around 9.5% higher than diesel oil).

Most tests were carried out with diesel cycle 4S ICEs, Detroit Diesel—DDC Series 60 (11.1 L) and 50 (8.5 L), manufactured between 1991 and 1998, and Cummins N14. These engines were already equipped with electronic injection and were ready to be used in trucks and buses.

The North American experience reports that, in power tests, the maximum reduction found with the use of B100 was 2.8%. Regarding increased consumption, there were results in which the difference in consumption for blends B0,

216 Transportation, energy use and environmental impacts

B20, B35, B65, and B100 does not exceed 5%. In all cases, these variations are considered imperceptible in practice.

Regarding atmospheric pollutant emissions, there is a trend of increasing NOx emissions and reducing the remaining regulated pollutants (HC, CO, and PM) when using higher concentrations of biodiesel in the blend.

EXAMPLE 5.2   A brief history of the use of biodiesel as automotive fuel in Brazil

In 1983 and 1984 tests were carried out in Brazil with a fleet of 16 trucks and buses traveling around 870, 000 km, and 6 tractors and 1 *moto-scraper* operating for around 5000 h. The fuel used was soy oil ethyl ester, pure or mixed with diesel oil in the proportions of 30% and 70%. The vehicles had normal driveability and performance, except in some cases in which a small level of injector coking was observed. The substitution of these components was enough to correct the performance characteristics of the vehicles. The injector coking problems were more common in engines that operated at higher rotations and with low cylinder capacity in urban application. Engines of higher cylinder capacity or with turbocharger had no problems. Energy performance was maintained while the injectors were clean. An average consumption increase was seen when using pure biodiesel.

Still in the 1980s, long-term tests carried out with soy oil methyl or ethyl esters had equivalent results among themselves but, if compared to diesel oil, the engines showed a 4% power loss and a 10% increase in specific consumption.

In the city of Curitiba, between January and March 1998, field tests with 40 urban buses were carried using a B20 blend of soy oil methyl ester. The tests were supervised by the city urbanization company (URBS). A similar fleet was kept running on diesel oil as reference. The tested vehicles did not have any of their components changed and the test accumulated a total of 426,617 km along which there was no noteworthy difference in vehicle operation, maintenance and drivability when compared to diesel oil. The average efficiency (km/L) of the vehicles running on biodiesel is 2.3% lower than that of diesel oil vehicles.

Urban buses tested in Curitiba adequately represent the technology used in the 1990s with mechanical-injection engines equipped with turbocharger and aftercooler. As with the experience presented for the technology used in the 1980s, the use of biodiesel and diesel oil blends in vehicles manufactured in the 1990s does not apparently cause major problems.

In 2001, Petrobras (Brazilian state oil company) made an assessment of the biodiesel content in diesel oil blends. Blends of 5% (B5) and 20% (B20) in soy oil methyl ester volume were tested. Results showed a progressive increase in the cetane number with the increased amount of biodiesel in the blend. The cetane number grew from 42.5, found for pure diesel oil, to 45 in B20. There was a significant improvement in lubricity after 5% biodiesel blend. This characteristic remained approximately constant in the case of B20. On the other hand, instability increased along with the increased biodiesel percentage in the blend, which is characterized by the higher number of particles in the fuel after exposure to the oxidizing atmosphere.

Energy sources for transportation **Chapter | 5 217**

A long-term test with a fleet of six Comlurb (Rio de Janeiro Urban Cleaning Company) trucks in Rio de Janeiro began in June 2003, using: B5 soy oil methyl ester (two vehicles); frying oil residue methyl ester (two vehicles); and low sulfur diesel oil (two vehicles). This test was carried out by the International Virtual Institute for Global Changes from Instituto Alberto Luiz Coimbra de Pósgraduação e Pesquisa (COOPE) a postgraduation unit of Federal University of Rio de Janeiro (IVIG/COPPE/UFRJ)), in partnership with Petrobras Research Center (CENPES), Robert Bosch, Cummings, and Ford. There was no verifiable change in performance or fuel consumption for vehicles that use a blend when compared to trucks that use diesel oil.

In 2004, the National Program for Biodiesel Production and Use (NPBPU) was created as an initiative of the Federal Government; it established the mandatory and progressive addition of biodiesel to petroleum diesel commercialized in Brazil so that, since 2010, the proportion of addition reached 5% in volume, thus the fuel is called B5.

In parallel, tests with biodiesel and petroleum diesel blends at different proportions were carried out in different Brazilian cities, especially the use of B20 (blend of 20% biodiesel and 80% petroleum diesel) in bus fleets in São Paulo and Rio de Janeiro in the second half of 2000. These tests proved that the use of B20 does not cause problems in engines designed to use B5 and that environmental benefits can be achieved regarding the reduction in the emissions of carbon monoxide (CO), hydrocarbons (HC), particulate matter (PM), and sulfur oxides (SO_x), besides a reduction in carbon dioxide (CO_2) that is approximately equivalent to the percentage of biodiesel added to diesel oil.

Regarding the use of 100% biodiesel, the most comprehensive experience happened in the city of Curitiba, where, since 2009, part of the bi-articulated bus fleet runs on B100 without any significant problems being found.

In March 2018, the addition of biodiesel to petroleum diesel commercialized for transportation use in Brazil reached 10%. This biofuel is mainly produced from surplus soy oil and from beef tallow, the latter on a smaller scale.

5.6 Advanced biofuels

Due to the specific characteristics of countries regarding their productive potential, related to land and water availability, solar irradiance and climate, biofuels may represent a promising alternative to conventional fuels. Some solutions capable of expanding the offer of biofuels, both in quality and quantity, are being researched all over the world. Because these products are still under development, it is not possible to identify specific feedstock or consolidated productive processes. Therefore, a brief description of conceptual focus will be presented next. It is highly recommended for the readers to deepen their knowledge about these alternatives through additional research.

5.6.1 Cellulose ethanol

The production of ethanol, or any other fuel, from cellulose represents an opportunity to use materials that are rich in vegetable fiber (such as bagasse and

218 Transportation, energy use and environmental impacts

straw from sugarcane and corn, the residues of wood extraction and agricultural handling) as feedstock in a process that involves chemical or biochemical reactions to break cellulose, hemicellulose, and pectin chains, polymers that constitute the fibrous structure of plants.

Biofuels made using these processes are usually called second-generation biofuels (2G), in contrast to those produced using traditional processes, such as sugarcane ethanol, presented in Section 5.3, which are called first-generation biofuels (1G).

The biomass to be used in this process is waste and/or residue of plant cultivation and handling that will not be reused as human or animal food, and could have a nobler destination than the traditional ones (such as composting to produce fertilizer, burning to produce heat, or destination to sanitary landfills), which would increase the offer of renewable fuel.

Furthermore, whenever the biomass to be used is associated with a conventional biofuel production process, such as those presented in Sections 5.4 and 5.5, the use of cellulose to produce fuel will increase the productive capacity of the facility, as long as the aspects of technical, economic, and environmental feasibility are considered.

At any rate, the supply of the feedstock to be used depends on the source of biomass. In the specific case of sugarcane bagasse and straw, the scenario will be the same as the one described for sugarcane ethanol (Section 5.4). The existing limitation regards the step of converting cellulose into ethanol, which is still complex, inefficient and expensive, since cellulose must be successively converted into other substances until it is transformed into sugar and converted into ethanol through the usual productive process.

5.6.2 Sugarcane diesel

Another fuel that is in experimental phase is sugarcane diesel. In this case, a modified enzyme transforms sugarcane juice into an intermediary substance that, after being hydrogenated, produces a hydrocarbon of 17 carbon atoms (C17), which can be considered a hydrocarbon of the range of diesel distilled from petroleum.

An alternative and renewable fuel with these characteristics is perfect for the application at conventional propulsion systems, which use diesel cycle ICE (CI), since its use is independent of any type of adaptation in storage, feeding, and ignition systems of engines that were developed for use in diesel oil, and in these cases are called *drop in* fuels.

For sugarcane diesel, the productive process of the feedstock to be used is also very similar to the one already described for sugarcane ethanol (Section 5.4), the difference being the fact that the product to be made available by the production plant is not an alcohol but a hydrocarbon, which requires changes to the final steps of converting sugarcane into a hydrocarbon and not an alcohol.

5.6.3 Enzymatic biodiesel

Different from the traditional chemical process of biodiesel production through the conversion of oils and fats through basic catalysis (Section 5.5), this process uses an enzyme capable of transforming oil and fats into esters (biodiesel) through a biochemical process.

The advantage of this process is that these enzymes are capable of acting on residual feedstock with low quality, much acidity or excess cellulose, without potentially compromising the productivity of the process. With this method, a series of residual feedstock could be introduced into the productive chain of biodiesel, such as residual frying oil, animal fat (bovine, swine, poultry, and fish), and vegetable oil residues with a proportional increase in the productive scale of this fuel.

The current disadvantage of this process lies in the cost of the enzyme and in the efficiency of the conversion of feedstock into biodiesel, which depends on the type of feedstock and impacts the product's final quality.

As with the production of fuels from vegetable residue, when the biomass to be used in this process comes from waste and/or residue, this process is considered a nobler destination than sending this material to the landfill, which further expands the offer of a renewable fuel.

In the case the substitution of the traditional chemical process of converting oils and fats for the biochemical process is being considered, the supply of the feedstock to be used will also be the same as the one presented for biodiesel (Section 5.5). In the case of using residual feedstock, each will have a specific supply chain depending on the production process to which it is associated.

5.6.4 Synthetic diesel obtained from biomass

Synthetic diesel is a fuel with identical chemical characteristics as petroleum diesel, and it has different production methods. As with sugarcane diesel, it is considered a *drop-in* fuel and it may be produced from biomass (*biomass-to-liquid*—BTL) and from the *hydrotreatment of vegetable oils* (HVO).

The production of synthetic diesel through the BTL method has three steps: generation of synthetic gas, conversion of the gas through the Fischer-Tropsch process, and generation of the synthetic process. In this case, the synthetic gas is produced through the gasification of cellulose biomass.

Synthetic diesel oil obtained through the HVO method is produced via the hydrotreatment of vegetable oils that come, for example, from canola oil, sunflower, soy, palm, or even from jatropha, algae, and animal fats. In this case, not competing with the food sector should be a goal. The hydrotreatment process consists in using hydrogen to remove the oxygen from the triglyceride (vegetable oil) and later refinement to produce a compound in the form of hydrocarbon. The process generates a gas, similar to LPG, which used to supply energy to the process, gasoline and diesel. The HVO fuel has a very high cetane number and its characteristics are similar to that of the BTL fuel.

220 Transportation, energy use and environmental impacts

Whenever the production of synthetic fuel is associated with some type of biomass originating from vegetable culture, as in the case of HVO applied to vegetable oils, the supply of feedstock will follow a process similar to the one described in Section 5.5. In case of using the BTL method, the feedstock used may even be residues similar to those used in the production of cellulose ethanol or enzymatic biodiesel, as already described.

5.6.5 Biokerosene

Biokerosene is the fuel formed by a mixture of hydrocarbons, both linear and cyclic, produced from renewable feedstock, with a composition similar to that of fossil kerosene; it is also a *drop-in* fuel.

As with biodiesel, the production of biokerosene may use vegetable oils rich in short-chain fatty acids that, after a transesterification process, result in a mixture of esters and glycerin. The heavier esters are separated and treated through chemical reactions to form a mixture of hydrocarbons and oxygenated hydrocarbons. The oxygenated compound is then submitted to a hydrogenation step that generates biokerosene or biogasoline.

Because it is a *drop-in* fuel, biokerosene has the potential to be used as a substitute for aviation kerosene (jet fuel), depending on the chemical stability of the product and its production cost.

When it uses vegetable oils and animal fat, as in the case of biodiesel, the supply of raw material to produce biokerosene follows a process similar to the one presented in Section 5.4.

5.6.6 Bio-oil

Bio-oil is a renewable fuel originating from biomass. It is produced through the thermal decomposition (pyrolysis) at temperatures of 500°C of feedstock such as sawdust, sugarcane and corn bagasse, agricultural residues, cattle-raising residues, and rice hull. The preliminary result of this process originates coal, aerosols, vapors, and pyroligneous acid that, after condensation, transforms into a black oil.

This product has physicochemical properties similar to those of petroleum fuel oil and, after being refined and having its properties enhanced, it may be used as fuel in diesel cycle ICEs, particularly for vessels.

Because it is a fuel derived from vegetable and animal residues, it has a lower feedstock acquisition price, which may reduce its production costs, depending on the performance of the process being used. On the other hand, the challenge that remains in the consolidation of bio-oil production is the cost and the performance of the production process, which still needs to be improved, even specifying the best sources of feedstock.

Because it primarily uses biomass originating from waste and/or residue, this production process is also considered to be a nobler destination to these materials than being sent to sanitary landfills. In this case, the supply of feedstock will depend on the productive process to which the residue is associated, following the

Energy sources for transportation **Chapter | 5 221**

same logic already presented to produce cellulose ethanol, enzymatic biodiesel, and diesel oil in the BTL form.

5.6.7 Biogas

Biogas is a substance obtained from the decomposition of organic matter, such as sanitary sewage, solid residues, and natural residues of plant pruning and vegetable crops. It may be naturally released into the atmosphere through the decomposition of solid residue in sanitary landfills or may be produced through the anaerobic digestion of sewage, animal manure, or other kinds of organic material.

Different from NG, biogas has a lower amount of methane in its composition, besides the presence of other gases such as CO_2. Thus, for biogas to be used as a fuel with commercial application in transportation, it must be submitted to a process of purification to remove impurities and increase the concentration of methane, starting to be called biomethane.

As with NG, biomethane may be used in Otto cycle engines that equip road vehicles for freight transportation or diesel cycle engines, in which case they need to be adapted with a *dual-fuel* system; in this scenario, biomethane will be mixed with intake air and diesel oil will be injected in a lower volume only to cause the beginning of the burn.

Once it is produced, biomethane may be directed to the same distribution network of NG and used in compressed form to power road vehicle fleets, as discussed in Section 5.2, and even to power locomotives and vessels, the latter usually in the *dual-fuel* form.

5.6.8 Dimethyl ether

Dimethyl ether (DME) is a compound produced from the gasification of biomass. It is considered a second-generation fuel, since it is produced from cellulose of vegetable residue. It has the same chemical formula as ethanol, but ethanol has a stronger molecular association due to the bond with hydrogen.

DME may be used in a diesel cycle engine and may have the same calorific value and injection point used for diesel oil. However, it has low lubricity and viscosity, requiring the use of an additive, which prevents it from being considered a *drop-in* fuel.

As in the case of fuels obtained through the BTL method, the feedstock used may even be residues similar to the ones used in the production of cellulose ethanol or enzymatic biodiesel, as already shown before, and its supply methods depend on the production processes associated with it.

5.7 Advanced energy sources

In addition to advanced biofuels, described before, other energy sources have been developed and improved to be used in transportation. Hydrogen and electric power stand out, as shown in the following.

5.7.1 Hydrogen

Hydrogen is considered a clean burn fuel because it only generates water vapor and is, therefore, a potential alternative to fossil fuels. On the other hand, it is important to assess the whole life cycle of the fuel, which, in the case of hydrogen, may increase air pollutant emissions during its supply, depending on the chemical production process that is used.

There are many ways of producing hydrogen, one of them is water hydrolysis, which may consume a significant amount of energy. Furthermore, when considering chemical and biochemical processes, hydrogen may be produced: through the process of thermochemical gasification along with a transformation of the gas; by means of a quick pyrolysis followed by the reform of the carbohydrate fractions of bio-oil; by the conversion of the synthetic gas produced by the biomass; by the supercritical or microbial conversion of biomass; or by the fermentation of dark hydrogen. It may also be produced from liquid compounds, such as ethanol, methanol, and ammonia.

Besides its burning in Otto cycle ICEs, in pure form or mixed with NG or biomethane, a more adequate opportunity to use hydrogen in transportation is its application as energy carrier in a fuel cell capable of generating electric power in an electric motor.

5.7.2 Electromobility

As presented in Chapter 4, the use of electric power in the propulsion of vehicles in transportation is a fast growing world trend. The use of electric power seems to be an alternative that is technically viable, environmentally friendly, and of potential economic viability for land transportation (road, rail, and pipeline) of passengers and freight. Even the air and water modes already have solutions for electric traction, considering the autonomy and weight limitations of the vehicles.

Due to its characteristics of energy efficiency, zero gas emissions in end use, and low noise generations, there is a significant trend indicating that battery electric vehicles (BEV) will prevail in transportation sectors, including bicycles, motorcycles, cars, light commercial vehicles, urban buses, and light trucks. Great effort is being made so that the batteries used in these vehicles become lighter and cheaper to enable a quantity of stored energy that guarantees the necessary autonomy for daily operations in urban areas.

In particular, the use of urban electric buses seems to be a trend for the near future, either in a design that only uses batteries (BEV), in association with energy obtained from air grids (trolleybus) or in the form of hybrid vehicles. Because they do not generate atmospheric pollutant emissions in end use and are associated with a regular operation of limited autonomy, electric buses are being implemented in different cities of the world as a clean alternative for urban passenger transportation.

Energy sources for transportation **Chapter | 5** **223**

Likewise, electric and hybrid trucks may be used in the segments of urban collection and delivery, primarily in urban centers or in short interurban trips, respecting the autonomy of the batteries and with little compromise to the vehicles' load capacity. For longer trips, hybrid combinations, especially those that may use devices to get energy from air grids when getting next to urban centers, may be interesting alternatives.

The expansion of the electric vehicle fleet will make it possible to also use it as an energy source in the cities, since, when they are not moving, their batteries could supply energy to the main power grid in moments of higher demand and would be later recharged in off-peak hours. Therefore, the electric vehicle fleet could operate as an equalizer of energy offer in electric power supply *smart grids*. With that, electric vehicles have their utility expanded beyond the use in transportation.

For all cases, it is important to conduct a careful assessment of the way electric power is generated, usually considering the energy generation life cycle assessment tool, as shown in Chapter 3. In order for environmental and social benefits to actually exist, it is necessary that electric power be generated from a clean and renewable source, such as solar, wind, hydro power, and biomass. This may be done individually or through the combination of its uses in order to take advantage of the best alternatives available in each country.

5.8 Final considerations

This chapter sought to present an overview of the energy alternatives for transportation, focusing on the road transportation mode, which is the most used one all over the world. For that, internationally consolidated energy alternatives have been considered, with more details given on those that have a more frequent application in the global scope.

Therefore, besides the conventional fuels of consolidated use all over the world, such as gasoline, diesel oil, and other petroleum derivatives, the chapter also addressed NG, ethanol, and biodiesel.

It could be seen that, for road transportation, NG is used in its compressed form (CNG). This fuel is mostly used for commercial vehicles, such as taxis, buses, and trucks, whose daily operation involves average mileages that enable the amortization of additional investments in adaptation through the use in a fuel that is cheaper than gasoline or diesel oil.

Ethanol is a biofuel that can be added to gasoline or even replace it in Otto cycle engines. As shown, it is a widely used alternative in Brazil where it is produced from sugarcane. Ethanol is also used in the United States on a smaller scale, where it is produced from corn, and in Europe, where it is most commonly produced from beet.

Nowadays, biodiesel also seems to be a predominant alternative worldwide to replace diesel oil. Its main feedstock sources are soy, rapeseed and palm oil, and beef tallow. It may also be produced from residual oils.

224 Transportation, energy use and environmental impacts

A set of advanced biofuels are already being experimentally produced and tested all over the world and may become alternatives to conventional fuels, depending on their technical, economic, environmental, and social viability. Examples of these biofuels are: cellulose ethanol, sugarcane diesel, enzymatic biodiesel, hydrogenated vegetable oils, biogas, biokerosene, bio-oil, and DME. On the other hand, electromobility emerges as a trend for transportation energy use in a future that seems ever closer.

5.9 Exercises

1. What are the conventional energy sources (fuels) for transportation worldwide?
2. What are the most common alternative energy sources (fuels) for transportation worldwide? Describe the main origins of these alternative energy sources.
3. List suggestions of alternative energy sources for rail freight transportation and justify your choice.
4. List suggestions of alternative energy sources for water transportation, justify your choice and indicate the possible limitations involved.
5. List suggestions of alternative energy sources for air transportation, justify your answer and indicate the possible limitations involved.
6. What cares must be taken when planning to extensively use electric power in road transportation?
7. What are the difficulties of introducing fuel cells for use in transportation?
8. Define biofuel. What questioning lies in this concept?
9. Describe at least three types of advanced biofuels indicating their range and limitations in the substitution of conventional fuels.
10. What are the kinds of feedstock used to produce biodiesel?

References

Bentley, R.W., 2002. Global oil and gas depletion: an overview. Energy Police 30, 189–205.

CONCAWE, 2014. Petroleum Substances. In: Workshop on Substance Identification and Sameness, Helsinki.

EBB, 2018. European Biodiesel Production. European Biodiesel Board, Statistics. http://www.ebb-eu.org/stats.php. (Access 31 July 2018).

Ferrés, J.D., 2001. Biodiesel: production and costs in Brazil (Biodiesel: Produção e custos no Brasil). In: Anais do Seminário Biodiesel. Brazilian Association of Automotive Engineering (Associação Brasileira de Engenharia Automotiva) (AEA), São Paulo, SP.

IANGV, 2018. Natural Gas Vehicle Fleet—2017. International Association on Natural Gas Vehicles. http://www.iangv.org/current-ngv-stats/. (Access 31 July 2018).

Parente, E.J.S., 2003. Biodeisel: A Technological Adventure in a Funny Country (Biodiesel: uma aventura tecnológica num país engraçado), 1ª ed. Fortaleza, CE, Tecbio.

Wright, K., 1990. The shape of things to go. Automakers turn to high technology in the search for car that is clean, safe and fun. Sci. Am. 262 (5), 58–67.

Further reading

de Acioli, J.L., 1994. Fontes de Energia, first ed. Editora Universidade de Brasília, Brasília.

Demirbas, A., 2010. Methane gas hydrate. Chapter 2, In: Natural Gas. Springer. http://www.springer.com/978-1-84882-871-1. Access 31 July 2018.

Rochan, M.H., Capaz, R.S., Lora, E.E.S., Nogueira, L.A.H., Leme, M.M.V., Renó, M.L.G., Olmo, O.A., 2014. Life cycle assessment (LCA) for biofuels in Brazilian conditions: a meta-analysis. Renew. Sust. Energ. Rev. 37, 435–459.

Shahid, E.M., Jamal, Y., 2011. Production of biodiesel: a technical review. Renew. Sust. Energ. Rev. 15 (9), 4732–4745.

Chapter 6

Air pollutant and greenhouse gas emissions (GHG)

General goal

The general goal of this chapter is to present the profile of air pollutant and greenhouse gas (GHG) emissions resulting from the operation of transportation and from the use of fossil fuels. Emphasis is naturally given to road transportation due to its importance.

At the end of this chapter, the reader should be able to:

1. Understand the concepts related to air pollution, the factors that influence this pollution, and its effects on human health and material goods (buildings, equipment, urban furniture, etc.).
2. Understand the concepts related to GHG emission and its consequence for the planet.
3. Analyze how transportation contributes to air pollutant and GHG emissions.
4. Identify the emission factors per mode of transportation and what actions may be taken to reduce atmospheric environmental impacts caused by the transportation sector.

6.1 Introduction

The activity of transportation contributes to the emission of air, water, and soil pollutants, with highlights to air pollution, since it is strictly associated with the operation of the different modes of transportation and the burning of fuels as an energy source.

There have always been discussions about the atmospheric pollution caused by transportation in urban areas, since this activity is one of the greatest contributors to this kind of problem.

The emission of gases originating from the activity of transportation reaches local, regional, and global levels, compromising the health of living beings, and contributing to global warming and, consequently, to climate change. This happens because the main energy source used by transportation is petroleum-derived fossil fuels.

Each mode of transportation causes air pollution in a different way and intensity, and the emission of all kinds of pollutants may have its intensity increased depending on deficiencies in the physical and maintenance conditions

---

Transportation, Energy Use and Environmental Impacts. https://doi.org/10.1016/B978-0-12-813454-2.00006-4
© 2019, Elsevier Editora Ltda. Published by Elsevier Inc. All rights reserved.

228 Transportation, energy use and environmental impacts

of vehicles and roads, on the kind of technology used in the propulsion systems, and in the way of managing the operation.

Considering the importance of this sector regarding this topic, there is extensive regulation at a national and international level aiming to decrease the emission of air pollutants. Furthermore, initiatives to improve technology and operations management may be applied to reduce air pollutant and GHG emission rates resulting from each of the modes of transportation.

This chapter addresses, in Section 6.2, air pollution produced by the different modes of transportation, focusing on the road mode and on its effects on the physical, biotic, and anthropic environments. The concepts related to the emission of GHG are presented in Section 6.3, highlighting their relationship with global warming and climate change. Next, Section 6.4 presents the emission factors per mode of transportation and which actions may be taken to reduce the environmental impacts on the atmosphere resulting from the transportation sector.

6.2 Air pollution

Atmospheric air is basically made of 78% of nitrogen (N_2) and 21% of oxygen (O_2), also having traces of other gases [argon (Ar)–0.93%; carbon dioxide (CO_2)–0.03%; neon (Ne)–0.0018%; helium (He)–0.0005%; methane (CH_4)–0.04% and krypton (Kr)–0.0001%]. This composition of atmospheric air allows the physical, biotic, and anthropic environments to harmonically coexist on the Earth's surface. Air pollution is understood as the modification of atmospheric air.

Air pollution results from the emission of gases, solids, and/or liquid aerosols, finely divided, all of which are known as air pollutants, since their existence, when they occur in volumes above the capacity of the atmosphere itself to dissipate them or dispose of them through their incorporation into the soil or into bodies of water, results in the modification of the composition of atmospheric air and compromises the health of living beings (animals and plants) and the integrity of material goods.

A pollutant is any substance present in the air that, due to its concentration, might make the air inappropriate or harmful to health, causing any inconvenience to public well-being, damage to property, animals or plants, that is, harmful regarding safety, the use and enjoyment of property and the normal activities of a community.

Air pollution may be classified as: (1) anthropogenic, the one caused by human action resulting from the activities of the industry, transportation, and energy production sectors, etc.; and (2) natural, the one caused by natural processes, such as volcanic eruptions, biological processes, soil dirt, and water droplets from the ocean carried by the winds.

The sources of anthropogenic air pollution may be fixed, when they concentrate on certain points of a geographical surface, almost all of them being of industrial nature; or mobile, when they are distributed throughout a broad geographical surface, which is the case of transportation.

Air pollutants may be classified as follows:

- Regarding their origin:
  - *Primary*: those directly liberated by the emission sources. In this case, some examples are: carbon monoxide (CO), nitrogen oxides (NO_x), hydrocarbons (HC), particulate matter (PM), and sulfur oxides (SO_x).
  - *Secondary*: those formed in the atmosphere through the chemical reaction between primary pollutants and natural atmospheric components, such as ozone (O_3).
- Regarding their physical state:
  - *Gases*: They are characterized by separate molecules with great mobility and that do not have defined form and volume, such as CO, NO_x, HC, SO_x, and O_3.
  - *Particles*: They are solid or liquid materials that are suspended in the air, in the form of dust, mist, aerosol, smoke, and soot, such as PM.
- Regarding their chemical composition:
  - *Organic*: Organic compounds or molecules are chemical substances that have carbon and hydrogen in their structure, often combined with oxygen, nitrogen, sulfur, phosphorus, and boron. Some examples of these are methane (CH_4) and the chlorofluorocarbons (CFC);
  - *Inorganic*: Usually, the inorganic compounds do not have carbon connected to hydrogen, such as NO_x, CO, and O_3.

6.2.1 Negative effects of air pollution on human health, on the existence of living beings, and on material goods

Air pollution has negative effects both for human health and for the existence and integrity of material goods.

Depending on their concentration on the composition of atmospheric air, air pollutants may cause respiratory, cardiovascular, skin and visual diseases, etc. Damages to health depend on the dose to which human beings are exposed as a function of the concentration of inhaled air and the time of exposure. Table 6.1 shows a selection of the air pollutants coming from the operation of transportation and their effects on health.

In the case of material goods, there is damage such as metal corrosion, accelerated degradation of paints and external coatings in urban and industrial environments, and rubber drying, making it crack, especially due to atmospheric ozone.

6.2.2 Air pollution caused by the transportation sector

The transportation sector is one of the greatest contributors to air pollutant emissions worldwide, especially in urban areas, since it depends on the burning of fossil fuels as a source of energy.

According to the European Environment Agency, in the European Union (EEA, 2017), in 2015, the transportation sector was responsible for the emission

230 Transportation, energy use and environmental impacts

TABLE 6.1 Potential health effects of air pollution

Pollutant	Potential health effects
Total suspended particles (TSP)	The smaller the particle size, the more prejudicial its effect on health will be. Cause more severe effects on people with lung disease, asthma, and bronchitis
Inhalable particles (PM_{10}) and smoke	Cause the worsening of respiratory diseases and may lead to premature death
Sulfur oxide (SO_x)	Cause discomfort in breathing, respiratory diseases, and the worsening of preexisting respiratory and cardiovascular diseases. People with asthma, chronic heart, and lung diseases are more sensitive to this air pollutant
Nitrogen oxides (NO_x)	Causes increased sensitivity to asthma and to bronchitis, and low resistance to respiratory infections
Carbon monoxide (CO)	Impairs reflexes, the capacity to estimate time intervals, learning, work performance, and visual acuity
Aldehydes (R-COH)	Cause irritation to the eyes, nose, and throat and are carcinogenic agents
Ozone (O_3)	Causes irritation to the eyes and respiratory tract and decreased respiratory capacity. Exposure to high concentrations may result in a feeling of chest tightness, coughing, and wheezing
Hydrocarbons (HC)	They are considered carcinogenic and mutagenic, causing irritation to the eyes, nose, skin, and respiratory tract

of 23% of carbon monoxide (CO), 57% of nitrogen oxides (NO_x), 11% of non-methane volatile organic compounds (NMVOC), 20% of particulate matter smaller than $2\,\mu m$ ($MP_{2.5}$), 13% of particulate matter smaller than $10\,\mu m$ (MP_{10}), and 18% of sulfur oxides (SO_x).

In this context, road transportation was mostly responsible for the emissions of CO (87%), NMVOC (82%), PM_{10} (60%), and NO_x (53%). Water transportation was the main factor responsible for the emission of SO_x, 89% of which associated with deep sea maritime transportation, and 6% to inland waterways transportation, due to the use of fuel oils with loosely controlled sulfur contents. The railway and air modes of transportation are responsible for marginal fractions of air pollutant emissions, rarely exceeding 5%.

A consultation made with the North-American Agency of Environmental Protection (EPA, 2016) shows that, in 2017, the transportation sector was mostly responsible for the emissions of CO (35%) and NO_x (39%). In the case of the NMVOC, $PM_{2.5}$, PM_{10}, and SO_2 (sulfur dioxide), the emissions associated with transportation in the United States represent fractions of 18%, 9%, 4%, and 5%,

Air pollutant and greenhouse gas emissions (GHG) Chapter | 6 **231**

respectively. When only considering the emissions of the transportation sector, road transportation answers for the highest fraction of emissions of all the air pollutants, being responsible for the emission of 89% of CO, 87% of NO_x, 24% of $PM_{2.5}$, 40% of PM_{10}, 63% of NMVOC, and 19% of SO_2.

EXAMPLE 6.1 Air pollution caused by transportation in developing countries—the case of Brazil

Although there are no inventories available that are as specific as the ones found for the European Union and the United States, it is estimated that, in Brazil, the participation of transportation in air pollutant emissions is very expressive. Among the modes of transportation, the road mode is the one that emits the highest volumes of air pollutants, since, at previously addressed in this book, it represents the highest use percentages both for passenger and freight transportation, which leads to the highest percentages of fuel burning.

The most recent data, which come from the National Inventory of Atmospheric Emissions by Road Automotive Vehicles developed by the Ministry of the Environment in 2012, report that 81% of CO emissions are associated with cars and motorcycles powered by gasoline or ethanol, and 92% of the emissions of NO_x are associated with vehicles powered by diesel oil (trucks and buses), which also answer for 96% of the emissions of PM and 29% of the emissions of NMVOC. These numbers show that vehicles powered by diesel oil predominantly contribute to the emission of NO_x and PM, while cars and motorcycles, which use Otto cycle engines and burn gasoline, ethanol, and/or natural gas, are the main agents responsible for the emission of CO and NMVOC.

As seen in Chapter 5, the main energy source for transportation are petroleum-derived fuels. These fuels, when burned, generate a gas emissions profile, as can be schematically seen in Fig. 6.1.

The inputs of the combustion process are air (formed mostly by N_2 and O_2) and fuel (made of hydrocarbons, contaminants, and additives).

The internal combustion engine transforms the chemical energy stored in the fuels into heat through the combustion with air. This heat causes the expansion of the combustion gases within the engine's cylinder, generating the reciprocating movement of the piston and the rotation of the crankshaft, which results in the movement of the vehicle via the operation of the transmission system.

In an ideal situation, which never occurs in practice, the complete burning of the fuel is expected, releasing water (H_2O) and carbon dioxide (CO_2). Usually, there is an incomplete burn in function of a set of natural conditions of the complex working of internal combustion engines. In this case, besides the gas products of the complete burn, there is the release of a series of gases, as can be seen in Fig. 6.1. A set of these gases may be considered as air pollutants, since they change the composition of atmospheric air in the areas around where they are emitted, such as: CO, NO_x, HC, SO_x, particulate matter (PM), and finely divided carbon (C). The use of a device for the post-treatment of gases emitted by

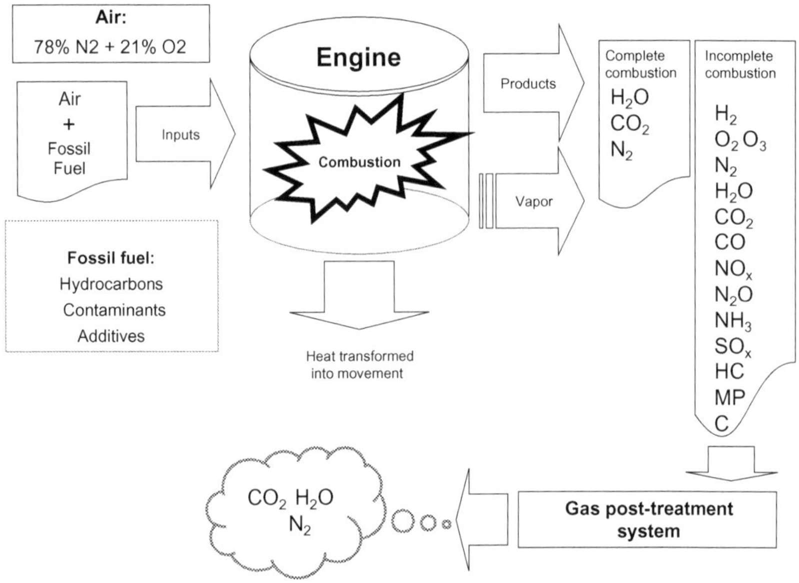

232 Transportation, energy use and environmental impacts

Legends: N_2 – Nitrogen, O_2 – Oxygen, H_2O – Water, CO_2 – Carbon Dioxide, H_2 – Hydrogen, O_3 – Ozone, CO – Carbon Monoxide, NO_x – Nitrogen Oxides, N_2O – Nitrous Oxide, NH_3 – Ammonia, SO_x – Sulfur Oxides, HC – Hydrocarbons, PM – Particulate Matter and C – Carbon.
Note: Additives aim to clean the fuel injection system, including fuel line, pump, fuel rail, injectors and intake valves. Its use allows the engine to operate under the conditions specified by the manufacturer for a longer time, thus reducing consumption and emissions and increasing the interval between maintenances. Contaminants may be: benzene, toluene, ethylbenzene, xylene. Among the organic substances, benzene is considered the most toxic and most water soluble of them.

FIG. 6.1 Profile of gas emissions resulting from fuel burning.

the engine makes it possible to reduce the final emission of these air pollutants in higher percentages than 50%.

Air pollutants emitted by transportation usually cause environmental impacts, which have local influence, affecting living beings (people, animals, and plants) and buildings located around the place of emissions.

For a set of air pollutants, the extent of the impacts may be higher, causing regional impacts. In this case, the comprehensiveness of air pollution may, depending on the amount of pollutants and on the dispersion conditions on the environment, reach large proportions. An example of that is acid rain, also called acid deposition, which is defined as precipitation in which the pH is acid, with values below 5.6. This phenomenon is caused by gases that may be transported up to 3000 km away.

In the case of transportation, the most common, and also regulated, air pollutants, which act locally, are CO, NO_x, HC and PM. Regarding the air pollutants of regional action, the following stand out, SO_x and NO_x. Table 6.2 shows the air pollutants, their characteristics, and emission sources.

Air pollutant and greenhouse gas emissions (GHG) Chapter | 6 **233**

TABLE 6.2 Local and regional air pollutants—characteristics and emission sources

Type	Characteristics	Emission sources
Total suspended particles (TSP)	Particles of solid or liquid material that are suspended in the air, in the form of dust, mist, aerosol, smoke, soot, etc. Size range < 100 µm	Combustion processes (soot and oil particles)
Inhalable particles (PM_{10}) and smoke	Particles of solid or liquid material that are suspended in the air, in the form of dust, mist, aerosol, smoke, soot, etc. Size range < 10 µm	
Sulfur oxide (SO_x)	Colorless gas with a strong odor, similar to the gas produced in the burning of matchsticks. It may be transformed into SO_3, which, in the presence of water vapor, quickly changes into sulfuric acid (H_2SO_4). It is an important precursor of the sulfates, on the main components of inhalable particles	Burn of fuels that have sulfur or through natural biogenic processes
Nitrogen oxide (NO_x)	Reddish brown gas with a strong odor and highly irritating. It may lead to the formation of nitric acid, nitrates (which contribute to an increase in inhalable particles in the atmosphere) and toxic organic compounds	Processes of combustion and of electric discharges in the atmosphere
Carbon monoxide (CO)	Tasteless, odorless, and colorless gas	Processes of incomplete combustion of fossil fuels and other materials that have carbon
Aldehydes (R-COH)	These are organic compounds that have the radical aldehyde, that is, $-HC=O$	Processes of incomplete combustion of oxygenated biofuels, such as ethanol
Ozone (O_3)	Colorless, odorless gas in environmental concentrations and the main component of photochemical smog	Oxidation of the oxygen that participates in the combustion
Hydrocarbons (HC)	They are organic compounds formed by atoms of carbon and hydrogen	Incomplete burn of fuels, evaporation of fuels, oils, and organic solvents, etc.

234 Transportation, energy use and environmental impacts

EXAMPLE 6.2   Profile of the atmospheric pollution caused by transportation in a megacity—the case of São Paulo

The Technological Company of Environmental Sanitation (Cetesb) of the state of São Paulo periodically produces the air pollutants inventory based on different sources; it highlights the mass of air pollutants resulting from the operation of road transportation in the Metropolitan Region of the state of São Paulo (RMSP) where the largest fleet of vehicles in Brazil operates. Table 6.3 shows the results for the year 2014 (CETESB, 2015), which presents the mass and relative weight percent of the pollutants emitted by the different types of vehicles.

The values shown in Table 6.3 confirm the statements of Example 6.1, where it was highlighted that the emissions of CO and NMVOC are mostly associated with cars and motorcycles powered by gasoline or ethanol, while NO_x and PM are strongly associated with the use of diesel in trucks and buses. The use of diesel is also the main contributor to the emission of SO_x.

6.3   Greenhouse gas (GHG) emissions

Global environmental problems reach the entire world population. Global warming, resulting from the emission of GHGs, may lead to disastrous consequences for life on Earth due to climate change and extreme events.

The most common GHGs released due to human activity (agriculture, industry, energy production, commerce, services, and transportation) are carbon dioxide (CO_2), methane (CH_4), nitrous oxide (N_2O), and chlorofluorocarbons (CFCs).

One way of estimating the joint impact of the emission of the different GHGs is associated with the concept of carbon dioxide equivalent (CO_{2e}), which represents in a single value the total GHG equivalent emissions, converting the non-CO_2 GHG into a single base. This correlation is conventionally carried out through the global warming potential (GWP) or the global temperature potential (GTP), which periodically establish the warming potential or the global temperature of a given GHG in equivalence to one ton of CO_2. Therefore, for a horizon of 100 years, considering the Second Assessment Report of the Intergovernmental Panel on Climate Change (IPCC) (GWP-SAR), one ton of CH_4 is equivalent to 21 tons of CO_2, and one ton of N_2O is equivalent to 310 tons of CO_2. For the CFC, this number may vary between 1700 and 8500, depending on the stability of the substance.

Among the problems seen with the emission of GHG are the climate changes caused by the greenhouse effect and the consequent increase in global temperature. The greenhouse effect was first observed by the French mathematician Jean-Baptiste Fourier, in 1827, who suggested that this phenomenon kept the Earth warmer than it would normally be.

Studies carried out in the last 40 years by the IPCC show a trend of increase of the Earth's average temperature. Worldwide, the average global sea level has also increased throughout the years, which may be a consequence of the melting of glaciers located in the polar ice caps. Moreover, there has been a decrease in

TABLE 6.3 Mass and percentage of pollutants in function of the type of vehicle and the type of fuel used

Category	Fuel	Air pollutant emission (t)					Air pollutant emission (%)				
		CO	NO$_x$	PM(1)	SO$_x$(2)	NMVOC	CO	NO$_x$ (%)	PM (1) (%)	SO$_x$ (2) (%)	NMVOC (%)
Cars	Gasoline C	111,039	14,218	59	151	23,245	30.3	7.2	1.1	3.2	29.0
	Hydrous ethanol	40,071	3,251	nd	nd	7,512	10.9	1.7	nd	nd	9.4
	Flex-gasoline C	20,478	2,085	39	108	8,071	5.6	1.1	0.7	2.3	10.1
	Flex-Hydrous ethanol	41,577	3,429	nd	nd	12,475	11.4	1.7	nd	nd	15.5
Light commercial	Gasoline C	18,799	1,917	11	39	5,346	5.1	1.0	0.2	0.8%	6.7
	Hydrous ethanol	2,747	312	nd	nd	675	0.8	0.2	nd	nd	0.8
	Flex-gasoline C	3,368	434	7	26	1,586	0.9	0.2	0.1	0.6	2.0
	Flex-Hydrous ethanol	8,965	748	nd	nd	2,384	2.4	0.4	nd	nd	3.0
	Diesel	1,973	8,968	382	414	526	0.5	4.6	6.9	8.8	0.7

Continued

TABLE 6.3 Mass and percentage of pollutants in function of the type of vehicle and the type of fuel used–cont'd

Category		Fuel	Air pollutant emission (t)					Air pollutant emission (%)				
			CO	NOx	PM(1)	SO$_x$(2)	NMVOC	CO	NO$_x$ (%)	PM (1) (%)	SO$_x$ (2) (%)	NMVOC (%)
Trucks	Semi-light	Diesel	527	2749	129	70	162	0.1	1.4	2.3	1.5	0.2
	Light		2,247	12,578	516	325	669	0.6	6.4	9.3	6.9	0.8
	Medium		1,482	8,484	410	200	477	0.4	4.3	7.4	4.3	0.6
	Semi-heavy		8,422	48,355	1,378	1,493	1,822	2.3	24.6	24.8	31.7	2.3
	Heavy		8,078	49,544	1,288	1,462	2,048	2.2	25.2	23.2	31.1	2.6
Buses	Urban	Diesel	4,375	22,156	656	21	957	1.2	11.3	11.8	0.4	1.2
	Micro-bus		317	1574	43	2	67	0.1	0.8	0.8	0.0	0.1
	Roadway		2,089	12,986	429	364	624	0.6	6.6	7.7	7.7	0.8
Motorcycles		Gasoline C	85,001	2,746	197	24	10,856	23.2	1.4	3.5	0.5	13.5
		Flex-gasoline C	2,701	192	13	4	426	0.7	0.1	0.2	0.1	0.5
		Flex-Hydrous ethanol	1,875	126	nd	nd	327	0.5	0.1	nd	nd	0.4
Total			366,131	196,852	5,557	4,703	80,255	100.0	100.0	100.0	100.0	100.0

snow covering in the North hemisphere over time. All of these facts compromise climate balance and potentialize the occurrence of extreme events such as storms, droughts, typhoons, hurricanes, tornados, floods, and landslides.

When considering the contribution of transportation in the emission of GHG, CO_2 is the main component, since its production is related to the burning of fossil fuels. From the estimates shown in the Global Calculator, developed by the Climate Knowledge and Innovation Community (CLIMATE-KIC, 2018) and the International Energy Agency for the year 2011, Fig. 6.2 shows the percent distribution of per activity sector of the emission of CO_{2e} regarding the energy sector, which the transportation activity is part of. It is also possible to see the percent distribution per mode of transportation of transportation-related emissions worldwide.

Fig. 6.2 shows that the transportation sector was the second largest emitter of CO_{2e} in 2011, answering for 21% of the total, less than half of the percentage attributed to energy generation (50%). Because it is the most used mode

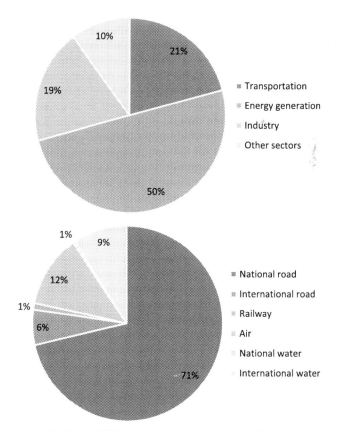

FIG. 6.2 Percent distribution of CO_{2e} emissions per activity sector and per mode of transportation for the world in 2011.

worldwide, road transportation is notably the largest emitter of CO_{2e} in the transportation sector, representing, individually, more than twice the emissions of all the other modes combined. On the other hand, the national railway and water (inland waterways) modes are the ones that least contribute to the emission of CO_{2e}, either due to their operational characteristics, which lead to better energy efficiency and a lower consumption of fossil fuels per transported unit, or due to the use of cleaner energy sources, as is the case of the railway mode, which, in many cases, uses renewable electric power.

This percent division of the emission of GHG by the different modes of transportation has not changed much over the last forty years, as indicated in Chapter 8 (Transport) of the 5th Assessment Report of world GHG emissions, produced by the IPCC in 2014. However, the problem becomes more serious over time. In 1970, the IPCC estimated that transportation has emitted a little <3 Gt of CO_{2e}. In 2010, this number went to a little over 7 Gt of CO_{2e}, increasing more than twice (Sims et al., 2014).

Nevertheless, according to the IPCC, concerning the activity of transportation, the emission of GHG other than CO_2 in 2010 contributed to <3% of the total. Furthermore, final energy use represented 98% of the emissions of these gases for this activity.

EXAMPLE 6.3 CO_{2e} emissions by transportation in developing countries—the case of Brazil

Different from the world distribution of CO_{2e} emissions by the different segments of the energy sector, transportation in Brazil, according to data from the Energy Research Company (EPE) for 2015 (EPE, 2016), answered for most of the GHG emissions in CO_{2e}, reaching 56% of the total and accounting for 226.5 million t of CO_{2e}, as shown in Fig. 6.3.

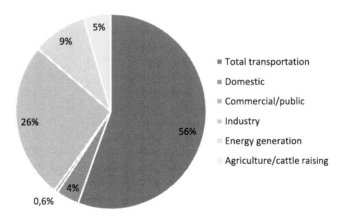

FIG. 6.3   Distribution of CO_{2e} emissions by the different segments of the energy sector in Brazil in 2015.

Air pollutant and greenhouse gas emissions (GHG) Chapter | 6 **239**

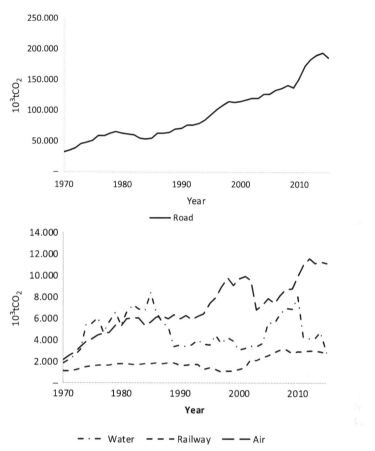

FIG. 6.4 Profile of CO_{2e} emissions by the transportation sector in Brazil between 1970 and 2013.

As in the rest of the world, the road mode is the main factor responsible for the emission of CO_{2e} in the transportation sector, historically answering for a fraction of more than 85% of the total and reaching around 95% in 2015 (Gonçalves and de D'Agosto, 2017). Fig. 6.4 shows the CO_{2e} emissions profile per mode of transportation in Brazil for the period between 1970 and 2015. Historically, it can be seen that the distribution of CO_{2e} emissions presented percentages that varied from 1% to 12% for the water mode, 1% to 3% for the railway mode, and 5% to 9% for the air mode, very similar numbers to the ones presented for the world.

6.4 Air pollutants and GHG emissions management

Managing the emission of air pollutants and GHG is important for the organizations that operate in the transportation sector worried about reducing their environmental impacts, either by their own policy or to meet some specific regulation. Fig. 6.5 summarizes a procedure that aims to do that.

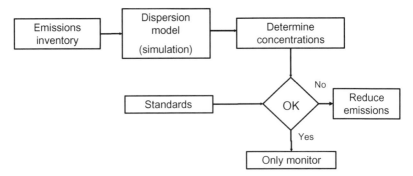

FIG. 6.5 Air pollutants and GHG management procedure.

Estimating air pollutants and GHG emissions by transportation is the first step in establishing the comprehensiveness potential of environmental impacts resulting from this activity. This estimate may be made using an inventory of air pollutants and/or GHG emissions.

Once these estimates are available, computational tools may be used to evaluate the mechanisms of dispersion of air pollutants and to estimate their concentration in the air. In this case, it is possible to use simulation tools to analyze the behavior and the results of the dispersion model.

Once the estimates of the concentrations of air pollutants or GHG in the atmosphere are available and standards for these measurements are established, it will be possible to determine what action should be taken. If the concentrations are in accordance with the parameters established by regulation, managers should monitor the process with new periodic evaluations. If the values are above the established ones, managers should take action to reduce emissions. Therefore, much has been done to reduce the emission of air pollutants through the burning of fossil fuels, through the introduction of emission prevention and control technology in internal combustion engines. Next, the procedure presented in Fig. 6.5 is detailed.

6.4.1 Air pollutant emissions inventory

Air pollutants management starts with the emissions inventory, which aims to check what types (quality) and amount of pollutants are emitted by the transportation activity in a given area. Fig. 6.6 proposes a procedure made of five steps that support the development of air pollutant emission inventories by the transportation activity.

On the first step, the study area is identified, highlighting the limits of geographical coverage. The second step aims to determine the sources that will be assessed and their location, and to identify the pollutants that will be inventoried.

Determining the internal and external sources in relation to the study area provides the bases for the definition of which fixed and mobile sources will be

Air pollutant and greenhouse gas emissions (GHG) Chapter | 6 **241**

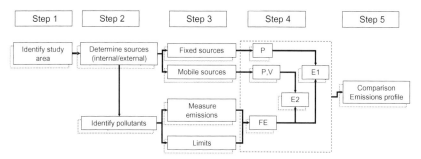

FIG. 6.6 Steps to the development of an inventory of atmospheric emissions. Legend: P—type of pollutant; V—volume of activity; FE—pollutant emission factor (g/s, g/L, g/km); Ei—emissions (g).

accounted for in the inventory (Step 3). After the identification of the pollutants (Step 2), it is possible to gather the emissions and the limits that must be considered as parameters (Step 3).

Step 4 aims to determine the types of pollutants of each fixed and mobile source and, in the case of the latter, the volume of activity responsible for the generation of pollutants. Mobile sources, in most cases, are represented by transportation and, the higher their activity, the higher their emission.

For each pollutant to be considered in the inventory, there are emission factors that, in the case of transportation, regard the amount of pollutant emitted per time of operation, unit of fuel consumed, and/or distance traveled.

Regarding local air pollutants, the determination of these emission factors is very specific for each situation and the form of operation, the type and the composition of the fuel, the vehicle maintenance conditions, the traffic profile, and the climate conditions that may influence these emission factors are worth highlighting. For CO_2, the main GHG, the emission factors are mainly associated with the fuel's carbon content. Table 6.4 shows a set of emission factors for a selection of air pollutants that are usually regulated by the legislation and for CO_2 per mode of transportation and fuel type.

Using the emission factors for each of the pollutants, and their respective volumes, it is possible to find out the emissions volume and to begin Step 5, which is responsible for comparing the profiles of emissions with the established limits or best practices standards.

Example 6.4 shows how to create the emissions inventory for a specific transportation situation based on the procedure presented in Fig. 6.6.

EXAMPLE 6.4 Applying the procedure of emissions inventory

Consider a highway of 10 km in length that has three lanes and a single direction. A total of 300 cars travel along each lane per hour. Each car carries 1.5 persons on average. The traffic of cars that consume gasoline causes air pollutant emissions, as shown in Table 6.5; for that reason, aiming to minimize air pollutant emissions,

TABLE 6.4 Emission factors for air pollutants and CO_2 for a selection of modes of transportation, vehicle technology, and fuel type

Mode [1]	Fuel	CO_2 (kg/L)	CO (g/km)	NO_x (g/km)	NMHC[10] (g/km)	PM (g/km)
Road	Diesel (Trucks[4])	2.603	0.004–0.275	0.511–1.645	0.004–0.032	0.003–0.016
	Diesel (Bus[5])		0.263–0.44	1.257–2.103	0.020–0.33	0.012–0.020
	Gasoline C[6] (22% of anhydrous ethanol)	2.061	0.25	0.03	0.014	0.011
	Gasoline C[7] (22% of anhydrous ethanol)		0.27	0.03	0.026	0.011
	Compressed Natural Gas[7,11]	1.999	0.56	0.29	0.026	–
	Anhydrous ethanol[2]	1.526	–	–	–	–
	Hydrous ethanol[2,8]	1.457	0.47	0.03	0.062	–
	Biodiesel[3,9]	2.431	1.234	14.73	–	0.438
Railway	Diesel[9]	2.603	1.56	15.20	–	0.38
	Biodiesel[9]	2.431	0.719	16.792	–	0.178
Water	Diesel[9]	2.603	2.15	14.28	–	0.62
	Fuel oil[12]	3.051	2.225	88.484	3.018	7.134
Air	Kerosene[13]	2.465	1.66–0.54	2.75 to 0.92	0.17–0.09	0.007–0.001

Notes: (1) Pipelines were not included because this mode usually uses electric power. (2) Sugarcane alcohol. (3) Soy oil biodiesel. (4) Semi-light and heavy trucks with technology equivalent to the Euro V European standard. (5) Urban and road microbuses and buses with technology equivalent to the Euro V European standard. (6) Gasoline car manufactured to meet the Brazilian Code of Federal Regulation 88.104–94. (7) Flexible-fuel car using gasoline C and manufactured to meet the Brazilian Code of Federal Regulation 88.104–94. (8) Gasoline car manufactured to meet the Brazilian Code of Federal Regulation 88.104–94. (9) The factors for CO, NOx, NMHC, and PM are given in g/hph; (10) Only the hydrocarbons in the fraction of the NMVOC are considered. (11) In the case of natural gas, the emission factor is of CO2 given in kg/m3. (12) the factors for CO, NOx, NMHC, and PM are in g/L. (13) the factors for CO, NOx, NMHC, and PM are in kg/t.km, considering that the highest values are for flights in distances of 500 km and the lowest values for flights above 3700 km.
Source: Mattos, L.B.R., 2001. A Importância do Setor de Transportes na Emissão de Gases do Efeito Estufa – O Caso do Município do Rio de Janeiro. Tese (Mestrado em Planejamento Energético). 179 p.; Universidade Federal do Rio de Janeiro, Coppe, Rio de Janeiro., Dubeux, C.B.S., 2007. Mitigação de Emissões de Gases de Efeito Estufa por Municípios Brasileiros: Metodologias para Elaboração de Inventários Setoriais e Cenários de Emissões como Instrumentos de Planejamento. Tese de Doutorado. PPE/Coppe/UFRJ. Rio de Janeiro., MMA (2013). Inventário Nacional de Emissões Atmosféricas por Veículos Rodoviários. Ministério do Meio Ambiente. Brasília, Brasil., Papanikolaou, A., 2014. Ship Design—Methodologies of Preliminary Design. Springer., and IMO (2014). International Maritime Organization. Third IMO

Air pollutant and greenhouse gas emissions (GHG) Chapter | 6 **243**

the local authorities decided to use one of the highway lanes to implement an exclusive-lane bus system. With that, it is expected that car traffic will be reduced proportionally to the reduction in the number of lanes available for its traffic. Consider that all the people who used cars and stopped using the express lane started to use buses. In this operation regime, it is expected that one bus, which uses diesel oil, transports 60 passengers. What is the expected variation in air pollutant emissions, per type of pollutant, with the implementation of the exclusive bus lane?

This is an example in which it is necessary to produce the baseline emissions inventory, considering the situation when only cars traveled along the way, and compare the results with the alternative situation, in which there are two car lanes and one bus lane. The emission factors are shown in g/km for the mobile sources (cars and buses) that travel along the studied road segment. The procedure presented in Fig. 6.6 may be applied as follows.

Step 1:The study area is a road segment used for the traffic of cars and buses with three rolling lanes. For the baseline, the three lanes are used for the traffic of cars and, in the alternative situation, two lanes are used for cars, and one for buses.

Step 2:Given that there is no other source of information, only the internal emission sources will be considered. For the baseline, the volume (V) of 300 cars per lane will be considered, amounting to $300 \times 3 = 900$ cars per hour in the segment. The alternative situation considers a volume of 300 cars per hour along two lanes ($300 \times 2 = 600$ cars per hour) and an equivalent bus flow that can carry the passengers that stopped using one of the lanes in the segment, that is $(300 \times 1.5)/60 = 7.5$ buses per hour in one lane. The air pollutants to be considered are shown in Table 6.5.

Step 3:The sources of air pollutant emissions are mobile and the basis of calculation will be of 1 h to evaluate the emission of the traffic flow along the 10 km of the study area.

Step 4:Calculation.
Calculation of the car traffic volume in baseline (V1): $3 \times 300 = 900$.
Calculation of the car traffic volume in the alternative situation (V2): $2 \times 300 = 600$.
Calculation of the amount of passengers per lane: $300 \times 1.5 = 450$ passengers per lane per hour.

TABLE 6.5 Emission factor per vehicle type and pollutant

Emission sources	Emission factor [FE] per type of pollutant [P] [g/km]			
	CO	NO$_x$	NMHC	PM
Car	0.25	0.03	0.014	0.011
Bus	2.50	2.00	0.020	0.020

244 Transportation, energy use and environmental impacts

Calculation of the bus traffic volume in the alternative situation (V3): 450/60=7.5–8.
Calculation of the emissions—baseline (considering 10 km of highway and three car lanes):
CO: $0.25 \times 900 \times 10 = 2250 \, g/h = 2.25 \, kg/h$.
NO_x: $0.03 \times 900 \times 10 = 270 \, g/h = 0.27 \, kg/h$.
HC: $0.014 \times 900 \times 10 = 126 \, g/h = 0.13 \, kg/h$.
MP: $0.011 \times 900 \times 10 = 99 \, g/h = 0.1 \, kg/h$.
Calculation of emissions—alternative situation (considering 10 km of highway, two car lanes and one bus lane).
Calculation of the emissions—two car lanes.
CO: $0.25 \times 600 \times 10 = 1500 \, g/h = 1.5 \, kg/h$.
NO_x: $0.03 \times 600 \times 10 = 180 \, g/h = 0.18 \, kg/h$.
HC: $0.014 \times 600 \times 10 = 84 \, g/h = 0.08 \, kg/h$.
MP: $0.011 \times 600 \times 10 = 66 \, g/h = 0.07 \, kg/h$.
Calculation of emissions—one bus lane:
CO: $2.5 \times 7.5 \times 10 = 187.5 \, g/h = 0.19 \, kg/h$.
NO_x: $2.0 \times 7.5 \times 10 = 150 \, g/h = 0.15 \, kg/h$.
HC: $0.02 \times 7.5 \times 10 = 1.5 \, g/h = 0.002 \, kg/h$.
MP: $0.02 \times 7.5 \times 10 = 1.5 \, g/h = 0.002 \, kg/h$.

Step 5: This step aims to evaluate the variation in emissions between the baseline and the alternative situation.
CO: $2.25 - (1.5 + 0.19) = 0.56 \, kg/h$ (decreased).
NO_x: $0.27 - (0.18 + 0.15) = -0.06 \, kg/h$ (increased).
HC: $0.13 - (0.08 + 0.002) = 0.048 \, kg/h$ (decreased).
MP: $0.1 - (0.07 + 0.002) = 0.028 \, kg/h$ (decreased).
It can be seen that there was an increase in the emission of NO_x (in mass per time unit) and a decrease in the emissions of all the other air pollutants with the introduction of the public collective transportation alternative in the studied segment. There was a total reduction in air pollutant emissions, even though the emission factors for diesel buses are higher than those of gasoline cars. This reduction results from the decreased traffic flow, since a bus can transport 60 passengers, which is equivalent to 40 cars.

When considering the calculation of CO_2 emissions, it is possible to use two approaches: (1) *bottom-up*; and (2) *top-down*. One way of applying the *bottom-up* approach is analogous to Example 6.4, where one could determine the volume of fuel consumed by the vehicles that operate within the study area and, then, multiply this volume by the emission factor of CO_2 in kg/L, shown in Table 6.4. If the study area is a state or a country, it is possible to evaluate the emission of CO_2 if all the traffic flows are known for each vehicle type throughout a given time, as well as the fuels these cars consume and their emission factors.

The *top-down* approach, in turn, adopts an aggregate perspective and allows the calculation of CO_2 emissions based on the energy consumption observed in a given study area. The choice of approaches depends on the quality and quantity of existing data; the *top-down* approach is less data intensive and its application is less complex, as shall be seen in Example 6.5.

Air pollutant and greenhouse gas emissions (GHG) Chapter | 6 **245**

EXAMPLE 6.5 Procedure for the application of the *top-down* approach

The top-down approach can be applied in a simplified way with six steps, as presented below. Note that this approach, just as it will be presented, applies to all the activity sectors of a region and not only to the transportation activity.

Step 1:Calculation of Apparent Consumption (AC) of fuels in their original units of measurement. AC represents the amount of fuel available in the country and it is calculated according to Eq. (6.1).

$$AC = PEP + IEP - EEP - B - E \qquad (6.1)$$

where
PEP is the annual domestic primary energy production, measured in the original unit;
IEP the annual import of primary and secondary energy, measured in the original unit;
EEP the annual export of primary and secondary energy, measured in the original unit;
B being the annual amount of energy embarked in international *bunkers*, measured in the original unit; and
E is the annual variation of energy stocks, measured in the original unit.

Step 2:Conversion of AC into a common energy unit—terajoules (TJ), according to the following equation:

$$EC = FC \times F_{conv} \times 45.2 \times 10^{-3} \times F_{corr} \qquad (6.2)$$

where
1 toe is 45.2×10^{-3} TJ (tera-joule = 10.12 J);
EC is the energy consumption in TJ;
FC the fuel consumption (m^3, L, kg); and
F_{conv} is the conversion factor of the physical unit of measurement of the amount of fuel for toe based on the higher calorific value (HCV) of the fuel.

Step 3:Transformation of the AC of each fuel into carbon content through its multiplication by the specific carbon emission factor of that fuel. The amount of carbon emitted in the burning of the fuel must be calculated according to the following equation:

$$CC = CC \times CEF \times 10^{-3} \qquad (6.3)$$

where
CC is the carbon content expressed in GgC;
EC the energy consumption in TJ; and
CEF the carbon emission factor (tC/TJ).

Step 4:Calculating the carbon content of each fuel destined to non-energetic purposes, and deducing this carbon content from the AC so as to calculate the real carbon content that may be emitted, according to the following equation:

$$FCC = CC \times FC_{Fix} \qquad (6.4)$$

where FCC is the fixed carbon content (GgC),
CC the fuel carbon content (GgC), and

246 Transportation, energy use and environmental impacts

FC_{Fix} the fixed carbon fraction.

This quantity of non-energetic use refers to the fuel used as raw material in the manufacturing of plastic, fertilizer, asphalt, lubricant, etc. The fraction of carbon stored in the biofuels is 100%, since the carbon is sequestered by the plantation used as feedstock.

After this calculation, it is necessary to calculate the liquid carbon emissions (LCE), subtracting the fixed carbon content (FCC) in GgC from the fuel carbon content (CC), also in GgC, according to the following equation:

$$LCE = FC - CC \tag{6.5}$$

Step 5:Correction of the values considering the incomplete combustion of the fuel, calculating the carbon content actually oxidated in the combustion.

As the combustion does not happen completely, it is necessary to take into consideration the carbon that will not be oxidized, according to the following equation:

$$RCE = LCE \times OCF \tag{6.6}$$

where
RCE is the real carbon emissions (GgC);
LCE the liquid carbon emissions (GgC); and
OCF the oxidized carbon fraction.

Step 6:Converting the quantity of oxidated carbon into CO_2 emissions. CO_2 emissions may be calculated according to Eq. (6.6). In function of the respective molecular weights, 44t CO_2 corresponds to 12t of C or 1t $CO_2 = 0.2727$t C.

$$ECO2 = RCE \times 44/12 \tag{6.7}$$

where
ECO2 is the CO_2 emission; and
RCE is the C emission.

6.4.2 Dispersion and concentration of air pollutants

The dispersion of pollutants affects their concentration and, with that, the potential impact on human health and on the integrity of material goods. The dispersion of air pollutants in air is affected by the variation in speed and direction of the winds, by the nature of the pollutant, by meteorological parameters (ambient temperature and atmospheric pressure), by the location of the source of the pollutant, and by the topography of the region.

In face of these variants, defining and controlling the concentration of air pollutants in the air by establishing a standard of air quality must be part of the process of environmental impacts management. The air quality standard legally defines the maximum limit for the concentration of an atmospheric component so as to guarantee the protection of people's health and well-being.

Air pollutant and greenhouse gas emissions (GHG) Chapter | 6 **247**

The air quality standards are based on scientific studies that evaluate the effects produced by specific pollutants, fixating the levels of pollution that may provide adequate security margin.

Primary standards are the concentrations of pollutants that, if surpassed, may affect people's health. These may be considered as the maximum tolerable levels of air pollutant concentrations, and demand the implementation of short-term and medium-term mitigation measures.

The secondary standards are the air pollutant concentrations below which it is possible to predict minimum adverse effects on the well-being of the population, as well as minimum damage to animals, plants, material goods, and the environment in general. They may be understood as the desired levels of pollutant concentration to base the establishment of long-term measures. Example 6.5 shows the standards of air pollutant concentration emitted most frequently in the transportation activity according to Brazilian regulations.

EXAMPLE 6.6   Air quality standards according to Brazilian regulations

Table 6.6 shows some of the main pollutants emitted by the transportation sector and the concentration standards established for Brazil. For the purpose of

TABLE 6.6 Air quality standards in Brazil

Pollutant	Average time	Primary standard ($\mu g/m^3$)	Secondary standard ($\mu g/m^3$)
PM	24 h[a]	240	150
	MG annual[a]	80	60
SO_2	24 h[a]	365	100
	MA annual	80	40
CO	1 h[a]	40,000	40,000
	8 h[a]	10,000	10,000
O_3	1 h[a]	160	160
Smoke	24 h[a]	150	100
	MA annual[a]	60	40
Inhalable particles (<10 μg)	24 h[a]	150	150
	MA annual	50	50
NO_2	1 h[a]	320	190
	MA annual	100	100

[a] *Cannot be exceeded more than once a year; MG—geometric mean; MA—arithmetic mean.*
Source: Conama—Resolution no. 3/1990.

248 Transportation, energy use and environmental impacts

comparison, the reader is encouraged to compare these standards to the ones prescribed by the World Health Organization (WHO), and by the European and North American standards.

To enable the identification of the concentration of air pollutants, there must be a monitoring of air quality, whose objectives are: (1) controlling air quality to keep the concentration of pollutants from offering risk to the health of living beings; (2) identifying the periods in which the concentration of pollutants exceeds the quality standards in order to, if possible, alert and guide the population to minimize damage; (3) identifying the factors that increase the concentrations of air pollutants to establish prevention programs; (4) establishing trends and analyzing historical data aiming to correlate the concentrations found with the characteristics (natural or not) of the analyzed phenomenon; (5) validating numeric forecasting models and improving the accuracy of model results; and (6) promoting information to create Environmental Impact Assessments (EIA) and Environmental Impact Reports (EIR).

6.4.3 Measures to control and limit vehicle emissions

Since many conditions influence the concentration of air pollutants, guaranteeing air quality implies using measures to control and limit air pollutant emissions by vehicles.

In the transportation sector, the measures to control and limit emissions may be divided into two groups: (1) those that aim to directly control the vehicle; and (2) those that aim to control the distances traveled by the vehicles.

In the first group, there are actions that focus on controlling the vehicle's operation, such as its obedience to emission standards; in this case, the following may be adopted: (a) mandatory *recall* and guarantee system if the vehicle is not meeting specifications; (b) tests in the assembly line to guarantee the working of the systems that comprise the vehicle, and (c) vehicle certification.

For that, there are vehicle labeling programs that collect and publish the results available about the working of the vehicles commercialized in a region and work as a guide so the user may choose less polluting equipment. In this context, it should be considered that the reduction of emissions has a direct relationship with the higher efficiency in fuel burning.

With the purpose of defining a basis for the vehicle emission indices that should be met in different parts of the world, the governments establish the maximum limits of emission by new vehicles. In the European Union, these limits are established by the EURO standards and, in North America, by the successive regulations of the Environmental Protection Agency (US EPA). Due to the importance of these standards, considering that most of the automotive industry is located within these two regions (Europe and the United States), this set of standards influences most other regions of the world. Example 6.6 presents the emission limits for heavy diesel-powered vehicles and light vehicles established by the Brazilian program.

Air pollutant and greenhouse gas emissions (GHG) Chapter | 6 **249**

EXAMPLE 6.7   Brazilian program of emission limits

Strongly influenced by the EURO standards for heavy vehicles and by the different steps of the North American regulation for light vehicles (cars and light commercial vehicles), Tables 6.7 and 6.8 show the emission limits established for Brazil.

All of these actions focus on the phase of operation of vehicles, but it is necessary to develop programs related to the energy spent in the manufacturing of these vehicles and in the final destination of solid waste (steel, plastic, rubber, tires) and liquid (lubricating oils). It is also necessary to pay attention to the questions related to roadways (construction and maintenance) and the construction, operation, and maintenance of the terminals that serve as a support to handling and transhipment needs. As seen in Chapter 3, expanding the scope of the assessment of environmental impacts resulting from the emission of air pollutants and GHGs by transportation may be made using the life cycle analysis tool.

Other actions related to controlling a vehicle's operation are those based on regulating vehicle equipment. With that in mind, there are many factors that influence combustion quality, among them the constructive characteristics of engines and their setup (air intake system and ignition).

Regarding the constructive characteristics of engines, different emission results may be achieved according to exhaust emissions by European gasoline vehicles, according to the type of traffic, emissions control, and engine characteristics, as shown in Table 6.9.

Fig. 6.7 shows the improvements that may be integrated to an internal combustion engine through complementary systems that help reduce air pollutant emissions. Below is a brief description of these systems.

(1) Recirculation of exhaust gases: The mixture of fuel with air (fuel + air − F/A) is diluted with the exhaust gases, which are carried through tubes and controlled by a valve until the combustion chamber. Exhaust gases may also be used before they leave the combustion chamber. It enables the reduction of the combustion chamber and the consequent reduction of NO_x emissions.

(2) Catalytic converters: These aim to increase the speed of reaction between oxygen, the unburned HC, CO, and NO_x present in the exhaust gases. This increase in reaction speed is achieved through the presence of precious metals such as platinum, rhodium, or palladium. Its efficiency depends on the A/F relation and, for that, the *lambda* sensor (a device that aims to evaluate the efficiency of combustion in the engine through the analysis of the exhaust gases). The most used devices are two: the oxidizing one (two ways), which acts on the emissions of CO and HC, transforming them into CO_2 and H_2O; and the oxidizing-reducing one (three ways), which, besides acting on CO and HC emissions, also acts on the NO_x emissions.

TABLE 6.7 Emission limits for diesel-powered heavy vehicles

Emission limits for diesel-powered heavy vehicles—PROCONVE							
PROCONVE	EURO	CO (g/kWh)	HC (g/kWh)	NOx (g/kWh)	PM (g/kWh)	S (ppm of S)	Validity
Phase P1	–	14.00[a]	3.50	18.00[a]	–	–	1989–1993
Phase P2	Euro 0	11.20	2.45	14.40	0.60[a]	–	1994–1995
Phase P3	Euro 1	4.90	1.23	9.00	0.40 or 0.70[1]	–	1996–1999
Phase P4	Euro 2	4.00	1.10	7.00	0.15	–	2000–2005
Phase P5	Euro 3	2.10	0.66	5.00	0.10 or 0.13[2]	–	2006–2008
Phase P6	Euro 4	1.50	0.46	3.50	0.02	50	2009–2012[3]
Phase P7	Euro 5	1.50	0.46	2.00	0.02	10	since 2012

[a] There was no legal requirement of: (1) 0.70 for engines up to 85 kW and 0.40 for engines with >85 kW; (2) engines with single cylinder capacity below 0.75 dm^3 and nominal power rotation above 3000 RPM; (3) the following will not be in effect: CO—carbon monoxide; HC—hydrocarbons; NO$_x$—nitrogen oxides; PM—particulate matter; S—sulfur.

Source: MMA, 2013. Inventário Nacional de Emissões Atmosféricas por Veículos Rodoviários. Ministério do Meio Ambiente, Brasília, Brasil.

TABLE 6.8 Emission limits for light vehicles

Vehicle Type	Pollutant							
Light	CO^d (g/km)	TC^a (g/km)	NMHC (g/km)	NO_x (g/km)		HCO^b (g/km)	PM^c (g/km)	Capacity and ELR
				Otto Cycle	Diesel Cycle			
Passenger	2.0	0.30	0.05	0.12	0.25	0.02	0.05	—
Commercial <= 1700 kg	2.0	0.30	0.05	0.12	0.25	0.02	0.05	—
Commercial >1700 kg	2.7	0.30	0.06	0.25	0.43	0.04	0.06	—

[a] *Only natural gas vehicles.*
[b] *Only for Otto cycle engines, except for natural gas.*
[c] *Only for diesel cycle engines.*
[d] *In the case of light vehicles, CO content in idle speed, only for Otto cycle engines: 0.50% vol.*
Source: Conama (2002). Resolução Conama no 297. Disponível em: www.mma.conama.gov.br/conama. Acesso em 30 mar. 2014.

TABLE 6.9 Emissions according to characteristics of engines in urban traffic[a]

Characteristics of the engine and the emissions control	Exhaust emissions (g/km)[a]		
	Carbon monoxide (CO)	Hydrocarbons (HC)	Nitrogen oxides (NO$_x$)
Two strokes	32.9	20.2	0.26
Four strokes (>2000 cc)	32.0	3.0	2.00
Four strokes (1400–2000 cc)	31.0	2.9	1.80
Four strokes (<1400 cc)	30.0	2.8	1.70
Catalytic converter without sensor λ	6.6	0.9	1.00
Catalytic converter with sensor λ	1.5	0.2	0.27

[a] *Average from 1970 to 1990.*
Faiz, A., Weaver, C.S., Walsh, M.P., 1996. Air Pollution From Motor Vehicles—Standards and Technologies for Controlling Emissions. World Bank, Washington, DC.

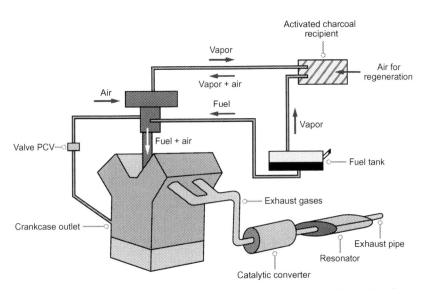

FIG. 6.7 Improvements integrated to internal combustion engines to reduce air pollutant emissions.

Air pollutant and greenhouse gas emissions (GHG) Chapter | 6 **253**

(3) Recirculation of evaporative emission gases: This involves using a device that closes the output of the engine's crankcase to the atmosphere, forcing the evaporated gases to go toward the air intake system to be sent back to the cylinder and be burned within the engine itself. The PCV valve controls pressure in the crankcase.

(4) Direct fuel injection: This method replaces the carburetors, resulting in a fast and precise control of the A/F ratio, which leads to a reduction in evaporative emissions. Currently, they are electronically controlled.

(5) Activated charcoal recipient: This is a device that receives the evaporative emissions from the tank and the carburetor in order to send them back to the engine to be burned. The HC vapors are adsorbed (trapped), and when air enters the system, it passes through the recipient, carrying HC to be burned in the engine.

Still regarding the vehicle operation control, another measure should be considered: the maintenance and operation of vehicles in use. Vehicles with maintenance problems consume more fuel, have a higher incomplete combustion factor and the catalyst may not have the adequate performance to reduce emissions.

The engine's operation/use profile also influences emissions. Table 6.10 shows idle speed emissions. Important changes are seen for some pollutants depending on the kind of operation.

The composition of the fuels also impacts the emissions profile with highlights, in this case, to the reduction of lead content and sulfur content, and the addition of oxygenated compounds, such as ethanol and biodiesel. Tables 6.11 and 6.12 show data related to the variation of the pollutants emission profile in function of fuel composition.

The second group of measures that aim to control the distance traveled by the vehicles, as seen in Chapter 3, is based on transportation policies, such as

TABLE 6.10 Influence of engine operation in air pollutant emissions

Type of operation	CO	HC	NO$_x$
Idle speed	1	1	1
Acceleration	0.6	0.4	100
Cruise	0.6	0.3	66
Deceleration	0.6	11.4	1

Effect of engine operation in exhaust emissions in relation to idle speed emissions. Relative emissions based on idle speed operation.
Source: Pierce, T., Geron, C., Bender, L., Dennis, R., Tonnesen, G., Guenther, A., 1998. Influence of increased isoprene emissions on regional ozone modeling. J. Geophys. Res.

254 Transportation, energy use and environmental impacts

TABLE 6.11 Average relative ethanol emissions by light vehicles in Brazil

Fuel	CO	HC	NO$_x$	Aldehydes
Hydrous Ethanol	100	100	100	100
95% ethanol–5% gasoline	125	110	100	nd
22% ethanol–78% gasoline	175	122	138	36
12% ethanol–88% gasoline	282	134	106	nd
100% gasoline	350	140	115	10

Relative emissions (base 100).
Source: Faiz, A., Weaver, C.S., Walsh, M.P., 1996. Air Pollution From Motor Vehicles—Standards and Technologies for Controlling Emissions. Washington, DC: World Bank.

increasing parking prices to inhibit the use of cars, and overtaxation of private vehicles aiming to reduce the purchase of cars and induce their replacement for more efficient modes of transportation, such as collective transportation. In this case, the government should present passengers with transportation characteristics that allow them to realize the advantages of using a public and collective mode of transportation instead of individual transportation (private vehicles).

6.5 Final considerations

Transportation is one of the main actors in the process of air pollution and GHG emissions, generating impacts to the environment, which may cause problems to human health, reduced quality of life, and damage to material goods.

Due to the use of fossil fuel energy (mostly), the transportation sector contributes to the emission of a high and varied amount of air pollutants, and each mode of transportation has different emission factors, due to their operational characteristics and use of technology, with highlights to the road mode, since it is the most widely used in the world.

The control of air pollutant emissions and GHG emissions is a process that involves producing an inventory, comparing results with established standards and taking action to reduce environmental impacts. Some approaches are used to inventory pollutants; the *top-down* and *bottom-up* approaches stand out.

Measures of control and limitation of air pollutant emissions are categorized into two groups: the first one focuses on a vehicle's direct control and, the

Air pollutant and greenhouse gas emissions (GHG) Chapter | 6 **255**

TABLE 6.12 Comparison of the emissions of an internal combustion engine operating, in the same type of vehicle, with diesel oil and gasoline

	Fuel used in the ICE without emissions control	
	Diesel oil in relation to gasoline	
Pollutants emitted	Light vehicle	Heavy vehicle
CO	90% less	98% less
NO_x	50%–70% less	50%–100% more
HC	90% less	90%–95% less
PM	600%–1000% more	600%–1000% more

Source: Faiz, A., Weaver, C.S., Walsh, M.P., 1996. Air Pollution From Motor Vehicles—Standards and Technologies for Controlling Emissions. Washington, DC: World Bank.

second one focuses on controlling the distances traveled by the vehicles. In both cases, there must be a joint action of the government, the society, and entities that use and operate transportation.

The theme that associates the activities of transportation with air pollution and GHG emission involves many variables, which makes the study complex, but there is still much room for improvement in this area, especially because the private initiative and the public authorities are constantly evolving regarding the improvement of technological, managerial, and political aspects.

6.6 Exercises

1. In a Brazilian city, the mayor wants to reduce the cases of respiratory diseases and, for that, he wants to reduce CO_2 emissions. Do you agree that this action will bring the potential benefits? What would you tell the mayor to support in achieving the objective proposed by him?
2. In the city of Rio de Janeiro, a project was created with the purpose of implementing measures that restricted the use of cars and encouraged the use of the subway. Considering that the subway uses hydroelectric power sources, what kind of air pollutants would be avoided in the operation of transportation with this project?
3. Regarding the operation of internal combustion engines, which pollutants, considering CO, HC, and NO_x, bring more problems in a city that has heavy traffic?
4. The owner of a carrier company has light vehicles that run on gasoline and has decided to replace its fleet with diesel-powered vehicles. He may use either light or heavy vehicles and he is in doubt about which vehicles to purchase, since he would like to contribute to the reduction of pollutant emissions. What would you recommend to the owner of this carrier considering that he does not have a preference for light or heavy vehicles?

256 Transportation, energy use and environmental impacts

TABLE 6.13 Air pollutant emission factors for cars

Vehicle	CO (g/km)	THC (g/km)	NMHC (g/km)	NO$_x$ (g/km) Otto cycle	NO$_x$ (g/km) Diesel cycle	HCO (g/km)	PM (g/km)
Car	2.0	0.30	0.05	0.12	0.25	0.02	0.05

5. With the economic crisis of 2009, the Brazilian government reduced taxation on vehicles, stimulating the population to purchase them. The result was the increased number of circulating vehicles and the consequent increase in the emission of air pollutants and GHG. To solve this problem, what measures might be adopted by the government to reduce the distance traveled by vehicles?

6. Explain the formation of vehicle emissions in an internal combustion engine.

7. What kinds of environmental impacts is fossil fuel combustion responsible for? What is their scope (global, regional, or local)?

8. What measures may be taken to control and limit vehicle emissions?

9. What are the main regulated air pollutants emitted by each type of vehicle?

10. What factors influence air pollution and what is the procedure adopted so that the air pollutant emission limits defined by Conama are followed?

11. The mayor of City A established the road rationing-based car plate digits, prohibiting part of the gasoline-powered car fleet from circulating in the city. With that, a daily reduction of 1,000,000 km in car traffic is expected. Based on Table 6.13, estimate the reduction in air pollutant emissions, specifying these pollutants.

References

CETESB, 2015. Emissões Veiculares no Estado de São Paulo 2015. Governo do Estado de São Paulo, Secretaria do Meio Ambiente, Companhia Ambiental do Estado de São Paulo, São Paulo, SP.

CLIMATE-KIC, 2018. The Global Calculator V23, Comunidade de Conhecimento e Inovação Climática, disponível em. http://tool.globalcalculator.org. (Acessado em 05/10/2018).

EEA, 2017. Emissions of Air Pollutants From Transport. European Environmental Agency. Available at https://www.eea.europa.eu/data-and-maps/indicators/transport-emissions-of-air-pollutants-8/transport-emissions-of-air-pollutants-5#tab-used-in-publications. (Accessed May 5, 2018).

EPA, 2016. Air Pollutant Emission Trends Data: Average Annual Emissions. Spreadsheet; Environmental Protection Agency, US. Available at https://www.epa.gov/sites/production/files/2015-07/national_tier1_caps.xlsx. (Accessed May 5, 2018).

EPE, 2016. Balanço Energético Nacional, Ministério de Minas e Energia, Empresa de Pesquisa Energética, Rio de Janeiro, RJ, Brasil.

Gonçalves, D.N.S., de D'Agosto, M.A., 2017. Future Prospective Scenarios for the use of Energy in Transportation in Brazil and GHG Emissions Business as Usual (BAU) Scenario—2050. Instituto Brasileiro de Transporte Sustentável (IBTS). Rio de Janeiro, RJ.

Air pollutant and greenhouse gas emissions (GHG) Chapter | 6 **257**

Sims, R., Schaeffer, R., Creutzig, F., et al., 2014. Transport. In: Climate Change 2014: Mitigation of Climate Change. Contribution of Working Group III to the Fifth Assessment Report of the Intergovernmental Panel on Climate. Cambridge University Press, Cambridge, United Kingdom and New York, pp. 2014.

Further reading

Conama, 2002. Resolução Conama no 297. Disponível em. www.mma.conama.gov.br/conama. (Accessed March 5, 1930).

Dubeux, C.B.S., 2007. Mitigação de Emissões de Gases de Efeito Estufa por Municípios Brasileiros: Metodologias para Elaboração de Inventários Setoriais e Cenários de Emissões como Instrumentos de Planejamento. Tese de Doutorado. PPE/Coppe/UFRJ. Rio de Janeiro.

Faiz, A., Weaver, C.S., Walsh, M.P., 1996. Air Pollution From Motor Vehicles—Standards and Technologies for Controlling Emissions. World Bank, Washington, DC.

IMO, 2014. International Maritime Organization. Third IMO Greenhouse Gas Study 2014. Executive Summary and Final Report.

Mattos, L.B.R., 2001. A Importância do Setor de Transportes na Emissão de Gases do Efeito Estufa – O Caso do Município do Rio de Janeiro. Tese (Mestrado em Planejamento Energético). 179 p, Universidade Federal do Rio de Janeiro, Coppe, Rio de Janeiro.

MMA, 2013. Inventário Nacional de Emissões Atmosféricas por Veículos Rodoviários. Ministério do Meio Ambiente. Brasília, Brasil.

Papanikolaou, A., 2014. Ship Design—Methodologies of Preliminary Design. Springer.

Pierce, T., Geron, C., Bender, L., Dennis, R., Tonnesen, G., Guenther, A., 1998. Influence of increased isoprene emissions on regional ozone modeling. J. Geophys. Res. 103 (D19), 25611–25629.

Chapter 7

Noise pollution, vibration, visual intrusion, and emission of solid and liquid waste

General goal

The general goal of this chapter is to present the environmental impacts resulting from transportation use and the action related to the monitoring and mitigation of noise pollution, vibration, visual intrusion, and emission of solid and liquid waste. At the end of this chapter, the reader should be able to:

1. Understand the concepts associated with the environmental impacts addressed in this chapter, which result from the use of modes of transportation, and identify their effects on the environment, on human health, and on properties.
2. Analyze how transportation contributes to potentialize the environmental impacts addressed in this chapter.
3. Identify which actions may be taken to reduce the environmental impacts addressed in this chapter.

7.1. Introduction

Besides energy consumption, air pollutant emissions, and GHG emissions, which are sources of environmental impacts related to the operation of transportation and directly associated with the use of energy, there are other, no less important, ways of causing environmental impacts associated with the operation of transportation that reduce the quality of life and cause damage to living beings and material goods, especially in large urban centers.

These impacts have influence on local and/or regional levels and are associated with noise pollution, vibration, visual intrusion, and emission of solid and liquid waste. This chapter presents a summary of each of these impacts, their consequences, and possible actions to reduce or eliminate their effects on living beings and material goods.

After this introduction, Section 7.2 addresses noise pollution in the form of noise emissions. Issues concerning vibration are discussed in Section 7.3. Section 7.4 addresses aspects related to visual intrusion and Section 7.5 focuses on the emission of solid and liquid waste. The final considerations are presented in Section 7.6.

Transportation, Energy Use and Environmental Impacts. https://doi.org/10.1016/B978-0-12-813454-2.00007-6
© 2019, Elsevier Editora Ltda. Published by Elsevier Inc. All rights reserved.

260 Transportation, energy use and environmental impacts

7.2. Noise pollution

Around 2500 years ago, there were already reports of deafness of people living near the falls of the Nile river due to staying near the source of the noise produced by the waterfall, which proves that problems caused to society by noise pollution have been known for a long time. Recently, in the Industrial Revolution (18th century), noise has become a byproduct of progress through the diffusion of large machines and vehicles in the production of goods and services.

Modes of transportation cause undesirable sounds, which influences the quality of life of the people who live in places where there is an intense flow of vehicles and constant exposure to the noise they emit when they are in operation.

7.2.1 Concept of noise pollution

Noise pollution is any change to the physical properties of the environment caused by the conjugation sounds, either desirable or not (the latter are called noise), that are directly or indirectly harmful to the health, safety, and well-being of living beings, especially human populations.

To better understand this topic, it is necessary to differentiate "sound" from "noise". Sound is a disturbance that is propagated through an elastic medium (air, water, etc.), at a speed that is characteristic of that medium. However, noise, for practical purposes, may be defined as an unpleasant sound, that is, a sound that disturbs people, although the physical properties of noise are the same as those of sound.

In order for sound to propagate and be noticed, three components are required: (1) a generating source (in the case of transportation vehicles); (2) propagation media (air, water, etc.); and (3) a receiver (people, animals). Therefore, actions to reduce sound pollution may be adopted focusing on one of these components. Fig. 7.1 illustrates the sound propagation system.

The following physical properties of sound are presented below to improve the understanding of sections to come: (1) pressure: sound may be defined as any variation in pressure exerted over a material medium that the human ear may detect, whether air, water, or any other propagation medium; (2) frequency (f): represents the number of pressure oscillations that pass through a point within one second, and it is measured in Hertz (Hz). The number of pressure oscillations per second is the sound frequency; (3) wavelength (λ): it is the distance between two successive wave peaks; and (4) speed (v). Frequency (f) and wavelength (λ) are correlated with the speed of sound (v) through Eq. (7.1).

$$v = f \times \lambda \tag{7.1}$$

The most common sounds consist in a rapid irregular series of positive (compression) and negative pressure (rarefaction) disturbances, measured through the static pressure.

Noise pollution, vibration, visual intrusion, and emission of waste **Chapter | 7** **261**

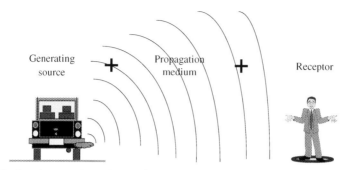

FIG. 7.1 Sound propagation and perception.

Sound pressure, measured in Pascal [Pa] or in Newton per square meter [N/m^2], is the difference between the atmospheric pressure of the environment affected by the disturbance and the ambient atmospheric pressure, considering that human hearing detects pressure values between 0.0002 and 20 Pa. Due to this large spectrum of pressure variation and due to the fact that human auditory perception of sound intensity increases is not linear, the values are converted to a logarithmic scale.

The scale used considers a reference value $P_0 = 2 \times 10^{-5}$ Pa (or 20 µPa), which is the threshold of hearing and uses Decibel (dB) as a unit of measurement. To transform the unit of Pa to dB, Eq. (7.2) is used so that the minimum audible sound pressure of 0.00002 Pa will be equivalent to zero dB.

$$L_p = 20 \log(P / P_0) \tag{7.2}$$

where $P_0 = 20 \mu Pa = 2 \times 10^{-5}$ Pa.

Human hearing does not react the same way to all frequencies. A sound pressure of 90 dB with a frequency of 100 Hz does not cause the same auditory sensation as the same pressure with a frequency of 2000 Hz. The decibel scale is, then, corrected to represent the auditory sensation, originating the A scale; thus, the unit of measurement is now called dBA.

The A scale [dBA] is used to measure the weighted pressure of sounds and attributes less weight to sounds below 500 Hz (low frequency) and more weight to sounds between 500 and 6000 Hz (high frequency), considering human auditory acuity.

The creation of the sound scale in dBA results from the fact the normal auditory perception of a young and healthy person varies between 20 and 20,000 Hz. Sounds below 20 Hz are called infrasounds and sounds above 20,000 Hz are called ultrasounds, imperceptible to the human ear.

Undesirable sounds (noise) may affect human health and may cause problems that are difficult to reverse. Continued exposure of people to noise above 85 dBA causes emotional stress and may increase blood cholesterol by 25%.

262 Transportation, energy use and environmental impacts

Noises lead to irritability, nervous system issues, dissatisfaction, and even physical discomfort. Hearing is also affected by noise, depending on the time of exposure and on sound pressure and it may lead to a definitive loss of this sense due to the following situations: (1) acute acoustic trauma: a single exposure or little exposure to very high sound levels, causing traumatic and irreversible loss of hearing; (2) temporary auditory change: temporary worsening of the hearing threshold, which gradually recovers after the exposure with due rest; and (3) permanent auditory change: it results from accumulated exposure to excessive noise (above 80 dBA), with constancy and for many years.

The physical characteristics of noise, combined with individual susceptibility, daily time of exposure, constancy of exposure, age, sex, race, and environmental characteristics, may increase the effects that are harmful to human health.

7.2.2 Noise generated by transportation modes

A significant amount of noise generated by the modes of transportation in operation is associated with the working of internal combustion engines and the transmission system. In this case, it is necessary to take into consideration exhaust gases due to fuel burning, vibration of parts, operation of ventilation systems, fluid flow (air, gases, and hydraulic fluid), friction between mechanical components (friction of the wheel with the axle and between the gears and mechanical couplings). Furthermore, the movement of vehicles causes noise resulting from the friction between the wheels and the way (tire-road and wheel-rail), braking, shifting gears, air flow around high speed vehicles, and water flow around vessels, with a substantial increment in these two last cases if there is turbulence. Besides, all the sound signals related to the working of vehicles (horns, whistles, and sirens) are examples of how transportation contributes to the production of noise.

Besides the traffic of vehicles, there is also noise associated with the operation of vehicles, equipment, and machines in passenger and freight terminals. This situation is particularly relevant considering that noise generation is concentrated in a relatively small area.

All this noise causes discomfort and health problems. Table 7.1 shows a selection of noise sources related to the activities of transportation, their levels, and the sensations and traumas caused to humans when exposed to them.

For the purposes of comparison, in a calm environment, with a comfortable sensation, sound intensity varies between 50 and 30 dBA. A soft wind ranges from 30 to 10 dBA, that is, transportation noise may be up to five times louder than a situation that is considered comfortable or acceptable for a human being.

There are a few factors that amplify the noise emitted by transportation. Traffic volume, for example, is one of these factors. From zero to 1500 vehicles per hour [vph], there is a growing volume of noise, which tends to stabilize at high levels from 2000 vph up. Speed is another amplifying factor, with noise

Noise pollution, vibration, visual intrusion, and emission of waste Chapter | 7 **263**

TABLE 7.1 Typical noise levels in transportation

Noise source	Loudness (dBA)	Sensation	Trauma
Jet plane at 5 m	140–130	Above pain threshold[1]	Permanent deafness
Car horn at 5 m Bus accelerating at 5 m	130–110	High discomfort, reaching the pain threshold	Instant deafness
Heavy truck at 5 m Motorcycle without a muffler	110–90	Extreme stimulus[2]	Dependence [3]
Traffic, felt on the streets and even inside residences	90–70	Highly stimulating	Beginning of dependency
Light traffic felt within residences	70–50	Acceptable	Beginning of discomfort

Notes: (1) The human ear has a very high sensitivity to this. Comparing air pressure (105 Pa), the variations in audible sound pressure are very small, varying from $20\,\mu Pa$ $(20 \times 10^{-6}\,Pa)$ and 20 Pa. A person's hearing threshold is $20\,\mu Pa$, while 100 Pa of sound pressure is such a high level that causes pain and, thus, is called pain threshold. (2) Hearing contributes to stimulating a part of the brain, called reticular formation that, in turn, controls muscular contraction or voluntary movement and the brain's general activity, determining our state of being awake or asleep. (3) At 80 dBA, the body releases biological morphines, causing pleasure and completing the state of dependency. The body reacts to try to adapt to the environment, inducing the releasing of endorphins, causing the body to become dependent. That is why many people can only sleep to the sound of radio or TV when in silent places.

being proportional to its variations. The age of the vehicle fleet is also a factor to be considered, and the higher the age, the more it contributes to increasing noise generated by engines and the vibration of parts.

The relative position between the source and the receptor, called the distance between source and receptor, may be verified as a mitigation to noise perception. The closer the source, the higher the effect of the noise. In a simplistic way, if the distance from the source doubles, it is possible to attenuate the noise in 3 dBA.

The configuration of the environment around the receptor must also be considered. In an urban environment, the distance between building structures (walls, facades, channels, and tunnels) must also be considered. The corridor formed by the buildings accentuates the noise, causing reverberation and, as its height, amplifies the noise for receptors that are higher, that is, in upper floors of buildings.

7.2.3 Regulations regarding noise

Regulations regarding noise have international precedents. Directive 2002/49/ EC of the European Parliament and of the Council, of June 2002, addresses

264 Transportation, energy use and environmental impacts

issues regarding the assessment and the management of environmental noise. In its definition, this directive highlights the noise produced by means of transportation, road, rail, and air traffic, and facilities used in the industrial activity.

In the United States, there is also a full legislation regarding noise pollution, using as an example Code 23 of the American Code of Federal Regulations, Section 772 (22 CFR 772) of 1982, which addresses the procedures to reduce road traffic noise and construction noise. Example 7.1 exemplifies the regulation of noise emitted by transportation in a developing country.

Example 7.1 Noise regulation in developing countries—the case of Brazil

In Brazil, a national council was created to regulate the environmental impacts resulting from different activities, among which were the ones related to transportation. In this sense, Conama's Resolution no. 1 establishes that noise levels for freight and passenger vehicles, both for the Otto cycle (spark ignition) and for diesel vehicles (direct and indirect injection, and compression ignition), must be regulated by the National Traffic Department (Denatran). This resolution associates noise levels to different vehicle categories that follow rules (Brazilian standards—NBR) established by the Brazilian Association of Technical Standards (ABNT), of national comprehensiveness. States and municipalities may establish a more restrictive limit. As an example, Table 7.2 details the maximum noise limits emitted by vehicles in acceleration, according to NBR-8433.

The National Program of Education and Control of Sound Pollution (SILÊNCIO) was instituted by Conama's Resolution no. 2, of 3/8/1990, considering the need for establishing standards, methods and actions to control excessive noise, which interferes in the health and well-being of the population. One of the purposes of Program SILÊNCIO is that of "fostering the manufacturing and use of machines, engines, equipment and devices with lower noise intensity when of their use in the industry, general vehicles, civil construction, house appliances, etc." Aiming to achieve it, in 12/7/1994 Conama's Resolution no. 20/1994 was established, instituting the mandatory use of the SELO RUÍDO (noise seal, in Portuguese) in electrical appliances produced and imported and that produce noise in their operation.

In this sense, Conama's Resolution no. 2 establishes, for motorcycles, scooters, tricycles, cyclomotors, bicycles with auxiliary engine and similar vehicles, national and imported, maximum noise limits with the vehicle in acceleration and stopped, as shown in Table 7.3.

7.2.4 Management of noises generated by the operation of transportation

Due to the problems caused by the noises emitted by transportation, it is necessary to develop actions to manage them in a way to reduce their potential impact

Noise pollution, vibration, visual intrusion, and emission of waste Chapter | 7 **265**

TABLE 7.2 Noise levels established by Conama's resolution no. 1 and NBR-8433

Category		Noise level or dBA level		
			Diesel cycle engines	
		Otto cycle engines	Direct injection	Indirect injection
Description				
A	Passenger vehicle with up to nine seats and mixed-use vehicle derived from car	77	78	77
B	Passenger vehicles with more than nine seats, freight or traction vehicle, mixed-use vehicle not derived from cars.	TGW up to 2000 kg	78	79	78
		TGW above 2000 kg up to 3500 kg	79	80	79
C	Passenger vehicle or of mixed use with TGW above 3500 kg	Maximum power below 150 kW (204 cv)	80	80	80
		Maximum power equal to or above 150 kW (204 cv)	83	83	83
D	Freight or traction vehicle with TGW above 3500 kg	Maximum power below 75 kW (102 cv)	81	81	81
		Maximum power between 75 kW and 150 kW (102 cv and 204 cv)	83	83	83
		Maximum power equal to or above 150 kW (204 cv)	84	84	84

Observations: (1) Vehicle designations according to NBR-6067. (2) TGW: Total Gross Weight. (3) Power: Maximum effective net power according NBR-5484. 4) Complement given by Resolution no. 242/1998: Vehicles with special characteristics for off road use will have their limits increased by: I – 1 dbA for engines with power below 150 kW. II – 2 dbA for engines with power equal to or above 150 kW.

TABLE 7.3 Maximum noise levels with vehicle in acceleration, measured according to NBR 8433

Category	Noise level 1st phase dB(A)	Noise level 2nd phase dB(A)[1]
Up to 80 cm³	77	75
81–125 cm³	80	77
126–175 cm³	81	77
176–350 cm³	82	80
Above 350 cm³	83	80

Note: (1) 2nd Phase: All the vehicles produced from January 1st, 2001 on.

to receptors. There are two approaches regarding analytic modeling to assess the generation of noise resulting from transportation: (1) empirical models; and (2) theoretical models. The manager must evaluate what the best approach for each situation is or consider the use of two approaches in a comparative way.

Regarding road transportation, the most used mode of transportation in the world, it is possible to illustrate a model to assess the generation of noise by road traffic, which applies a combination of a theoretical (Phase 1) and an empirical (Phase 2) approach, according to Fig. 7.2.

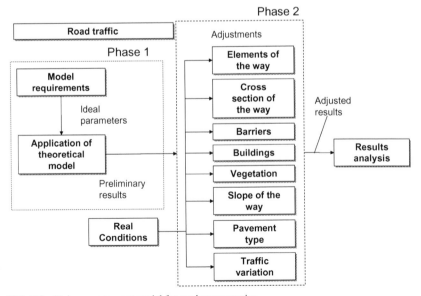

FIG. 7.2 Noise management model for road transportation.

Noise pollution, vibration, visual intrusion, and emission of waste **Chapter | 7** **267**

It is observed that the model starts (Phase 1) establishing the conditions that will result in the ideal parameters to be considered for the application of the theoretical model. This model, in turn, generates preliminary results, which will be adjusted (Phase 2) based on the real conditions regarding the way, traffic, and facilities, under an empirical approach. Finally, a results analysis is carried out aiming to propose actions that minimize noise or its effect. It can be seen that although an application for the road mode is being presented, an approach that considers Phases 1 and 2 could also be applied for the rail, water, and air modes, while specific adjustments would have to be made to Phase 2, where the peculiarities of each mode must be considered.

Physical characteristics of the way, be it a roadway, a railway, or a waterway, such as its cross section, help establishing the distance between the noise source and the receptor. Other elements, such as barriers and vegetation, help amplifying the dispersion of sound pressure waves. A set of adjustment items considered in Fig. 7.2 will be shown next. It supports the understanding of the empirical approach of noise management in road transportation.

An action that may be taken toward reducing the noise of vehicles traveling on a roadway concerns the roughness of the pavement being used. Eq. (7.3) shows a relationship between pavement roughness and the speed of the vehicle on a roadway.

$$NPS = K + 30 \log V \left[dBA \right] - \text{at 7.6m of the source} \tag{7.3}$$

where V is the average flow speed [mph]; $K = 28$ is the very rough pavement; $K = 23$ is the moderately rough pavement; and $K = 18$ is the little rough pavement.

Empirical models to describe the behavior of sound pressure as a function of traffic speed may be established for a road segment, as shown in Example 7.2.

Example 7.2   Road noise curves

Fig. 7.3 shows the results obtained for a road segment for the assessment of the noise produced by the operation of an engine, of friction of air with the body of vehicles (aerodynamic noise), and the rolling of the tire on the lane (rolling noise) generated through the flow of road vehicles. These measures were established for a level road with asphalt concrete pavement.

Regarding the actions related to minimizing the propagation of noise generated by the flow of vehicle traffic, it is possible to implement solid barriers (walls) or to plant vegetation along the right-of-way. Therefore, the noise barriers may be artificial, built for this purpose, or natural, using native or planted vegetation. Examples 7.3 and 7.4 illustrate the application of solid and planted barriers.

268 Transportation, energy use and environmental impacts

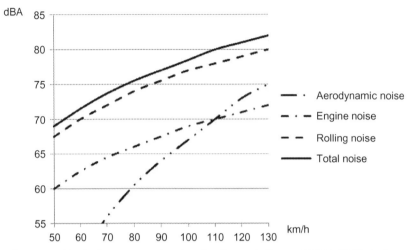

FIG. 7.3 Profile of noise curves as a function of traffic speed. *(Source: ABEDA (2012). Avaliação do ruído causado por diferentes revestimentos asfáltico. Comitê Técnico da Abeda—Associação Brasileira das Empresas Distribuidoras de Asfalto. Asfalto em Revista, Ano IV, vol. 22, 16–20.)*

Example 7.3 Application of solid noise barriers

Fig. 7.4 illustrates the case of implementing a solid barrier along the right-of-way of an at-grade (level) road with two directions (two lanes), in the form of a wall and indicates, in the chart that correlates the measure H^2/RB with noise intensity [dB], how much reduction can be obtained with the implementation of this barrier regarding its height (H) and the distance between the noise sources and the receptor.

In Fig. 7.4, RB is the distance between the axis of the way (center of the way) and the barrier of height H, and DB is the distance between the exhaust pipe (noise source) of a vehicle that passes through the way and the barrier of height H. In both cases (RB and DB), the measurement is made horizontally.

The chart shows three curves. One for $H^2/dB=0$ (no barrier), one for $H^2/dB=0.3$ (the barrier has an interference of 30%), and one for $H^2/dB=1$ (the barrier has an interference of 100%). The vertical scale of the chart (dB) measures the reduction of sound intensity provided by the barrier of height H. If $H^2/dB=0$, there is no expected reduction of sound intensity, which naturally dissipates with the distance from the observer. With $H^2/dB=0.3$, it is already expected there will be a reduction in noise intensity provided by the barrier of around 5 dB, which increases as the observer moves away. In the case of the ratio $H^2/dB=1$, a reduction of around 10 dB in noise intensity is expected.

Example 7.4 Application of a barrier formed by vegetation

Fig. 7.5 illustrates a barrier formed by vegetation and its impact in reducing noise propagation. In this case, on an at-grade way, with two traffic directions (two lanes) and 30 m of vegetation along the wayside (road side), with average height of 4.6 m, the expected reduction is of 5 dBA.

Noise pollution, vibration, visual intrusion, and emission of waste Chapter | 7 **269**

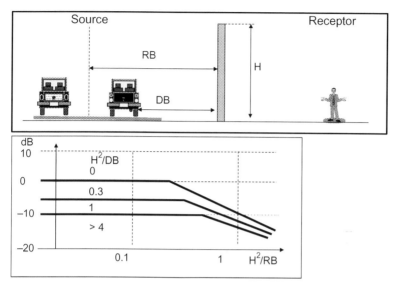

FIG. 7.4 Ratio between the distance and height of barriers and the minimization of noise propagation. Legend: RB—distance between the axis of the way (center of the way) and the barrier; DB—distance between the exhaust pipe (noise source) of a vehicle that passes through the road and the barrier; H—barrier height.

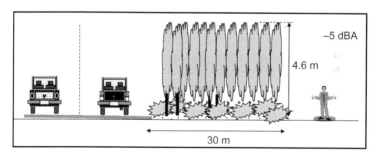

FIG. 7.5 Natural noise barrier.

The amplification of noise generation must also consider the angle of the way, especially when there is traffic of heavy vehicles. If there is a positive slope (going up) and truck traffic, which need to accelerate more and make more noise to overcome the slope, there is an expected amplification of traffic noise. In these cases, up to 2% of slope, there is no expected increase in noise levels. With the slope in 3% and 4%, the amplification will be of 2 dBA; for a slope between 5% and 6% the amplification will be of 3 dBA. For slopes above 7%, the amplification will be of 5 dBA.

It is worth noting that these adjustment interventions are related to road transportation; however, they may be easily adapted to the rail mode. Furthermore, the remaining modes also generate noise, as can be seen in Table 7.4.

270 Transportation, energy use and environmental impacts

TABLE 7.4 Characteristic noises coming from the operation of modes of transportation

Water	Railway	Road	Air	Pipeline
Noises associated with the operation of vessels (engines, hydrodynamic flow, waves, horns, and whistles) and equipment from freight and passenger terminals (vehicles, machinery, and equipment).	Noise produced by the activity of vehicles and equipment (engines, aerodynamic flow, rolling, horns, and whistles) in the proximity of the terminals and throughout the railway lines	Noise produced by automotive vehicles in the cities (urban ways) and along rural roads. Noise produced by automotive vehicles and equipment in passenger and freight terminals.	Noise produced in the proximity of airports by aircraft, mainly due to the acceleration of engines (turbines) in take-offs, aerodynamic braking, the impact of landing gears on the soil on landings, and the operation of vehicles, machinery, and equipment that support ground operations.	Noise produced at the pumping and compression stations, and during valve maneuvers.

Noise pollution, vibration, visual intrusion, and emission of waste Chapter | 7 **271**

7.3. Vibration associated with the operation of transportation

The vibration that propagates through solid media, due to the operation of transportation, affects not only the people who are around this operation, but also those that drive the vehicles. In some cases, vibration may cause irreparable damage to the health of living beings and to material goods and, thus, this issue must receive attention.

7.3.1 Concept of vibration

Vibration is understood as any movement that a solid body performs around a fixed point. This movement may be regular, of sine type, or irregular, when it does not follow any particular standard. The environment in which the vibration directly acts is called a vibration environment. Vibration is defined by the standards ISO 2631-1 (1997) and ISO 5349-1 (2001), in three variables: (1) frequency (Hz); (2) maximum acceleration suffered by the body (m/s^2); and (3) direction of movement, which is given in three spatial axes: x (from back to front), y (from right to left), and z (from down to up).

In human beings, vibration may affect the whole body or only parts of the body, such as the hands and arms. The vibration of the whole body occurs when there is a vibration of the feet (standing) or of the seat (sitting position).

7.3.2 Effects of vibration on human health

The operation of machinery, vehicles, and the manipulation of tools produce vibrations that are transmitted to the body. Each part of the body may both dampen and amplify the vibrations and the amplifications occur when parts of the body start to vibrate in the same frequency, leading to resonance.

A physical system has the tendency of oscillating at a specific frequency of oscillation called preferential vibration frequency. In resonance, there is the transfer of energy from an oscillating system to another when the frequency of the first one coincides with one of the harmonic frequencies of the second one.

Severe vibrations suffered by the hands (caused by vibrating tools) may cause neurological and circulatory damage, changes to muscular strength, and hand dexterity. Vibrations applied to the whole body, caused on drivers and passengers due to the operation of vehicles such as buses and trains, may lead to resonance of the internal parts of the body and mainly damage the muscles and the skeleton, particularly the spine.

The damage and the disturbance caused by the exposure to vibration, which are known as professional or occupational diseases, are often incurable and irreversible. Thence the need of implementing programs to identify and prevent this kind of risk.

In humans, these vibration may cause the following sensations of discomfort: (1) 0.25–1 Hz—nausea; (2) 2–3 Hz—resonance in the head for horizontal movements, also resulting in nausea; (3) 4–6 Hz—resonance of the whole

272 Transportation, energy use and environmental impacts

body; (4) 7–9 Hz—abdominal resonance and (4) 10–12 Hz—nonspecified torso resonance.

In the case of vibrations caused by the traffic of road vehicles that occur usually at frequencies within 1 and 45 Hz, extremely unpleasant levels are reached, tolerable for few minutes. It can be seen, then, that the sensitivity of the human body starts in the set of organs of the inner ear, responsible for maintaining balance, and reaches muscles, tendons, and skin, as shown in Table 7.5, which shows the sensitivity of the human body to vibrations.

7.3.3 Vibrations caused by transportation

In transportation, there is a set of variables that affect the production of vibration through their operation. They are the following:

(1) Weight of the vehicles: heavier vehicles require more effort of the engines, which increases vibration.
(2) Speed of the way: the increased speed requires acceleration, which may increase the vibration of engines.
(3) Braking and acceleration characteristics of the vehicle: if the braking is too sudden or the acceleration is too strong, the level of vibration increases.
(4) Type of pavement: rougher pavements increase the vibration imposed on the vehicles.
(5) Nature of the soil under the pavement: less rigid soils may absorb vibrations, just as those that are more rigid may increase the vibration imposed on the vehicles.
(6) Distance that separates the receiving vehicle: the vibration will have greater impact if the source is closer to the receptors.

Table 7.6 shows that the main sources of vibration of a selection of North-American and Europena industries/activities are related to transportation

TABLE 7.5 Sensitivity of the human body to vibrations

Frequency (Hz)	Sensitivity	Sources of vibration
0–2	Vestibular system,[1] associated with the auditory system and to balance	Vessels, trains, cars, and aircraft
2–30	Biomechanics, related to body resonance	Cars, aircraft, and machinery
>20	Muscles, tendons, and skin	Tools and machinery

Notes: (1) Vestibular system, also known as the gravitoceptor organ, is the set of organs of the inner ear of the vertebrates responsible for detecting the movements of the body, which contributes to maintaining balance.
Source: Chaffin, D.B., Anderson, G.B.J., Martin, B.J., 1999. Occupational Biomechanics. Society Automotive Engineers, Inc.

Noise pollution, vibration, visual intrusion, and emission of waste Chapter | 7 **273**

TABLE 7.6 European and North-American industries/activities with high levels of exposure to vibration

	Industry/activity	Main sources of vibration
European industries with clinical evidence of occupational exposure to vibration of the human body	Agriculture	Operation of tractors
	Civil construction	Operation of heavy vehicles
	Logging	Operation of tractors
	Mining	Operation of heavy vehicles
	Transportation	Vehicles (passengers and driver)
Potential exposure to vibration in the North-American industries	Driving of trucks/buses	Vehicle movement
	Operation of tractor and agricultural machines	Tractors and harvesters
	Foundry	Forklift and bridge cranes
	Forklift operation	Vehicle movement
	Siderurgy and metallurgy	Forklifts, bridge cranes, and trucks
	Quarry	Machinery and heavy vehicles
	Mining (underground/free air)	Machinery and heavy vehicles

Source: Wasserman, D.E., 1987. Human Aspects of Occupational Vibration. Elsevier Science Publishers, USA.

vehicles or to equipment that support them, which shows that transportation is related to this type of environmental impact.

There are also impacts caused by the vibration of material goods, such as cracks in buildings close to roads and railways. There is also observable discomfort caused to inhabitants by the vibration of buildings and other real estate due to the traffic of vehicles on the streets.

Considering what has been shown by now, it is possible to associate the production of noise to vibration, with the latter being limited to the propagation through solid bodies. Noise caused by the operation of transportation cause vibrations and may lead to all the harmful consequences seen before.

7.4. Visual intrusion

Visual intrusion, also known as visual pollution, is one of the problems associated with cities, particularly urban centers. The implementation of transportation systems (roads, vehicles, terminals, and controls) contributes to the deconstruction of the natural landscape, causing discomfort and loss of quality of life for people living in places affected by this kind of environmental impact.

7.4.1 Conceptualization of visual intrusion

Visual intrusion is the designation of a phenomenon that contributes to the progressive deconstruction of landscapes in cities and rural areas. It is possible to define it saying that it is a notion or concept, at the level of visual perception, of the environment in which one is inserted.

Visual intrusion is based on a value judgment, of aesthetic basis, encompassing everything that somehow contributes to decreasing the visual quality of urban and rural landscapes. Visual intrusion may be perceived without much effort, but it may also be subtle, and only a careful observer identifies it.

The concept of visual intrusion translates into: (1) degradation of the landscape due to human action and natural hazards; (2) highly polluted environments due to the lack of awareness by the population; and (3) a consequence of human occupation without spatial planning.

Visual intrusion has repercussions on the level of life, on public health, and on environment and quality of life. For this reason, it is important to pay attention to this kind of impact.

7.4.2 Visual intrusion caused by transportation

The infrastructure of transportation and the vehicles circulating are elements that promote visual discomfort to people that pass through the same place where the system was implemented.

Visual intrusion by transportation regards land use and occupation by transportation systems, and it affects aesthetic quality and interferes in the privacy of people.

Transportation systems, in their implementation and operation, change and deconstruct the local natural landscape, impacting not only the life of people, but of the animal and plant life around them. Because of that, there is a growing number of empirical studies about the interaction between transportation and land use in urban areas, where there is a higher concentration of people living and higher traffic intensity.

The accessibility given by transportation is considered an important variable for different types of land use and it is an essential factor for the location of stores, offices, and residences. Locations with high accessibility tend to have a faster development than other areas, and that leads to demand for land use and occupation.

Noise pollution, vibration, visual intrusion, and emission of waste **Chapter | 7** **275**

As an example of visual intrusion caused by transportation, there many elements competing for scarce free space, mainly in urban centers: (1) semaphores and bad location of their automation boxes, which could be buried; (3) vehicle lines in urban traffic; (3) poles and information signs concerning traffic; (4) parking meters; (5) cement blocks to prevent the parking of vehicles; (6) holes on the street; (7) cars parked on the sidewalk due to lack of parking space; (8) parking of trucks and buses or passenger vehicles on central sites; and (9) other elements associated with roads, vehicles, terminals, and control, according to Table 7.7.

7.4.3 Strategies of land use and occupation integrated to transportation

Some strategies may be adopted by the public power to improve land use and occupation, using transportation as a stimulating variable for that purpose. This way, there is a better organization of urban space, contributing to the reduction of visual intrusion. Table 7.8 shows some strategies and the conditions for their implementation.

Some indicators that may be used to evaluate the strategies and help in the choice and implementation of those more appropriate for a given situation: (1) populational density; (2) residential density; (3) number of commercial and service companies; (4) diversity of commercial use; (5) amenities for pedestrians (sidewalks and crossings); (6) extension of bicycle lanes; (7) extension of lanes with *traffic calming*; (8) parking space; and (9) revitalized area.

Other indicators may be used to monitor the effects of these strategies after their implementation, such as: (1) passengers transported by urban public transportation; (2) offer of public transportation; (3) average daily traffic on the

TABLE 7.7 Visual intrusion caused by the modes of transportation

Water	Railway	Road	Air	Pipeline
Infrastructure of ports and vessels docked in bays or close to the coastline.	Infrastructure of ways, terminals, and maneuver yards. Construction of viaducts, level crossings, and line protection walls.	Traffic jams in cities, infrastructure of roadways, and operation terminals.	Infrastructure of airports and their access ways.	Areas for the passage of pipelines through forests and cities.

276 Transportation, energy use and environmental impacts

TABLE 7.8 Land use and occupation strategies and respective implementation requirements

Strategy	Implementation requirements
1. Increased populational/ residential density	Next to urban transportation stations and terminals, within a maximum distance of 500 m, that is, within a radius of 500 m centered on the station
	Next to a transportation corridor (e.g., bus, trains, and LRT), within a range of 500 m along this corridor
2. Land use diversity	Foster the implementation of different types of commerce and services within residential blocks, serving the population in a maximum radius of 500 m, through the implementation of sidewalks and crossings for pedestrians and bicycle paths
3. Accessibility for pedestrians	Implementation of sidewalks that facilitate the access to stations and to the commerce within the blocks, as defined in strategies 1 and 2
4. Bicycle path	Implementation of ways, parking lots and signaling especially made for cyclists, especially when associated with strategies 1 and 2
5. Parking areas	Only in the proximity of stations or transportation corridors, at a maximum distance of 300 m between them
6. Traffic Calming[1]	Implementation of traffic calming measures within the areas mentioned in strategy 2 and within historical centers and areas of tourist attraction
7. Revitalization of areas	When next to stations or transportation corridors both for residential and commercial use

Note (1): *Traffic calming* refers to measures that aim to slow down or reduce the traffic of motored vehicles in order to improve safety for pedestrians and cyclists and the environment for inhabitants of the area.
Source: Campos, V.B.G., de Melo, B.P.M., 2005. *Estratégias integradas de transporte e uso do solo visando à redução de viagens por automóvel. In: XV Congresso de Transporte e Trânsito, 2005, Goiânia.*

ways; (4) hours of traffic congestion; (5) car traffic; (6) traffic accidents; (7) air pollution level; and (8) offer of public transportation.

Some other actions may be taken aiming to reduce visual intrusion caused by transportation, as seen in Example 7.5.

Example 7.5   Mitigating visual intrusion on a freight railway

Fig. 7.6 shows the possibility of planting trees along the margins of a freight railway, which mitigates the intrusion caused by the construction of the way and also enables a joint action in containing noises resulting from the operation of the compositions.

Noise pollution, vibration, visual intrusion, and emission of waste **Chapter | 7 277**

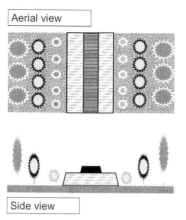

FIG. 7.6 Planting of trees along railways to mitigate visual intrusion.

7.5. Generation of solid and liquid waste through the operation of transportation

The emission of solid and liquid waste in the environment resulting from the operation of transportation contributes to soil, water, and air pollution, bringing harm to human, animal, and plant quality of life. The topic of air pollution was addressed in this chapter. This section summarizes impacts on soil and water.

7.5.1 Conceptualization of solid and liquid waste

The operation of transportation generates solid, liquid, and gas waste that is released into the natural environment, made of soil, water bodies, and atmospheric air.

Water pollution includes the release (in rivers, lakes, and oceans) of substances that dissolve and stay in suspension or are deposited over the bottom of water bodies and accumulate, interfering in the functioning of the water ecosystem.

Water contaminants are inorganic and organic chemical compounds, radionucleotides, and microorganisms. Liquid effluents are the greatest polluters of water bodies and that is why much effort is dedicated to control it. The liberation of energy in the form of radioactivity and/or heat is called thermal pollution of water bodies.

Soil and subsoil pollution regards the deposition of solid waste (e.g., metals, glass, plastic, paper, solid chemical waste, etc.) that does not degrade fast or, in some cases, that does not fully degrade through the action of organic and inorganic forces. This type of pollution also includes the accumulation in the soil of liquid chemical substances that are harmful to life, despite solid substances.

278 Transportation, energy use and environmental impacts

Although there is diversity in the amount of pollutants regarding their origin, in general lines effluents are classified into: (1) domestic waste: result of waste coming, mainly, from trash and sewage; (2) industrial waste: resulting from productive activities, such as toxic waste, production waste, and trash, in addition to waste generated by the activity of transportation; (3) agricultural waste: waste originating in crops and harvests, especially pesticides and fertilizers; (4) urban rain waste: results from the rainwater in sewage networks and often carries urban waste along; and (5) solid waste storage residue: especially leachate, which is a liquid pollutant of dark color and strong and unpleasant odor, originated in processes of decomposition of organic waste. Leachate is present in landfills due to the abundance of decomposing organic material.

To avoid or minimize environmental damage, effluents need to undergo treatments, aiming to decrease the pollutant load before being discarded in the soil or in a receiving body (river, lake, or sea). The degree of this treatment will depend on the quality of the effluent and the receiving body.

The uncontrolled emission of solid and liquid waste in the environment causes problems related to the death of fish and other water animals, contamination of groundwater tables and drinking water reservoirs, visual pollution, blocking of sewage systems, and unpleasant odors, generating a decrease in the quality of life and well-being of the population.

7.5.2 Waste generated by the operation of transportation

In the case of transportation, a set of waste is emitted in solid or liquid form and may be prejudicial to the health of living beings and to the environment, such as: (1) tires; (2) plastic, originating from parts of the vehicles; (3) metal parts; (4) rubber; (5) lubricant oils that are discarded or are leaked; (6) greases; (7) fuels that leak during the operation or fueling of fuels; (8) in the case of vessels and aircraft, waste classified as domestic (food, crew sewage, etc.); (9) water resulting from car washing; and (10) water resulting from tank washing, in the case of hazardous products.

Example 7.6 Regulating the treatment of solid and liquid waste in the operation of transportation—the case of Brazil

In Brazil, Law no. 12.305/2010 established the National Policy of Solid Waste, describing its principles, objectives, and instruments, as well as directives regarding integrated management and solid waste management, including hazardous products, the responsibilities of waste generators and the Public Authorities and the applicable economic instruments. Transportation service waste are those originating in ports, airports, customs terminals, road terminals, railway terminals, and border crossings.

In this Law, article 33 requires manufacturers, importers, distributors and traders of some specific automotive vehicle waste (such as batteries, tires, and

Noise pollution, vibration, visual intrusion, and emission of waste Chapter | 7 **279**

lubricant oils, their residues and packages) among other types of waste, to structure and implement reverse logistics systems through the return of products after their use by the final customer independently of the urban cleaning and solid waste management public service.

Another important aspect of the law is that it understands solid waste management as a set of actions taken, directly or indirectly, in the steps of collection, transportation, transhipment, treatment, and environmentally adequate final destination of solid waste and environmentally adequate final destination of residue, according to the Municipal Plan of Integrated Solid Waste Management or with the Solid Waste Management Plan. With that, transportation, besides being a source of waste emission, is also part of the waste management system due to its operation.

7.6. Final considerations

Transportation contributes to sound pollution, mainly in urban centers, where there is an accumulation of road and railway vehicles in circulation. Despite the focus on road transportation, noises are produced in all modes of transportation, causing damage to the health of living beings. Many actions may be taken to mitigate transportation noise, ranging from actions regarding the vehicle itself to the implementation of natural or artificial sound barriers.

Vibration is another impact caused by transportation that is harmful to health and material goods. This impact may be caused by the emission of noise and by the traffic of vehicles. Mitigation actions may be taken to attenuate the effects of vibration.

Visual intrusion may be increased by the construction of transportation and vehicle operation infrastructure, damaging landscapes and decreasing people's well-being. This is also a very common impact in urban centers due to the accumulation of vehicles, signaling, and concentration of ways and terminals in a given place. Better land use and occupation by transportation contributes to improve inhabiting conditions in cities, minimizing visual intrusion.

The emission of solid and liquid waste by transportation pollutes the soil, water, and even air through the accumulation of materials such as gases, aerosols, particles, metals, plastic, glass, fuels, and lubricants, which are part of vehicles and their operation. Controlling the emission of these residues is beneficial to the environment in the function of reuse and its correct destination.

The impacts resulting from the transportation operation presented in this chapter show the comprehensive ability of this sector to impact the environment, especially at local and regional levels. Sound pollution, vibration, visual intrusion, and emission of solid and liquid effluents are important fields of study that still need to be better explored by the professionals that act on the area of environment.

This chapter shows a diversity of impacts in the operation of transportation in physical media such as the soil and water bodies, different from the atmosphere, commonly addressed in transportation and environment studies. That

280 Transportation, energy use and environmental impacts

is why the assessment of environmental impacts resulting from transportation must be integrated with knowledge areas such as biology, botany, agronomy, etc., leading to possibilities of improvements to the environment and the well-being of the population.

7.7. Exercises

1. Define sound and noise, indicating the difference between them. How can noise be considered sound pollution?
2. What are the physical characteristics of sound and how does it propagate?
3. What effects do noises above 85 dBA have on people's health?
4. What are noise sources in transportation?
5. Which mode of transportation causes more noise? Why?
6. What are the noise sources in transportation that, from 50 dBA on, may cause reactions that range from discomfort to permanent deafness on people?
7. What are the factors that cause and amplify noise in road transportation?
8. What is the legislation about noise emission in transportation?
9. What are the analytic models for the management of sound pollution? Explain it.
10. A road has problems regarding noises caused by the traffic of vehicles; these noises directly affect the quality of life of the population that lives around it. By measuring noise levels in this road, an average of 94 dB was found. An engineer proposed the construction of an artificial barrier of 2 m that should be at an average distance of 4 m of the exhaust pipes of vehicles. Another engineer proposed a different solution: instead of building a physical barrier, a green corridor could be planted with 4.6 m of height and 30 m of width. Which engineer proposed the best solution so that noise levels on this road may be reduced to 84 dB?

Further reading

ABEDA, 2012. Avaliação do ruído causado por diferentes revestimentos asfáltico. In: Comitê Técnico da Abeda—Associação Brasileira das Empresas Distribuidoras de Asfalto. Asfalto em Revista, Ano IV. vol. 22, pp. 16–20.

Campos, V.B.G., de Melo, B.P.M., 2005. Estratégias integradas de transporte e uso do solo visando à redução de viagens por automóvel. In: XV Congresso de Transporte e Trânsito, 2005, Goiânia.

Chaffin, D.B., Anderson, G.B.J., Martin, B.J., 1999. Occupational Biomechanics. Society Automotive Engineers, Inc.

Wasserman, D.E., 1987. Human Aspects of Occupational Vibration. Elsevier Science Publishers, USA.

Index

Note: Page numbers followed by "*f*" indicate figures, "*t*" indicate tables, and "*b*" indicate boxes.

A

AC. *See* Apparent consumption (AC)
Acid rain, 232
Acute acoustic trauma, 262
Administrative facilities, 61
AEAF. *See* Anhydrous ethyl alcohol fuel (AEAF)
Aerodynamic resistance force (ARF), 125
  railway transportation, 163
  road transportation, 126, 128–129, 130*t*
  water transportation, 165
AFQRJOS. *See* Aviation Fuel Quality Requirements for Jointly Operated Systems (AFQRJOS)
Agricultural waste, 278
Airbus, 33*b*
Airdromes, 31
Air pollutants, 228
  classification, 229
  dispersion and concentration of, 246–248
  emission, in vehicles, 235–236*t*
  emission factors for cars, 256*t*
  emissions inventory, 240–246, 241*b*
  gases, 229
  inorganic compounds, 229
  local and regional, 233*t*
  management, 239–254, 240*f*
  organic compounds, 229
  particles, 229
  primary, 229
  secondary, 229
Air pollutant emissions, 254–255
Air pollution, 228–234
  air pollutants, 228–229
  in Brazil, 231*b*
  anthropogenic, 228
  classification, 228
  natural, 228
  potential health effects, 229, 230*t*
  by transportation sector, 229–234, 231*b*
Airports, 31–32, 32*f*
Air quality standards, 247*b*

Air transportation, 3–4, 40, 174–175
  controls, 33
  energy demand, 171–172
  energy supply, 172
  energy use, 172–174
  history, 30
  terminals, 31–32
  vehicles, 30–31, 31*f*
  ways, 30
AKI. *See* Anti-Knock Index (AKI)
Anhydrous ethanol, 86, 119*f*
Anhydrous ethyl alcohol fuel (AEAF), 201, 201*t*
Animal traction, 5, 12–13
Anthropogenic air pollution, 228
Anti-Knock Index (AKI), 191
Apparent consumption (AC), 244–245, 245*b*
Appian Way, 5
ARF. *See* Aerodynamic resistance force (ARF)
Argon (Ar), 228
Artificial inland waterways, 21
ASIF methodology, 99
ASI methodology, 98–99
Asphalt plants, 61
Atmospheric air, 228–229, 244
Atmospheric pollution
  Brazil, 106
  São Paulo, 234*b*
Atmospheric residue, 189
Automotive vehicle waste, 278–279
Aviation Fuel Quality Requirements for Jointly Operated Systems (AFQRJOS), 192
Azipod, 167

B

BAT. *See* Batteries (BAT)
Batteries (BAT), 132, 143*b*
Battery electric vehicles (BEVs), 104, 104*b*, 106, 139, 222
BDC. *See* Bottom dead center (BDC)
BEV. *See* Battery electric vehicles (BEVs)
Bicycles, 87–88, 91*t*

281

282 Index

Bike sharing system, 12*b*
Biodiesel, 87, 106
  distribution, 215
  enzymatic, 219
  in Europe, 209
  feedstock processing, 210–211
  in Germany, 209
  oil extraction method, 211*t*
  supply process, 209
  synthetic diesel, 219–220
Biogas, 181–184*t*, 221
Biokerosene, 181–184*t*, 220
Biomass-to-liquid, 219
Bio-oil, 220–221
Boeing, 33*b*
Borrow pits, 61
Bottom dead center (BDC), 134–136
Brassica oleracea, 209
Brazil
  air pollution caused by transportation in, 231*b*
  air quality standards, 247*b*
  as automotive fuel in Brazil, 201*b*
  CO$_{2e}$ emissions, 238*b*
  emission limits, program of, 249*b*
  ethanol emissions by light vehicles in, 254*t*
  noise regulation, 264*b*
  treatment of solid and liquid waste in operation of transportation, 278*b*
Brazilian Association of Technical Standards (ABNT), 264
Brazil transportation
  biofuels, 87
  gasoline, 86
Breaking systems (breaks), 16–17
BRS. *See* Bus Rapid System (BRS)
BRT. *See* Bus rapid transit (BRT)
Buses, 9, 9*f*
Business Council for Sustainable Development, 87–88
Bus Rapid System (BRS), 96–97
Bus rapid transit (BRT), 36–38, 37*b*, 57, 57*b*, 96–97
Biofuels, 180–185, 217, 221, 223–224

C

Cana planta, 204
Cana soca, 204
Capsule pipelines, 27–28
Carbon content (CC), 244, 245*b*, 246
Carbon monoxide (CO), 138–139, 191, 193, 216–217, 216*b*, 229–230

Cars, 9, 10*f*
CC. *See* Carbon content (CC)
Celestial navigation, 22
Cellulose, 203
Cellulose ethanol, 217–218, 220–221
Cetane number, 191, 216*b*
CFC. *See* Chlorofluorocarbons (CFCs)
Chassis
  buses, 10
  truck, 8–9
China inland waterway, 26*b*
Chlorofluorocarbons (CFCs), 229, 234
CI. *See* Compression ignition (CI)
Civil airdromes, 31
CNG. *See* Compressed natural gas (CNG)
CO. *See* Carbon monoxide (CO)
CO$_2$ emissions
  bottom-up approach, 244
  in Brazil, 238*b*, 239*f*
  percent distribution, 237*f*
  top-down approach, 244, 245*b*
Coastal navigation, 21
Collective transportation, 96–97
Community facilities, 61
Compact car, 90, 91*t*
Compressed natural gas (CNG), 118*f*, 180, 193–194
  as automotive fuel, 197, 198*f*
  dual-fuel vehicles, 200
  ethanol, 200
  fast fueling, 195–196
  Otto cycle engine, 197
  refueling vehicles with, 195–196
Compression ignition (CI), 191
Compression ratio (CR), 126, 134
Conama's Resolution no. 1, 264
Conama's Resolution no. 2, 264
Construction phase, 39. *See also* Infrastructure construction
Container ship, 22, 23*f*
Containers over road semitrailer, 35, 37*f*
Conventional fuels
  crude oil, 185, 189
  diesel oil, 185–186
  distribution, 189–190
  end use, 190–192
  exploration, 186–187
  gasoline, 185–186
  hydrocarbons, 185
  kerosene, 185–186, 192
  petroleum-derived, 185, 186*t*
  production, 187–188
  refining, 188–189, 190*f*

Index **283**

storage, 188
transportation, 188
vacuum distillation, 189
CR. *See* Compression ratio (CR)
Curitiba's public transportation, 37*b*
Cuts, 62
Cycling, 12*b*

D

Davis formula, 158
Decibel (dB), 261
Decibel A scale (dBA), 261
Deforestation, 60
Dehydration process, 213
Demand analysis, 55
Demand planning, 93–97
Demobilization phases, 49–51t, 52, 82–83
Design phase, 39, 56–57
DI. *See* Direct injection (DI)
Diesel cycle engines, 191
Diesel-electric railway propulsion, 160, 160*f*, 164
Diesel oil, 86–87, 93, 119*f*
Dimethyl ether (DME), 221
Direct injection (DI), 136
Dispenser, 196
DME. *See* Dimethyl ether (DME)
Domestic waste, 278
Drag, 171
Drainage, 62
Dredging, 62, 82*b*
Drilling surveys, 187
Drop, in fuels, 218
Dual-fuel vehicles, 200

E

EA. *See* Energy accumulator (EA)
Earthworks, 62
EC. *See* European Community (EC)
ECE. *See* External combustion engines (ECE)
ECU. *See* Energy conversion unit (ECU)
EEA. *See* European Environment Agency (EEA)
EEP. *See* Energy Efficiency Program (EEP)
Effective power, 160
Efficiency management system, 107–109
Effluents, 277, 279
EIA. *See* Environmental impact assessment (EIA)
EIR. *See* Environmental Impact Report (EIR)
Electric motors (EMs), 132, 170

Electric propulsion system, 132, 175
advantages, 142
batteries, 143*b*, 144*t*
challenges, 142
classification, 141
configuration, 139, 141*f*
with fuel cell, 143, 145*f*, 146, 146*b*
Electronic navigation, 22, 30
EM. *See* Electric motors (EMs)
EMP. *See* Energy Management Program (EMP)
Energy accumulator (EA), 133, 133*f*
Energy consumption, 85–86
Energy conversion unit (ECU), 138–139, 147–149, 166
Energy demand
in air transportation, 171–172
in pipeline transportation, 169
in road transportation, 125–132
in water transportation, 165–166
Energy efficiency, 100, 106
and consumption measures, 102–103
direct consumption of useful energy, 101–102
evolution in road transportation, 103–106
in propulsion system, 104, 105*t*
Energy efficiency management system in transportation (EEMST), 100, 108–109, 108*f*
life cycle, 108, 111*f*
structure, 109, 110*t*
Energy Efficiency Program (EEP), 107–109, 110*t*
Energy Management Program (EMP), 107–109, 110*t*
Energy sources (ESs), 85–86, 116*f*, 125, 175, 178–179, 181–184*t*
advanced biofuels, 217–221
biodiesel, 208–217, 212*f*, 213*t*, 216*b*
conventional fuels, 185–192, 185–186*t*
electromobility, 222–223
ethanol, 200–208, 201*b*, 201*t*
hydrogen, 222
natural gas, 192–200, 193–194*t*
Energy storage units (ESU), 147–150
Energy use, 8, 26, 45, 86–87, 125, 157, 175
in air transportation, 172–174
ASIF methodology, 99
ASI methodology, 98–99
freight transportation, 88–89, 89*f*, 92–93, 92*t*
life cycle assessment, 109–120
management planning, 97–99
number and length of trips, 90

284 Index

Energy use *(Continued)*
  passenger transportation, 87, 88*f*, 90
  in railway transportation, 163–165
  transportation demand planning, 93–97
  in water transportation, 167–169
Engine cycle, 133, 135*f*
Environmental impact assessment (EIA), 39, 49–51*t*, 52, 248
Environmental Impact Report (EIR), 39, 52, 56, 248
Environment studies, 279–280
Enzymatic biodiesel, 219
ESs. *See* Energy sources (ESs)
Esterification, 210
ESU. *See* Energy storage units (ESU)
Ethanol, 86, 106, 115
  as automotive fuel in Brazil, 201*b*
  distribution, 207
  end use, 207–208
  feedstock production, 204
  juice fermentation, 205
  physicochemical characteristics, 200, 201*t*
  production, 205–207
European Community (EC), 209
European Environment Agency (EEA), 229–230
Evaporation, 213
Expropriations, 60, 65–67*t*
External combustion engines (ECE), 132, 133*f*
Electromobility, 222–223

F

Fastening, 15
Fast fueling, 195–196
FCC. *See* Fixed carbon content (FCC)
FCs. *See* Fuel cells (FCs)
Feedstock production, 203
Final energy use, in road vehicles, 152–157
First-generation biofuels (1G), 218
Fixed carbon content (FCC), 244, 245*b*, 246
Flettner rotors, 168
Flexible-fuel vehicles, 86, 106, 202
FNCS. *See* Forces needed to change speed (FNCS)
Force of resistance to inclination (FRI), 127–128, 130*t*
Forces needed to change speed (FNCS), 124, 128, 158
Forces of residual resistance (FRR), 165
Forces of resistance to curve (FRC), 128, 130*t*, 158
Forces of resistance to motion (FRM), 123–124, 160–161, 169, 171

Forecasting model use, 55
FRC. *See* Forces of resistance to curve (FRC)
Freight cars, 16, 16*f*
Freight railway, mitigating visual intrusion on, 276*b*
Freight railway terminals, 18–19, 19*f*
Freight transportation, 40
  energy use, 90, 92–93, 92*t*
  evolution of modal split, 88–89, 89*f*
  modal distribution, 43, 44*f*
  use of physical space, 43, 43*f*
  road vehicles, 6, 7*t*
  waterways, 22, 23*f*
FRI. *See* Force of resistance to inclination (FRI)
FRM. *See* Forces of resistance to motion (FRM)
FRR. *See* Forces of residual resistance (FRR)
Fuel cells (FCs), 132, 145*f*, 146, 146*b*
Fuel consumption, 100, 101*f*, 103
Fuel production, 210
Fuzzy input, 2

G

Gas emissions, from fuel burning, 231, 232*f*
Gasoline, 86–87, 104*b*, 118*f*
Gas pipelines, 27–28, 195
Gas turbines, 139, 140*t*
Gauge, in railway, 15
GDP. *See* Gross domestic product (GDP)
General-use road vehicles, 141
Geochemical techniques, 187
Geological techniques, 187
Geophysical techniques, 187
GHG. *See* Greenhouse gas (GHG)
Global positioning system (GPS), 19, 22, 30
Global temperature potential (GTP), 234
Global warming potential (GWP), 234
Glycerin, 208, 214, 220
GPS. *See* Global positioning system (GPS)
Graph Theory, 54
Gravel, 61
Gravimetry, 187
Greenhouse gas (GHG), 98, 106
Greenhouse gas (GHG) emissions, 234–240, 254
  carbon dioxide, 234
  global warming, 234
  management, 239–254, 240*f*
Gross domestic product (GDP), 87
Gross energy, 100
GTP. *See* Global temperature potential (GTP)
GWP. *See* Global warming potential (GWP)

H

HC. *See* Hydrocarbons (HC)
HCV. *See* Higher calorific value (HCV)
He. *See* Helium (He)
HEAF. *See* Hydrous ethyl alcohol fuel (HEAF)
Helium (He), 228
Hertz (Hz), 260
Higher calorific value (HCV), 244–245, 245b
High-speed train (HST), 63, 82b
Hinterland, 24
HPS. *See* Hybrid propulsion systems (HPS)
HST. *See* High-speed train (HST)
Human-traction bicycle, 90, 91t
HVO. *See* Hydrotreatment of vegetable oils (HVO)
Hybrid car, 90, 95, 106
Hybrid propulsion systems (HPS), 132, 146–150, 149f
Hydrated ethanol (HE), 86, 119f
Hydrocarbons (HC), 191, 216–217, 216b, 229
Hydrodynamic drag, 165
Hydrotreatment of vegetable oils (HVO), 219
Hydrous alcohol, 202, 215
Hydrous ethyl alcohol fuel (HEAF), 201, 207
Hyperloop, 170
Hz. *See* Hertz (Hz)
Hydrogen, 185, 192, 221–222, 224

I

IANGV. *See* International Association for Natural Gas Vehicles (IANGV)
ICAO. *See* International Civil Aviation Organization (ICAO)
ICE. *See* Internal combustion engine (ICE)
IEA. *See* International Energy Agency (IEA)
IID. *See* Injection devices (IID) devices
IMO. *See* International Maritime Organization (IMO)
Impact energy use, 90–93
Improved inland waterways, 21
Indicated power, 160
Induced drag, 171
Industrial facilities, 61
Industrial waste, 278
Informal terminals, 10–12
Infrastructure construction
  actions, 57, 58–59t
  asphalt plants, 61
  borrow pits and waste pits, 61
  concrete and crushing plants, 61
  deforestation, 60
  demobilization phase, 49–51t, 82

drainage, 62
dredging, rock blasting, and earthworks, 62
environmental impacts, 63, 65–67t
implementation and installation of guideway accessories, 63
machinery and equipment, operation of, 63
mitigation measures, 63–82, 69–80t, 82b
paving, 62
regular and special civil engineering structures, 62
sites, 60–61
slope stabilization, 62
trails, accesses, and service, 61
Injection devices (IID) devices, 190–191
Inland navigation, 21
Inland waterways, 88–89
Intelligent transport system (ITS), 12
Inter City Express, 163
Intergovernmental Panel on Climate Change (IPCC), 99, 234
Internal combustion engines (ICEs), 90, 101–103, 175, 177–179, 231
  activated charcoal recipient, 253
  catalytic converters, 249
  components, 133, 134f
  compression-ignition, 178–179
  with diesel oil and gasoline, 255t
  direct fuel injection, 253
  engine cycle, 134, 135f
  evaporative emission gases, recirculation of, 253
  exhaust gases, recirculation of, 249
  strokes, 135, 136f
  total displacement, 135
International Association for Natural Gas Vehicles (IANGV), 194
International Civil Aviation Organization (ICAO), 30
International Energy Agency (IEA), 86, 237
International Maritime Organization (IMO), 169
International transportation, 40, 41t, 43
Interstate transportation, 40, 41t
Interurban transportation, 40, 41t
Intrusion, 259, 274, 279
IPCC. *See* Intergovernmental Panel on Climate Change (IPCC)

K

Kerosene, 185–186, 192
Krypton (Kr), 228

286 Index

L

Land clearing, 60
Land pipelines, 27
Land use, 279
LCA. *See* Life cycle assessment (LCA)
LCE. *See* Liquid carbon emissions (LCE)
LCI. *See* Life Cycle Inventory (LCI)
LCM. *See* Life cycle model (LCM)
Leachate, 278
LF. *See* Lift force (LF)
Life cycle assessment (LCA), 109
  application, 115*b*
  fuels, 112, 113*t*
  impact assessment, 112–113, 114*f*
  interpretation phase, 114–115, 115*f*
  inventory analysis, 112
  stages, 109, 111, 112*f*
Life Cycle Inventory (LCI), 115, 115*b*
Life cycle model (LCM), 115, 115*b*, 117
Lift force (LF), 171
Light rail transit (LRT), 17, 17*f*, 96–97
Liquefied natural gas (LNG), 181–184t,
  193–195
Liquefied petroleum gas (LPG), 181–184t, 189
Liquid carbon emissions (LCE), 244, 245*b*,
  246
Liquid effluents, 277, 279
LNG. *See* Liquefied natural gas (LNG)
Locotractors, 16
LPG. *See* Liquefied petroleum gas (LPG)
LRT. *See* Light rail transit (LRT)
Lung, 196

M

Maglev propulsion system, 162, 163*f*
Magnetometry, 187
Maneuver operation controls, 29
Maritime transportation, 21
Markings, in waterways, 25
Mechanical transmission system
  (MTS), 132, 133*f*, 136–137, 190
Methane (CH_4), 197
Metropolitan trains, 17, 18*f*
Military air bases, 31
Mining pipelines, 27–28
Mitigation measures, 48, 52, 57, 82
Mixed terminals, 23–24
Mixed vehicles, 6, 7*t*
Monitoring, reporting, and verifying (MRV)
  process, 56
Mowing, 60

MTS. *See* Mechanical transmission system
  (MTS)
Multimodal transportation, 33
  conditions for, 38, 38*f*
  freight, 34–35, 37*f*
  modes, 34, 34*t*
  passenger, 35–38
Municipal Plan of Integrated Solid Waste
  Management, 279

N

National Natural Gas Plan, 106
National Policy of Solid Waste, 278
National Program for Biodiesel Production and
  Use (NPBPU), 216–217, 216*b*
National Program of Education and Control of
  Sound Pollution (SILÊNCIO), 264
National Traffic Department, 264
Natural forces of resistance to motion
  (NFRM), 124
  for railway transportation, 158, 159*t*
  for road transportation, 125, 130, 130*t*
  vessels, 165
Natural gas (NG), 86–87, 106, 180. *See also*
  Compressed natural gas (CNG)
  composition, 192, 193*t*
  compressed natural gas service station,
  196*f*
  dispenser, 196
  distribution, 195–196
  exploration, 194
  fleet of vehicles, 194, 194*t*
  physicochemical characteristics, 192, 193*t*
  production and processing, 195
  transportation, 195
Natural gasoline (C_5^+), 188
Natural gas processing unit (NGPU), 192,
  195
Nautical charts, 21, 25
Neon (Ne), 228
NFRM. *See* Natural forces of resistance to
  motion (NFRM)
NG. *See* Natural gas (NG)
NGPU. *See* Natural gas processing unit
  (NGPU)
Nitrogen oxide (NO_x), 138–139, 168–169, 173,
  191, 229–230
NMHC. *See* Non-methane hydrocarbons
  (NMHC)
NMVOC. *See* Non-methane volatile organic
  compounds (NMVOC)
Noise, 259–260, 279

Noise pollution, 259–269
  concept, 260–262
  management, 264–269, 266f
  regulations regarding noise, 263–264
  by transportation modes, 262–263, 270t
Noise regulation, in Brazil, 264b
Non-methane hydrocarbons (NMHC), 193,
    242t
Non-methane volatile organic compounds
    (NMVOC), 229–231
NPBPU. See National Program for Biodiesel
    Production and Use (NPBPU)

O

OCC. See Operation control center (OCC)
Oil pipelines, 26–28
Oil tankers, 92t, 188
On-grade pipelines, 27
Operation control center (OCC), 19–20, 29
Otto cycle engines, 135, 197

P

Planning phase, 49–51t, 52
Pallets, 35
Parasitic drag, 171
Particulate matter (PM), 191, 216–217, 216b,
    229, 231–232
Passenger car, 13–14, 16
Passenger transportation
  airplanes, 107
  energy use, 90, 91t
  evolution of modal split, 87–88, 88f
  modal distribution, 40, 42f
  per capita income, 87
  port terminals, 25
  use of physical space, 40, 42f
  railways, 17, 17f
  road terminals, 10, 11f
  waterways, 21
Passenger vehicles, 6, 7t
Paving, 62
PEMFC. See Proton-exchange membrane fuel
    cells (PEMFC)
Permanent railway, 14–15
Petroleum, 86, 88–89
Petroleum derivatives, 178–180, 203, 209, 223
Petroleum-derived fuels, 231
PF. See Propulsive force (PF)
Piggy-back, 159t, 161b
Pipeline transportation, 3, 43, 88–89,
    174–175

controls, 29–30
  energy demand, 169
  energy supply, 170
  gas and capsule pipelines, 28
  history, 26
  Hyperloop system, 170
  land pipelines, 27
  modal split, 43
  oil and mining pipelines, 27–28
  in Russia, 29b
  subsea pipelines, 27
  terminals, 28–29, 28f
  water pipelines, 28
Planning phase, 39, 52
Plimsoll lines, 25
PM. See Particulate matter (PM)
Polymer electrolyte membrane fuel cell, 145
Port, freight, 24, 24f
  Hinterland, 24
  landside, 24
  products handled, 25
  waterside area, 24
Potassium hydroxide (KOH), 212, 214
Power delivered to the generator (PowG),
    160
Powered rolling stock, 15
PowG. See Power delivered to the generator
    (PowG)
Proálcool, 201
Production facilities, 61
Propulsion systems (PS), 96, 123–125, 175,
    180, 186
  air transportation, 171–174
  combustion engines, 138–139
  electric vehicles, 139–146
  energy conversion and transmission,
    150–152, 151f
  energy efficiency, 104, 105t
  final energy use, 152–157
  hybrid technology, 146–150
  internal combustion engine (ICE), 133–137,
    133f
  mechanical transmission system, 133f,
    136–137
  pipeline transportation, 169–171
  railways, 157–165
  water transportation, 165–169
Propulsive force (PF), 123, 158
Proton-exchange membrane fuel cells
    (PEMFC), 145–146, 146b
PS. See Propulsion systems (PS)
Public civilian airdromes, 31–32
Pyrolysis, 220, 222

288 Index

R

Railbuses, 16–17
Railway terminals, 17–19
Railway transportation, 34, 40, 43, 157–158
    controls, 19–20
    diesel-electric propulsion system, 160, 161b
    energy use, 163–165
    Maglev propulsion system, 162, 163f
    NFRM, 157–158, 159t
    permanent way, 14–15
    rolling stock, 15–17
    terminals, 17–19
    wagonways, 13
Rankine cycle engines, 132, 138, 140t
RB. *See* Regenerative braking (RB)
RCE. *See* Rotary internal combustion engines (RCE)
RCES. *See* Regular civil engineering structures (RCES)
RE. *See* Renewable energy (RE)
Rebound effect, 96
Reciprocating ICE, 133–136, 133f
Reformer (REF), 143–145
Regenerative braking (RB), 150
Regular civil engineering structures (RCES), 6, 62
Reinjection, 195
Renewable energy (RE), 115, 115b, 117
Reservoirs, 187
Ressoca, 204
Road noise curves, 267b, 268f
Roads, 5–6, 6f
Road terminals, 10–12
Road transportation, 86–89, 99, 120, 123, 125, 157, 237–238
    conventional propulsion systems, 133–137, 134f
    direct energy consumption, 101
    energy consumption measures, 102
    energy conversion and transmission systems, 150–152
    energy demand, 125–132
    final energy use, 152–157
    historical evolution of energy use, 103–106, 104b
    NFRM, 125, 130, 130t
    nonconventional propulsion systems, 138–150
Road vehicles, 6–10, 40
    characterization, 6, 7t
    propulsion systems for, 132, 133f
    traffic control, 12
Rock blasting, 62

Rolling resistance forces (RRF)
    railway transportation, 126, 158
    road transportation, 126, 126t
Rolling stock, 15–17
Rotary internal combustion engines (RCE), 132, 133f
Routes
    air, 30
    waterway, 21
Royal Road, 5
RRF. *See* Rolling resistance forces (RRF)
Russia's pipeline network, 29b

S

São Paulo
    bus rapid transit, 37–38
    atmospheric pollution, 234b
SCES. *See* Special civil engineering structures (SCES)
Second generation biofuels (2G), 218
Seismology, 187
Self-propelled equipment, 63
Seoul subway, 20b
Service aircraft, 175
Service paths, 61
SFF. *See* Surface friction force (SFF)
SI. *See* Spark-ignition (SI)
Signaling, in waterways, 25
Silk Road, 5
Slope stabilization, 62
Slow fueling, 195–196
Smart grids, 223
Sodium hydroxide (NaOH), 212, 214
Solid and liquid waste
    conceptualization, 277–278
    generation, 278–279
    treatment regulation, in operation of transportation, 278b
Solid noise barriers, 268b, 269f
Solid Waste Management Plan, 279
Solid waste storage residue, 278
Sound, 260
    physical properties, 260
    pressure, 261
    propagation, 260, 261f
SO_x. *See* Sulfur oxides (SO_x)
Soy oil, 214
Spark-ignition (SI), 177–178
Spark ignition engine (SIE), 133, 135
Special civil engineering structures (SCES), 6, 62
Stations, 3–4

Index **289**

Stirling engines, 132, 138–139, 140*t*
Stops, 4
Subsea pipelines, 27
Subway, rail, 17, 41*t*
Sugarcane, 203
Sugarcane diesel, 218
Sulfur oxides (SO_x), 168–169, 208, 216–217, 216*b*, 229–230
Surface friction force (SFF), 165, 174
Suspended pipelines, 27
Synthetic diesel, 219–220

T

TC. *See* Torque coupling (TC)
TD. *See* Total displacement (TD)
TDC. *See* Top dead center (TDC)
TDW. *See* Tons deadweight (TDW)
TE. *See* Total energy (TE)
Technological society, 94
Telematics, 94–95
Temporary auditory change, 262
Terminals, 3–4
  airways, 31–32
  pipeline, 28–29, 28*f*
  railway, 17–19
  road, 10–12
  in water transport, 23–25
TIN. *See* Transit integrated network (TIN)
TOD. *See* Transport-oriented development (TOD)
Tons deadweight (TDW), 22
Top dead center (TDC), 134, 136
Torque coupling (TC), 149–150
Total displacement (TD), 135
Total energy (TE), 115, 115*b*, 117
Traction units (TU), 147–149, 160
Traffic calming, 275, 276*t*
Traffic control, 12–13
Traffic volume, 262–263
Traffic zones (TZ), 53–54
Trams, 17, 34, 41*t*
Transesterification, 209–210, 212
Transit integrated network (TIN), 36–37, 37*b*
Transportation modes, 82–83, 96–97
Transportation system, 1
  air pollution, 229–234, 231*b*
  design phase, 56–57
  divisions, 3
  elements, 2, 2*f*
  life cycle, 39–40, 48, 48*f*, 49–51*t*
  modes of, 4–33
  operational schemes, 40–43

  planning phase, 52, 52*b*
Transportation zones (TZ), 55
Transport-oriented development (TOD), 52
Transrapid, 163
Tree felling, 60
Tribal society, 94
Trip distribution, 55
Trip generation, 55
Trucks, 8, 8*f*
TU. *See* Traction units (TU)
TZ. *See* Transportation zones (TZ)
TZ. *See* Traffic zones (TZ)

U

UAVs. *See* Unmanned aerial vehicles (UAVs)
UGS. *See* Unified Gas System of Russia (UGS)
Underground pipelines, 27
Unified Gas System of Russia (UGS), 29, 29*b*
Unmanned aerial vehicles (UAVs), 173–174, 174*b*
Unpowered rolling stock, 15
Urban/municipal transportation, 40, 41*t*
Urban passenger transportation, 90
Urban rain waste, 278
Usefull energy, 101–102
Useful power, 160

V

Vibration
  concept, 271
  definition, 271
  environment, 271
  on human health, 271–272, 272*t*
  of material goods, 273
  sources, 272–273, 273*t*
  by transportation, 272–273
Vacuum distillation, 189
Vegetable oils, 208
Vegetation, noisebarrier formed by, 268*b*, 269*f*
Vehicle, 3
Vehicle emissions, control measures, 248–254
Vehicle labeling programs, 248
Vessels, marine, 22–23
Visual intrusion
  conceptualization, 274
  land use and occupation strategies, 275–276, 276*t*
  mitigating on freight railway, 276*b*
  by transportation, 274–275, 275*t*
Visual pollution. *See* Visual intrusion

W

Wagonways, 13
Wankel engine, 132, 138, 140*t*
Waste, 259, 277, 279
Waste pits, 61
Water bodies, 279–280
Water contaminants, 277
Water pipelines, 27–28
Water pollution, 277
Water transportation, 40, 43, 165–169
  aerodynamic resistance force, 165
  in China, 26*b*
  controls, 25–26
  energy demand, 165–166
  energy supply, 166–167
  energy use, 167–169
  freight service, 22, 23*f*
  history, 20
  inland navigation, 21–22
  terminals, 23–25
  vessels, 22–23
Way, 3
Well to wheel (WTW)
  assessment, 109
World Health Organization
  (WHO), 247–248, 247*b*

Printed in the United States
By Bookmasters